Performance and Appropriation: Profane Rituals in Gardens and Landscapes

Performance and Appropriation: Profane Rituals in Gardens and Landscapes

Performance and Appropriation: Profane Rituals in Gardens and Landscapes

Performance and Appropriation: Profane Rituals in Gardens and Landscapes

Dumbarton Oaks Colloquium on the History of Landscape Architecture XXVII

Held at Dumbarton Oaks May 2–3, 2003

Performance and Appropriation: Profane Rituals in Gardens and Landscapes
edited by Michel Conan

Published by Dumbarton Oaks Research Library and Collection
Washington, D.C.

Distributed by Harvard University Press, 2007.

Published by Dumbarton Oaks Research Library and Collection and
Spacemaker Press. Distributed by Harvard University Press, 2007

Library of Congress Cataloging-in-Publication Data

Architecture, Dumbarton Oaks Colloquium on the History of Landscape (27th :
2003)
Performance and appropriation : profane rituals in gardens and landscapes
/ edited by Michel Conan.
p. cm.
"Dumbarton Oaks Colloquium on the History of Landscape Architecture XXVII,
held at Dumbarton Oaks May 2-3, 2003 ."
ISBN 0-88402-313-3
1. Gardens—Symbolic aspects—Congresses. 2. Gardens—Psychological
aspects—Congresses. 3. Landscape architecture—Congresses. 4. Landscape
assessment—Congresses. 5. Rites and ceremonies—Congresses. 6. Public
spaces—Psychological aspects—Congresses. I. Conan, Michel. II. Title.
SB470.7.A73 2003
712.09—dc22

2005036023

Printed in China

CONTENTS

Performance and Appropriation: Profane Rituals in Gardens and Landscapes

Performance and Appropriation: Profane Rituals in Gardens and Landscapes

Performance and Appropriation: Profane Rituals in Gardens and Landscapes

Performance and Appropriation: Profane Rituals in Gardens and Landscapes

The Significance of Bodily Engagement with Nature

Michel Conan

A character in a satirical drama, the "Théophraste moderne," performed in Paris in 1695, mused on stage upon his habit of walking in the Tuileries gardens, thirty years after they had been redesigned for private use by the king and his court. The play brought all the more laughter for the verisimilitude of the caricature it sketched of common ritual behavior in the great central allée of the garden:

> Do I visit the Tuileries for the sake of taking a walk? This is certainly my purpose. Walking twice up and down an alley exhausts me: I look for a place on the lawn where to sit, if none is available on a bench. There, withoutpaying heed to my better judgment, I censor the habits, the clothing, the demeanor, the look of all passers-by; they do much the same to me.[1]

The setting itself seems to have engaged the visitors in some unusual behavior,[2] as if it invited a new kind of social agency.

A second example, taken from a text published in 1788, underlines the undefinable sense of agency exercised by the garden itself. A prudish woman was accounting for her experiences at the Tuileries garden, and

> she added that, there is almost no woman who did not wish to become a coquette when walking across the Tuileries garden, that there is an undefinable sense (*un je-ne-sais-quoi*) that lingered in this place, which is capable of turning around and muddling up any person's mind, and that even devout women had owned up to her that they grasped their hearts in their two hands when walking swiftly along the arcades where one meets as many nice ribbons as (there are) stones.[3]

This undefinable sense of place did not prescribe new kinds of action, but suggested new forms of social life that a prude, however tempted, could resist. Therefore, it did not impose upon visitors an intentional will encoded at its creation by a skillful

---

[1] Pierre Jacques Brillon (1671–1736), *Le Théophraste moderne, ou Nouveaux caractères des moeurs* (Paris, M. Brunet, 1701). Quoted in Marcel Poëte, *Au Jardin des Tuileries: L'art du jardin, la promenade publique* (Paris: A. Picard, 1924), 294.

[2] This emergent property of the garden seems to have struck contemporary observers. See "Les promenades de Paris" (1695) in Evaristo Gherardi, *Le Théâtre italien de Gherardi, ou le recueil général de toutes les comédies et scènes françaises jouées par les comédiens italiens du roi pendant tout le temps qu'ils ont été au service de sa majesté* (Paris: J.B. Cusson and P. Wiite, 1700), 6: 136:

> La Grande Allée (. . .) C'est là que tous les ambulans / Viennent mettre à l'encan leur
> taille et leur visage / C'est là qu'on se donne un public rendez-vous / Que tous les beaux
> objets se trouvent / Et que tous ils se désapprouvent / Parce qu'ils se ressemblent tous
> [The Large Alley (. . .) This is where all walkers / put their figure and their face in
> auction, / this is where everyone comes to a public date, / where all these beautiful
> objects meet one another, / and disapprove of one another / because they look like one
> another].

Another play, "*Arlequin aux Tuileries*" (1700), by Gherardi provides other glimpses into the life of the Tuileries.

[3] Mercier, *Les Entretiens du jardin des Thuileries de Paris* (Paris: Buisson, 1788), 48–49.

iconographical program, but rather, it embodied a cultural horizon of ideal nature. This ideal derives from the success of descriptions of the pastoral world in which sixteenth-century novels, poems, and plays located an ideal of courtier life. The Pastoral tradition achieved great success among the literate public far beyond the confines of the aristocratic courts in the early seventeenth century.[4]

The Tuileries embodied this ideal of freedom and civility. It framed the visitors' inventions of new forms of social interaction that became ritualized over time. We need not believe that it resulted from the metaphysical presence of some Genius of the Place. The ritual practices that were established in the Tuileries after the 1620s, when it became a common meeting place for the well-to-do in Paris, had created a sense or a culture of place in the *Grande Allée* that seemed to invite even newcomers to such uncouth behavior, greatly embarrassing for some, and much enjoyed by others. Many other rituals established different cultures of place in other parts of the garden. They were predicated upon rituals of courtship, prostitution, political slandering, and high-society gossip.[5]

This is, of course, a very special garden at a time when very few gardens were open for social interaction to a large number of city-dwellers. Yet its history raises a question about how rituals established the cultural significance of gardens, and it questions the reliance on a study of a garden's iconography as a major source for discussing its meanings.

In the Tuileries gardens, rituals of walking in the *Grande Allée* do even more than create a sense of the agency of place; they provide visitors with a new sense of self, a sense of gentility, as well as contribute to the emergence of cultural mores, meanings, and attitudes that sustain these new senses. This link between a new cultural trait and a new sense of self can be easily understood, as this new sense of self was achieved through interactions with other visitors to the gardens, which aroused mutual approval, envy, or desire of one another's appearance. Thus, it rested upon the development of fashion and the fashionable display of self, an enduring feature of Western culture. When considering gardens as sites of specific ritual practices, we may reach an understanding of their active role in the development of three levels of social categories: one spatial, another personal, and the last cultural. It suggests that garden rituals may put into motion processes of cultural production, making gardens into efficient machines or agents of cultural change.

Is this a largely shared feature of gardens around the world and throughout history? This is the first major challenge addressed by this book. It implies a bold departure from questions usually raised in historical studies of gardens, which describe gardens as representations of intentions or cultural concerns that originated elsewhere, as passive mirrors of cultural change. Instead of asking what meanings are symbolically inscribed in the garden and whether they are organized to convey one or several messages, we shall ask: "How do gardens and landscapes trigger their users into engaging in some performance, and what are the ontological, personal, cultural, and social outcomes of the whole set of performances in a garden?"

Studies of ritual practices lead to questions about the outcomes of performances in gardens, and stress the role of users, of their interactions among themselves, and of the emerging cultural experiences in which they engage. One may fear, therefore, that such an emphasis upon actions performed in gardens and landscapes may entail a loss of attention to spatial, material, and formal aspects of gardens. I want to argue the contrary, that attention to ritual practices may provide new approaches to the importance of garden spaces for our understanding of cultural change. Gardens may offer unique

[4] The pastoral tradition was born out of attempts at revivals of Greek and Latin elegiac and bucolic poetry in vernacular language in Italy at the end of the fifteenth century. In his youth a Neapolitan poet, Jacopo Sannazaro (1456–1530), wrote a work alternating verse and prose entitled "Arcadia" that was the first to achieve a great success in this genre; it was translated and imitated, and in the sixteenth century ran to about sixty editions; the first was in Venice, 12 May 1502. This work was later emulated by Tasso, Ariosto, and Marini in Italy, who contributed much to the fame of this new genre. It was also emulated in Spain, and both Italian and Spanish pastoral poems and eclogues became very influential in France at the end of the sixteenth century and a little later in England. From songs, and verses, pastoral themes were transported first into sentimental novels and then into dramas. They were also absorbed into painting, and were to influence the opera, and later, as we all know, they became a source of inspiration for musicians, including Beethoven, Ravel, and Debussy.

[5] For a short presentation of these other ritual practices, see Michel Conan, "A Tale of Two Gardens: Urbane Wilderness in the Tuileries Gardens and Saint-James Park," in Richard Blythe, ed., *Wild Cities/Urbane Wilderness* (Launceston: School of Architecture at the University of Tasmania, 2002), 12–20.

opportunities for social encounters. Whenever these social encounters develop into ritual practice, they call upon the garden-users to become actors in the development of new mores or new ideas, and the natural setting itself contributes to a transformation that can be studied in terms borrowed from rhetoric. The natural setting becomes imbued with new meanings and propensities.

There are many kinds of activities in the modern world that look very much like rituals, but rest upon rather recent traditions without any clear origin or source of legitimacy. Commencement celebrations, baseball games, concerts, museum visits, weekends on the beach, visits to Disneyland or the Vietnam memorial, school trips to Washington, D.C., are not considered time-honored rituals, and yet we may be interested in the social, cultural, or moral significance of these activities because they contribute to the forms of civility that exist in different countries. Sometimes they clearly contribute to a sense of cultural identity, as can be seen with several types of sporting events, for instance. Others, such as the rituals of interaction studied by Erving Goffman, contribute to the development of the modern sense of individual responsibility and autonomy.[6] Ritualized practices, such as television-watching, discussed by Joshua Meyrowitz in his book on the impact of electronic media on social behavior, *No Sense of Place*, contribute to the erosion of systems of authority in the society at large.[7] Still others, like the new rituals of work life introduced by the incipient industrial world in late-nineteenth-century Sweden, studied in Jonas Frykman's and Orvar Löfgren's book, *Den Kultiverade Människan*, have engaged an in-depth transformation of the sense of time and the sense of nature among Swedish communities previously attuned to the temporality of rural activities.[8] All of these studies show that we ought to pay more attention to form than content in order to understand the transformation of culture cultural rituals perform. Neither the content of the greetings or discussions between two persons engaged in interaction, nor the topic of the television show being watched, nor the nature of the industrial activity in which Swedish people would engage in a particular place characterizes the ritualization of these activities; but the forms of agency—the ways of behaving, speaking, thinking—which were imposed upon and circumscribe these activities do. Thus, ritual studies have repeatedly called our attention to the large cultural impact of miniscule activities in which large numbers of people engage on a more or less regular basis throughout their lives in modern societies. In fact, we are interested in practices that fall into some limited patterning of social interactions, and thus enable social actors to frame, negotiate, and articulate their existence as social, cultural, or moral beings. The lay-ritual practices in gardens and landscapes belong to these kind of activities. All of them change over time. Some of them tend to look more and more like rituals as time goes by, whereas others disappear or lose their ritual character. Instead of discussing well-established rituals, as in the previous Dumbarton Oaks volume, *Sacred Gardens and Landscapes: Ritual and Agency*, we shall pay attention to the dynamics of garden practices that resemble those of well-established rituals. This raises two questions: What triggers the development of ritualized practices, and what triggers their decline?

Therefore, we may wonder why ritualized practices developed in gardens and why they disappeared. Many gardens have not been designed for the ritual practices they shelter. This was certainly true of the royal gardens in Paris with respect to the practice of public gossip. Studying ritualized practices in gardens may help us understand the significance of gardens beyond the intentions of their patrons and designers once we have discovered the living, material, and symbolic attributes that contribute to this significance. In order to understand the role of gardens in the development of ritualized practices, we shall need some descriptions and interpretations of these practices that link them to the materiality and the meanings attached to the gardens or to some of their parts. We should, in particular, attempt to achieve an understanding of garden space and of its role in triggering certain types of behavioral, cognitive, or emotional responses.

[6] Erving Goffman, *Interaction Ritual: Essays on Face-to-Face Behavior* (New York: Pantheon Books, 1967).
[7] Joshua Meyrowitz, *No Sense of Place: The Impact of Electronic Media on Social Behavior* (New York: Oxford University Press, 1985).
[8] Jonas Frykman and Orvar Löfgren, *Den Kultiverade Människan* (Lund: LiberLäromedel, 1979); Frykman and Löfgren, *Culture Builders: A Historical Anthropology of Middle-Class Life*, adapted and translated by Alan Crozier from *Den Kultiverade Människan* (New Brunswick, N.J.: Rutgers University Press, 1987).

Anthropological literature about rituals is very rich. Unfortunately, it has not paid much attention, until very recently, to the spatial dimensions of ritual activities. Victor Turner,[9] using models proposed by Arnold van Gennep,[10] has stressed the separation of ritual practices from ordinary life, and has argued that ritual practices allowed the development of a *communitas*,[11] a sense of being together that dissolves the distinctions between people in everyday life, an "anti-structure," as he also calls it. The example of the Tuileries gardens does not seem to uphold this model, as the gossip in the *Grand Allée* turns every spectator into a critic of all passers-by, and as it allows quite opposing attitudes of vain and devout women, it stands as a far cry from the sense of *communitas*. Therefore, we need to examine the specific features of ritualized practices in gardens, rather than simply subsume them under well-known models, in order to understand the meaningfulness of gardens, the specificity of their spaces, and the cultural significance of the rituals they shelter. In order to discover how garden practices contribute to cultural change, an understanding of the symbolic nature of these practices, which engage both mind and body, must be gained. Following a lead proposed by Victor Turner, we may try to see how "in the interchange between the sensory and the ideological pole of ritual practice the conceptual is given the power of the experiential thus making the obligatory desirable."[12]

Moreover, it is not possible to understand a ritual's activities and its meanings without paying attention to a larger domain of ritualized activity, both in spatial and temporal terms. This is, in fact, a general feature of ritual studies that Van Gennep highlighted, which has been constantly re-asserted: a ritual event should not be studied in isolation, but as part of a larger world of ritual practices. Rituals derive their meanings and efficacy from the system of ritual practices to which they belong. This poses some practical questions: How can we define these systems? How far should we broaden our investigations? What is the proper context for studying and understanding garden activities? How do gardens contribute to a specific role in the development of systems of ritual practices? We might also wonder how these ritualized garden activities have contributed to the introduction of new gestures in cultural life, and have helped spread ideologies or struggle against ideological domination. Since gardens are only part of the larger space where the lifeworld takes place, we should always explore how ritualized activities in the gardens constitute enacted meanings that make sense within a larger domain of social, cultural, or moral activities.

Presentation of the Chapters of the Book

The authors of this book have liberally borrowed from different theoretical perspectives in ritual studies. Wary of dogmatic imposition of a theoretical model, several refrained from any theoretical reference, whereas others preferred to borrow simultaneously from competing theories.

This theoretical eclecticism has some value, as it suggests different models of interpretation than those used by other garden scholars who would like to engage in similar research. Yet, it is somewhat unfortunate because it obscures a common emphasis on the study of ritualized practices as performances that are formative of shared cultural orientation beyond the avowed goal they pursue. Thus, it makes sense to read the whole book with this line of interpretation in mind. As Pietro Scarduelli remarked, the performative interpretations of rituals hold that there is more than meets the eye to a performance.

> The theoretical models that present rituals as communication process (Leach), as instrument for the
> maintenance of an equilibrium in man-environment relationship (Rappaport), as a performative action
> (Tambiah), or as expressions of an unconscious combinatorial calculus (Smith, Izard, Cartry) display, beyond

[9] Victor Witter Turner, *The Ritual Process: Structure and Anti-Structure* (Ithaca, N.Y.: Cornell University Press, 1977; 1st ed. 1969).

[10] Arnold van Gennep, *Les rites de passage: Étude systématique des rites de la porte et du seuil, de l'hospitalité, de l'adoption, de la grossesse et de l'accouchement, de la naissance, de l'enfance, de la puberté, de l'initiation, de l'ordination, du couronnement des fiançailles et du mariage, des funérailles, des saisons, etc.* (Paris: E. Nourry, 1909; repr. Paris: Éditions A. & J. Picard, ca. 1981) (van Gennep, *The Rites of Passage*, trans. Monika B. Vizedom and Gabrielle L. Caffee; intro. Solon T. Kimball [Chicago: University of Chicago Press, 1960]).

[11] The word *communitas* is derived from *communalitas*, a Latin word meaning "community." Thus, we should understand *communitas* as a collective sense or way of being in society, not as a social form like a community.

[12] Quoted in Peter McLaren, *Schooling As a Ritual Performance, Toward a Political Economy of Educational Symbols and Gestures* (Lanham, Md.: Rowman and Littlefield, 1999).

all their specific differences, a common feature (that they share with Malinowski's theories and with structuro-functionalism): they postulate that things are not what they seem to be, that scholars cannot rest satisfied with observing the superficial aspects of human behavior, but have to look for themselves beyond the ideas that social agents develop to describe their own rituals.[13]

Performative interpretations of rituals seek to understand how the dramatic performance of any ritualized action achieves both intended and unintended consequences for the participants themselves. The range of possible consequences is very large and may lead to surprising discoveries.

Peter McLaren's *Schooling as a Ritual Performance* highlights the role of cultural hegemony in ritualized interactions, demonstrating the usefulness of performative interpretation of rituals and their capacity to open for discussion aspects of cultural transmission and dynamics usually unheard of in studies of education. It provides an intriguing parallel for garden studies. At the end of the book, he remarks that "the instrumental rituals were only tangentially part of the art of teaching."[14] The instrumental rituals refer to the common practices and gestures acquired in the school environment and that were performed as if natural when greeting one another, sitting or standing in class, addressing each other in a formal way or whispering in an informal one. He noted that these behaviors and gestures were formative both for teachers and students, albeit in different ways. Ritual makes symbols, metaphors, and root paradigm incarnate, into enfleshed, enacted meanings. "They sanctified the workplace, hedged the cultural terrain with taboos, shored up the status-quo and created a student-body conditioned to accept such a state of affairs."[15]

The instrumental rituals of school education engage all participants in the acquisition of bodily gestures and of responses to specific situations. These acquired forms frame interactions between teachers, between students, and between teachers and students. They also circumscribe the meanings of these interactions. All persons concerned embody these forms and meanings, experiencing them naturally and enacting them unreflectively. The instrumental rituals of the school shape the personality and self-image of students and teachers. They are not directly useful to the understanding of English grammar, mathematical operations, or any other disciplinary content, "rather they were more important in creating a cultural world, a moral order."[16] The school as an institution performs more than it claims, and is unaware of some its cultural impacts.

In the general context of unequal power relations between students and teachers, acquisition of a new system of habitual practices resulted from a succession of situations of cultural domination or resistance. It imposed a new way of responding to others in any situation, a way of making sense of situations, and a way of acting, as if the school or the places themselves had imposed a new sense of agency. McLaren notes that in this particular school, "Rituals regulated the systems of intelligibility of the students and persistently undermined the belief that students are the tenants of their own will."[17]

The attention to ritualized performance in gardens and landscapes leads in a very similar way to the discovery of habitual practices that became embodied in gestures, interactions, and ways of speech. Whether in the enclosure of gardens or in open landscapes, the conditions that led to the development of such habitual practices cannot be divorced from their cultural and social context. It should not be a surprise that relations of power and of cultural hegemony play an important role in several of these studies, as most of the gardens that draw the attention of garden historians were created in very unequal societies. Besides the immediate aims they already pursued, ritualized practices in gardens and landscapes contributed to the formation of newly shared cultures, moral orders, forms of self-construction, and even political struggles. The different authors in this book have stressed one or the other of these dimensions of cultural change and they are presented accordingly. This book is divided into three parts: Garden and Landscape Performances: Contributions to Cultural Changes; Achieving a Social Construction of the Self; and Struggling for Political Changes. The chapters in each part are introduced in chronological order. I shall introduce their content briefly before discussing some of the general questions raised by this book as a whole.

---

[13] Pietro Scarduelli, ed., *Antropologia del rito, interpretazioni espiegazioni* (Turin: Bollati Boringhieri, 2000), 46.

[14] McLaren, *Schooling As a Ritual Performance*, 204.

[15] Ibid., 218.

[16] Ibid., 204.

[17] Ibid., xiv.

Garden and Landscape Performances: Contributions to Cultural Changes

Erik de Jong opens the book with a genealogy of walks in the Dutch landscape in "Taking Fresh Air: Walking in Holland, 1600–1750." He questions the exclusive attention to landscape and garden walks since the advent of the picturesque tour and the development of the landscape garden; and he introduces his study's perspective, proposing that walking the space of garden and landscape is "a ritual-like activity where the body responds to an environment that it is at the same time creating, organizing, appropriating."[18] Landscape-walking developed for a variety of reasons, and took different forms in early seventeenth-century Holland. De Jong's review leads him to devote special attention to garden walks in rural domains, and their representations in poems and engravings as they were practiced in the mid-seventeenth century. These documents reveal the nexus of relationships between walking demeanors in a garden, the garden's design and nurture, and the new construction of self it afforded to wealthy city-dwellers. He also accounts for the role of medical treatises, religious concerns, botanical curiosity, and antiquarianism in the development of multiple levels of culture, regarding a walk during the surveyed period. He is able to demonstrate a complex path of development of cultural models of walking in the countryside. Much of the interest of his presentation stems from the balance he proposes between the formative role of walking for the development of a new sense of urbanity among well-to-do Dutch city-dwellers, the attempts at manipulating these rituals as tools of civilization directed at the more unruly city-dwellers, and the resistance that they opposed to the latter. It reveals a walk's role in constructing a landscape of an urban elite, and in anchoring a sense of the legitimacy of a town-dweller's hierarchy in a bodily experience in the fresh air outside the city. It suggests that bodily practices did not simply contribute to a history of behavior, but also to visual and cultural appropriation and a limited shaping of nature in and out of cities, and, more importantly, to the development of elite cultures and perspectives on their civilizing roles.

In the second chapter, "Royal Gardens, Fashionable Promenades, and Public Opinion in Seventeenth- and Eighteenth-Century Paris," I describe the progressive development of rituals of public discussion of the news in the royal garden that was open to the public from the beginning of the seventeenth century until the revolution at the end of the eighteenth century. The public dissemination of news by the *novellists*[19] did not start in royal gardens and it never was a monopoly of garden activities, but it did give rise to specific rituals of interactions between novellists, their public, and the spies of the secret police in the royal gardens. Small groups of novellists and listeners would appropriate specific emplacements in the royal gardens, in convents, cafés, and a few other meeting places that fortified a network in which opinions could be freely debated. This gave rise to a collective belief in the existence of public opinion and in its capacity to exercise perfect judgment on issues of public interest. The novellists themselves speaking daily in the royal gardens came to be seen as embodiments of public opinion. The news and the opinions they presented were avidly discussed, but the abstract idea that they embodied public opinion was never critically examined; instead it was daily experienced daily by garden visitors. The appropriation of garden emplacements naturalized the belief in the existence of public opinion, making even the sharper critical minds blind to the phenomenon.

Even though none of the gardens I surveyed had been designed for rituals of public gossip and political slandering, but were instead temporarily appropriated for these purposes, other gardens have been designed as settings for specific rituals. The chapter by Alessandro Tosi, "Stages of Knowledge, Settings for Brotherhood:, Settings for Brotherhood, Gardens and Freemasonry in Tuscany During the First Half ofinduring the First Half of the Nineteenth Century," deals with a well-known and little-studied example of such gardens. Freemasonry was a secret society and some of its eminent members had their gardens designed as settings for the performance of initiatory rites. Much confusion has arisen, however, from unwarranted attributions of Masonic meanings to many landscape gardens. Tosi's careful documentation shows how varied the repertoire of garden follies and sculptures used in these gardens was, and how it spread throughout Tuscany in the early nineteenth century.

---

[18] See Chapter 1, p. 22.

[19] They were called "nouvelliste" in France, but the word is no longer in use, as the practice has vanished out of existence. In order to avoid confusion with the English term "novelist," I have introduced that of "novellist," with a double l, as an anglicized form of "nouvelliste."

The initiation rituals remain a matter for conjecture, but the variety of the garden iconography is suggestive of individual contributions to cultural change in Masonic culture and orientations. This will to embrace changing situations was demonstrated after 1814, when the moderate order of the Freemasons gave way to new societies with more overt political connotations. The presentation of the garden of Niccolo Puccini, built between 1825 and 1841, offers a telling example of the introduction of public rituals, officially dedicated to the celebration of agriculture, in a garden inspired by Masonic ideas. It is only then that we may get a glimpse of the contributions of these garden rituals to the formation of new political and cultural ideas in Italian society.

Susan Warren Lanman attempts a much more direct study of the formative role of ritualized garden practices in "Meaning and Change in the Walled Kitchen Gardens of Nineteenth-Century Britain." She draws eclectically upon functionalist and performative theories of ritual in order to highlight the role some ritual practices played in maintaining cultural traditions while others contributed to change.[20] Kitchen gardens usually do not receive as much attention as elite gardens, and the kitchen gardeners are often ignored. Lanman resists the temptation simply to invert this perspective and ignore the landowners. Instead, her study concentrates on rituals of interaction between estate owners and gardeners. It shows that these interactions made sense in a different way for both groups, as for each group they belonged to a different system of practice. She stresses that even though rituals of interaction in kitchen gardens could sustain the solidarity between masters and gardeners, they rested on different understandings of garden space, production, and life. Thus many garden rituals of interaction she presents contributed to the social and cultural status quo. By contrast, her study of rituals of interaction when kitchen-garden production became a commodity to be sold on the marketplace shows how a new economic context stimulated new forms of interaction and led to new cultural definitions of authority in the kitchen garden.

Sylvie Brosseau is also interested in changes in behaviors over time, in the appropriation of space, and in the formative role of some habitual landscape practices in Japanese culture. She introduces her study, "Tokyo's Modern Parks: Spaces and Practices," by giving a detailed history of the development of the popular enjoyment of cherry blossoms that paved the way for some modern park practices. She deliberately avoids any formal definition of ritual practices. She insists, however, that the practices she studies occur in times and spaces that are set apart from the profane everyday world, and that their cultural value derives both from the bodily engagement with natural elements, and from the formalized acts they demand. Her chapter shows how rituals of appreciation of cherry blossoms started as rare rural religious practices and became, through a complex history, popular urban practices that take place both in anciently appropriated hunting grounds and in modern city parks. These rituals, however, are practiced differently by various groups of city people.

She explains how these ritual practices can be seen as dramatic performances in which each participant is both actor and spectator. Each drama is expressive of the group life in some institution (school, work, and club) and contributes to the reactivation of its community spirit. This gives rise to a bodily engagement with nature that anchors the sense of community renewal into the experience of the renewal of nature in the spring, and it makes the seasonal change into a socialized event. Brosseau proposes more than a purely functionalist interpretation of performance, an understanding of the modes of engagement with nature that allow ritual uses of modern parks to mediate between Japanese tradition and modernity. She sees Japanese park rituals as guardians of institutions that facilitate cultural change at large, and thus lead to the invention of new ritualized garden practices.

Achieving a Social Construction of the Self

Catherine Benoît moves the discussion of the formative role of garden rituals from the domain of cultural change to social and cultural construction of self, in "Silent Performances in Guadeloupean Dooryard Gardens: The Creolization of the Self and the Environment." Her chapter presents the discovery of gardens and garden practices belonging to a group of

---

[20] Susan Warren Lanman, this volume.

non-Western people whose culture she does not share, and she candidly introduces her chapter with an evocation of the misunderstandings she experienced throughout her research. Her chapter reveals how the imposition of Western ideas about space, gardens, and self-identity precludes any understanding of the role of dooryard gardens in the life dynamics of their Guadeloupean creators. It also demonstrates that the systematic attention to all ritual practices in these dooryard gardens could reveal their role in the appropriation development of an adult Guadeloupean selfhood. This is not to say that garden rituals are meaningful for adults alone. On the contrary, the whole life from birth to death, through all sorts of purification and healing practices, is inextricably linked to the dooryard garden. Yet, learning about these ritual practices can call into play dangerous relationships with the spirits of the dead. Children are spared these, but have to learn them later in life when building a house and making a family. Thus, when learning how to make a garden that enables healing, restorative, and protective performances, one becomes a self-fulfilled Guadeloupean. This view of the cultural role of gardens for self-development is as foreign to the European elite of Guadeloupe, as is the Western view of gardens as conservatories of botanical knowledge or of traditional modes of plant cultivation is to the Guadeloupean maker of a dooryard garden. This chapter also makes an interesting point on methodology for garden studies. It highlights the difficulty of achieving an understanding of the engagement with gardens and their personal and cultural significance in a different culture. It shows, however, what can be gained when the scholar candidly confronts her own views of nature, and efficiently brackets these cultural assumptions.

Kendall Brown reaches for an understanding of the performative role of a much more specific type of event in "Performing Hybridity: Wedding Rituals at Japanese-Style Gardens in Southern California." He even narrows the larger part of his discussion to events celebrated in a single garden, the Earl Burns Miller Japanese garden on the campus of California State University at Long Beach. The present manager of this garden uses it as a setting for a variety of social events and in particular for staging unconventional wedding ceremonies. Inspired by psychological theories and a good sense of enterprise, she has created a frame of appropriation of different locations in the garden, allowing her to negotiate details of the ceremony with each wedding party, and so to accommodate any specific religious or practical requirement. It is clear that this ritual leaves much to the invention of the participants and it offers a very interesting example of the appropriation of a garden for a rite of passage. The detailed description of the ritualized use of the garden during the ceremony shows precisely how the ritual enables friends and family to join in the performance of a marriage by a couple. But is this the only formative role of this ritual? In order to answer that question, Brown moves the study to a different plane. He demonstrates first that these marriages concern mostly couples with different religious or cultural identities who seek to achieve a new hybrid identity. Then he proposes that the Japanese-style garden, which is a hybrid of two cultures, allows multiple cultural appropriations. Thus, wedding parties transform this Japanese-style garden, in spite of some claims to authentic Japanese design, into an icon of the "American melting pot."

Struggling for Political Changes

In "Academy Landscapes and the Ritualization of Cultural Memory in China under the Mongols," Linda Walton proposes a study of "a dynamic *process* that both produced and negotiated power relationships."[21] This process involves landscape only indirectly, but in a very significant manner for the Chinese. During the period of Mongol imperial rule, Chinese scholars in the neo-Confucian academies started producing inscriptions that commemorated the memory of cultural heroes of each academy and their engagement with the academy's landscapes. Walton studies these inscriptions in six of these academies, arguing that the production of each one has to be understood as a contribution to a larger process of ritualization of everyday practice in the academy. She implies that both reading and writing these inscriptions was part of ritualized life. These inscriptions were communicated to and formally accepted by the Mongol administration rulers in a formal show of deference to the Yuan regime. Thus they can be understood as contributions to the cultural hegemony of the Mongol rulers. By contrast,

---

[21] Linda Walton, this volume, p. 155.

the textual content of the inscription designated the landscape as a support of Chinese cultural memory. Walton argues that the introduction of these inscriptions into the ritualized practices of life at the academies changed the daily appreciation of the landscape into a form of cultural resistance by enhancing the memory of Chinese scholars mentioned in the inscriptions, some of whom were celebrated for their resistance to foreign powers. The argument hinges on the well-known importance of landscape appreciation by all Chinese scholars, and on the practice of roving through the landscape by members of the academies. Walton's study proposes an example of a ritualized landscape practice that secretly played a role in political struggles.

Battles between nations are overtly political in a way that their celebratory representations are not. "British Naumachias: The Performance of Triumph and Memorial," by Patrick Eyres, confronts this issue. The Romans practiced performances of the representation of a naval battle in a garden and the Italians emulated them in a few Renaissance gardens. From there, garden naumachias passed to England in the eighteenth century, where they were practiced for the pleasure of many different audiences and have continued to be performed up to the present day.

Eyres mostly focuses on practices in Georgian and in contemporary England. Relying on the later writings of Victor Turner, he emphasizes the public's role in the performance, calling attention to the belief system they articulate during the event and through which they come to share a sense of fusion and cohesion. This is where the ritualized show impinges on the political scene by reinforcing, and eventually spreading, a collective ideology.

Eyres argues, with Catherine Bell, that the appropriation of the garden by the ritual event endows it with social symbolism, making it a symbol of the sacred fatherland. He draws upon multiple examples of garden naumachias that pursued this ideological purpose. The examples emphasize the idea that a garden may derive some of its meaning from the ritual, but other elements of the cultural context impinge on the nature of the sense of *communitas* a garden produces. Large cultural transformations, such as the trend toward peaceful exchange rather than warfare in contemporary Europe, may imbue the particular performance of any garden naumachia with very different meanings. The cultural context of these rituals gives an unending fluidity to the collective identification they seek to promote in coeval politics. This does not preclude that each participant may appropriate this ideology for its own purpose, including turning it upon its head. One may see the search for pleasure by the audience as a way of resisting the ideological agenda of the ceremony.

In the last chapter, "Rituals of Transgression in Public Parks in Britain, 1846 to the Present," David Lambert returns with force to a question that had been lightly touched on by de Jong in the opening chapter. Whenever gardens are transformed into instruments of cultural imposition they are likely to give rise to habitual practices of transgression. There is nothing mechanical, however, in the course of the development of transgressive performances. Lambert stresses the role of public authorities in the definition of rules meant to frame the domain of pleasurable practices that are permitted. He demonstrates how several urban parks in the mid-nineteenth century grew out of an institutional appropriation of popular common grounds by landscape improvement and imposition of rules of conduct. He describes the invention of traditions to be celebrated in the parks as part of a general attempt at manipulating unruly citizens to make them—through a rite of passage in the park—into a civilized and rule-abiding crowd. He also stresses the role of high-society groups and institutions in the performance of some of these invented traditions and of public enforcement of the general conduct rules, which in turn gave rise to rituals. These may have reinforced the solidarity of the dominant groups of each local society, but they also triggered derision, resistance, and transgression. Some of these activities became habitual for some groups of park users, and even took forms that were clearly identified and labeled by the park police, thus indicating that their ritual-like nature was acknowledged by authorities. It is most interesting to read how the legitimacy of some of these activities was publicly discussed, and sometimes gave rise to a new appropriation of the park by former transgressors. The history of the appropriation of park emplacements for public protest that Lambert traces dovetails with the interpretation that I proposed of the dynamics of public appropriation of the royal gardens in seventeenth- and eighteenth-century Paris. He takes his observations in a different direction, insisting on the complementary nature of the civilizing and transgressive rituals, rather than on the latter's emancipatory power. This difference illustrates that garden rituals may be engaged in political struggles for social or cultural change, but that rituals do not resolve the issues.

This Volume's Contributions to Garden Studies

Garden studies as we know them originated with travelers' interests in the design of Italian Renaissance gardens in the nineteenth century.[22] They benefited greatly from the confrontation of historical traces on the ground with archival material, but remained focused upon an understanding of the succession of design styles. A major change was introduced by students of Erwin Panofsky, who broadened the study to the cultural meanings encoded in garden sculpture, architecture, and inscriptions, as well as in the landscape design itself. David Coffin, who played a major role in this development of garden studies has told how Sir Geoffrey Jellicoe, a major student of Italian garden design, responded to the first conference on the history of Italian gardens at Dumbarton Oaks in 1971: "After politely commending the participants for their papers, he added an admonition to the effect that we should always remember that the essence of the Italian garden was its design." Coffin added:

> Although the four papers at the colloquium often referred to elements of design, it was obvious that their major thrust was the meaning, the iconography, and the social context of the gardens. This, however, was not so much a generational difference as a difference in training and interests. Of the five participants in the colloquium, four of us were trained as art historians who approach the gardens as we would any work of art. Sir Geoffrey and many of his contemporaries were architects or landscape architects who looked to the Italian gardens primarily for what they might contribute to their own work, hence their concentration on design.[23]

Nevertheless, it was clear that garden designers', artists', and patrons' intentions remained the central focus of this new garden history. In a similar way, the variety of ritual behaviors in very different cultural contexts that have been presented may give the impression that we have learned very little about garden form or iconography. It is true that garden intentions were not a direct concern of this symposium. Therefore, we may wonder whether the symposium really contributes to garden studies, or whether it has taken gardens only as a pretext for a broad discussion of applied social anthropology, and thus risks losing sight of the "essence" of gardens, as Sir Geoffrey would say. In spite of these reservations, this symposium definitely makes an important contribution to garden studies, and at the same time it reveals in several ways the potential interest of garden studies for social anthropology. It proposes first that garden studies should acknowledge differences between gardens not only according to design style but also according to forms of ritual agency and social functions. Second, it calls attention to garden rituals as a means of communication that gives precedence to bodily engagement in social practice over discourse. Finally, it invites a renewed understanding of garden or landscape spaces and their role in social or cultural change.

A few authors in this book have mentioned the style of the gardens they studied, but no one has engaged in a detailed study of the role of a particular style with respect to ritualized practices. Thus, design style seems to be only one among many interesting aspects of gardens, but not a central one when studying garden practices and rituals. More precisely, there are gardens that were designed in order to accomplish ritualized practices such as the naumachia at Peasholm Park, the *hanami* in the ancient parks reappropriated by Yoshimune, and the Masonic itinerary in Tuscan gardens of the early nineteenth century. By contrast, there are also landscapes and gardens that were not designed for ritual practices and yet have become appropriated by specific groups of people who introduced unplanned ritualized activities. These are places such as the countryside landscape around Amsterdam and Haarlem, the landscapes in the vicinity of Chinese academies under the Yuan rulers, the gardens such as the Earl Burns Miller Japanese garden at California State University, Long Beach, the Tuileries gardens in Paris, and the Victorian public parks in England. Strangely enough, this way of distinguishing between the presentations about gardens that were designed for a ritual practice and those where the ritual practice is introduced later does not cover all of the presentations in the book. There are gardens that are neither designed for ritual practices nor appropriated by some external group of users who bring in their own ritualized habits. These are gardens built and produced as a result of ritual practices, gardens in which

---

[22] There were many earlier writings about gardens and garden history, but they did not lead to the development of a new domain of studies in which authors are engaging with one another until the end of the nineteenth century.

[23] David Coffin, "The Study of the History of the Italian Garden until the First Dumbarton Oaks Colloquium," in Michel Conan, ed., *Perspectives on Garden Histories*, Dumbarton Oaks Colloquium on the History of Landscape Architecture XXI (Washington, D.C.: Dumbarton Oaks, 1999), 33.

gardening, rather than design, is the defining reference. We have evidence of several examples of these gardens in contemporary Guadeloupe and in nineteenth-century England.

Of course, such gardens are not usually studied in garden history, and yet they comprise a large number of different kinds of vernacular gardens that deserve attention. As we have seen in the two examples presented in this volume, such gardens may turn out to be central to any effort at understanding the culture, social status, contradictions, and anxieties in which some groups of people live. Two chapters directly introduce us to an understanding of the construction of culture by such groups, living in a context of social domination and cultural hegemony. There is little doubt that these studies demonstrate how garden studies can raise new questions for social anthropology and contribute to their understanding. But this statement is not true only of these two chapters. All of the chapters engage with questions discussed by the social sciences. They show that garden studies can develop in different ways, either standing by themselves in a nook of art history, or opening themselves to debate with other academic fields.

There is a common belief in contemporary academia that garden studies do not constitute a serious field of study. They are accused of being engaged in the most frivolous aspect of the leisure societies of the past. Gardens are viewed as domains of art that allow no critical reflection, as opposed to painting or literature, for example, and invite simply some indulgence in aesthetic contemplation and a paradisiacal *rêverie*. As a whole, the chapters in this book do not conform to these stereotypes. They present landscapes and gardens in which personal activities of groups that range from a few persons to thousands of visitors, contributed to a process of cultural development, a process of personal development, or the development of a political agenda. These are clear examples of the potential contributions of garden studies to the pursuit of scholarly research on different aspects of cultural changes, irrespective of the particular society one is considering. This raises a very intriguing question for garden studies: Do these processes depend in a specific way on some universal characteristic of gardens and landscapes? Is such a universal property possible when gardens are so different in their physical appearances, their ecologies, and the aesthetics that presided over their creation? Is there a common feature shared by all these gardens other than being a carefully enclosed piece of land? And if gardens share, at least in principle, the fact that they are all enclosures of cultivated land, how could such a property apply as well to unbounded landscapes?

The chapters of this book cannot provide answers to such broad questions, yet they all point to a common property of the gardens under study: the rituals that they sheltered contributed to a means of social communication deriving their expressive power from bodily engagement in a natural setting.[24] Ritualized performances can be generally interpreted as formative of new aspects of culture. The interactions between performers and between performers and audience make these ritual practices into a means of communication within the society where they are performed. Ritualized performances in gardens and landscapes, however, share a specific property among others: they derive their expressive power from bodily engagement in a natural setting. This deceptively simple idea is actually quite rich in consequences. People who are engaged in ritual practices in gardens interact with one another in ways that stimulate a sense of sharing an experience, being active in the development of that experience rather than passive bystanders, and being part of some meaningful activities. So a certain kind of communication is established between them, as it was between the skinny-dippers of Hyde Park, or the wedding participants in the Miller garden, without any need for long, discursive exchanges. Performers and audience interact, and they may even exchange roles. The class defiance of authority in the first case, or the experience of transcendence in the second, need no words to be commonly experienced and understood, and would actually be very difficult to articulate for the persons engaged in the ritual enactment.

[24] In the conclusion of his book, Ronald Grimes writes: "Ritual knowledge is nothing if not sensual. A rite is an activity that engages the hand and pricks the ear: it catches the eye and lifts the heart. Every ritual system cultivates a ritual sensibility, a way of being in the world that is at once ideological and sensory. Although rites may be taught by way of a book or learned as a formula, the aim is to create a repository of knowledge at the sensory level. Most of us know people who cook by taste, garden by instinct, or play music by ear." Ronald L. Grimes, *Deeply into the Bones: Re-Inventing Rites of Passage* (Berkeley: University of California Press, 2000), 344.

This book provides a few insights into the complexities of such a communication process. First, it involves a dialectic of regulation and improvisation. In the two examples cited just above it is quite clear that the boys are counter-dependent with respect to municipal rules. They act as if they were obeying the opposite of the municipal rule: it is prohibited to skinny-dip in the pond so they do it. By contrast, they have to improvise their actions, in particular the interaction with the policewoman when she arrives on the scene.

The participants in the Miller garden rituals are engaged in a very different regulated improvisation. They are certainly improvising their theatrical role, but they have also been invited to negotiate the rules with the master of ceremony. There are more examples to be found in the chapters about the Netherlands, the royal gardens in Paris, and the parks in Victorian England. They simply show that such ritualized activities demand initiatives and personal engagement from the participants. These people are partly the producers of the message that they receive. Of course, this makes it difficult for them to contest the message!

Second, in each case we can also recognize that the ritual practices encompass a certain form of bodily investment. This may demand walking at a leisurely pace in warm clothes in the countryside, standing among a shouting crowd, silently watching a young bride who walks in a dream, or reveling with friends under cherry blossoms. Each of these forms of bodily investment produces an embodiment of meaning in gestures. (I borrow this term of gesture from Peter McLaren's study, *Schooling as a Ritual Performance*, in which a gesture introduces a patterned set of activities and social interactions that follows a particular rhythm over time.) Thus, one has to move from the description of the bodily engagement with the landscape or the garden to a description of the collective gestures to which each body contributes. Then it is possible to move from our understanding of these gestures to an interpretation of the meanings that the ritual embodies. As we have seen, one may be helped in this task by coeval descriptions, by theatrical productions, or by cartoons satirizing the events. In short, we have to call on coeval commentaries that propose their own interpretation of the events.

Third, one may also try to unravel the way gardens and landscapes themselves frame these events. There seem to be two major modes of framing that introduce either a metonymic or a metaphoric mode of appreciation of nature. This may be too simplistic a reading of the book, yet it is very important for studies of garden rituals to reach an understanding of the way gardens provide a specific perspective, a particular horizon of understanding and of expectation to the participants in ritual activities. By a metonymic mode of appreciation of nature, I mean that gardens are seen as participating in a larger natural domain, and that engaging with the garden affords the users a vicarious experience of this larger domain. At Peasholm Park the lake offers a metonymy of the ocean and thus the garden becomes a metonymy of the British Empire, the naumachia profiling against the background of the British Empire. At Long Beach, California, the Miller garden provides a metonymy of Japan as a land of mystical fusion with nature. In the *meisho* of Edo, the cherry blossoms constitute a metonymy of spring, the renewal of nature, the eternal return of harmony. In each case, we see that the metonymy introduces a specific sense of nature.

Let us turn to the metaphoric mode of appreciation of nature. It derives from the acknowledgment of some aspect of the garden or landscape as a clue that transports the imagination into a completely unrelated domain of experience. It seems that this metaphoric framing of the experience of nature is even more common. I shall only mention a few examples: fresh air as a metaphor of common culture in seventeenth-century Holland; the whole garden standing for a pastoral world peopled with courtly and civilized shepherds all sharing in an equal status and freedom at the Tuileries and the Luxembourg; or the territory of a public park in Victorian Britain standing for a land of freedom confiscated by municipal power. Of course, none of these references should be understood as the meaning of these gardens. I am proposing instead that these are the horizons of understanding within which participants in garden rituals could make sense of their own situation and of the actions in which they engaged. This leads to the fourth aspect of garden rituals as communication processes availing themselves of bodily engagement.

In fact, these actions very often rest on interactions between sensory aspects of bodily experience and ideological content of different moments in the ritualized practices. Thus, the frame of aesthetic appreciation impinges directly on the meaning of the ritualized experience, so we can understand how the garden itself contributes significantly to the production of the meanings communicated through the ritual practices. We can read how the excesses of noise and gladiatorial sights at Peasholm were intimately linked with the ideas of sublimity of the British Empire. And, to give a second example, we can read how sweeping the earth around the house, bathing in the garden, healing a family member, caring for the plants, and disposing them strategically in or around the house were many sensual experiences, each carrying its own meanings in a Creole Guadeloupean garden. Here again, almost all the chapters provide some examples of this intimate linkage between sensory and ideological dimensions of the ritual experience.

This has a profound consequence for our understanding of space. It means that we are invited to discern that gardens and landscapes frame more than the horizon of perception of the participants in ritualized activities, that they frame the activities themselves in three different ways. They provide, first, a material setting; second, a horizon for understanding and perceiving it; and, third, a horizon of expected agency and of temporality of action. In other words, we can see that attention to ritual activities has led us to an understanding of these gardens or landscape spaces as much more than purely material spaces. They are greater than whatever can be accounted for by a description of their geometry, and their natural and artificial components. These are spaces of collective experience, and as such, materiality, horizon of perception, horizon of agency, and temporality characterize them. Spaces of ritualized garden practices embody cultural propensities. Many seventeenth-century Parisians participating in the rituals of the *Grande Allée* in the Tuileries, for example, felt that the garden space compelled them to engage in mutual criticism against their better judgment. The different chapters of the book, in a similar way, show how such propensities may either contribute to the reproduction of the social order, and of shared cultural beliefs, or may, in different circumstances, be conducive to cultural change.

As a result of this approach to rituals as communication processes, this book makes important claims about gardens. It proposes that ritualized garden or landscape spaces may constitute springboards for social or cultural change. In short, the various chapters highlight two different gestural modalities that characterize ritual uses of gardens or landscapes in ways that are conducive to social or cultural change. The first one consists in the appropriation of emplacements as a way of contesting the agency of an existing space by newcomers who may thus develop into a growing social group; and the other consists in walking in an existing space by simply envisioning it from a new perspective. The two modes are strikingly different, and further research would probably result in the discovery of more.

Let us begin with the appropriation of emplacements by newcomers who develop there a new sense of perception, a new mode of agency, and a new temporality, perhaps achieving over time a sense of group identity. Brown discusses how, in a few Japanese-style gardens in California, the introduction of wedding ceremonies by garden managers leads to couples and marriage attendants appropriating certain emplacements in these gardens. This allows a significant number of people interested in promoting an American path toward multicultural life to congregate there. This is not yet a group aware of its own existence, but the identity of this group is already acknowledged by the garden managers and it may become more visible as more light is shed on this phenomenon. In contrast, we have seen how novellists in Paris came to form a group so clearly aware of its own existence that it evolved a specific form of organization and internal control. We also can read how, in Japan, different groups make specific uses of gardens or public parks, appropriating, even for as short a time as one evening, a place under cherry trees in a meisho. There the formation of culturally defined groups merges the general process of dissemination of Westernized leisure into the Japanese population.

Let us turn to the second mode, the new perspective brought to a space one discovers in a promenade that leaves all pre-existing appropriation of the land unchanged. Two examples will do. The first one, in the opening chapter, concerns the citizens of Amsterdam and Haarlem. They walked in the countryside without interfering with the activities taking place there, without transforming its material organization, or the cultural rhythms of activities taking place. They simply used the experience of being in these places as a springboard for seeing themselves transported into a different world. And through later ritualized exchanges of these experiences, they came to acknowledge themselves as a group of like-minded people, as urbanites sharing the same culture.

The second example concerns the laborer women in the Victorian English gardens who walked in the landscape park in search of plants for feeding or healing their families. They were certainly making use of the land, and yet they neither changed its material arrangement, nor the actions the landlords pursued there, nor the temporality of high-class entertainment. Yet, seeing it through their own cultural interests and knowledge of plants, they transformed the garden from a place of higher-class leisure into a place of family sustenance. This mode could be termed a cultural appropriation of the landscape, as it produces a new interpretation of the landscape that contributes to the cultural identity of the people who practice it.

Thus, bodily engagement with nature through ritualized practices of gardens contributes to slow cultural changes, transforming categories of perception of natural spaces, self, and legitimate actions. It may establish a new metonymic or metaphoric understanding of nature in a particular place, and endow it with a sense that one is called there to particular types of action, thus demanding improvisation on the part of its users. Over time, this may lead to large numbers of people being engaged in the acquisition of new gestures that seem to issue from Nature herself. This is how gardens and landscapes contribute to the development of ways in which humans see themselves as part of nature, and some cultural changes become naturalized, eventually inscribed in new garden forms. Thus, ritualized uses of gardens and their formative roles for culture seem to be part of the founding layers of the cultural struggles that symptomatically surface in all sorts of intentional actions and open conflicts, or in debates and polemics.

Performance and Appropriation: Profane Rituals in Gardens and Landscapes

Performance and Appropriation: Profane Rituals in Gardens and Landscapes

Performance and Appropriation: Profane Rituals in Gardens and Landscapes

Performance and Appropriation: Profane Rituals in Gardens and Landscapes

Taking Fresh Air: Walking in Holland, 1600–1750

Erik A. de Jong

In memoriam Derk Persant Snoep, "who had a genius for sauntering"

(after: Henry David Thoreau, *Walking*)

Introduction

Signs that invite us or forbid us to walk are all around us. When walking in the streets of Holland, the icon of a little green or red man invites us to go or asks us to stop. In New York, the words WALK or DON'T WALK do the same. Words and images thus evoke the unlimited diversity that is walking the city, where the walker, as de Certeau says, "constitutes, in relation to his position, both a near and a far, a here and a there," appropriating topography, defining space, and often as a "man of crowds," as Edgar Allan Poe wrote.[1] Walking affirms one's goal, transgresses boundaries, respects—or disrespects—certain rules, and thus becomes part of social space. As a physical movement it may be intent on equating a hurried walk with a specific amount of time, or it may become its opposite: the pursuit of leisure. Walking may be done alone, or together with someone, or in groups, and this social context changes its meaning and process. Walks may be accompanied by speech—or they may be silent. During the peace demonstrations in New York City, in the spring of 2003, and elsewhere in the world, walking in a march became an expression of personal or communal conviction, accompanied by shouting and signs, banners and Bibles. It showed that walking could be laden with significance that cuts across differences of class and may become a highly personal expression, even when among many. The Monthly Global *Silent* Walks, called "Living Peace by Walking Peace," are spiritual walks that begin at the highly symbolic Imagine Circle, at Strawberry Fields in Central Park, New York City.[2] Walking may take on a diversity of meanings, intentions, and usages.

In modern studies, walking is almost exclusively associated with the advent of the landscape style in country and town (Fig. 1).[3] Specific social uses of the walk were indeed invented through the medium of the landscape park, as we find them described in Jane Austen's *Pride and Prejudice* from 1813: her characters use the avenue walk for sociability, they retreat to the flower garden for pleasure, and use the shrubbery for private walks and intimate talks as a chance to break away from the confinement of the house.[4] It is true that nineteenth-century landscape treatises devote much attention to the making and the effect of paths and walkways, showing how the walk was to be the backbone of a design method that saw the offering of

---

[1] M. de Certeau, *The Practice of Everyday Life* (Berkeley: University of California Press, 1988), 97–99.

[2] Leaflets issued by the Community of Mindfulness/NY Metro/BPF, NYC, which also publishes *Walking Meditations* by the Buddhist teacher Thich Nhat Hanh.

[3] Giuliana Bruno, *Atlas of Emotion: Journeys in Art, Architecture and Film* (New York: Verso, 2002). Michel Conan, ed., *Landscape Design and the Experience of Motion*, Dumbarton Oaks Colloquium on the History of Landscape Architecture XXIV (Washington, D.C.: Dumbarton Oaks, 2003).

[4] Mark Laird, *The Flowering of the Landscape Garden: English Pleasure Grounds 1720–1800* (Philadelphia: University of Pennsylvania Press, 1999), 18, referring to Jane Austen's *Pride and Prejudice*.

1. *Walking the landscape park of Duin en Daal near Haarlem, handcolored etching in Adriaan Loosjes*, Hollandse Arcadia of Wandelingen in de Omstreeken van Haarlem *(Haarlem 1804)*

experience and varied enjoyment within a consistent narrative as its main goal.[5] More particularly, walking has been interpreted as an urban invention, related to new concepts of urbanity in the nineteenth century. "*Flanerie*," defined by Victor Fournel in 1858 as "a most enchanting word," has been discussed more than once from many angles. Fournel defined it as an "infinite investigation through streets and promenades; drifting along . . . with serendipity, without pondering where to and without urging to hurry . . . giving yourself over, captivated and enraptured, with all your senses and all your mind to the spectacle." Flanerie became a new way of experiencing the urban world.[6]

Gudrun König, in her beautiful study on the history of the walk in Germany in the period from 1780 to 1850, interprets the walking of promenades, gardens, and landscapes as a major contribution toward the invention of nonfeudal identities of contemporary citizenry and a crucial instrument in the birth of specific modern civic and democratic concepts of landscape, nature, public space, and personal leisure time for both men and women.[7]

Yet, this attention to the late eighteenth and nineteenth centuries' origins of our modern walk disregards that walking gardens, avenues, and landscapes in the Western European tradition is infinitely more varied in its manifestations. We need to look at the walk and walking in a broader way, trying to fathom the historicity of this phenomenon and its multifarious performances: the walk represents an important unifying and structural principle in the design of garden and landscape architecture and the discovery of landscape from past to present. It must be considered the hinge that steered more than anything else the changing options for use, experience, and design and contributed fundamentally to both personal and cultural developments.

Is it a coincidence that in recent landscape theory, movement, process, and walking have gained new attention? Bernard Lassus wrote in 1998 that "we have . . . to cross the road each day, to take paths by walking on slow or fast grounds to get to work, to hurry or to wander around in passages of light or shade, of sun or foliage, later on to walk in the garden, to breathe its smells, to listen to its murmurs. That, we do by *successions of ambiances*, a concept it is difficult not to evoke as soon as we understand that where a landscape appears, we are already in place."[8] Both the city and the landscape are invoked here, different senses of time and place, different modes of physical movement and sensory perception. Lassus's words may help us discover how much walking is about the presence of place, about succession in time, about discovery by virtue of the body

[5] Michael Seiler, "Wege, Bewegung und Sehen im Landschaftsgarten," *150 Jahre Branitzer Park: Garten-Kunst-Werk. Wandel und Bewahrung* (Cottbus/Branitz: Kolloquium der Stiftung Fürst Pückler Museum—Park und Schloss Branitz, 1996), 110–21.

[6] Anke Gleber, *The Art of Taking a Walk: Flanerie, Literature, and Film in Weimar Culture* (Princeton, N.J.: Princeton University Press, 1999), and "Great Thinking Machines," *The Urban Park: Special Issue of Lotus International* 30, no. 1, 1981.

[7] Gudrun M. König, *Eine Kulturgeschichte des Spazierganges: Spuren einer bürgerlichen Praktik 1780–1850* (Vienna: Böhlau Verlag, 1996).

[8] Bernard Lassus, "The Obligation of Invention," in *The Landscape Approach* (Philadelphia: University of Pennsylvania Press, 1998), 67–77.

2. Romeyn de Hooghe, map of the region between Amsterdam and Haarlem, etching, ca. 1700, Haarlem, Streekarchief Kennemerland

and the senses moving; spaces are left behind, boundaries crossed, new worlds discovered. It is modern tourist theory, where walking is part of travel, that sees such an activity as a form of ritual inversion where the routine of everyday life is exchanged for an experience shaped by the specific temporal and spatial contingencies of a tour.[9] It is proposed here that such a perspective on present usage may shed light on historic performances of walking the landscape as a common practice and on its meaning as an important activity for different groups of people.

Walking in Holland

Walking represents a continuous tradition in Dutch culture of the early modern and modern period. Its importance has recently drawn the attention of designers, who are rediscovering the walk and walking as a vital activity that has always been crucial in shaping our experience of place. A recent report states that modern urban design has degraded walking space to the sidewalk strip.[10] Modern urbanism has forgotten how the walk as a consciously designed green space used to be an integral part of public space and formed an important link between inner city, suburb, and surrounding landscape. The study notes that almost ninety percent of the Dutch practice this diversion in one way or another, from a short (Sunday) walk in their own neighborhood, to walking in parks, gardens, and landscapes at home and abroad.[11] Its practice is fueled by modern concepts of health, but even more so by social practices that value the everyday experience of one's own urban surroundings, the discovery of a natural environment or the extraordinary discovery of far away and unknown landscapes. It is also a practice that is characterized by repetition, be it a daily exercise or the more obligatory and formal family "Sunday" walk. The walk may thus

[9] Tim Edensor, *Tourists at the Taj: Performance and Meaning at a Symbolic Site* (London: Routledge, 1998), Introduction.
[10] Th. J. M. de Bruin and J. E. Burger, *De ommetjesmaker en zijn habitat* (Amsterdam: Stichting Op Lemen Voeten, 2004). I thank the authors for allowing me a preview of their conclusions.
[11] See also *Op Lemen Voeten: Tijdschrift voor Wandelaars* 25, no. 2 (2003). This issue, published on the occasion of this journal's twenty-fifth anniversary, was called *De acht mooiste wandelingen van 25 jaar/the most beautiful walks of the past 25 years.*

hover between a traditional custom or a compulsive activity. But it may also present itself with more performative dimensions, where it tries to create a multifaceted sensory experience, modeling a new world. All these different practices of the body moving in time and space define the walk and walking as a ritual-like activity where the body responds to an environment that it is at the same time creating, organizing, and appropriating.[12]

A historical perspective will be able to show how this activity is capable of transforming traditional uses and meanings, reformulating again and again the meaning of bodily movement in relation to its surroundings. Material for such an inquiry will be taken from the Dutch Republic where a well-defined urban environment developed as early as the beginning of the seventeenth century and throughout the eighteenth century, and where the opposition between aristocratic and townsmen's uses of landscape did not exist to the same degree as elsewhere in Europe. Moreover, the Dutch landscape—especially in the west, where we will mostly focus on the region around and north of Amsterdam and Haarlem—represented a unique topography with its flat expanse of land, covered by immense skies with the horizon always in sight (Fig. 2). Outside the towns of Amsterdam and Haarlem, a variety of landscape types met the eye of those traveling and walking: waterways, lakes and polders, agricultural lands, pastures with cattle, farmhouses, villages with churches and bleaching fields, (ruined) castles and modern country seats with their green gardens. The ultimate borderland of the dunes offered, from its sandy tops, views inward where the hand of man could be recognized in many ways, yet also gave way to views outward to a less controllable, boundless landscape of beach and sea. This part of the landscape of the Dutch Republic—at the same time offering Amsterdam and Haarlem as main urban centers—offers us a unique context to see how "taking fresh air" functioned as an experience of landscape for different people. This material should add to our understanding of the different historic meanings of walking as it developed as an activity in diverse contexts all over Europe.[13]

The Activity of Walking

What do we know about walking in the Dutch burgher Republic of the seventeenth and early eighteenth centuries? Johan van Beverwijck, in his *Schat der Gesontheyt* (Treasure of health), the most popular medical encyclopaedia of the seventeenth century (published in 1643), strongly advocated walking.[14] His concept was based on the theory of the *humores*: just as stagnant water in a well starts stinking, so the human body must be set in movement. Yet walking may not demand too much of a person. Van Beverwijck considered it a light exercise for healthy and older people in order "to augment warmth, move the spirits and to dispose of bad substances." He advised walking on an empty stomach and in the shade under trees to avoid overheating the body (Fig. 3). Such walking for pleasure should not "pose a danger for limbs to exhaust themselves" as another writer put it in 1725.[15] A poem by Jacob Cats, inserted in Van Beverwijck's medical manual, takes up a humanistic tradition that perceived taking fresh air on a walk as a sanguine counterpoint to melancholic temperament: he wrote that scholars must walk moderately, as restless walks through fields characterize melancholic natures.[16] Trees, landscape, and fresh air are the perfect locations to chase sadness through amusement (*vermaak*) and relaxation; for painters moreover, they represent the perfect environment to observe nature, wrote Karel van Mander, the Haarlem painter, poet, and theorist, about forty years earlier in 1596 and 1603.[17] In Gerard de Lairesse's theoretical manual on painting from 1707, we even find that *looking* at painted landscapes could provide relaxation and pleasure.[18]

[12] Catherine Bell, *Ritual: Perspectives and Dimensions* (New York: Oxford University Press, 1997), chap. 5.

[13] I am preparing a full-length study of walking in Dutch culture from the sixteenth through the twentieth centuries.

[14] Johan van Beverwijck, *Schat der Gesontheyt, Verciert met Historyen, Kopere Platen, als oock met Verssen van heer Iacob Cats* (Amsterdam, 1643), 680–85.

[15] P. Straat, "Op het verheerlykt Watergraafs- of Diemermeer," in Matthaeus Brouërius van Niedek, *Het Verheerlykt Watergraefs- of Diemermeer By de Stadt Amsterdam* (Amsterdam: Andre and Henry de Leth, 1725) (unpaginated).

[16] Huigen Leeflang, "Het landschap in boek en prent. Perceptie en receptie van vroeg zeventiende-eeuwse Nederlandse landschapsprenten," in Boudewijn Bakker, Huigen Leeflang, *Nederland naar 't leven: Landschapsprenten uit de Gouden Eeuw* (Zwolle/Amsterdam: Waanders/Museum het Rembrandthuis, 1993), 29.

[17] Karel van Mander, *Het tweede beelt van Haerlem: 't Stadt Haerlems Beeldt, in welck men speurt met lesen: Haer oudtheyt, aerdt, ghedaent' en heerlijck wezen* (Haarlem: Gillis Rooman, 1596), verse 9, and Hessel Miedema, ed., *Karel Van Mander: Den grondt der edel vry schilder-const [1603–1604]* (Utrecht: Haentjens Dekker and Gumbert, 1973), chap. 8, verses 1–8. Leeflang, "Het landschap in boek en prent," 29.

[18] Gerard de Lairesse, *Het Groot Schilderboek waar in de schilderkonst in al haar deelen grondig werd onderwezen* (Amsterdam: de erfgenaamen van Willem de Coup, 1707), 344.

That the act of walking for a broad middle class was intimately tied to the experience of pleasure and amusement, and thus part of early Dutch concepts of leisure, becomes clear from some of the criticism against it.[19] The Dordrecht Synod (1574), in which the essence of Protestant morals and ethics was decided, requested that civic authorities prohibit buying, selling, working, drinking, and walking on Sundays during church hours. More than a hundred years later, in 1687, criticism was still being voiced against the idleness of walking and people parading proudly in gardens and public promenades and on the cities' bulwarks (Fig. 4). In 1713, a Rotterdam teacher continued to protest vehemently against Sunday visits to gardens and like places of pleasure.[20] Such sources suggest that indeed a great deal of walking was done, both as a healthy activity according to medical insights, but also as true relaxation and pleasure that for many must have stood in marked contrast to the heavy physical exercise of laborious and functional walking and moving forward as a means to earn a living, both in town and country (Figs. 13 and 15). By walking and taking fresh air in green public spaces on a Sunday—the accepted day of rest—the strains of the workday week became temporarily dissolved for the broad middle and lower classes, and replaced everyday life with another system of experiencing and knowing the world. For the elite, summer offered relaxation in private gardens.

3. *Constantijn Huygens, "A woman walking in the garden of Hofwijck," pen and ink, ca. 1654, Berlin, Kupferstichkabinett, Staatliche Museen Preussischer Kunstbesitz*

Because most of this activity was done both in the city and in spaces where there were trees, gardens, and fields, walking came to represent an experience in which one could pass from the ordinary and the everyday to something extraordinary, in which the systems of social and civic behavior changed and a more relaxed mode could be taken on, offering a prospect of physical or moral health, chasing time, seeking pleasure, amusement, alone or in the company of others. Such is the impression gained from the 1624 diary of the The Hague schoolmaster David Beck (1594–1634).[21] He used his (extensive) leisure time to walk for hours in town and see well-known people such as the stadholder, royal visitors, and literary figures like Constantijn Huygens and Jacob Cats. He also took long walks around The Hague as far as Delft to visit and speak to a friend. Walking for him constituted a basic condition for how he spent his time, and shared and exchanged knowledge and news.

We do well to remember that the Dutch word for walk (*wandeling*) denotes both the act and the place where one could walk: the paths under the trees on the bulwarks, the avenues and lanes around and leading outside cities, the paths in a garden (Fig. 4). Nowhere does the popularity and use of the walk become more apparent than from the many songbooks, garden poems, arcadias, and other publications produced in the seventeenth and eighteenth centuries, as well as a wealth of visual material, each reflecting different social practices in walking the landscape.

[19] For the use of the term "broad middle class," see Simon Schama, *The Embarrassment of Riches: An Interpretation of Dutch Culture in the Golden Age* (New York: Knopf, 1987), 174.

[20] S. D. van Veen, *Zondagsrust en zondagsheiliging in de zeventiende eeuw* (Nijkerk: Callenbach, 1889), 8 and 68. Wendy Jansen, "Verfrissing van lichaam en geest. Aspecten van de wandeling in de 17ᵉ en 18ᵉ eeuw," *Holland* 28 (1996): 30.

[21] Sv. E. Veldhuijzen, ed., *Spiegel van mijn leven: Een Haags dagboek uit 1624 / David Beck* (Hilversum: Verloren, 1993).

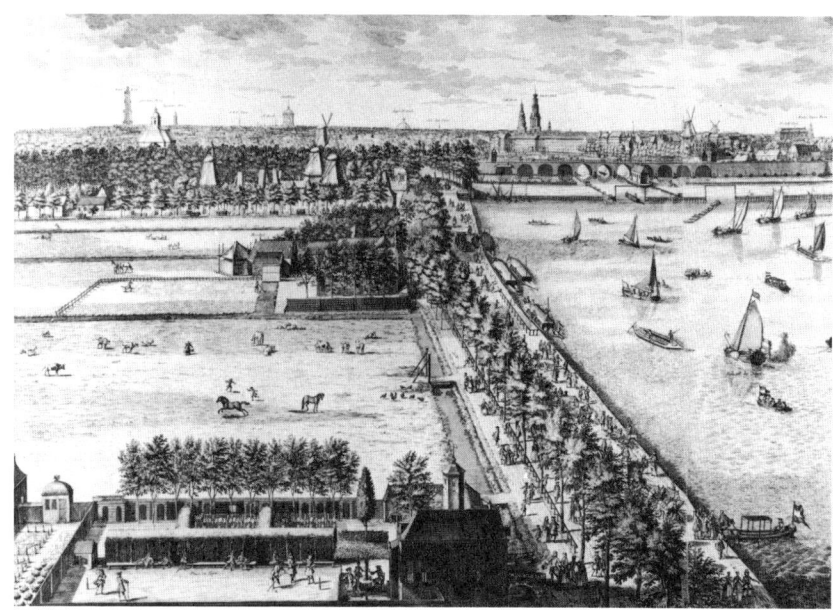

The Landscape around Amsterdam and Haarlem

At the beginning of the seventeenth century, the surroundings of Haarlem, west of Amsterdam, became known, both to those living in Amsterdam and to the citizens of Haarlem themselves, for their varied landscapes of lush agricultural fields, villages, castle ruins, the sandy dunes and the sea, that were easy to explore on foot (Fig. 2). Many songbooks from the beginning of the seventeenth century, published in Haarlem and Amsterdam, illustrate in text and image amorous walks through the dunes, which maps and other documents call the "wilderness," a place without a system of well-defined and regular paths (Fig. 5).[22] Haarlem's landscape is called a "sweet dale," and the songs celebrate its most prominent promenades leading into a refuge for spring courtship rituals where men would carry girls into the sea and roll them dry from dune tops and where young women were allowed to

4. *A. van der Laan, "View of Amsterdam with the 'Peacock Garden' along the Amstel River," engraving, early 18th c., Amsterdam,* Historisch-topografische Atlas van het Gemeentearchief Amsterdam

cover men with grass, flowers, or hay, the so-called *grazelen*, part of spring courtship ritual (Fig. 6).[23] Inns, fairs, and village festivals also were popular destinations of these walks, sometimes in combination with a cart. The role of the dunes in this context is important, as its "wilderness" in seventeenth-century Dutch evoked a disordered space.[24] This disorder in the songbooks—as reflecting the practice of walking—is the prerequisite for the *experience* of pleasure, since order evoked urban and social order, which was exactly what was escaped here.

Pleasure of landscape is also the theme of one of the first series of landscape etchings by Claes Jansz. Visscher produced in the northern Netherlands, illustrating twelve "Pleasant Places" around Haarlem, published in Amsterdam in circa 1611–1614, reedited with a commentary in 1728 (Figs. 7 and 8).[25] These *"Plaisante Plaetsen"* seem to be a direct reference to the tradition of the *locus amoenus*, here transposed onto the larger landscape. The series frontispiece offers these images to those who have no time to come to the environs of Haarlem and invites "ye, who like to look at the varied appearance of landscape and the ever different but always lovely bends in roads, come, let your eager eyes go over these stately scenes, offered by the wooded surroundings of Haarlem." The structural sequence of such etched landscape series as Visscher's seems to replicate a real walk.[26] Read through the lens of the commentary a century later, this walk confronted the viewer/walker with a diversity of landscape scenes: the sea with all its dangers, the safe fishing with nets on the beach, dunes that protect the countryside, the beach as a

[22] Leeflang, "Het landschap in boek en prent," and idem, "Dutch Landscape: The Urban View. Haarlem and its Environs in Literature and Art 15th–17th century," *Nederlands Kunsthistorisch Jaarboek* 48 (1997): 52–116.

[23] D. P. Snoep, "Een 17e eeuws liedboek met tekeningen van Gerard ter Borch de Oude en Pieter en Roeland van Laer," *Simiolus* 3, no. 2 (1968): 85–86.

[24] Erik de Jong, *Natuur en Kunst: Nederlandse tuin- en landschapsarchitectuur 1650–1730* (Amsterdam: Thoth, 1993), Introduction.

[25] Boudewijn Bakker, "Nederland naar 't leven; een inleiding," and Leeflang, "Het landschap in boek en prent," in Boudewijn Bakker and Huigen Leeflang, *Nederland naar 't leven*, and their catalogue on pp. 8–9. Walter Gibson, *Pleasant Places: The Rustic Landscape from Breugel to Ruisdael* (Berkeley: University of California Press, 2000), chap. 2.

[26] C. M. Levesque, "Place of Persuasion: The Journey in Netherlandish Landscape Prints and Print Series" (Ph.D. diss., University of Michigan, 1988).

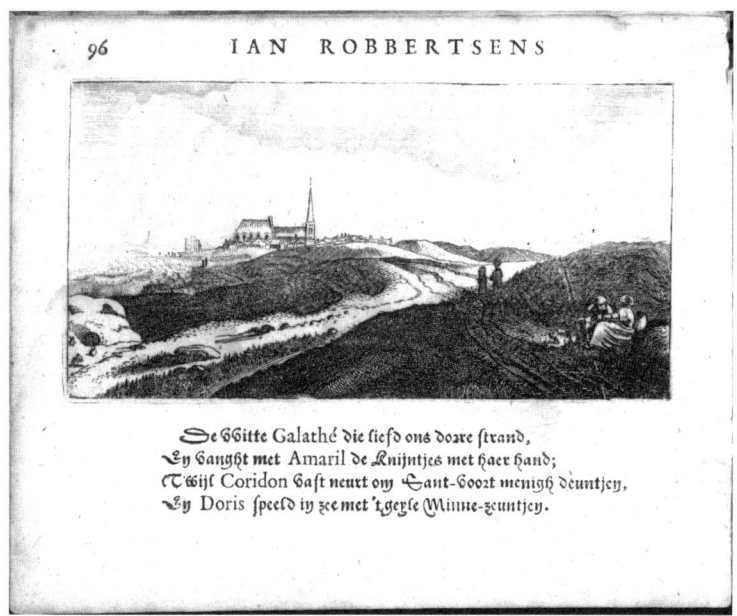

De witte Galathé die liefd ons doore strand,
En ganght met Amaril de Knijntjes met haer hand;
Twijl Coridon Gast neurt om Sant-Goort menigh deuntjey,
En Doris speeld in zee met 't geyle Minne-geuntjey.

5. *Jan van de Velde II, "View towards the dunes with the village of Zandvoort in the background," in M. Campanus ea.,* Amsterdamse Pegasus *(Amsterdam: Cornelis Willemsz Blaulaecken, 1627), The Hague, Royal Library*

6. *Gerard ter Borch de Oude, "The ritual of 'Grazelen'," songbook of Gerard ter Borch de Oude and Pieter van Laer, pen and brown ink, ca. 1620, Rotterdam, Stichting Atlas van Stolk*

place for amorous walks. It also confronted the walkers with bleaching fields, which still in 1728 evoked a eulogy on weaving, the profit of clothes, as well as the contribution of flax cultivation and weaving to general economic prosperity. Such scenes, we may remark, revealed the intimate connection between landscape and its natural resources with human activity, on both of which much of the urban industry and trade in Haarlem depended. Through the sequence of illustrations or a real walk, landscape became part of urban memory. Material has been put forward that Visscher's connection with the reformed Dutch New Church in Amsterdam may account for another layer of meaning in such walks.[27] Calvin saw the created world as a book, which must be used and inhabited, but also studied and praised for its *ordo naturae* or *ordo creationis* (the order of nature or of creation). In his *Institution*, Calvin allowed for more than just the necessary use of creation and encouraged its enjoyment.[28] The Dutch Religious Creed, as drafted during the Synod of Dordrecht in 1619, also emphasized that the world before our eyes is like a beautiful book, where all creatures small and large serve God's greatness and where God's providence could be read through a multitude of signs: stranded sperm whales on the beach, for example, as divine premonitions of calamities.[29] At the beginning of the great flowering of Dutch landscape representation, Visscher's illustrated walks may have wanted to invoke this aspect of the experience of landscape, providing both an image and a guide to the praise of God's creation sung during the Sunday sermon. Presented as part of religious experience, the secular act of walking the landscape may have become the motive

[27] Boudewijn Bakker, "Levenspelgrimage of vrome wandeling? Claes Janszoon Visscher en zijn serie 'Plaisante Plaetsen'," *Oud Holland* 107, no. 1 (1993): 106–13.

[28] W. Balke, "Calvijn over de geschapen werkelijkheid in zijn psalmencommentaar," *Wegen en gestalten in het gereformeerd Protestantisme* (Amsterdam: Bolland, 1976), 89–103, M. de Kleijn, *De invloed van het Calvinisme op de Noord-Nederlandse landschapschilderkunst 1570–1630* (Apeldoorn: Willem de Zwijgerstichting, 1982), 45–56. See also Boudewijn Bakker, *Landschap en Wereldbeeld van Van Eyck tot Rembrandt* (Bussum: Thoth, 2004), part 3 (Ph.D. diss., Vrije Universiteit, Amsterdam, 2003).

[29] Bert Sliggers and A. A. Wertheim,*'Op het strand gesmeten': Vijf eeuwen potvisstrandingen aan de Nederlandse kust* (Zutphen: Walburg Pers, 1992). Eric Jorink, "Van omineuze tot glorieuze tekens: Veranderende opvattingen over kometen," in Florike Egmond, Eric Jorink, and Rienk Vermeij, *Kometen, monsters en muilezels: Het veranderende natuurbeeld en de natuurwetenschap in de zeventiende eeuw* (Haarlem: Arcadia, 1999), 89–105.

7. and 8. *Claes Jansz. Visscher, two views of the surroundings of Haarlem, nos. 2 and 8 in the series* Plaisante Plaetsen: *the beacon near Zandvoort and the bleaching fields in the vicinity of the Haarlemmerhout. Etchings, Haarlem, Streekarchief Kennemerland.*

and pretext for the growing and enduring popularity of both walking and (depicted) landscape. Yet, the fact that orthodox preachers and others scorned it as an all too pleasurable action for the broad middle class, proves that for many the experience of landscape represented a diversity of meanings rather than specific religious edification only.

Walking: A Search for Knowledge

Another example will show how much the profane and the sacred were part of the practice of walking in relation to the development of scientific and amateur curiosity in the seventeenth century. The Haarlem teacher van Westerhoven mentions in his book the *Creator Glorified* (1685) the lonely wanderings he undertook in the region around Haarlem, looking for herbs and plants.[30] Such walking stems from the tradition of undertaking a walk in order to botanize in the wild, an activity documented as early as the sixteenth century with the rise of botany as a science. Used for the professional study and collection of botany during the sixteenth century, more than a century later this tradition was still very much alive, but had also evolved into a more general activity to know and observe the larger landscape. From the botanical tradition the author also took the form of the colloquy, here staged between two Haarlem men, Paulus Verus and Petrus Novus, and Johannes Rotgans from Amsterdam.[31] Van Westerhoven's book treats everything that may be met on a walk through the landscape (Fig. 9). Dunes, plants, trees, animals, and specific places are all studied and observed, and used as a means to praise God and his creation. Interestingly enough, Rotgans, who comes from the city of Amsterdam and represents someone less educated, is disappointed in the Haarlem surroundings, for he prefers amorous adventures, eating fish, laughing, or making music in the landscape, thereby proving that walking the landscape indeed served those kinds of activities.

Coenraad Decker's large engraving in the book shows us three gentlemen on the top of the dunes, with the vast expanse of landscape at their feet (Fig. 9). The silhouette of Haarlem is centrally placed, with Amsterdam much further in the

[30] Huigen Leeflang, "Ruisdaels natuur," *Jacob van Ruisdael: De revolutie van het Hollandse Landschap* (Zwolle/Haarlem: Waanders/Frans Hals Museum, 2002), 21–29.

[31] Compare for these botanical traditions the remarks on Euricius Cordus (1486–1535) and his *Botanologicon* from 1534 in Edward L. Greene, ed. Frank N. Egerton, *Landmarks of Botanical History* (Stanford: Stanford University Press, 1983), 361–67.

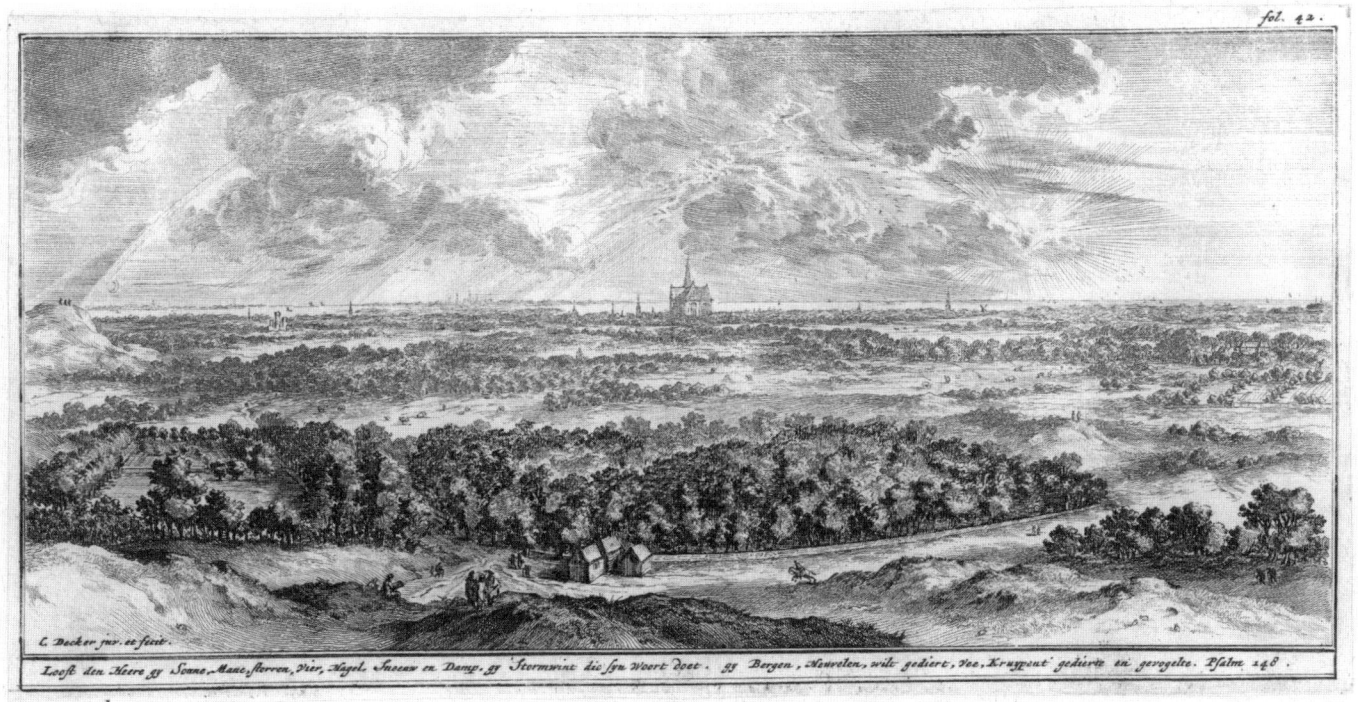

Looft den Heere gy Sonne, Mane, sterren, Vier, Hagel, Snaeuw en Damp, gy Stormwint die syn Woort doet. gy Bergen, Heuvelen, wilt gediert, Vee, Kruypent gediert en gevogelte. Psalm 148.

9. *Coenraad Decker, "View of Haarlem from the Dunes," etching in Jan van Westerhoven Jr, Den Schepper verheerlijckt in den Schepselen (. . .) (Haarlem, Jan Gerrit Geldrop, 1685), Haarlem, Streekarchief Kennemerland*

distance on the left. The landscape becomes a giant platform, a theater, much as in Ruisdael's famous views on Haarlem from the late 1640s (Fig. 10). They show an inversion of the standpoint of those who live in the city, since the town from where they come is but one of the elements in the larger whole of the landscape: it is the landscape that flaunts the city and not the other way around. Therefore, Rotgans, when seated on a dune top, feels he may now look on the world in a different way. It is Verus who explains to him that most people look with their eyes open, but with their thoughts elsewhere, or that they see things and their appearances, but do not search for their meanings.[32] The preferred way of looking is of course to observe and learn the character and nature of things as to their purposes and why they exist. This was a tenet that in the science of natural history was often linked to Virgil's famous "rerum cognoscere causas" (*Georgics* Book II, v. 490), in which sky and earth provide the landscape setting to get to "know the cause of things." Sitting in the wilderness of the dunes on one of its sandy tops after a long walk, the elevated position in the landscape provides a moment of enlightenment, a century before the dune top would become a "lieu de mémoire," a national symbol of all of Holland's historic Republican strivings toward freedom and liberty.[33]

[32] The ideas presented by Deckers, as well as many other literary works, painted landscapes (such as Ruisdael's landscape paintings), and designed gardens, ground themselves in Mennonite ways of interpreting the created, divine world. The specifics of their concepts still need further exploration, but for some explanation for the Mennonite approach to nature, see Erik de Jong, *Nature and Art: Dutch Garden and Landscape Architecture 1650–1740* (Philadelphia: University of Pennsylvania Press, 2000), 108–11.

[33] Erik de Jong, "Op uw Duinen, zoet Holland," *Ons Bloemendaal* 16, no. 4 (1992): 16–22.

The walk is also an important feature in the many seventeenth- and eighteenth-century garden and country-house poems that treat the country life of a specific owner at a specific country place, or the country place itself. The audience for these poems—those who had them composed and their readers—must be situated among the urban elite. Dutch country seats were in general not assets of landed, noble gentry, but of administrators, merchants, and other citizens. The specific Dutch genre of the garden poem flowered during the seventeenth and eighteenth centuries with thirty-eight poems written between 1613 and 1710, and many more after that date.[34] In rhetorical terms an extensive *narratio* takes the form of a walk, which thus becomes both the ordering principle of the poem as well as the objective for the fusion of poetic language with actual description. The poet—sometimes also the owner of the garden—never walks alone; the reader becomes the one that walks with him and is led into the world of the garden. Often the time frame of the walk is a day, but with references to all seasons, with the effect that the visit refers to both real and ideal time. The poems are highly didactic: a description almost never comes without a moral lesson, thus making the garden a place of meditation, a

10. *Jacob van Ruisdael, "View towards Haarlem with bleaching fields," oil on canvas, ca. 1648, Kunsthaus Zurich, Ruzicka Stiftung*

space for the *vita contemplativa*. As part of that ideal, the poems also devote much space to issues of gardening, botany, and horticulture, activities that probe the visible and invisible world.

As with Visscher's landscapes, nature in the garden is often referred to as God's second book, conveying a moral lesson on God's greatness, in other cases inviting personal, empirical research and physical activities. Walking under the trees of his own garden, the courtier and writer Constantijn Huygens, secretary to the Prince of Orange, combines in his influential garden poem "Hofwijck" (1653) refreshment of the soul with physical relaxation, reflecting, as he walks, on the course of the heavenly bodies, climate, the sea, the earth and her metals, plants and animals, and last but not least, man himself and the functions of his body—and this no doubt reflected a true personal practice (Fig. 3).[35]

[34] P. A. F. van Veen, *De soeticheydt des buyten-levens, vergeselschapt met de boucken: Het hofdicht als tak van georgische literatuur* (The Hague: Van Goor, 1960). Willemien de Vries, *Wandeling en verhandeling: De ontwikkeling van het Nederlandse hofdicht in de zeventiende eeuw (1613–1710)* (Hilversum: Verloren, 1998), and, by the same author, "The Country Estate Immortalized: Constantijn Huygens Hofwijck," in John Dixon Hunt, ed., *The Dutch Garden in the Seventeenth Century*, Dumbarton Oaks Colloquium on the History of Landscape Architecture XII (Washington, D.C.: Dumbarton Oaks, 1990), 81–97.
[35] De Vries, *Wandeling en verhandeling*, chap. 4.

Huygens's lived body, when walking, moved him not only through space, but also put him in touch with the psychological aspects of thinking and remembering, thus nurturing his physical and moral awareness.[36] Within the traditional privileging of country life over life in the city, this performative function of the walk discovered and appropriated the garden as an actual place. At the same time, it generated the memory of the garden and its space as an idealized, virtuous, and moral construct of nature, art, and creation.[37] Through the perspective of the garden another construction of the self was engendered, distinct from what life in the city brought. We know of several instances where owners came to regard life in the garden as their true, physical, and moral destiny, from which they were forced to return—be it refreshed—to their busy and necessary urban *vita activa*, that, however, was regarded as a great *ennui*.[38]

When we compare some of these poems with existing suites of watercolors and engravings—their numbered *vedute* also reflecting the sequence of a walk—both word and image help us to see how walking such gardens was indeed intent on following a consciously orchestrated narrative. In the gardens at Heemstede (near Utrecht, east of Amsterdam), begun in 1680 for a high official within the States of Utrecht, with strong personal ties to the Amsterdam elite, two poems written between 1691 and 1699 help us define the main axis as a walking and viewing axis, quite distinct from other axes serving coaches and horses (Fig. 10).[39] The walk on this axis, organized within a closed composition, leads through a dense "wood," then continues along high hedges with architectural features made of lattice works, past a series of ponds, an area for deer, a *volière*, then back along the deep avenues through an orchard with a grotto, along a parterre, and ends at an outdoor orangery, where large collections of exotics were exhibited. A pavilion on the main axis oriented on the four points of the compass offered a moment of rest and contemplation.

Walking the garden in the summer was a sequential experience of wood, water, wilderness, the domain of horticulture, and that of art and technology, all represented through the design vocabulary of the garden, confronting the visitor with almost all the variety within the spheres of nature and art. A painted sequence of these sights, represented as allegories of the four seasons, and accompanied by allegories of the four elements, was to be seen in the pavilion on the main axis, overlooking outdoor orangery and parterre, providing a quiet moment to remember and review the walk made.

The poets call the circuit "entertainment by steps" and present walking as a true narrative that develops with the perspective unfolding in different axes and on paths: foreground is a stage from which one moves toward the background which, when reached, changes into foreground. The movement of the body enlivens the experience of perspective: in several country house poems from the seventeenth and eighteenth centuries we may read that views in gardens were perceived as a *living* "painting" or "stage," whether they were seen from a fixed point or experienced by the body moving through the perspective of an alley or walk, changing dimensions of perception. It is instructive to learn that in some instances, such bodily movement was compared with the functioning of binoculars or a telescope, where far-away scenery was brought near in an ongoing process of movement and change.[40] Discovering the variety of nature by the body moving, halting, and continuing is hailed in almost all garden poems as the key to experiencing, enjoying and understanding the garden in all its aspects.

[36] Edward S. Casey, *Remembering: A Phenomenological Study* (Bloomington and Indianapolis: Indiana University Press, 1987), 144–216 (part 3, chap. 8 [Body Memory] and chap. 9 [Place Memory]).

[37] This also becomes apparent in the many seventeenth-century travel journals in which the Dutch garden increasingly becomes a source for study and knowledge, from its technology and maintenance, to plantings, waterworks, issues of design, and positioning in the landscape. For a recent study see Erik de Jong, "Nicodemus Tessin Travels in Holland in 1687," *Konsthistorisk Tidskrift* 72, nos. 1–2 (2003): 33–47.

[38] Joseph Elias Van der Meulen, mayor of Utrecht, expressed on 11 December 1749 his regrets about leaving his garden to return to the city for the winter, as follows: "Me voilà donc arrivé aux quartiers d'hiver. Il faut pourtant que je vous dise, que ce n'est pas sans regret que je viens ici m'ennuier d'une manière affreuse et je quitte ma campagne, bien aimée, mon bijou, ou mon sans souci, car il n' y a point de nom assez précieux à lui donner"; see P. Coumans, "Geld en Geluk: De familie Van der Muelen in gezinshistorisch perspectief 1600–1800," *Jaarboek Oud-Utrecht* (1984): 106, note 19.

[39] Erik de Jong, *Nature and Art*, Chap. 4.

[40] Erik de Jong and Marleen Dominicus-van Soest, *Aardse Paradijzen: De tuin in de verbeelding van Nederlandse kunstenaars, I 1460–1760* (Den Bosch/Haarlem: Noord-Brabants Museum/Frans Hals Museum, 1996), 61–63.

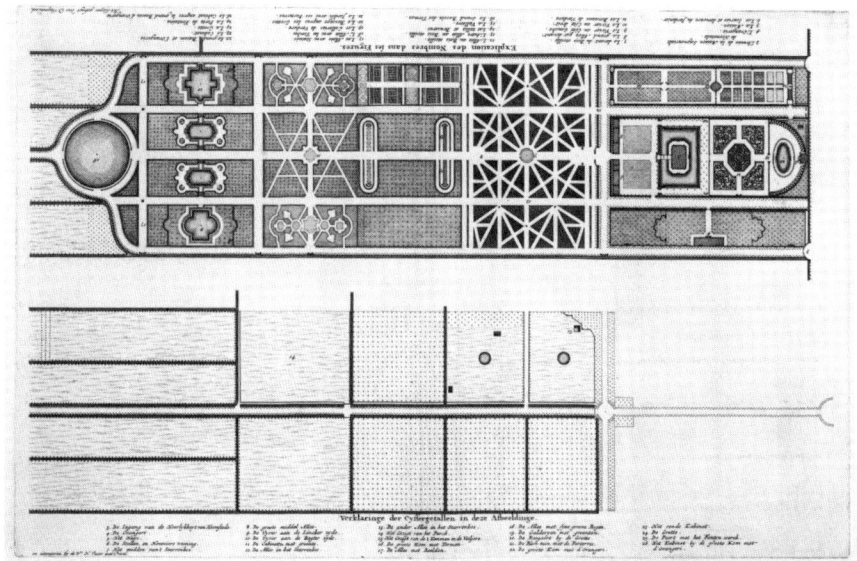

11. *D. Stoopendaal, Plan of the garden Heemstede, copper engraving after 1700/1702, Amsterdam, Rijksmuseum, Rijksprentenkabinet*

Walking the Garden as a Social Activity

Gardens like Heemstede, as evidenced by its topographical *vedutes* from circa 1700, were also social spaces (Fig. 11). Some of the postures and gestures in these garden engravings depict moments of greeting and conversation and seem to be inspired by engraved French examples of people politely gesturing, such as Sebastien Le Clerc's *Divers Desseins de Figures* from 1679.[41] Admired French concepts of civility reached the Dutch upper classes through, among others, De Courtin's popular *Nouveau Traité de la Civilité* from 1671. Translated in 1672, it was heavily edited, thus creating an adapted version for the Dutch elite, that next to such publications relied heavily on oral channels.[42]

Central to polite behavior was the wish to develop a growing self-control over the body: "without affectation . . . . erect, without stiffness or constraint, free and easy in its natural gestures" and, when walking, placing the feet "in such a way that the edifice of the body will rest well on them" as the gait should be "well ordered, without swaying the body to and fro," as a Dutch source from 1735 aptly describes.[43] It was a comportment that consciously sought a marked distinction from what was considered the rambunctious and swaying Italian and Spanish style (Fig. 13).[44] In contrast with the use of landscape in our earlier songbooks, such civil behavior while walking the garden showed as much improvement on human nature as art had had through design on nature in the garden. It was a frequently used educational metaphor in the seventeenth and eighteenth

[41] For the role of ceremonial movement in North European gardens see the studies by Cornelia Jöchner, "Barockgarten und zeremonielle Bewegung: Die Möglichkeiten der *Alée couverte*. Oder: wie arrangiert man ein *incognito* im Garten," in Jörg Jochen Berns and Thomas Rahn, *Zeremoniell als höfische Ästhetik in Spätmittelalter und Früher Neuzeit* (Tübingen: Max Niemeyer Verlag, 1995), 471–83, and "Die höfische Gesellschaft im Garten: Soziale Interaktion als Bildstrategie barocker Gartenveduten," in Wolfgang Adam, ed., *Geselligkeit und Gesellschaft im Barockzeitalter* (Wiesbaden: Harrassowitz Verlag, 1997), 833–55, and Erik de Jong, "Oord van Eden, Oord van Heden: Over de esthetica van de Nederlandse tuin- en landschapsarchitectuur," *Jaarboek Monumentenzorg* (Zwolle: Waanders, 1998), 121–28.

[42] Antoine de Courtin, *Nouveau Traité de la Civilité qui se pratique en France parmi les honnestes gens* (Amsterdam: Daniel Elzevier, 1671), translated as *Nieuwe Verhandeling van de welgemanierdheidt, welke in Vrankryk onder de fraaye lieden gebruikelyk is* (Amsterdam: 1672). See Herman Roodenburg, "The 'Hand of Friendship': Shaking Hands and Other Gestures in the Dutch Republic," in Jan Bremmer and Herman Roodenburg, eds., *A Cultural History of Gesture* (Ithaca, N.Y.: Cornell University Press, 1991), 152–90.

[43] *Het Groot Ceremonie-boeck der beschaafde zeeden, welleevendheid, ceremonieel, en welvoegende hofflykheden . . .* (Amsterdam: C. van Laar, [1735]), 68, 169–79. For the importance of upright posture, see Georges Vigarello, "The Upward Training of the Body from the Age of Chivalry to Courtly Civility," in Michel Feher, Ramona Naddaff, and Nadia Tazi, eds., *Fragments for a History of the Human Body* (New York: Zone and MIT Press, 1989), 2: 149–96.

[44] Herman Roodenburg, "The 'Hand of Friendship'."

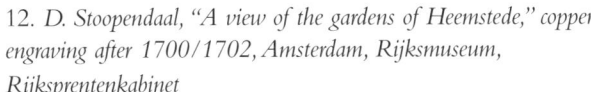

12. *D. Stoopendaal, "A view of the gardens of Heemstede," copper engraving after 1700/1702, Amsterdam, Rijksmuseum, Rijksprentenkabinet*

13. *Ludolf de Jongh, "Two women walking in a garden with gardeners at work," oil on canvas, 1676, Princeton, The Art Museum of Princeton University, on loan from an anonymous collection*

centuries to compare the bridling and taming of animals and nature (training dogs, plants, and hedges) with the right behavior, correct civility, and appropriate education of children and adults (Fig. 14).[45]

Walking enabled the full display of such comportment for both men and women of the Dutch elite, fusing a pleasing, exciting, and instructive educational diversion with the possibility of affirming one's social position in the arena of the garden. The walk, as reflected in poems and *vedute*, will have contributed to a sense of awareness of one's place in the civilized world, something that could not be experienced in the public space of the city. Indeed, the elite may have wished to distinguish itself quite consciously within its own social spheres from middle- and lower-class behavior, thus stressing how physical comportment represented moral values. We may imagine how these elegant summer walks in gardens contrasted painfully with the winter walks of less fortunate farmers and others, who broke off branches of trees in the Heemstede gardens to be used as firewood. Diederick van Velthuysen, both as a magistrate in the province and as owner of the jurisdiction that was attached to his country house and garden of Heemstede as personal privilege, issued severe punishments for the violation of valuable trees in his and other gardens.[46]

Conflicting Arenas

Dutch garden paintings and engravings document for us how the space of the pleasure garden was in fact a conflicting arena of the realities of work, class, and behavior. Gardeners on foot, going about their work, and, bent forward, carrying their tools and utensils, represented in their dress and movements and in the actions of their bodies the opposite of the elegant and leisurely performance of patrons, walking around with family and guests (Figs. 13 and 15).

From other visual sources we may learn how garden imagery was used to represent the ideal moral implications of garden walking. Such implications become clear from the personal deliberations in a manuscript written circa 1730 by Nicolaas

[45] Jan Baptist Bedaux, "Inleiding," in Jan Baptist Bedaux and Rudi Ekkart, eds., *Kinderen op hun mooist: Het kinderportret in de Nederlanden 1500–1700* (Ghent/Amsterdam: Ludion, 2000), 19–24.
[46] Erik de Jong, *Nature and Art*, 84.

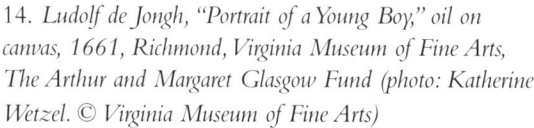

14. *Ludolf de Jongh, "Portrait of a Young Boy," oil on canvas, 1661, Richmond, Virginia Museum of Fine Arts, The Arthur and Margaret Glasgow Fund (photo: Katherine Wetzel. © Virginia Museum of Fine Arts)*

15. *Walking the Garden of Buitenrust in the Diemermeer. Engraving from Matthaeus Broërius van Niedek and Daniel Stoopendaal,* Het Verheerlykt Watergraefs- of Diemer-meer *(Amsterdam: Andries and Hendrik de Leth 1725), pl. 38, Washington D.C., Dumbarton Oaks Research Library and Collection*

Bidloo (1674–1735), the Dutch physician to Tsar Peter the Great.[47] Added to his series of nineteen drawings of the garden he designed for himself from 1702 onward in the German suburb of Moscow (Russia), he instructed his children on why he tried to record his "most favorite pastime," the garden (Fig. 16). "Preserve my handiwork," he wrote, "and you will always be able to see what simple pleasures refreshed your father. And should you not have the opportunity of owning this garden, then *walk* through these drawings of your father, and if you feel so inclined, follow his footsteps in seeking such a useful, honest and pleasing diversion." Bidloo's *adhortatio* shows us how a series of drawings could be considered a substitute for the experience of a garden walk: both reflected a sequence of time and a succession of views. Yet, the drawings are not only a specific record of a particular place. They also embody memory and allude to how the walking experience is connected to the original intent of its designer and the way he considers the garden as "a simple pleasure" and "a useful, honest and pleasing diversion." In the drawings of the garden, Bidloo's children were expected to recognize the ambition of their father: creating order and harmony in a world otherwise full of vanity (to quote Bidloo). The garden does not only invite a walk in thoughts, it also asks to "follow in footsteps" actively as a metaphor for living honestly and justly and in accord with the lessons of divine creation, to which Bidloo more than once refers in his text.

This insight from the spheres of private early-eighteenth-century life, contrasts with how engravings illustrated behavior in public green spaces. An image from 1725 shows us the Middenlaan, the main artery of the Plantage in Amsterdam,

[47] Erik de Jong, "Virgilian Paradise: A Dutch Garden near Moscow in the Early l8th Century," *Journal of Garden History* 1, no. 4 (1981): 305–45, with a full translation of this Dutch text in English.

16. *Nicolaas Bidloo, View in his own garden in the German Suburb of Moscow, Russia. Pen and ink ca. 1730. Leiden, University Library.*
17. *The "Middelwegh" in the New Plantation in Amsterdam, seen towards the Muidergate, engraving from Matthaeus Broërius van Niedek and Daniel Stoopendaal,* Het Verheerlykt Watergraefs- of Diemer-meer *(Amsterdam: Andries and Hendrik de Leth 1725), pl. 3B, Washington D.C., Dumbarton Oaks Research Library and Collection*

Gezicht op den MIDDELWEGH of MUIDER STRAET in de Nieuwe Plantagie naer de Muider Poort toe. || *Vüe du Grand Chemin du Plantage vers la Porte de Muyden.*

a complex of gardens within the city walls of Amsterdam created from 1682 onward (Fig. 17). It also functioned as the main avenue that led outside the city in the direction of the Diemermeerpolder (and further to the east), where again many gardens, walking avenues, and inns attracted hosts of people for a pleasurable outing. The avenue is shown as a well-ordered and clean tree-lined street, busily peopled with pedestrians, individually or in groups, carriages, and dogs. Everybody behaves in an exemplary fashion as part of polite society (Fig. 18).

Contemporary poetry underlined this ideal and extensively praises the Arcadian beauty of the Plantage's design, its space and its avenues.[48] But this image is make-believe, whereas archival sources affirm that the engraving reflects quite specific, even propagandistic, attitudes toward walking, that is, as a social activity controlled by public space. From the many city regulations, written up by the Amsterdam city authorities regularly since 1684 (only two years after the creation of the Plantage), we learn that the avenue formed an arena of conflicting activities. Transgressive behavior of those walking there and using its space was a rule and not an exception. Trees, the main ornament of the avenue's design, were time and again damaged by having their branches broken off (fruit vendors amongst others used these to cover their baskets with merchandise, others stole the wood to build a fire). People cut into the bark of trees, hung laundry from their branches, or peed against their trunks. Animals roamed free in space; garbage polluted the waters; heaps of dung, sand, and stones lay around; the pavement was dirtied with mud and filth. Garden pavilions along the avenue were used for permanent living—housed whores, inns, or other drinking establishments—while garden yards were often subdivided and sublet for activities of trade and industry, all violations of the city's strict rules. Where design and regulations in the Plantage represented agents of control and were coded

[48] Richter Roegholt, "Driehonderd jaar Plantage," in Richter Roegholt, D. Hillenius, and H. E. Coomans, *Wonen en wetenschap in de Plantage: De geschiedenis van een Amsterdamse buurt in driehonderd jaar* (Amsterdam: Universiteit van Amsterdam, 1982), 9–21. For the engraving, see Matthaeus Brouërius van Niedek, *Het Verheerlykt Watergraefs- of Diemermeer* (1725), and for the poem Daniel Willink, *Het Amsterdamsche Tempe of Nieuwe Plantage* (1712).

18. *The "Middelwegh," detail*

19. *Abraham Zeeman, titlepage of Claes Bruin,* Kleefsche en Zuidhollandsche Arkadia

(. . .) verrykt met aantekeningen van den Heere L. Smids, *1716, Amsterdam University Library*

in "ideal" imagery and poetry, in reality walking and using the space of the "Plantage" provided many with a license for transgressive behavior. Opposing the intentions of design and order became an agent of quite another realization of "self." But such transgressions in turn legitimized the repeated issuing of new rules for maintaining order and the increasing severity of punishment.

Landscape, Walking, and Antiquarianism

In 1728 the antiquarian Andries Schoenmaker (1660–1735), based in Amsterdam, wrote to his grandson of the three important things in life.[49] First of all, he mentions spiritual exercise (religion); second, temporary exercise (trade or craft, inherent to life in the city); and, third, permissible exercise as one's pastime. For Schoenmaker, the latter meant an interest in history and, in particular, visiting and documenting villages, towns, country houses, churches, ruins, and castles in the landscape. Schoenmaker's passion pointed to an increasing interest in the antiquarian and other cultural aspects of landscape that are mirrored in the many arcadia, landscape treatises, topographical and antiquarian literature, publications that find their origin in the early and mid-seventeenth century, but enjoyed a high popularity in the 1720s, when the rise of new topographical illustration and the need to collect and publish resulted in the first full-fledged documentation of the province of Noord-Holland, with Amsterdam at its center (Amsterdam itself, interestingly enough, was not documented).[50]

[49] Jeanine Otten, "Opdrachtgevers: Andries en Gerrit Schoenmaker," in Luuc Kooijmans, Erik de Jong, and Hans Brokken, eds., *Pronk met pen en penseel: Cornelis Pronk (1691–1759) tekent Noord-Holland* (Amsterdam: De Bataafsche Leeuw, 1997), 111.

[50] For the arcadias, see Hans Groot, "Achttiende-eeuwse arcadia's: Tussen literatuur en geschiedenis," *Holland* 17 (1985): 241–52. Wendy Jansen, "'Laag bijdegrondse geleerdenpoespas': Een revisie van het beeld van de zeventiende en achttiende-eeuwse aracadia's," unpublished Master's thesis, University of Amsterdam, 1993, and idem, "'Laag bijdegrondse geleerdenpoespas': Onderzoek naar de zeventiende- en achttiende- eeuwse arcadia," *Spektator* 23, no. 2 (1994): 127–37. For the development of Dutch antiquarianism in the early eighteenth century, see Luuc Kooijmans, Erik de Jong, and Hans Brokken, eds., *Pronk met pen en penseel* and in that volume especially Pieter Jan Klapwijk, "Topografie in literair perspectief: De relatie tussen literatuur en topografische tekenkunst in het begin van de achttiende eeuw," 127–51.

20. *C. Pronk, "De Buurchurch te Egmond-Binnen," wash, 1740–45, Haarlem, State Archives Noord-Holland*

21. *C. Pronk, "View of Schermerhorn," pen, wash in grey, 1728, Haarlem, State Archives Noord-Holland*

Where garden poems described garden landscapes, mostly in a monologue, arcadias treated landscape at large, as in the *Kleefsche en ZuidHollandsche Arkadia* from 1716 (Fig. 19). In the form of a dialogue between several people, often with allegorical names like Happy-at-Heart or Witty, the arcadias as a literary subgenre discuss in verse a vast array of themes associated with walking, from monuments to gardens, from planted avenues to local history, from natural scenery, villages, and churches to transportation, morals, customs, literature, and the classics. These geographical and historical descriptions are profusely annotated with artful erudition and often give way to philosophical and religious discourse, which makes these texts both subjective in tone and promotional in character. These imaginary but recognizable walks may be set on the outskirts of a town, among its avenues and lanes, or take on the detailed description and inquiry of the larger landscape beyond the city walls, thus becoming part of a more extensive travel, where walking, barges, and coaches were alternatively used.

This growing vogue for walking and documenting the landscape was connected with new techniques of topographical drawing by artists like Cornelis Pronk (1691–1759) and others. They furnished the engraved illustrations for the arcadias, taking them from a stock of documentation they had amassed on behalf of their patron collectors while traveling and walking throughout the Republic, systematically painting and sketching local signs as part of what was often termed the past of the Fatherland (Figs. 20 and 21). Traveling and walking through the province of Noord-Holland from 1727 to 1733, Pronk's most popular topics were ruins, churches, city gates, castles, and villages in the landscape.

Much of this kind of walking the landscape accompanied by making observations, notes, and drawings, may be interpreted as an outcome for a need for empirical observation, which in Holland was stimulated by the Dutch reception of Isaac Newton's ideas. A scientific approach called physico-theology was combined with the insight that God is manifest in all of nature and its laws. Some of the early antiquarian publications are called *Cabinet* or *Treasury*, in reference to the seventeenth-century cabinets of curiosity with their collections of art and nature (Fig. 22). The interest they had generated in collecting and studying the world through all its manifestations was now transposed onto the larger landscape as one vast cabinet of divine creation and human history. The effect of all this extensive walking, traveling, and documenting was immense: it brought a new, firsthand consciousness of the appearance, the character, and the history of landscape within local boundaries. It was, above all, important in the construction of notions of a shared national Fatherland where landscape and history represented a common identity.

22. *A. van Buysen, "A Cabinet of Curiosity" in Levinus Vincent,* Wonder toneel der Nature *(Amsterdam, 1706)*
23. *H. de Leth, titlepage of M. Brouërius van Nidek,* Het Zegepralent Kennemerlant, Vertoont in veele Heerelyke Gezichten (. . .) *(Amsterdam, 1732)*

Developing a Landscape Perspective

Looking at identity and history from a landscape perspective became fundamental for ongoing explorations of the landscape around Haarlem. We find it codified on the frontispiece of the *Triumphant Kennemerland* (1732), one of the main antiquarian publications of its day illustrating Haarlem's environs through ruins, medieval castles, villages and churches, modern country houses, and gardens. In the small vignette the landscape presents the city of Haarlem, soaring toward the sky, while on the central image it offers an elevated knoll, and on it Brinio, legendary hero and lord of the Caninefates, the earliest inhabitants of this region, about whom Tacitus wrote (Fig. 23). Stone landmarks, ruins of old castles, and emblems of natural prosperity surround this natural historical feature in the landscape.

The book suggests that these monuments from the past are succeeded by the modern gardens and houses illustrated in it. They are the new landmarks and continue the honorable, rich cultural and natural history of this region. Remarkably enough, some of the gardens illustrated show wide vistas beyond the confines of their design, bringing both the city and the ruined castles into the view of those walking in the garden, linking past and present, city and country, visually and ideologically.

Does this mean that design and social practices of the elite within the closed system of a garden were now diluted by other, more scientific, observations and practices? It seems highly likely that the antiquarian approach generated attitudes that looked at landscape in a more encompassing way and brought forward new views on the intimate relations among nature, landscape, history, and the city. The continued practice of traveling and walking was discovering wider horizons as part of increased curiosity in the phenomenology of the landscape. This practice was to continue throughout the eighteenth and the nineteenth centuries into the twentieth, generating continuously changing social practices and concepts of nature, landscape, and culture in relation to the returning themes of natural science, religion, history, and identity.

Walking the Landscape and the Formation of Urban Identity

Much of the topography produced in the late seventeenth and early eighteenth centuries puts an emphasis on the city's boundaries: the bulwarks and fortifications with their gates (Fig. 24). Some garden poems start their description outside these walls, while many arcadias devote much attention to the walks on bulwarks, outside of them, and those leading out into the countryside. Practically and symbolically, walls defined the city; they protected it in times of war, but also defined what it meant to live in the city.

Of the three social groups within the Dutch city, *inhabitants* lived permanently in the city, but had no access to civic rights, whereas *strangers* lived there temporarily. It was the *burgher* (also called *poorter* because he lived within the gates or *poorten*), who enjoyed civic rights, though this does not mean that in Amsterdam, for example, burghers socially formed a homogenous group for they were represented by all classes. The *poorter*-status was desirable because it offered the burgher legal, economic, political, and social privileges and thus a protection within the confines of the city.[51]

24. *C. Pronk, "View of the Spaarnwouder City Gate in Haarlem," pen, wash in grey, ca. 1740, private collection*

Anyone leaving the city through its gates did in fact cross an important boundary, as he became separated from what defined him as a burgher, an inhabitant, or a stranger. He now entered into a new realm, the border region of the landscape and that which lay beyond toward the horizon, both direction and goal. One may compare entering this territory on foot with entering a threshold state, where one's position as a citizen became both confirmed yet also challenged.[52]

In Amsterdam, this liminal state knew gradations, while the jurisdiction of the city still extended for about seven and one-half kilometers. So-called *banposts*, put up along the most important arterial roads in the form of pyramids, symbolized the legal order of the city and marked the territory where judicial authorities could exert their power.[53] Burghers could pass these terms freely but were reminded that for others, such as those banished from the city, they marked an exclusionary boundary.

It is only telling that next to his series of *Pleasant Places*, Claes Jansz. Visscher produced circa 1610 a series of four etchings, illustrating views that all had to do with the jurisdictional boundaries of Amsterdam (Fig. 25, and compare Fig. 2).[54] Read in conjunction with his other series, where the walk leads out to the landscape beyond Amsterdam into the landscape around Haarlem, we may conclude that such walking indeed was felt to cross protective boundaries and represented a temporal separation from one's everyday life in the city.

[51] Erika Kuijpers and Maarten Prak, "Burger, ingezetene, vreemdeling: Burgerschap in Amsterdam in de 17ᵉ en 18ᵉ eeuw," in Joost Kloek and Karin Tilmans, *Burger: Een geschiedenis van het begrip 'burger' in de Nederlanden van de Middeleeuwen tot de 21ste eeuw* (Amsterdam: Amsterdam University Press, 2002), 113–33.
[52] Arnold van Gennep, *The Rites of Passage* (Chicago: The University of Chicago Press, 1960), foreword, chaps. 1, 2, 3, 9, and 10. Victor Turner, The *Ritual Process. Structure and Anti-Structure* (New York: Aldine de Gruyter, 1995; 1st ed. 1969), chap. 3.
[53] Anne Van Dooren, "Sublieme limieten," in Agnes Schreiner, Henny Bouwmeester, and Anne van Dooren, *In de ban van het recht/Captured by Justice* (Amsterdam: 1991), 62. Marc Glaudemans, *Amsterdams Arcadia: De ontdekking van het achterland* (Nijmegen: Sun, 2000), 47–53.
[54] Boudewijn Bakker and Huigen Leeflang, *Nederland naar 't leven*, cat. no. 9.

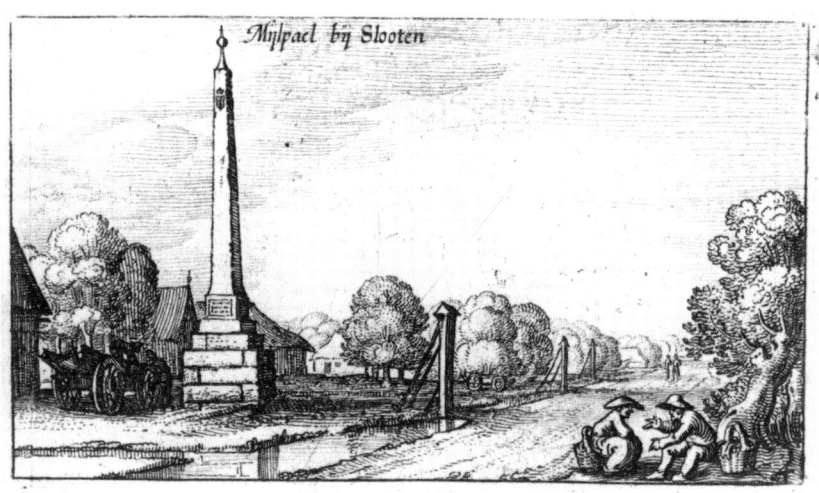

25. *Claes Jansz. Visscher, "The ban post near the village of Sloten," etching, ca, 1610, Amsterdam,* Historisch-topografische Atlas van het Gemeentearchief Amsterdam

One might make a comparison with the Greek *polis* and its *chora*, the countryside territory that continuously had to be mastered through ritual in order "to secure," as Pérez-Gómez puts it, "the survival of the world from one instant to the next."[55] As the *polis*, the Dutch seventeenth-century cities of Amsterdam and Haarlem were both highly organized and ordered urban spaces. They contrasted with the rather unpredictable world without, ranging from ordered agricultural fields, reclaimed and organized polders (where a sense of urban and social order could be recognized) to the wilderness of the dunes, the beach, and the endless sea.

Walking that landscape, that complex liminal space, could then be seen as a ritual-like performance during which the structure of everyday life was challenged. It offered both a confrontation and an opportunity.[56] To some it offered the freedom of dalliance and amorous play, healthy exercise, and the pleasure to see and visit things and places. To others it presented the opportunity to construct gardens as socially protected spaces, allowing them the privilege to retire within an ideal construction of art, life, and nature. To still others, walking allowed for the possibility of collecting knowledge and understanding about the world with its plants and trees, its history, customs, buildings, and villages.

The landscape must have looked like a miraculous open-air *wunderkammer*, where topographical features seemed to mimic urban features. The dunes west of Haarlem, for example, protected the fertile cultural landscape as "bulwarks" against the wild sea, replicating the fortified walls of the city. Both functioned as a real and symbolic border with regard to territories that lay beyond. Both fortifications and dunes provided the opportunity to look down onto the landscape, creating views into a panoramic distance where the flat landscape seemed to provide all elements with their proper place under the vast expanse of the sky. For many, therefore, the secular act of walking the landscape must have been a confrontation with a magnificent creation. Its variety and expressiveness solicited response during the frame of a walk where ordinary, urban behavior was suspended for a different experience of time needed to live and read through what the landscape had to offer.

In Pieter de la Court's theoretical treatise *Considerations on the State* from 1662, acquired, not inherited, power calls forth the best in people and education is the main tool to achieve it. Experience, knowledge, and argumentation are part of civic virtue and a good citizen is both its condition as well as its product.[57] The burgher needs to be a *mercator sapiens*, a wise merchant, who knows how to value both pleasure and utility, as De la Court put it. Walking beyond the boundaries of the city into the landscape may well have been part of the education to gain such "wisdom," much in the same way traveling to foreign countries—the "*groote tour*" or "grand tour"—was considered an essential part of good education, hence its definition as

[55] Alberto Pérez-Gómez, "Chora: The Space of Architectural Representation," *Chora: Intervals in the Philosophy of Architecture* 1 (1994): 1–34, quote on p. 10. Indra Kagis McEwen, *Socrates' Ancestor: An Essay in Architectural Beginnings* (Cambridge, Mass.: MIT Press, 1997), chap. 4, "Between Movement and Fixity: The Place for Order."

[56] Heidi de Mare, "The Domestic Boundary as Ritual in Seventeenth-Century Holland," in Heidi de Mare and Anna Vos, eds., *Urban Rituals in Italy and the Netherlands* (Assen: Van Gorcum, 1993), 108–32.

[57] Hans W. Blom, "Burger en Belang: Pieter de la Court over de politieke betekenis van burgers," in Kloek and Tilmans, *Burger*, 110–11.

an "*educatiereis*" or "educational voyage."[58] As such, the ritual act of walking the landscape became part of a complex interplay between the use of urban space and the use of the landscape. The walk was capable of assimilating new insights, offered new knowledge, and connected members of different groups, allowing each of these groups their own experiences. It supported their identity and memory, instilled a sense of place and locality, and produced pleasure and moral meaning as a response to the act of moving the body. As a ritual-like performance, the walk signified more than just a physical movement in time. For a citizen of Amsterdam and Haarlem, walking the landscape made apparent that his status and identity as a burgher or inhabitant was defined by what lay not only *inside* but also *outside* the boundaries of the city's walls.

We may understand this most clearly when we realize how in the course of the seventeenth and eighteenth centuries Amsterdam became surrounded by a true arcadia of pleasure and utilitarian landscapes, ranging from strings of hundreds of country houses along the rivers Vecht, Angstel, Amstel, and Spaarne, country seats in the industrial peat landscape of 's Graveland and along the dunes near Haarlem, along the Wijkerlake, and in the Beemsterpolder (Fig. 26 and Fig. 2). All these larger and smaller sites were connected through waterways and paths, set in rich agricultural fields, and bordered by the wilderness of the dunes to the west. This was Amsterdam's true landscape.

Official descriptions of Amsterdam's location and environment were mostly described in economic and legal terms, while its urban landscape proper was looked upon as a swamp.[59] It led some to compare the city of Amsterdam with its tree-lined canals, many gardens, hundreds of ship masts in the harbor, and thousands of trees driven into the soil to provide the fundament for architecture, with a forest or a countryside arcadia.[60] The urban was seen through the eyes of the cultivated landscape, not the other way around.

Nearby Haarlem linked its identity in a different way with the positive qualities of its surrounding landscape. In its official city descriptions it constructed an intimate relationship between its *situs* (topography), its *res* (material life), and its *populus* (burghers).[61] This could range from the rich natural resources the landscape had to offer (clear dune water to brew beer, sand to

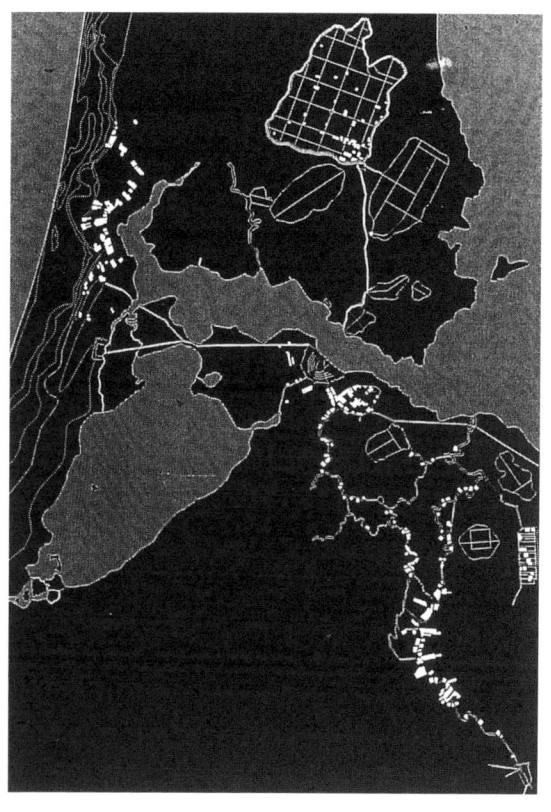

26. *Reconstruction of the 17th- and 18th-c. pleasure landscape around Amsterdam with the Beemster polder to the northeast, the string of countryseats along the Wijkermeer in the northwest, countryseats to the west of Haarlem near the dunes and the Diemermeer, the villas along the rivers Angstel and Vecht and in the peat district of 's Graveland to the east. Map prepared by the Department of Landscape Architecture, Delft Technical University under supervision of Prof. Clemens Steenbergen.*

[58] For concepts about traveling and its role in education in the Dutch Republic, see A. Frank-van Westrienen, *De Groote Tour: Tekening van de educatiereis der Nederlanders in de zeventiende eeuw* (Amsterdam: Noord-Hollandsche Uitgeversmaatschappij BV, 1983), 28–49.

[59] Leeflang, "Dutch Landscape: The Urban View," 73–80.

[60] Erik de Jong and Wouter Reh, "De Tuin en de Stad: De Amsterdamse grachtentuin in vogelvlucht," in Willemien Dijkshoorn, Erik de Jong, and Lodewijk Odé, eds., *Amsterdamse Grachtentuinen. Keizersgracht* (Zwolle: Waanders, 1997), 15–49.

[61] Frans P. T. Slits, *Het Latijnse Stededicht: Oorsprong en ontwikkeling tot in de zeventiende eeuw* (Amsterdam: Thesis Publishers, 1990), 252–300. Henk van Nierop, "Lof en beschrijving van Haarlem bij Samuel Ampzing," and Erik de Jong, "Historisch landschap: Haarlem als hoofdstad van het Hollands Arcadië," in Koos Levy-van Halm, Epco Runia, Bert Sliggers, and Derk Snoep, eds., *De Trots van Haarlem: Promotie van een stad in kunst en historie* (Haarlem: Frans Hals Museum/Teylers Museum, 1995), 13–21 and 127–35.

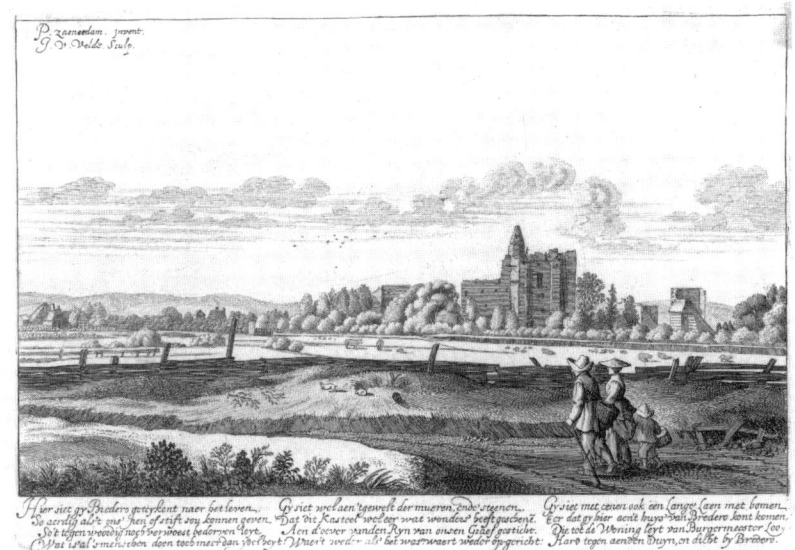

build the city) to countryside pleasures based on its diversity of landscape. Samuel Ampzing's *Praise and Description of Haarlem*, published in 1628 with illustrations designed by Pieter Jansz. Saenredam, shows five out of its eight topographical illustrations devoted to landscapes outside the city, while his text extols the prosperity and utility, the beauty and the safety of the natural environment. Walking acted as the active agent in the creation of such landscape propaganda and confirmed such a vision through its ritualized experience (Fig. 27).

At the End of the Walk

Having taken "fresh air," a return to the confines of the city awaited those walking—in seventeenth- and eighteenth-century terms they came back "refreshed": physically, intellectually, and morally transformed. Arcadias, garden poems, and engraved or painted landscape

27. *Jan van de Velde II after Pieter Jansz. Saenredam, "Landscape view with the ruins of castle Brederode," etching in Samuel Ampzing,* Beschrijvinge ende Lof der Stadt Haarlem *(Haarlem: Adriaen Rooman, 1628), Haarlem, Streekarchief Kennemerland*

views in the confinement of the home must have evoked for some the experience of walking and its connection to time, creativity, pleasure, history, and morality. For others, on a more basic level, standing on the bulwarks and looking out toward the horizon beyond the city walls, the knowledge of having walked in the landscape must have brought a sense of orientation, of level, distance, and frontier very different from the vagaries of daily urban routine. In whatever way, eye and mind must have followed many times in the footsteps of a real walk, transforming the experience of place into a physical and mental memory, into a sense of place. Without the experience of walking the landscape, one's identity as an urban inhabitant could not be properly defined nor understood.

Notes
I thank Michel Conan, Washington, D.C.; Stephen H. West, Arizona State University, and two anonymous reviewers for their insightful, enthusiastic, and instructive comments.

Performance and Appropriation: Profane Rituals in Gardens and Landscapes

Performance and Appropriation: Profane Rituals in Gardens and Landscapes

Performance and Appropriation: Profane Rituals in Gardens and Landscapes

Performance and Appropriation: Profane Rituals in Gardens and Landscapes

Royal Gardens, Fashionable Promenades, and Public Opinion in Seventeenth- and Eighteenth-Century Pairs

Michel Conan

Joachim Alexandre Metra (1714–1786) used to sit every day on a wooden bench under a large horse chestnut tree on the Feuillant terrace at the Tuileries, in the midst of a large circle of chairs reserved for a privileged group of friends to whom he repeated the news he had learned earlier that day.[1] He belonged to a bourgeois family and, after he inherited a large annual income, he gave up his job in the tax administration to devote himself entirely to his passion for telling the news to passers-by at the Tuileries. He was the best known of the many people telling the news every day in public places, known as *novellists*,[2] in Paris. Metra always wore the same clothes and spoke calmly, presenting news and developing its consequences in a moderate and modest voice. He was always surrounded by a silent crowd of listeners. The garden guards allowed no one but his friends to sit there. He became so popular, even among aristocrats, that he became an opinion leader in high society as well as among the Parisian population at large. Whenever an important event occurred, Louis XVI would ask his close courtiers: What does the Metra chap say about it?[3]

At his death in 1786, Metra's ritual performance embodied and expressed public opinion in Paris. Other novellists engaged in similar rituals. We shall see how these rituals came into existence, how royal gardens contributed to their development, how such ritual practices contributed to the development of a new agency of garden places, and how this yields some tentative insights into relationships among royal gardens, rituals of emplacement, and public opinion. Because I have already mentioned public opinion several times, I should remind the reader that the reality of public opinion goes unquestioned nowadays, it is routinely measured, and we are all very familiar with its role in public affairs, but this has not always been the case. We shall see how this shared belief came into existence.

Royal Promenades and New Forms of Urban Civility

The development of the public discussion of government affairs, which was formally prohibited by law, coincided with three major changes in Parisian life in the early seventeenth century: the irresistible growth in the numbers of carriages, gardens, and conversation circles in the city. To a large extent, each of these was inspired by Italian precedents, but they resulted in a specific course of cultural change in Paris. These three domains of practical change are related. The construction of a *corso* for aristocratic carriages by Queen Margot was followed by the construction of the *Cours La Reine* by Queen Marie de Medicis. This daily attracted a group of bourgeois who came to watch a conspicuous display of riches by aristocrats in their carriages. At the same time a growing number of wealthy Parisian citizens—aristocrats, noblemen and -women, churchmen, bourgeois, and

---

[1] Leclerc de Sept-Chênes, *Eloge de J-A. Métra, Le nouvelliste*, ed. Originales Londres, 1986 avec une préface de Maurice Tourneux (Paris, 1827).
[2] The French name "nouvelliste" is no longer in use. So it would not be appropriate to call them "newsmen." Instead, I have translated this term as *novellist*, with a double l, in order to avoid confusion with novelist.
[3] *Mémoires de la Marquise de Villeneuve Arifat*, ed. H. Courteault (Paris, 1900).

robins (the recently ennobled bourgeoisie that grew tremendously at the end of the sixteenth and early seventeenth centuries)—became frequent users of several royal gardens: the Luxembourg, the Tuileries, and the Arsenal gardens, and sometime later the Palais-Cardinal gardens (1624). In each of these gardens, people would walk up and down the alleys, then some would sit on the benches or the lawn, or lean along a balustrade and watch the strollers. This prompted the development of the promenade, a new form of social intercourse, and of some voyeuristic rituals.[4]

The development of private gardens took off all around Paris a little before 1620. At the same time a conversation circle organized by Catherine de Vivonne, the Marquise de Rambouillet, in her house near the Carrousel and the Tuileries, was taking off.[5] These conversations were ritualized practices that allowed a happy few to engage in intellectual intercourse irrespective of social rank or gender. A relationship developed over the years between garden promenades and conversation practices. Conversation circles, then known as *ruelles*,[6] would slip from the lady's alcove into her gardens, and pursue, in smaller groups, all sorts of conversational games. Thus promenades became for a growing group of mundane persons, *les mondains*, an exercise in the aesthetics of civility. A similar development took place in public gardens. Groups of people walking in an alley would engage in conversation, some of them catching others' attention, and growing slowly in number or losing participants according to the topics of conversation. There were differences, however, between the royal gardens, as if they specialized in different modes of conversation—the Luxembourg, for instance, attracted more serious conversation, the Tuileries more light-hearted ones. Of course, there were many more uses of gardens and many users did not belong to the mundane world. So this new civility and its participants attracted social climbers who attempted to ape distinguished manners as best they could. Their failures provided fuel for conversations in the lady's alcoves.[7]

Thus, we can see rituals of promenades in the royal gardens as a development of urban civility that parallels at its beginning the development of the ruelles society culture, named after the lady's alcove, the ruelles, where the guests assembled in the host lady's chamber. It was very different, however, because, unlike in the ruelles, no one was responsible for conducting the interactions between participants. In addition to the number of potential participants to any group, conversation was broader and more diverse in the gardens than in any lady's alcove, and there was constant interaction among groups promenading and people or groups sitting along the alleys and observing, criticizing, and reflecting on the events at the promenade.

Visits to these garden promenades led to the development of new implicit rules of behavior, establishing a clear separation in dress, bodily deportment, and social behavior from those of common life in the city: in the Tuileries, for instance, it came to be seen as ridiculous for a woman to walk in the company of her husband, and it became standard practice for men and women alike to engage in conversation with an unknown person of the opposite sex, or to break into a conversation—even to contradict a speaker. Royal gardens became an extraordinary magnet for the wealthy Parisian population, allowing the development of previously unheard-of social intercourse between men and women, among young people, and among members of the bourgeoisie, the church, and the nobility, as well as between factions of the aristocracy and the mundane world. These meetings gave rise to a completely new fluidity in interactions between members of different social classes.

To a large extent, these royal gardens were a melting pot. Yet, they only allowed a limited *communitas*, as a great part of the population was excluded. It reached a zenith in the interregnal period separating the death of Louis XIII (1643) from the political coup by Louis XIV in 1661, which ushered in the second phase of absolutism in France. An ever-growing number of daily visitors would crowd the Tuileries as well as the Cours La Reine, Luxembourg, Cours de l'Arsenal, or private gardens opened to the public by their owners, such as the gardens of La Folie-Rambouillet. Garden designers took note of this

---

[4] Michel Conan, "A Tale of Two Gardens: Urbane Wilderness in the Tuileries Gardens and Saint-James Park," in the conference proceedings *Wild Cities/Urbane Wilderness* (Tasmania: School of Architecture at Launceston, 2002), 12–20.

[5] Victor Cousin, *La société française au XVIIe siècle d'après le Grand Cyrus de mlle de Scudéry* (Paris: Didier et cie), 1858.

[6] *Ruelles* were groups of people gathering in the alcoves of a lady's chamber to engage in sophisticated conversations under her direction.

[7] See *Polyandre* (1642) by Charles Sorel, quoted in Elizabeth Kugler, "The Promenade as Performance: A Study of the Landscape and Literature of Seventeenth-century Paris." Ph.D. diss., Johns Hopkins University, 1998.

phenomenon and paid increased attention to the establishment of a main alley as flat as possible in an aristocratic garden; the longer it was, the larger the crowd it could attract, and henceforth the wider it had to be as noted by Dezallier d'Argenville in 1709.[8]

When Colbert called on Le Nôtre to provide a new design for the Tuileries, it is most likely that Colbert had in mind that Louis XIV would restore the Louvre and that the Tuileries would be his private garden. Le Nôtre believed that modern royal gardens were bound to remain open to the Parisian public and needed to accommodate large crowds. Thus, he provided a new design with fewer alleys, a double alley on the major axis, and large by-alleys beneath two long terraces on each side of the garden. In a similar vein, one can see that long, flat promenades were designed in all major gardens, very often perpendicular to the main axis when they allowed a significantly larger flat or nearly flat walking area as in the Luxembourg, Chantilly, Saint Germain en Laye, or Choisy for the Grande Mademoiselle.

However, cultural changes took an altogether different course in aristocratic gardens and in the royal gardens open to the public in Paris, because they gave rise to very different rituals of interaction, such as group walks and entertainment, or sentimental pursuits among a self-selected society in the aristocratic gardens; and conversation, conspicuous display of clothes, public gossip, news peddling, or prostitution among a mixed-class society in the public gardens. Learning the news from the novellists was a distinguishing feature of gardens open to the public, and that is the focus of attention for the rest of this chapter.

The "Echo" and the "Mazarinades"

It should be stressed that this phenomenon was completely unplanned for. It was, in fact, anathema to the official view of public order defended by the king, parliament, and the church. And it developed very slowly, making its entry into the royal gardens because they attracted a large crowd of visitors. In the old Tuileries garden, there was an artificial echo at the end of the main alley opposite the palace. It was made of a semicircular wall. Speaking or singing aloud in front of it would produce an echo that allowed the last two syllables of a sentence or verse to be heard after the speaker was silent. This was a place sought by many lovers who would make a display of themselves and of their love for a lady of their choice.[9] During the regency, it came to be used as a place for reading libels and satirical poems known as Mazarinades against Concini, the queen's favorite, and against the prime minister, Cardinal Mazarin, hence their name. The authors of such pamphlets could be punished on the gallows. Reading a banal poem in front of the Echo was not punishable, however, even if the repetition of a few syllables by the Echo made it into a scathing pamphlet. So the Echo became a place sought for watching and performing this kind of political slandering.

This remained a trifle among the large variety of social activities taking place at the Tuileries. When Le Nôtre reorganized the garden, he destroyed the Echo and did away with this marginal political activity, but this did not curb the development of novellist activity in this garden, because it was not rooted in any functional property of design, but in cultural trends that had been on the upsurge for a long time and would avail themselves of any place where large numbers of Parisian citizens would gather and enjoy a sense of freedom.

---

[8] Antoine-Joseph Dézallier d'Argenville, *La théorie et la pratique du jardinage. Où l'on traite à fond des beaux jardins appellés communément les jardins de propreté, comme sont les parterres, les bosquets, les boulingrins, &c. Contenant plusieurs plans et dispositions generales de jardins; nouveaux desseins ... & autres ornemens servant à la décoration & embélissement des jardins. Avec la maniere de dresser un terrain...* (Paris: J. Mariette, 1709), 41.

[9] Marcel Poëte, *Au Jardin des Tuileries, l'art du jardin, la promenade publique* (Paris: Auguste Picard, 1924), 191. According to John Evelyn's 1644 visit, the Tuileries were the best place in the world to enjoy both solitude and social intercourse. He was particularly captivated by the artificial echo that repeats words so distinctly that there is always some beautiful nymph who delights in making him repeat her songs: from under a certain tree the voice seemed to fall from the clouds, from another, to issue from the depth of the earth. See also p. 192. Sauval describes the echo: it was formed by a semicircular wall covered with greenery from top to bottom and hidden by palisades and arbors (*tornelles*). "Voices could be heard along the entire diameter of the wall and could be produced from different places a few meters away." (I assume they were inside the semicircle.) See the illustration by Merian (XVIIe s.), 273.

The Origin of the Novellists' Network

The citizens of Paris were extremely keen for news, yet there was little available in print. The first journals to be created were quickly placed under a monopoly and governmental censorship. Publishing activities were more and more restricted as time went by. *The Gazette*, created by Theophraste Renaudot in 1631, had a *privilège*, a royal monopoly for political news, and merely chronicled the life at court in France and abroad; the *Journal des Savants*, created by Eugène Savin in 1665, provided literary criticism under state control after 1781; and the *Mercure Galant* in 1672 chronicled the leisure and pleasures of Parisian higher society (it came under royal control in 1724). In 1563, Charles IX prohibited any publication that was not explicitly authorized by the king. In 1571, it was made clear how harsh the punishments could be for trespassers of the law. Louis XIII extended the punishments to the printers, bookshop keepers, and all booksellers. In 1624, it was expressly forbidden to publish any news concerning the state. Louis XIV and the Parliaments went further and prohibited any criticism of a person engaged in government. The so-called liberal government of Philippe d'Orléans after Louis XIV's death aggravated the penalties, adding the threat of corporal punishment.[10]

In 1728, under the "beloved" King Louis XV, trespassers of these laws could be considered "threats to public order and peace" (*perturbateurs du repos public*) and banished from their province on a first offence and from the kingdom on the second; printers would be put to the gallows on a first offence and sent to the *cadena perpetua* for the second. In 1757, capital punishment became the fate of anyone convicted of "having authored, sponsored or printed writings" that "tend to challenge religion, to set trouble in the minds, to slight the government's authority, to foster public disorder, or unrest."[11] This was not enough. In 1764, any publication concerning public finance was prohibited, and, in 1767, the Parliament of Paris forbade any discussion of religious questions. This parody of laws was put into effect. I have drawn attention to this aspect of governmental institutions in order to highlight the significance of the development of a population of novellists who disseminated as much gossip as they did information throughout the city of Paris.

Public broadcast of news by self-appointed persons is likely to have begun at the end of the sixteenth century, a time of great unrest in the city of Paris because of religious wars. The Augustinian Cloister was, in 1585, already a center of discussion of political news,[12] and the booksellers on the Augustinians' quay received all sorts of journals from England, Brussels, and the Netherlands, which remained a source of information for novellists.[13] During the first half of the seventeenth century, novellists would gather and tell the news mostly on the Pont Neuf and, after mid-century, in the Galleries of the Palais, the court of justice.[14] Both places attracted large crowds and held many small shops visited by lots of people who could join a novellist's circle of listeners. Yet from the early seventeenth century onward they gathered in a growing number of places, either convents or gardens, open to the polite public. The convents where they convened also opened onto gardens accessible to the public such as the Celestine, near the Arsenal gardens, the Cordeliers near the Sorbonne, and the Temple, street of the corderie. The gardens they used were very large, such as the Arsenal gardens, the gardens of the Prince de Soubise planted with dense horse-chestnut trees, and with a gallery in the shape of a demi-lune,[15] the Jardin du Roi where the royal botanical collections were kept, and the gardens of the Luxembourg, the Tuileries, and the Palais-Cardinal.

---

[10] In 1728, under the "beloved" King Louis XV, trespassers of these laws could be considered "threats to public order and peace" (*perturbateurs du repos public*) and banished from their province on a first offence and from the kingdom on the second; printers would be put to the gallows on a first offence, and sent to the *cadena perpetua* for the second.

[11] This was not enough. In 1764, any publication concerning public finance was prohibited, and in 1767, the Parliament of Paris forbade any discussion of religious questions.

[12] *Mémoires-journaux de Pierre de Lestoile* (Paris: Librairie des bibliophiles, 1875–83), vol. 1: 301; vol. 2: 117, 181; vol. 5: 41, 131, 237, 325.

[13] Francois Colletet, *Les Tracas de Paris ou seconde partie de la Ville de Paris en vers burlesques* (Paris, 1692), in Paul Lacroix, ed., *Paris ridicule et burlesque au dixseptième siècle . . . nouvelle édition . . . par P. L. Jacob* (Paris: A. Delahays, 1859), 279.

[14] Frantz Funck-Brentano, *Les nouvellistes / Avec la collaboration de M. Paul d'Estrée. Ouvrage contenant six planches hors texte* (Paris: Hachette et cie, 1905), 115.

[15] Funck-Brentano, *Les nouvellistes*, 140.

Brief Descriptions of Ritualized Behaviors

Convents were convenient gathering places because the cloisters provided refuge from the rain, and monks who were curious to hear the news would treat the novellists to a meal, but the promenade in the gardens was the magnet that attracted the public. Two young Dutchmen described the gardens of the convent of Celestine monks in 1657: "The near-by garden is behind the convent. One finds vine-covered arbors first, and then large alleys bordered with beech trees neatly trimmed." There were small beds of rare flowers and artificial grottoes with statues of painted wood.[16] The gardens of the Arsenal offered a long walk (approximately 670 meters), all the way along the city wall from the Bastille to the river Seine. The cloister of the Cordeliers was a later promenade, built in 1683. It contained a parterre with a fountain in its cloister, and novellists engaged there in the most radical criticism of the monarchy and its cynical aristocracy as early as 1725, according to police reports.[17]

At the Luxembourg gardens, some novellists would walk under the elm trees of the quincunx; some walked the longer alleys that ran between the terrace and the vegetable gardens of Notre Dame des Champs forming two rows facing one another (*l'allée des soupirs* alongside the chateau, *la grande allée* starting at the *rond d'eau*, *l'allée des Carmes* near the rue de Vaugirard); some would gather at the crossing of several alleys or in a circle of chairs placed for their convenience at the allée des Carmes; still another group would stay under a very large dark yew tree. From the end of the seventeenth century to the middle of the eighteenth, this was the favorite walk of the Parisian bourgeois. The tone of conversation was serious and the novellists dealt with politics, economics, and religion, adopting a more moderate attitude than their colleagues at the cloister of Cordeliers.

A greater variety of novellists was to be found at the Tuileries: in the *Grande Allée*, *galant* novellists would echo the news of ruelles society, read the latest poems, sing the latest songs, and everywhere small groups would gather to listen to all sorts of gossip including, of course, about war, finance, and government affairs, as well as all possible scandals and mundane events. There were, however, a few places used solely by novellists, such as a bench at the very end of the garden, and a circle of benches in the shade around the rond d'eau.[18] The terrace along the water, shaded by elm trees, filled a special function: the critical examination of the day's news at 6 p.m. by groups of novellists, a feature to which I shall return.

The Palais Royal became, after the mid-eighteenth century, the major gathering of political novellists who used to walk either in the central alleys, or on the benches in the shadow around the rond d'eau,[19] or along the *boulingrin*. In the second half of the eighteenth century a number of novellists would gather around a very large horse chestnut tree known as the Tree of Cracovie. To say one held "a degree in Cracovie studies" became a commonplace way of describing a compulsive liar.

Ritualized Practice and Organization

To disseminate news, novellists had to discover it. So almost all of them listened to other novellists, whose news they repeated in their own way, or fished for fresh news, engaging anyone in the garden to offer them some news or organizing a network of informers. Thus, we can see that in spite of differences in the form of presentation, the news all proceeded from a criss-cross of information and disagreements.[20] In fact, novellists depended very much on the willingness of their audience to believe them and were constantly exposed to contradiction by someone who claimed a greater authority on the topic at hand. Very quickly, in the first half of the seventeenth century, novellists started to specialize in discussing either politics, or military

[16] Funck-Brentano, *Les nouvellistes*, 133–34. From 1608 to 1611, Antonio Perez, a former minister of Philippe II, was the very successful chair of a circle of novellists (136).

[17] Funck-Brentano, *Les nouvellistes*, 142–43.

[18] Laurent Bordelon, abbé (1653–1730), *L'Ambigu d'Auteuil, ou Veritez historiques; composées du Joueur. De l'Inconnu. Du Nouveliste. Du Sincere. Du Financier. Du Subtil. Du Critique. De l'Hypocrite. Et de plusieurs autres personnages de differens caracteres* (Paris: chez la veuve Jacques de Courbe, 1709).

[19] Bordelon, *L'Ambigu*, 203–4.

[20] In fact, novellists depended very much on the willingness of their audience to believe them and were constantly exposed to contradiction.

and foreign travel, or literary affairs. The latter were called the Parnasse novellists, and they developed their own specializations: drama, opera, ballet, music, painting, and architecture.

Yet, the most interesting phenomenon was the development of small groups that practiced news criticism and mutual support. Active novellists would spend a great part of the day collecting news, either actively interviewing visitors in the garden, meeting informants, or listening to other novellists. Thus, they would share the news with a group of novellists with whom they had become affiliated. These groups used to call themselves a society, a company, or an office. All of them formed a small deliberating assembly with a chair and a secretary. The author Du Camp d'Orgas calls them the "chamber" in a satirical poem on novellists:

> The chamber breaks off
> Did you say the chamber? Yes it is a whole body (*corps*)
> With its chair, its barrister. . . . [21]

They would assemble at a given hour. At the Tuileries, most of them would gather under the elm trees on the Water Terrace along the Seine after 6 p.m. The chair would open the session. All news would be listed on the agenda, and then began the reflection hour, a critical examination meant to decide which news could be trusted and which should be discarded. Late participants would join the group without greeting anyone or saying a word, to avoid interrupting the speaker. Such behavior would have been against the rituals of interaction for members of polite society elsewhere in the garden. Yet, here, a different ritual prevailed. It is worth noting that these practices followed a set of sensible rules once disbelief about the news source was suspended. They can be accounted for entirely as a set of performative actions that quenched the well-educated population's thirst for fresh news.

Because these novellists were self-appointed, it is rather difficult to know who they were. Satirists and the police, however, have left much information about them. In the mid-eighteenth century, the author of *Les Moeurs de Paris* distinguished three main groups: retired army officers, specializing in military affairs; bourgeois, mostly engaged in political news and usually very critical of the government; and workers. The description is obviously incomplete, as several aristocrats and members of the robe nobility[22] were known for many years as prominent figures in one of the gardens. So there is little ground to look at social class as a force in developing the role of novellists, and I would rather insist on the spatiality at work.

Many people who listened to the news in the garden would repeat it later in other places so that some news would travel around Paris in a day or two. These rituals of production, selection, and dissemination of news rested on a spatially distributed network of novellists who operated from a limited number of emplacements mostly located in three royal gardens open to the public and smaller gardens in three cloisters. Yet, we would entirely miss the significance of these rituals if we did not pay attention to the larger number of specific performances to which they gave rise throughout the city. We shall come back to two aspects that are directly linked: reinterpretation and repression. We shall examine how they contributed to the development of the commonly shared idea that public opinion exercises the best possible judgment. The idea of public opinion was a major cultural development, as it tended to substitute human judgment for divine will. However, this judgment—public opinion—was to be exercised by the public, but no one could say who the people were whose judgment embodied public opinion.

Public Opinion and Urban Ritual Performances

Let me first define the distance I have traveled away from the history of ideas, and then introduce the dialectics of opacity and reflexivity or, seen from different points of view, the dialectics of emplacements and ideas. To study the

[21] Du Camp, Pierre, sieur d'Orgas, *Satires ou réflexions sur les erreurs des hommes, et les nouvellistes du temps* (Paris: Chez Gabriel Quinet, 1690).
[22] M. L(a) P(e)y(r)e, *Moeurs de Paris* (Amsterdam, 1747). See, for example, Artur de Lionne, p. 88. See also p. 97.

development of public opinion, we might start from the origins of the idea and try to follow up its impact on social practices. We might trace back the origin of public opinion to the concept of *doxa* in Aristotle and then argue that this idea gave rise to social practices such as gatherings in ladies' alcoves or public debates in royal gardens, collective judgment in the Salon de Peinture at the Academy, or in the parterre of the royal theater. This would leave us, however, with two intractable problems: Why did such phenomena wait until the seventeenth century to appear, and why did they not all start at the same time? Instead, we shall proceed in reverse order, and ask how did urban ritual practices give rise to different forms of collective judgment? And how were they interpreted by a variety of different reflective observers of Parisian society as instances of the same conceptual entity: public opinion? Yet, before that, we should examine the existence of the public and some of its most prominent manifestations.[23]

The Ruelles Gatherings

Public gatherings became an important feature of daily life in leisure society of seventeenth-century Paris as soon as the Tuileries and the Cours La Reine opened, but I wish to call attention again to the almost minuscule ruelles society gatherings. Before the time of the Fronde (1648–1653), their number was extremely limited, but even then they played an important role in the development of public judgment and critical assessment of cultural changes. In *Polyandre* (1642), Charles Sorel (1602–1674) provides an example of the reflective relationship between public gardens and mundane society in the salon. The ridicule of characters whom he saw or met during a promenade, first at the Luxembourg, and then at the Cours La Reine, became the material for a satirical examination of new forms of collective behavior presented and discussed in a witty manner in a ruelle gathering. Thus, the lady's chamber became a place where a very small group of mundane people comprising robins, noblemen, and members of the *Parnasse* society passed aesthetic judgment on drama, poetry, and literature as well as ethical judgment on issues of gender, private behavior, and the emerging forms of public life in the public gardens.[24]

Let me insist here on the role of reflexivity in the dialectic of ideas and behaviors, or praxis and culture that I am trying to introduce. New ideas were discussed in the ruelles society, and their production was directly mirrored in contemporary novels by Scarron or the Scudérys, inviting a history of ideas. However, the discussions themselves can be seen as responses to social practices at court and in the city. The civility and refinement in speech as well as behavior in a ruelles gathering were a reaction against depravity at court. This moves us one step further, and invites us to settle for a history of social practices that would account in materialistic fashion for the development of ideas. This is not the direction I am proposing. Instead, I would like to see both the links between social practice and ideologies, and trace their mutually shared influences, and the distance that persists between ideas and the practices they inspire. In that respect, the reflexive interpretation of social practices, just as they occur, is of the greatest interest, as it may impact on new developments of such social practices. Yet, it cannot mold them, because they are embodied in a way that always remains partially opaque to reflection. I want to show that public gardens as embodiments of social praxis not only contributed to this opacity but also perpetuated a social agency that could diffract, bias, or contradict new interpretations of social life in a most efficient way. Of course, gardens were only part of a larger embodiment of ideas about the good city life from which they cannot be separated lest we either ignore or distort their agency in broad cultural changes.

The Salon de Peinture Society

Institutional practices such as the Salon de Peinture or the theater also gave rise to such embodiments of new ideas about city life. Such acknowledgment immediately forces us to pay attention to politics in our analysis. Let me start with the development of public appreciation and judgment on painting in Paris in the mid-seventeenth century, because it contributes to the development of the idea of public opinion and to its embodiment in royal gardens. At the precise moment when the

---

[23] It will show how different the public was then and now, and also in what sense there is a continuity between then and now.
[24] Kugler, "The Promenade as Performance," 1998.

Fronde civil war was about to disrupt the first mundane ruelles society life in the city, another coup engineered by Le Brun and supported by Anne of Austria struck a fatal blow to the corporation of painters supported by Anne's foe, the Parliament of Paris, and instituted, in 1647, the first Academy of Painting inspired in its principles by the Academy of Saint Luke in Rome. This institution was meant to substitute for the arbitrariness of aristocratic taste, the filter of public judgment embodied in a small number of independent, firm, and righteous men wholly devoted to truthfulness and public good. It intended to establish rules for the art of painting, to teach young artists, and to exercise its duties under public scrutiny.

The academy failed as a teaching institution, as it became entangled in fights with the corporation, and Anne of Austria was compelled to rally public support among the Parisian leisure classes, and later the entire population, by organizing public lectures about art and public exhibitions of painting. Thus, a tension between practices of aesthetic judgment by groups of people of various social provenance and the classical ideal of judgment by the public—illustrated by the famous story of Apelles placing his paintings in a public place and hiding among the public to learn from its criticism—became an object of reflection as early as 1662.[25] The novellists echoed these debates; in 1673, Donneau de Vizé complained in the *Mercure Galant* of their pedantic insistence on technical language,[26] thus contributing to the dissemination of a modern attitude toward art against which Samuel de Sorbière was already railing in 1662.[27]

I assume that art criticism became established as a topic for public gossip at least during the 1660s, but it could have already made its way there after 1647, when the academy was first established, or by 1655, when Le Brun led his second coup against the corporation of painters. Thomas Crow has shown how the idea of public judgment expressed by Roland Fréart de Chambray (1606–1676) reflects his support of the ideal and the contradictions of power under the absolutist monarchy: the king exercises power under the control of the nation (the people who represent God), but the nation has to be controlled and reared in such a way that they dispense the love they owe to a king who rules after his anointment by God.[28] Thus, we can see that art gossip in the garden did not please the staunchest supporters of the absolutist monarchy, and was already lively before the first Salon de Peinture opened its doors in 1664.[29] This may help us to understand the growing audience for the first salons of painting, in spite of the reluctance of the members of the academy to present their works.[30]

The academy did not form public taste, as was later demonstrated by the success of the "Rubenist" school of painting against which the academy fought, and by the late adoption by the academy of the "Rubenist" approach to painting when it came under the direction of Roger de Piles after 1699. Besides, the interruption of the salons of painting from 1704 to 1737 shows that the academy did not campaign for a developing role of the public. No such discontinuity of activity is noted among the novellists, including the galant novellists, because the Salon de Peinture was not yet the major source of innovation in the public eye. Yet, we should not downplay the importance of the few salon exhibitions between 1664 and 1737, because they brought together large audiences that embodied the idea of a judging public, and invited discussions of the capacity of a real crowd to embody the ideal of a truthful and discerning public eye. These gatherings differed greatly from the groups in the literary ruelles, or from the *pelotons*, the organizations of novellists, in two major ways: they recruited a much broader and fluctuating segment of the Parisian population, and they lacked a capacity for internal criticism. Yet, they gave a bodily appearance to the public as connoisseur, thus giving a new ring to debates of public taste, and to their dissemination through art gossip.

[25] Roland Fréart, sieur de Chambray, *Idée de la perfection de la peinture démonstrée par les principes de l'art . . .* (Au Mans: de l'imprimerie de Jacques Ysambart, 1662).

[26] Funck-Brentano, *Les nouvellistes*, 80; quotation from the *Mercure Galant* 1673, III, 164.

[27] Thomas E. Crow, *Painters and Public Life in Eighteenth-Century Paris* (New Haven, Conn.: Yale University Press, 1985). Translated into French by André Jacquesson as *La peinture et son public à Paris au dixhuitième siècle* (Paris: Macula, 2000), 40.

[28] Crow, *La peinture et son public*, 42.

[29] It was opened on 25 August, the day of Saint Louis, when people of all ranks were admitted to the Tuileries, and this date was later maintained.

[30] From 1664 to 1673.

The Dramatic Theaters

The spatial organization of another absolutist institution, the monopoly of dramatic representations held by four theater companies in Paris until 1789—the French Theater, the Italian Theater, the Opéra, and the Comical Opera—gave rise to another embodiment of the public as connoisseur that also was echoed in royal gardens. Theater plays give rise to three different forms of representation: the impersonation of characters by the actors, which introduces an imaginary fluidity of society and gender; the representation of conflicts and their developments in a ritual way, to which Victor Turner called attention in his last work on ritual; and the audience's enactment of public judgment, in which any particular audience stands for the public at large.

We know that students in grammar schools were encouraged to perform drama from at least the mid-sixteenth century in France. Montaigne even compared theatrical plays to religious gatherings, underlining their role in the improvement of the townspeople's behavior.[31] Theater plays were read and criticized in the Blue Room of Madame de Rambouillet and in later ruelles, and the monarchy on Richelieu's initiative tried to control and make use of the popularity of this art form among all classes of inhabitants. People of some distinction and wealth would sit at the theater of the Académie Française in a loggia or, even better, on the stage itself, while a very diverse audience made up of lawyers, authors, artists, bourgeois, craftsmen, religious men, servants, retired army officers, and thieves would stand side by side in the parterre.[32] Very quickly, it became apparent that the response of the parterre—the people standing on the ground floor—to a play, especially on its first representation, decided its failure or success, as Corneille learned from experience in his old days. Thus, the audience very quickly came to represent a judge speaking in the name of the general attendance, as if the haphazard gathering of people on a particular evening formed a trustworthy representation of the general public. So, we can see how the abstract idea of a general public of the theater could be embodied by a group of people comprising all classes of society except the poorest and the highest strata.

The news from the theater world was discussed in public gardens by a special group of novellists, the Parnasse novellists, who contributed to the debate of the ancients against the moderns, and who were still willing to criticize Racine and Corneille many years after their deaths.[33] However, they had much more to discuss than theater, and they did not seem to have been very engaged in an interplay between the public of garden gossip and the public of the parterre until the middle of the eighteenth century, when a craze for theater swept through France.[34] It is worth noting, however, that a specialization in theater chronicle already appeared among Parnasse novellists in the 1720s.[35] They were called the "theater caterpillars" and used to form small groups, conversing under the elms or chestnut trees in the quincunxes at the Luxembourg and Tuileries gardens. They announced new plays, provided a review before a show, and a critique of the plot and the performances afterward. They impersonated the role of the parterre and articulated public judgment in a way that was never achieved by the emotional and riotous crowd in the parterres.

Thus, we can observe a slow development of novellist practices that mirrors changes or development of a public demand for news and contributes to the formation of public opinion. The strong reaction of Parnasse novellists against the first journals of literary criticism testifies to the acute awareness of their role in fashioning the taste of their contemporaries. New social practices that were perceived as expressive embodiments of public opinions surged in a variety of places in Paris. We have just noted the ruelles gatherings, the Salon de Peinture, and the dramatic theaters because they introduced significant

[31] Plays were read and criticized in the Blue Room of Madame de Rambouillet and in later ruelles, and the monarchy, on Richelieu's initiative, tried to control and make use of the popularity of this art form among all classes of inhabitants. Maurice Lever, *Théâtre et Lumières, les spectacles de Paris au XVIIIe s.* (Paris: Fayard, 2001), 312.

[32] Lever, *Théâtre et Lumières*, 35–37.

[33] Funck-Brentano, *Les nouvellistes*, 74. *Le journaliste amusant ou Le Monde serieux et comique* (Paris, 1731).

[34] It would take too long to account for the struggles between popular shows at the Foire Saint Germain or the Foire du Lendit and the official theaters that resulted in the creation of private theater, after Madame de Pompadour created the *théâtre des petit cabinets* in Versailles in 1747, and later the tacit acceptance, under public pressure, of more than a hundred theaters in the city of Paris after 1760.

[35] The last survivor of the Moliere company, the actor Pierre Le Noir de la Thorillère, played a significant role in this development until his death in 1731. Funck-Brentano, *Les nouvellistes*, 75.

innovations into Parisian life. We might have also studied the cafés, the bookshops, and the fairs. It would have further underscored that the ritualized practices of news-peddling in the royal gardens contributed to a large network of developments of social practices that were understood by Parisian society as expressions of public opinion. It was important, however, to show that all these phenomena were echoed by the novellists in the royal gardens, thus allowing even further the voice of the novellists to sound like the voice of public opinion itself. I shall turn to the attempts at controlling them, which show how much they were perceived during the last fifty years of the absolute monarchy as a real embodiment of public opinion.

Satire and Illustration as Forms of Reflexivity

Thus, we are confronted with a snowball process, whereby the embodiment of a variety of forms of public opinion is supported, on the one hand, by the general thirst for public participation in the world of mundane and libertine life, and of intellectual and political affairs, and, on the other hand, by the reflexivity of several categories of actors who display an awareness of the difference between the vanity of gossip and its underlying political content. This is clearly evidenced in some eighteenth-century writing about the novellists at the Tuileries and in the activity of the secret police.

Let us turn first to Mercier's *Discourses of the Tuileries Garden in Paris* published in 1788. This fictional narrative pretends to report a series of observations made by the author when visiting the Tuileries gardens and listening to conversations to which he seldom contributes. It adopts a satirical tone. Thus, under the pretense of mocking actual events, he advances his own agenda; that is, he echoes the political debates that fill the gardens with their rumors. He defends the necessity of reforms at all levels of society. He listens to the

> natural eloquence with which little men, whose figures and garments seemed to betray a complete lack of instruction and intelligence, and yet spoke with such good sense of the necessary reforms to be made at the court where they seemed to have spent all their life."[36]

Constant references to the gardens, the crowd of visitors, the delight of watching the general departure of all visitors at dinner time with a flow of ladies' hats that looked like a "walking parterre of flowers," remind the reader that such discourses could only proceed from conversations in this royal garden. In his second discourse, Mercier paints a crowd of chatterboxes shuttling between the most inconsequential prattle and serious reflections on mores, institutions, and government. However, he accounts in much greater detail for social or political issues. He deals at great length with reforms of general education, the law and medical schools, and the clergy, and he concludes that "the tax administration could not fail to enter our plan for reform."[37] This is a dangerous topic and he refrains from presenting his proposals for this reform. When he wishes to make a more daring proposal, he first makes fun of the speaker, then exposes his point of view, and then concludes that it is impossible: "The 'Frondeur' told me first that the world was going down the drain . . . because he is prone to fancies that make him writhe with moral pain he invents events by himself in order to be able to raise his claims."[38] Then he explains that "He would have liked to make all men happy, as if it were possible; and as if a 'frondeur' blinded by his passion for universal criticism, was able to carry such an enterprise." He later blames "anglomania," reminding his readers of the freedom of expression allowed by the political institutions in England and forbidden in France. The last discourse is devoted to a ferocious satire of the ancient regime. It is called "the ultimate project." It pretends to mock all those reformers who, deprived of

ROYAL GARDENS, FASHIONABLE PROMENADES, AND PUBLIC OPINION IN SEVENTEENTH- AND EIGHTEENTH-CENTURY PARIS

52

[36] Sébastien Mercier, *Les entretiens du jardin des Thuileries de Paris, par M. Mercier auteur des Entretiens du Palais-Royal* (Paris: chez Buisson, Libraire, 1788). Second Entretien: Des réformes, 11 ("Et souvent nous fûmes étonnés de la justesse et de l'éloquence avec laquelle parloient de petits hommes, qu'on eût jugé au vêtement ainsi qu'à la figure des gens sans instruction et sans talent; on eût dit qu'ils avoient vieilli à la cour, tant ils parloient bien des réformes qu'on devrait y faire . . .")

[37] Mercier, *Les entretiens du jardin des Thuileries*, "Les fermiers ne pouvaient manquer d'entrer dans notre plan de réforme." Second Entretien: Des réformes, 18.

[38] Mercier, *Les entretiens du jardin des Thuileries*, 18.

practical experience, are eager to let the rest of the world know their magic solutions to society's problems. One of these mumbles in his ear the solution to all problems. He tells him:

> Here it is, the ultimate reform project. The monarchs will take for themselves all the goods and properties of all their subjects, and all the workers, the merchants, the artists, the colonizers will work only for them; and after this great move they will distribute all the wealth of which they are the sole owners to every class of citizens according to their needs. . . . I want to say that the prince being the owner of all existing goods will order dress and shoes to be made for each individual according to his needs and his social status. . . . So the king will act as the head of a family providing himself for the shoes and the garments of his sons, for the heating of their house, for their dwelling, for the lighting, and for the money they need for their leisure.[39]

This fictitious account pursues *ad absurdum* the will to control and the greed of the monarchy, in a very amusing satirical piece of fantasy. The absurdity of the whole story going into the detailed description of the organization of dinner service at all the homes of the kingdom and of different menus according to each person's social status, of course, serves as a mask behind which an implicit criticism can be expressed.

Attempts at Controlling the Novellists

Caution was necessary because the police had multiplied their spies. The king and his circle believed they were under attack from a few malevolent individuals who worked from a secret room in Paris toward the ruin of the regime and their reputation, and they used the police to track them relentlessly. Robert Darnton has shown brilliantly that they never succeeded because there were no leaders, but rather a large population engaged in a turmoil of criticism.[40] The police were extremely present in the gardens and daily reported dozens of stories told by the novellists or overheard between garden visitors.

This antigovernment activity was a great source of concern for the king and his ministers. In spite of the image we have inherited of an absolute monarchy controlling all activities in the country, its capacity to maintain order and to control individuals was far less extensive than that of contemporary Western governments, but it was much more ruthless and wily in its efforts at control. Thus, revolts flared ceaselessly in the country, the high nobility and the parliaments were always tempted toward sedition, and the people of Paris aided several revolts against the king in the sixteenth and early seventeenth centuries.[41] So the Paris police prefect was instructed by Louis XIV to use spies who mimicked the attitudes of the novellists by seeking news and rumors, in particular in the higher strata of society, and who spied on the novellists. These spies were helped by a great number of minor spies who seem to have worked in the hope of receiving generous financial rewards that rarely materialized. They nevertheless wrote regular accounts of their "itineraries" throughout the city. The archives for the 1720s and 1730s still exist and give an idea of their activities. For the most part, they deal with trivia, yet from time to time they report an alarming rumor.

At the Tuileries garden on 24 August 1725, novellists reported news that stimulated their audience to demand the hanging of the most important financier of the monarchy, the brothers Paris, Samuel Bernard, and "all the other rascals that starve the people to death." It was said that they bought large quantities of wheat to sell abroad, and that the Marquise de Brie, the prime minister's mistress, was one of the main beneficiaries of a plot that would starve many Parisians to death.[42] These

[39] Ibid., 205–6.

[40] Robert Darnton, "Presidential Address to the American Historical Review: An Early Information Society, News and the Media in Eighteenth-Century Paris," *The American Historical Review* (February 2000) http://www.historycooperative.org/journals/ahr/105.1/ah000001.html (accessed 6 Dec. 2005).

[41] Funck-Brentano, *Les nouvellistes*, 285.

[42] Bibliothèque de l'Arsenal, Archives de la Bastille ms 10153, f 52v.

conversations were duly recorded and despite the fact that they were outlawed, the novellists were not prosecuted. The police lieutenant and the government thought, with some reason, that prosecution would force such people to hide in private homes and that it would become much more difficult to monitor them. Thus, the ritualized transgression of the law by novellists allowed rumors to spread and become common beliefs in a matter of one or two days in Paris. Such common beliefs embodied public opinion, and made it palpably present through the voice of celebrated novellists such as Metra at the Tuileries. Louis XVI himself believed, as we have already seen, that public opinion about his government was expressed daily by Metra's voice.

Emplacements and Rituals of Interaction in the Royal Gardens

How can we understand the role of gardens in the development of a shared belief in the existence of public opinion that always passed true and fair judgment over the arts as well as politics? Whatever the role of the novellists at the Luxembourg, Tuileries, Arsenal, or Palais Royal gardens in this process, we cannot claim that garden practices resulted in the establishment of a common belief in the existence of public opinion. This would be an overstatement, for at least two reasons. First, there were many other places such as convents, the Palais de Justice, the Pont Neuf, cafés, bookshops, as well as the Salon de Peinture and the theaters, that contributed to this conceptual construction. Second, there are only a limited number of emplacements within gardens that triggered ritualized activity by the novellists. Thus garden emplacements should be seen as part of a network of emplacements within the city where some ritualized activities could be experienced by contemporary citizens as expressions of public opinion and public judgment.

Please allow me a side remark here about garden studies. Emplacements engaging the same public in one kind of ritualized activity are to be found in different gardens and city places because they correspond to the dynamics of a single social practice. We can therefore see that concentrating all our attention on a single garden would not allow the pursuit of such an investigation as the one I am presenting. Instead, attention to the development of a simple practice calls attention to a network of places—many of which are royal gardens—and to the appropriation[43] of some emplacements in the gardens.

Let me underline the distinction between place and emplacement—a word I borrow from Foucault, with a slight twist.[44] A place results from the appropriation of a parcel of land by an institution. It may be delimited clearly as a church, a cemetery, or a school, but it need not be. A rural home may be a farm building, or the farm and its surrounding buildings, yards, and gardens, or the farm and its fields, or even the parish depending on the context in which the home is evoked. In similar fashion, a marketplace, or a royal hunting ground may expand or contract according to circumstances.

Yet, in all of these situations, the appropriation of land by an institution establishes a horizon of understanding of place, of agency, and of social roles inasmuch as the institution can maintain it. Because no institution is absolutely powerful, any place has its own trespassers and poachers. Royal gardens in Paris were parcels of land appropriated by the king's household, and yet the king, who lived most of the time outside of Paris, had very little control over their use by the crowd of Parisians once he allowed them to visit his gardens. These people could easily engage there in ritualized forms of interactions that reappropriated some part of the land at specific times of the day. I use "emplacement" to refer to these phenomena that called

[43] Places, objects, and even people can be put to a variety of uses in any given society. Proper uses are those considered legitimate according to law or custom, and all others are improper. So the property of a place, an object, or a person results from the legitimacy of its uses. Ownership of land, objects, or people (through marriage or parenthood in our own society) is one mode of appropriation among others since appropriation is the process through which individuals or groups of individuals acquire the legitimate rights of use of a particular object. Ritualized use of an emplacement by a particular group of people, as long as this group is not challenged by other groups, establishes a customary right of use, and thus the appropriation of the emplacement by the user group. By contrast, attempts at appropriation of an emplacement by a group may lead to very serious conflicts with other groups or with the authorities when the legitimacy of its uses of the emplacement is challenged publicly.
[44] Michel Foucault, "Different Spaces," lecture given in March 1967, trans. Robert Hurley in Michel Foucault, *Aesthetics, Method and Epistemology*, ed. James D. Faubion (New York: The New Press, 1998), 175–86.

on a form of ritualized interaction on a parcel of land and for a specific duration of time, thus allowing a certain type of social relationship to be obtained, such as the relationships among the novellists, and between them and their public. Thus, like any other space, an emplacement should be defined along three dimensions: physicality, praxis, and temporality.

Each of these emplacements was defined by its location, the actors, and the audience it attracted, as well as the rules of interaction and improvisation it promoted. The royal gardens attracted an audience composed of the aristocracy, clergy, robe nobility, and all members of the leisure society of the time who gathered there. So each garden had a somewhat specific audience, but many rituals such as the walk in the Grande Allée, sentimental encounters, fashionable display, musical entertainment, conversation, or gossip about mundane or political news would spread from one garden to the next. Thus, we can see how a network of emplacements extending over the city allowed the development of the promenades, public display of clothing and carriages, or adolescent courtship, to name a few, which took place in royal gardens. Each of these ritual practices was loosely tied to the others because their emplacements either overlapped or merged ambiguously into one another. Instead of the rigid sense of a limit that seems to be requested by the analysis of many rituals by Victor Turner, here we are bound to observe the opposite: within the royal gardens, limits of emplacements are ambiguous and individuals may join any ritualized event, or leave it as they please.

Thus, as opposed to rituals analyzed by van Gennep in Europe or by many social anthropologists in Africa and Melanesia, these ritualized practices do not result from a social requirement experienced by all members of society, or even all members of a particular group. To the contrary, these ritual practices are entertained by free-willed individuals in a place where constraints on public behavior are somewhat relaxed. Because the different kinds of emplacements all depend on ritual practices of reappropriation of some institutionally defined space, I propose to call these rituals of emplacement, and to see them as contributing to the development of the modern idea of public space. So the performance of garden rituals resulted in the appropriation of specific emplacements in the gardens.

Thus, I propose to understand space as a social phenomenon—rather than a transcendental category of the mind—through which institutional domains are reappropriated by ritual practices of interaction that result from free initiatives. Of course, the idea of freedom is relative to the cultural context. Here, it means that these initiatives were not axiologically driven. And space becomes public space whenever the participants in its emplacements are seen by themselves and by others as representative of the public rather than of any particular group. We can see the novellists' activities and their audiences as making a public space out of the reappropriation of part of the royal gardens throughout the city of Paris. The space of the novellists comprised all of the emplacements to which they contributed: it had a territorial, a social, a behavioral, and a temporal dimension. Thus, I am arguing that space results from ritual performative actions achieving a reappropriation of the land. This calls attention to the different levels at which we can acknowledge the performative action of garden rituals.

The performances of these ritual practices achieved several results at the same time. First, they achieved results sought by the participants. In this case, they quenched the thirst for news of an educated population. Second, they created a new form of social life by appropriating a place and establishing a pattern for use that was offered to any passer-by as a recognizable feature of Parisian social life. This is the embodiment of a specific social practice as an emplacement in the gardens.[45] Third, they gave

---

[45] The idea of embodiment is borrowed from phenomenology. It calls attention to the production of forms that can be later recognized as cultural forms. Thus, the idea of a nation can take form—become embodied—in a number of objects such as the parliament building, the flag, monuments. But there is more to this form than simply material objects: the chambers and the institutions that give existence to the judiciary, legislative, and executive power are certainly even more important aspects of the form of a nation. They are certainly present at any given moment of history through the existence of material objects and people who represent them, but these representations are obviously not to be mistaken for the form that they represent anymore than an actor is to be mistaken for Hamlet. The tune of the national anthem provides another example of this difference between the tune that is part of the form of the nation, and a particular performance of the tune that is a mere representation. All these aspects of the form of a nation contribute to its embodiment. So we can understand that the new social practice is embodied in the garden and in the ritual practices to which they give rise. This is how any particular performance of ritual in the garden can be recognized by coeval visitors as the typical form of this social practice. The emplacement and the ritual both contribute to this form. When considering them separately we lose the possibility of recognizing the figure that is represented as a whole. Analytical separation of space, material objects, and practices would prevent us from understanding how new social practices could be perceived and become an object of reflection for their actors.

rise to the creation of categories of interpretation and understanding of this new form of social life itself. Because this form is partially embodied in a natural setting, it seemed to belong to the natural order itself, and the new categories of interpretation appeared to only reveal aspects of the natural order. The sense of being strongly invited to participate in these garden rituals, or the sense that public opinion was a fact of life were imposed on the minds of all participants as belonging to the order of nature. Thus, the development of critical thinking among an educated Parisian population stimulated the multiplication of these rituals, and their embodiment in gardens derailed the population's ability to make sense in a critical manner of the cultural forms to which its own critical thinking gave rise. Let us turn to this third level of garden ritual performance.

Royal Gardens, Rituals of Emplacement, and Public Opinion

Many of the practices by the novellists of rituals of emplacement were clearly held in defiance of social control by the state or the church. It may seem strange that royal gardens, of all possible meeting places, would have become such sanctuaries under a regime of political absolutism and authoritarian imposition of Catholic practices at church. However, the reasons are simple: royal gardens were designed and perceived as idyllic places where, according to the pastoral tradition, all inhabitants were free from the anxieties of oppressive life, and could indulge in the civilized pursuit of sentimental affairs. The Tuileries palace and gardens could thus be seen by Catherine de Medicis as the palace and gardens of Appolidon[46] as described in Amadis de Gaule (1540–1559) that had been used earlier for the design of the Castle of Chambord.[47] This view held sway over Parisian people as well as garden managers throughout the seventeenth and mid-eighteenth centuries. It was strongly reinforced by the different exercises of freedom they allowed, because the city police were barred from the royal domain that had its own royal police, quite determined to fight for its authority against any possible encroachment by the city police.

This invites particular attention to the ontological nature of the royal gardens. Thirty years ago, Michel Foucault in his discussion of utopia and heterotopia had casually mentioned gardens as heterotopias, characterizing them as attempts at embodying a utopia that fall prey to reappropriation by an ensemble of relations between individuals so "they may suspend, neutralize, or reverse the set of relations that are designated, reflected or represented by them."[48] He wrote, "Since early antiquity the garden has been a sort of blissful and universalizing heterotopia."[49] He certainly meant to call attention to the difference between court, city, or countryside, and garden spaces, which resulted from the human relations they were meant to designate. This analysis supports Foucault's emphasis on the utopian attributes of gardens, but it calls attention as well to the institutional framework that sustains the existence of this utopian dimension, to its capacity to shelter new systems of social relationships from dominant institutions, thus fostering the development of a public space, that is of a network of various emplacements allowing a specific type of freely attended ritualized practices to develop.

Yet, there is something paradoxical about these ritual practices in the royal gardens: they result from whimsical impulses of idle individuals, and they prompt such annoyance that authors write satirical plays against them and the police step up their efforts to spy on them; but neither the satirists nor the police seem able to highlight some really consequential aspect of their activity. As the century goes on, however, the weight of the political opinions they establish becomes increasingly obvious. Individual misdemeanors are spied upon and eventually repressed, but the development of the belief in public opinion as a reality is never discussed. It clearly imposes itself on the mind of the staunchest and most articulate defenders of the monarchy because it proceeds from the opacity of ritual practices of emplacement rather than from discourse.

I propose that this paradox is the stuff of which the fabric of cultural change in gardens is woven. It calls particular attention to the distinction we have made between the object of the ritual as it was perceived by the actors themselves, such as

[46] See Frances A. Yates, *The Valois Tapestries* (London: Warburg Institute, University of London, 1959). See Tine L. Meganck, "A Tapestry Designed by Karel Van Mander" and Hans Buijs, "The Princeton Tapestry" in the exhibition catalogue (Princeton: The Art Museum at Princeton University, 6 March–10 June 2001).

[47] André Chastel, *Culture et demeures en France au XVIe siècle* (Paris: Julliard, 1989), 99–103.

[48] Foucault, *Aesthetics, Method*, 178.

[49] Foucault, *Aesthetics, Method*, 182.

the novellists, and the abstract idea of an embodied public opinion to which it gave rise. The aim of the rituals of emplacement that the novellists, their public, and their police spies acknowledged made them blind to the ideological or cultural constructions these rituals were accomplishing. The aims, practices, and discourses of the novellists were discussed, approved, or ridiculed depending on the point of view of the person reflecting on them, but the abstract idea of the superior judgment of public opinion was not, because it was not articulated in speech but, rather, embodied in action and space.

The ideas articulated by the novellists were open to critical discussion; the abstract idea that they embodied could only be experienced. Ritual enactments of collective judgments allowed the idea of public opinion to be commonly accepted at the same time that its origins remained opaque to the understanding and critical investigation of its own producers. On the contrary, they conceived public opinion as a metaphysical force to which they were subjected, and out of which they derived their own strength. In other words, the emic point of view shared by all actors rendered opaque an ideological production that is recognizable from an etic perspective.

We should not think of the royal gardens as agents of cultural change, however tempting it may be to speak of the agency of certain emplacements in the Tuileries gardens, as authors of the seventeenth and eighteenth centuries have done, or as a hasty reading of *Art and Agency* by Alfred Gell might suggest. Cultural change was made possible by the existence of these gardens, but it was only achieved by the networks of ritualized actions that could thrive there. Yet, we also should see that the reflexive activity from Donneau de Vizé to Mercier on the novellists' activities was part of a larger movement of reflection on the new collective rituals taking place in the gardens, at the Salon de Peinture, in the theaters, in the convents, and the cafés. These were all public emplacements that allowed innovative collective behaviors. The critiques or praises of these activities allowed a public sphere to develop and to construct a self-representation with the idea of public opinion. The royal gardens of the late seventeenth and eighteenth centuries, however, played a unique role in this development because they allowed the embodiment of public opinion by the novellists. Thus, public opinion became palpably evident, a living thing speaking up in public, for all to hear and see, a real phenomenon beyond any doubt. They could not doubt that "Public opinion exists and expresses common judgment." This is how the royal gardens contributed to the formation of a myth fundamental to later democracies.

Performance and Appropriation: Profane Rituals in Gardens and Landscapes

Performance and Appropriation: Profane Rituals in Gardens and Landscapes

Performance and Appropriation: Profane Rituals in Gardens and Landscapes

Performance and Appropriation: Profane Rituals in Gardens and Landscapes

Stages of Knowledge, Settings for Brotherhood: Gardens and Freemasonry in Tuscany during the First Half of the Nineteenth Century

Alessandro Tosi

During the past twenty years, considerable developments in studies, from a historical and sociological perspective, of the phenomenon of eighteenth- and nineteenth-century Freemasonry have made possible a deeper understanding of the contribution made by this secret brotherhood to the architectonic language of the period and, in particular, to a new interpretation of one of its most significant elements—the landscape. Indeed, one area of research has focused on the close ties between Freemasonry and picturesque and landscape gardening that characterized the period of the Enlightenment and manifested itself in many forms during the second half of the eighteenth century.[1]

Masonic lodges regarded the garden and picturesque gardening as a plastic medium uniquely suited to give expression to their rituals and ideals. However, although the designation "Masonic garden" may be appropriate given the close conjunctures in formal choices and symbolic, esoteric language between the two terms, one must be wary of applying the concept in a simple, univocal manner. Scholars such as Anthony Vidler, James Stevens Curl, Magnus Olausson, Géza Hajós, Helmut Reinhardt, and Carlo Cresti have underlined the complexities and pitfalls presented by apparently straightforward typological definitions. They appropriately distinguish between gardens that can be interpreted as Masonic allegories and those that functioned as "settings for Masonic ritual," and warn against laying undue emphasis on the iconological component, which could lead to a misinterpretation of the significance of landscape designs in which the use of specific symbolic typologies actually constituted a response to the latest shifts in taste.[2]

[1] As James Stevens Curl has observed: "the design of gardens, based on English exemplars, which became fashionable in France, Germany, and elsewhere . . . [constitutes one of the] . . . remarkable aspects of endeavour in Europe that have distinct Masonic associations" (J. S. Curl, *The Art and Architecture of Freemasonry: An Introductory Study* [London, 1991], 116). In addition, see A. Vidler, "The Architecture of the Lodges: Ritual Form and Associational Life in the Eighteenth Century," *Oppositions* 5 (1976): 75–97 (also in *The Writing of the Walls* [Princeton, 1987]); A. von Buttlar, *Der Englische Landsitz 1715–1760: Symbol eines liberalen Weltentwurfs* [Mittenwald, 1982]; M. Mosser, "Le Rocher et la colonne—un thème d'iconographie architecturale au XVIIIème siècle," *Revue de l'Art* 58/59 (1983): 53–74; M. Olausson, "Freemasonry, Occultism and the Picturesque Garden towards the end of the Eighteenth Century," *Art History* 8, no. 4 (1985): 413–33; H. Reinhardt, *L'influence de la franc-maçonnerie dans les jardins du XVIIIème siècle*, in *Massoneria e architettura*, ed. C. Cresti (Foggia, 1989), 87–94; I. Svirida, "Le jardin naturel et la franc-maçonnerie," in *Actes du Septième congrès international des Lumiéres* (Budapest, 1987; Oxford, 1989), 310–13; G. Hajós, "La Franc-Maçonnerie et le jardin anglais du XVIIIe siècle avancé en Autriche," *Actes du Septième congrès international des Lumiéres* (Budapest, 1987; Oxford, 1989), 1503–15; J. S. Curl, "The Landscape Garden and Freemasonry," *AQC* 116 (2003): 83–121.

[2] Olausson, "Freemasonry, Occultism and the Picturesque Garden," 426; Reinhardt, *L'influence de la franc-maçonnerie*; Hajós, "La Franc-Maçonnerie et le jardin anglais," 1509; G. Hajós, *Romantische Gärten der Aufklärung: Englische Landschaftskultur des 18. Jahrhunderts in und um Wien* (Vienna–Cologne, 1989), 45–59; C. Cresti, "Architetti e ingegneri massoni nella Toscana del Settecento e Ottocento," in *Massoneria e architettura* (1989): 137–42.

In contrast, there were gardens whose primary function was genuinely one of ritual. Such constructions became renowned within select circles and served as models for landscapes conceived, designed, and built as settings for Masonic rites. Some of the earliest examples include the Parc Monceau commissioned by the Duke de Chartres and various landscape gardens in Germany and Austria—Louisenlund in Schleswig, the summer residence of Landsgraf Charles of Hesse-Cassel, the Royal York zur Freundschaft in Berlin, Basil von Amann's estate at Aigen near Salzburg.[3] All of these gardens drew on a repertoire of symbols with unmistakable Masonic connotations. The hermetic layout of the Parc Monceau included a Gothic building, an alchemist's laboratory, a grotto, and a pyramid designed by Carmontelle, whereas the park of Louisenlund comprised an initiation route that passed by an artificial lake and a cavern, before ending at a Gothic-cum-Masonic tower erected between 1779 and 1784. Most important, in each of these gardens was a pavilion that served as the seat of the Masonic lodge and confirmed the ritual function of the site.

The same symbolic elements linked to the iconography of Freemasonry recur in various English-style gardens built at the end of the eighteenth century by patrons and architects, who documents show were members of the fraternal order. Thus, Drottningholm near Stockholm—with its Gothic tower erected in 1792–93 by Louis Jean Desprez based on a design by Gustavus III—and the garden of Mauperthuis near Paris—with its lake, pyramid, and tower designed by Charles-Nicolas Ledoux in the 1760s for the Marquis of Montesquiou and later completed by Alexandre-Théodore Brongniart (all three of whom were Freemasons; indeed, Brongniart and the marquis belonged to the same lodge)—can be read as Masonic allegories.[4]

Nevertheless, typical of the historiographic snares that may be encountered by those seeking to discover the intentions underlying a given project is Le Désert de Retz, the famous garden on the edge of the Forest of Marly near St-Germain-en-Laye (Paris) built by François Racine de Monville at the end of the 1770s, perhaps in collaboration with the architect François Barbier. Its architectonic elements replete with symbolic meaning—the Gothic church, the Temple of Repose, the obelisk, pyramid, hermitage, and grotto, as well as a completely novel conceit, the "Colonne Détruite" realized in 1781 and declared "the most extraordinary folly in Europe"—were greatly admired. It became the model for numerous gardens built throughout Europe in the picturesque style. The presence of so many of the codified esoteric elements, combined with the (albeit undocumented) Masonic interests of Monville, may easily lead one to assume that the layout of Le Désert de Retz was prescribed by Masonic ritual. However, this thesis is belied by the absence of documented evidence and by incongruities in the chronology of the garden. In addition, as pointed out by Diana Ketcham, the physiognomy of the garden itself makes the Masonic conception implausible, consisting as it does of "a small open valley, where nothing is hidden, the site is not conducive to a ritual progression where the initiate views only one scene at a time."[5]

This example may serve to underline the methodological snares that await those who embark on the study of a fascinating but complex and elusive symbology, in a context that becomes all the more intricate at the beginning of the nineteenth century as the model of the landscape garden spread across Europe and other fashionable trends arose such as the Egyptian Revival.

The role of Italy in this period was significant and, as is amply documented in the literature, important examples of gardens whose design included many Masonic symbols and references can be found from Veneto and Emilia to Naples and Sicily. The work of Giuseppe Jappelli, which includes the celebrated Cittadella Vigodarzere at Saonara (Padua), constitutes one

[3] Olausson, "Freemasonry, Occultism and the Picturesque Garden," 417–21; Hajós, "La Franc-Maçonnerie et le jardin anglais," 1509; D. Ketcham, *Le Désert de Retz: A Late Eighteenth-Century French Folly Garden: The Artful Landscape of Monsieur de Monville* (Cambridge, Mass.: The MIT Press, 1994), 126.

[4] Vidler, "The Architecture of the Lodges," 89; Olausson, "Freemasonry, Occultism and the Picturesque Garden," 421–22; Curl, *Art and Architecture of Freemasonry*, 129–31; R. Middleton, "The Château and Gardens of Mauperthuis: The Formal and the Informal," in *Garden History: Issues, Approaches, Methods*, Dumbarton Oaks Colloquium on the History of Landscape Architecture XIII, ed. J. Dixon Hunt (Washington, D.C.: Dumbarton Oaks, 1992), 219–41.

[5] D. Ketcham, *Le Désert de Retz*, 19. See also Olausson, "Freemasonry, Occultism and the Picturesque Garden," 415–17; M. Baridon, "The Garden of the Perfectibilists: Méréville and the Désert de Retz," in *Tradition and Innovation in French Garden Art: Chapters of a New History*, ed. J. Dixon Hunt and M. Conan (Philadelphia: University of Pennsylvania Press, 2002), 121–34.

of the most complex and fascinating instances of this phenomenon to be found in Europe.[6]

Tuscany offers a particularly striking case in point, for not only was the first Masonic lodge on the peninsula established in Florence between 1731 and 1732, the Grand Duchy in fact played a central role in the intellectual and cultural events of eighteenth-century Italy. This is reflected in the 1739 trial of Tommaso Crudeli, the activities of Philipp von Stosch and Horace Mann in Florence, and in the fact that some of the most prominent intellectuals of the period were Freemasons, such as the naturalist Giovanni Fabbroni, Felice Fontana (director of the Museum of Physics and Natural History in Florence), and Giorgio Santi (director of the Botanical Garden of Pisa). Indeed, Fabbroni, Fontana, and Santi were also enrolled in the prestigious Parisian lodge of the "Neuf Soeurs,"

1. *Georges Le Rouge, "Vue de la Glacière" (the Icehouse Pyramid at Le Désert de Retz), Paris 1785*

which was founded in 1776 and counted among its members Benjamin Franklin and Thomas Jefferson.[7]

In this context, at the end of the century various projects appear to reflect a conscious search for a new repertoire of symbols, beginning with Giuseppe Manetti's layout of the park of the Cascine, envisaged as a microcosm, and a translation into public and concrete form of the physiocratic *Royaume Agricole* promoted by Pietro Leopoldo.[8] Here, Manetti sought to invent an architectonic language that would give expression to the political ideals of the Grand Duke, and the architectural conceits he incorporated could not have been more significant in terms of their symbolic content: the Casa del Capoguardia (Guardhouse) with its echoes of the Masonic temple, the two "emblematic fountains" of Narcissus and Pegasus, and above all the "Ghiacciaia" (ice house), which had been commissioned personally by Pietro Leopoldo based on the prototype of the pyramid of Caio Cestio (as reproduced in an etching by Piranesi) and that bore significant parallels with the Icehouse Pyramid at Le Désert de Retz (Fig. 1), as documented in the engravings published in Paris by Georges Le Rouge in 1785.[9]

[6] *Massoneria e architettura* remains a fundamental source for anyone interested in studying the influence of Freemasonry on architecture in Europe. Some observations on this cultural phenomenon in Italy may be found in J. Dixon Hunt, *The Picturesque Garden in Europe* (New York, 2002). On the cultural ambience of Veneto and the work of Giuseppe Jappelli, see *Giuseppe Jappelli e il suo tempo*, ed. G. Mazzi (Padua, 1982); M. Azzi Visentini, *Il giardino veneto tra Sette e Ottocento e le sue fonti* (Milan, 1988); L. Puppi, "Giuseppe Jappelli e la Massoneria: Una profezia inquietante," in *Massoneria e architettura*, 175–80; M. Azzi Visentini, "Il giardino Cittadella Vigodarzere a Saonara," in *Il giardino italiano dell'Ottocento nelle immagini, nella letteratura, nelle memorie*, ed. A. Tagliolini (Milan, 1990), 177–93; R. W. Gastil, "Jappelli's Gardens: 'In dreams begin responsibilities'," in *The Italian Garden: Art, Design and Culture*, ed. J. Dixon Hunt (Cambridge, 1996), 274–301; *Il giardino dei sentimenti: Giuseppe Jappelli architetto del paesaggio*, ed. G. Baldan Zenoni-Politeo (Milan, 1997); B. Mazza Boccazzi, "Simbologia massonica nel giardino veneto tra Settecento e Ottocento," *Studi Veneziani* 44 (2002): 241–51; G. M. Cazzaniga, "Percosi iniziatici e giardini: La villa Torre de' Picenardi," in *La scuola classica di Cremona* (Cremona, 2004), 45–62.
[7] See C. Francovich, *Storia della massoneria in Italia: Dalle origini alla Rivoluzione francese* (Florence, 1974), 49–85, 397; Z. Ciuffoletti, "Per la storia della massoneria in Toscana," in *Le origini della massoneria in Toscana*, ed. Z. Ciuffoletti (Foggia, 1989), 9–42; F. Bertini, "La massoneria in Toscana dall'età dei lumi alla Restaurazione," in *Le origini della massoneria in Toscana* (Foggia, 1989), 43–163; S. Goretti, "Logge e massoni nella Firenze postunitaria (1861–1866)," *Rassegna Storica Toscana* 41, no. 1 (1995): 65–83.
[8] A. Rinaldi, *La caccia, il frutto, la delizia: Il parco delle Cascine a Firenze* (Florence, 1995), 65.
[9] Rinaldi, *Il parco delle Cascine a Firenze*, 88.

2. Giuseppe Manetti's Icehouse at the Cascine

Manetti does not appear to have been a member of the Freemasons and, as Alessandro Rinaldi perceptively observes, the overall design of the Cascine does not conform to a diachronic, hermetic conception of space (Figs. 2 and 3). For this reason, any discussion of the iconological significance of this project—or others by Manetti such as the itinerary designed for the "giardino moderno [new garden]" of Poggio Imperiale in Florence, with its pyramid dedicated to "the antique virtues" built in 1811[10]—must remain for the most part speculation. Nevertheless, these projects do offer a clear demonstration of how motifs more or less explicitly connected with Masonic ideals and linked to a vision of landscape, which embraced new conceptual models and new forms of sociability, began to permeate Tuscan culture in this period.

The Freemasons were already well established and quite active at the beginning of the nineteenth century. With the annexation of the Grand Duchy by Napoleon at the end of 1807 the fraternal order in Tuscany received a significant new impetus and Masonic lodges dedicated to Napoleon, to his sister Elisa, Princess of Lucca and Piombino and later Grand Duchess of Tuscany, and to her husband Felice were established in cities all over the territory, from Florence, Pisa, Arezzo, and Lucca, to Leghorn, Portoferraio, and Piombino. Among the members of the lodges were celebrated scholars and writers, and other conspicuous figures in politics and the arts: intellectuals including Francesco Fontani, Giovanni Rosini, Giovanni Alessandro Carmignani, Gaetano Cioni, and Francesco Mariti; the celebrated physician Paolo Mascagni of Siena; the booksellers Giuseppe Molini and Giuseppe Landi; the engravers Raffaello Morghen, Pietro Ermini, and Filippo Cinganelli; the painters Antonio Luzzi, Francesco Huet, and Gaetano Piattoli; the sculptor Giovanni Battista Comolli; and architects such as Roberto Bombicci, Pasquale Poccianti, and Luigi Cambray Digny.[11]

Therefore, membership in the brotherhood of the Freemasons became a characteristic choice among a large sector of the ruling class. At the same time, one of the tangible forms that this activity took was precisely the search for a new "space of brotherhood" that went beyond the architecture and decoration of the lodges to create a relationship between symbols and rituals interconnected by a multiplicity of subtle links, a relationship that was destined to evolve over time, undergoing significant transformations.[12] It is no coincidence that the poetic and literary themes attached to the Masonic culture, which were widely shared and quickly disseminated, converged in a renewed feeling for landscape.

[10] M. Dezzi Bardeschi, "Il linguaggio segreto: Architettura e massoneria a Firenze, 1803–1845," in *Massoneria e architettura*, 168; D. Mignani Galli, "Un'idea di giardino moderno per un giardino prospettico," in *Il giardino romantico* (Florence, 1986), 46–55.

[11] E. Stolper, "Contributo allo studio della massoneria italiana nell'era napoleonica," *Rivista massonica* 68, no. 7 (1977): 399–424; Bertini, "La massoneria in Toscana"; F. Cristelli, *Storia della loggia massonica "Napoleone" di Firenze, attraverso i suoi verbali (1807–1814)* (Florence, 1992); F. Cristelli, "Massoneria e società segrete in Toscana nell'età napoleonica," *Rassegna Storica Toscana* 40, no. 2 (1994): 311–38. The first Masonic lodges to be established were the Napoleon Lodge in Florence, which was founded on 25 December 1807 and based on modern ritual (in 1814, its name was changed to the Galileo Lodge), the Elisa Lodge in Florence, the Napoleon Lodge in Leghorn, the Felice Lodge in Lucca, and the Napoleon Lodge in Arezzo. The documents conserved in the Archivio di Stato di Firenze constitute essential reading on this subject (Archivio di Stato di Firenze, *Buongoverno Segreto*, 4).

[12] On the "space of brotherhood," see Vidler, "The Architecture of the Lodges," 83. For example, concerning the decoration of the Pisan lodges see M. Montorzi, *Giustizia in contado: Studi sull'esercizio della giurisdizione nel territorio pontederese e pisano in età moderna* (Florence, 1997), 295.

At the beginning of the nineteenth century, Francesco Fontani—librarian of the Biblioteca Riccardiana, member of the "Elisa" Lodge in Florence, editor of *Rime e delle prose di Tommaso Crudeli* printed in 1805, and a prominent figure in intellectual and Masonic circles—provided an emotive interpretation of landscape, one impregnated with moral and symbolic implications, in the text which he wrote for the volume of engravings *Viaggio pittorico della Toscana* (1801–3). This landscape would later incorporate Manetti's Icehouse at the Cascine, a "contemporary" symbol described and illustrated in the second edition of *Viaggio pittorico della Toscana*, which was published in 1817–18[13] (Fig. 3).

Therefore, we find Manetti's pyramid in the background of the French painter François-Xavier Fabre's *Portrait of Doña Maria-*

3. *View of Manetti's Icehouse at the Cascine, in Francesco Fontani,* Viaggio pittorico della Toscana, *Florence 1817–18*

Elena de Palafox y Silva of 1818 (Fig. 4), and then in the emblematic family portrait commissioned in 1834 by Vincenzo Antinori (Fig. 5), director of the Museum of Natural History in Florence, from Giuseppe Bezzuoli—a prominent exponent of the Romantic movement in painting and author of some of the frescoes at Niccolò Puccini's Villa di Scornio. This charming domestic conversation piece testifies to a new mode of experiencing landscape: the park of the Cascine forms a fitting background to a romantic, bourgeois portrayal of feelings and affections in a literal and mental space that is at once private and public.[14]

The Appropriation of Space

In recent years, many important studies have been published on the redesigning of Florentine gardens in the English style during the opening years of the nineteenth century, and their possible connections with Masonic symbolism have been carefully examined.[15] Among these, the Torrigiani Garden provides the best-known example of a "philosophical" layout. Commissioned by the Marquis Pietro Torrigiani, who under the reign of Napoleon served in various official capacities and who was inducted into the Florentine "Napoleon" Lodge in 1808 (during the Restoration he also was suspected of harboring ties with the Carbonari, a new secret society that bore close affinities with the Freemasons), this garden was one of the largest,

[13] The "Veduta della Ghiacciaia situata in uno de' viali delle Cascine" is inserted in the second edition of *Viaggio pittorico della Toscana*, vol. 2 (Florence, 1817). Linked to the wisdom of ancient Egypt and to the rituals of the Freemasons, the pyramid recurs as a symbolic element in the minutes of the meetings of the Florentine Lodge. See Cristelli, *Storia della loggia massonica*, 22. On the symbology of the Masonic landscape, see F. Fedi, "Le paysage, image maçonnique du monde moral chez Bertola," in *Symboles, signes, langages sacrés: Pour une sémiologie de la Franc-maçonnerie*, ed. G. M. Cazzaniga, Pisa, 1995, 45–68.

[14] On this painting, see *Mostra di disegni italiani del XIX secolo* (Florence, 1971); *Pittura italiana del primo '800* (Milan, 1992); A. Tosi, "Romantici in giardino: Immagini e parole nella Toscana dell'800," in *"Giardini di piacere giardini del sapere": Forme e colori del giardino storico* (Turin, 1997), 317–34.

[15] In particular, see Cresti, *Architetti e ingegneri massoni nella*; Dezzi Bardeschi, *Il linguaggio segreto*; P. Maresca, "Architetti e committenti massoni nella Toscana del XIX secolo: I giardini come 'iter' simbolico e iniziatico," in *Massoneria e architettura*, 171–73; P. Maresca, *Boschi sacri e giardini incantati* (Florence, 1997).

most elegant, and most celebrated in Florence.[16] In 1813 Torrigiani asked Luigi Cambray Digny, a fellow member of the Florentine "Elisa" Lodge, to oversee the renovation of the garden, and in 1819 Gaetano Baccani was appointed to assist him. Cambray Digny's initial plan was dominated by classical and mythological references and close correspondences to Manetti's architectural inventions at Poggio Imperiale but, mirroring the Masonic interests of both the patron and the architect, these gradually evolved into a more elaborate program of symbolic allusions. Within this program, the garden was conceived as the setting for a ritual itinerary that anticipated many of the ideas and designs of Giuseppe Jappelli for the Cittadella Vigodarzere garden at Saonara.[17]

4. *François-Xavier Fabre,* Portrait of Doña Maria-Elena de Palafox y Silva, *1818 (private collection)*

The Torrigiani Garden provides us with perhaps the most striking and convincing example of a garden that directly reflected ritual practices through symbolic elements in a diachronic conception of space. From the entrance in Via dei Boffi, which was guarded by two white marble sphinxes designed in 1817 by Marquis Torrigiani, the route followed a path marked by the "Egyptian statue representing Osiris" (Fig. 6), as the *Guida al Giardino Torrigiani* published in 1824 observes, who "held in his hands the tablets upon which were inscribed the rules for gaining access to and traversing the Garden."[18] Although this was actually a statue of Antinous, a motif that can clearly be traced to the vogue *retour d'Egypte* and that Gaetano Baccani would borrow for the two statues that dominate the atrium of the palace of Prince Camillo Borghese constructed in via Ghibellina at the end of 1821,[19] the explicit reference in the *Guida al Giardino Torrigiani* to a figure of great significance in Masonic symbolism points to the desire to confer an initiatory dimension to the garden.

The itinerary of the Torrigiani garden continues with a series of symbolic elements in which we can find suggestive echoes of the gardens of Parc Monceau and Louisenlund such as the "chemistry laboratory," the "ruined basilica built in the Gothic style and dedicated to Saint Peter," which served "to camouflage a reservoir and a machine for pumping water," the "Convent," "Merlin's Grotto," a grove of citrus trees and a botanical garden dedicated to Linnaeus "filled with the most rare and exotic plants," a hypogeum "in the midst of cypresses and other lugubrious plants," and across a "dark way" the hermitage of Saint Salvatore, a cemetery and the "Sacred Grove."[20]

[16] M. P. Maresca, "Da Osiride al Torrino (Il Giardino Torrigiani)," in *Il giardino romantico*, 56–60; M. P. Maresca, "Il Giardino Torrigiani a Firenze: L'invenzione romantica di un parco tra natura e allegoria," *Arte dei giardini: Storia e restauro* 2 (1993): 55–77; Maresca, *Boschi sacri e giardini incantati*; *Giardini parchi paesaggi: L'avventura delle idee in Toscana dall'Ottocento a oggi*, ed. G. Pettena, P. Pietrogrande, and M. Pozzana (Florence, 1998), 99–100; M. Zoppi, "La città e i giardini: Storie di piante, fiori e uomini," in D. Cinti, *Giardini & Giardini: Il verde storico nel centro di Firenze* (Milan, 1997), 35–36. See also *Guida al Giardino Torrigiani* (Florence, 1824).

[17] See Gastil, "Jappelli's Gardens," 288–89; M. Levorato, "Giuseppe Jappelli e l'arte del giardino: La variabilità del gusto," in *Il giardino dei sentimenti: Giuseppe Jappelli architetto del paesaggio* (Milan, 1997), 96–108, esp. 98.

[18] *Guida al Giardino Torrigiani*, 9. On the sphinxes carved by the sculptor Peruzzi, see Maresca, "Il Giardino Torrigiani a Firenze," 67.

[19] See A. Tosi, "Pittori d'Egitto," in *La Piramide e la Torre: Due secoli di archeologia egiziana*, ed. E. Bresciani (Pisa, 2000), 209–99.

[20] *Guida al Giardino Torrigiani*, 11; see also V. Cazzato, "Fenomenologia del neogotico in villa," in *Il Giardino Italiano dell'Ottocento*, ed. A. Tagliolini (Milan, 1990), 37–56, 45. On the initiatory meaning of the symbols of death and rebirth, see the chapter "Initiation" by W. O. Kaelber in *The Encyclopedia of Religion*, ed. M. Eliade (*Enciclopedia delle religioni*, vol. 2, *Il Rito* [Milan, 1994], 301–11).

5. *Giuseppe Bezzuoli, "Portrait of the Family of Vincenzo Antinori," 1834 (private collection)*
6. *"Egyptian statue representing Osiris," Florence, Torrigiani Garden*

In the Torrigiani Garden, it was precisely the allusion to a ritual progression, to the "gradual education" entailed in the Masonic rite that was of significance, in an itinerary marked by progressive stages of knowledge and naturalistic scenarios: "Magical and full of wonders is the journey made in stages from the most melancholy objects and the gloom of the forest which one has just crossed, to the vast and laughing prospects that spread out before one's gaze."[21] The arrival point was the neo-Gothic tower realized in 1821 by Baccani, "a monument fully worthy of the genius and daring of its founder" (Fig. 7).[22] Three stories high, symbolizing the three stages of the initiation rite, and decorated with family portraits and coats of arms, the tower boasted a library and an observatory equipped with "astronomical instruments." This tower became the quintessential symbol of the garden, and was portrayed in romantic landscapes such as the scene painted on a large Ginori vase in 1820 by Clementina, the daughter of Pietro Torrigiani, in which the tower is shown under construction.[23] It also appears in the background to the elegant *Portrait of the Marquis Pietro Torrigiani* (Fig. 8) painted in the 1820s. Indeed, Baccani's "torrino" furnished the prototype for the astronomical observatory in the ideal garden poetically envisioned by Angelo Maria Ricci in *La Georgica de' fiori*, his "poema didattico-didascalico [didactic-instructive poem]" published in Pisa in 1825.[24]

[21] *Guida al Giardino Torrigiani*, 10 ("Magico e sorprendente è il passaggio che si fa a grado da più tristi oggetti, e dal cupo del bosco che si è percorso, ai vasti e ridenti prospetti che si affacciano alla vista"); also quoted in Maresca, "Il Giardino Torrigiani a Firenze," 70.
[22] *Guida al Giardino Torrigiani*, 21. See also C. Cresti, "Esperienze neogotiche in Toscana," in *Giuseppe Jappelli e il suo tempo*, 208, 213; Cresti, *Architetti e ingegneri massoni nella Toscana*.
[23] *Guida al Giardino Torrigiani*, 29.
[24] See A. Tosi, "Fruit and Flower Gardens of the Neoclassical and Romantic Periods in Tuscany," in *The Italian Garden: Art, Design and Culture*, ed. J. Dixon Hunt (Cambridge, Cambridge University Press, 1996), 215.

7. The "Torrino" by Giuseppe Baccani, 1821, Florence, Torrigiani Garden
8. "Portrait of the Marquis Pietro Torrigiani," 1820–30 (private collection)

This figurative and literary imagery refers yet again to themes of a culture traversed by a multitude of recognizable motifs. Furthermore, the Marquis Torrigiani—"munificent Protector of Artists and Men of Letters"—possessed "perhaps the only [copy] in Tuscany" of Vivant Denon's *Voyage dans la Basse et la Haute Égypte*, which was used by Giuseppe Bardi to prepare the Italian edition of Denon's work. Printed in Florence by Giuseppe Tofani in 1808, *Viaggio nel Basso ed Alto Egitto illustrato dietro alle tracce e ai disegni del sig. Denon* was dedicated to Luigi Rangoni—"most worthy knight of the Iron Crown" and a particular devotee of the "abstract Sciences," as Bardi notes in his preface addressed to "all lovers of the fine arts and literature." *Viaggio nel Basso ed Alto Egitto* represented one of the most emblematic and significant manifestations of Masonic culture in Tuscany and appeared in the same period in which the Florentine lodges were founded. The erudite librarian Francesco Fontani was the author of the translation, and the vision of landscape that imbues his *Viaggio pittorico della Toscana* is expressed in this text as well.[25] This emotive and moral reading of landscape emerges in other literary documents such as the verses of Antonio Vignozzi, a printer from Leghorn who in 1810 published *Vocabolario de' liberi muratori italiano e francese corredato dei loro regolamenti basati sulle costituzioni generali e del catechismo massonico addetto ai primi gradi, indispensabile ai F. dell'ordine*, which included a poem entitled "*La morte di Adonirham* [The death of Adonirham]":

[25] Tosi, *Pittori d'Egitto*, 299; see also Dezzi Bardeschi, *Il linguaggio segreto*.

Nella stagion cocente in sull'albore
Messaggero del giorno, le fresch'auree
Io giva a rintracciare al bosco amico;
Ed ivi meditando di natura
Il variopinto aspetto, immagin liete
O lugubri affollavansi al mente!
Indi mia debil fiacca cetra estempore
Ne formava concetto, e per diporto
Sopra candida certa io lo vergava.
Un dì che all'ombra di verzuto Platano,
Circondato di teneri arboscelli
D'Acacia, io stava assiso meditando . . .

[In the midst of the scorching season, Dawn,
The Messenger of day, its fresh breezes
I used to seek in the friendly wood;
And therein meditating on nature
Its varicolored aspect, merry images
Or lugubrious crowded my mind!
Therefore my weak and weary cithara extempore
Formed of it an idea, and for pleasure
On snow-white sheets I wrote.
One day when in the shade of the green plane tree
Surrounded by tender saplings
Of Acacia, I sat meditating . . .][26]

The same atmosphere and associations were evoked by the settings created in the Torrigiani Garden, where the appropriation of spaces was used to lend visible form to moral values shared by a brotherhood. In its symbols therefore, the garden summarized and distilled a particular reading of the landscape, providing an extension of the initiatory space that characterized Masonic architecture. It is interesting to note in this context that the Marquis Torrigiani provided a seat for the lodge from 1811 to 1814 in a house owned by him in Via del Giglio.[27]

The illusionistic effects and *trompe l'oeil* used by the marquis to enhance his scenes and landscapes seem to have been designed to respond to the demands of this symbolic agenda. On the walls of the "stable" at the Cascina, "one could admire various bas-reliefs painted with great skill and genius by Giovanni Luzzi of Florence" (although these were more probably the work of Antonio Luzzi, member of the Napoleon Lodge and the author of its charter),[28] whereas the convent was decorated "with medallions painted in the style of the famous ceramics known as *della Robbia*" and "to remove every constricting sense of boundaries, he even had forests, aqueducts, and ruins painted on the city wall that delimited the garden on its western side."[29]

[26] This edition (printed in Livorno by Vignozzi, 1810) was a translation of the original work by Bazot: see Cristelli, *Storia della loggia massonica*, 45.

[27] Cristelli, *Storia della loggia massonica*, 100, 103, 338. See also Vidler, "The Architecture of the Lodges," 89.

[28] Cristelli, *Storia della loggia massonica*, 175; *Guida al Giardino Torrigiani*, 10.

[29] *Guida al Giardino Torrigiani*, 7, 11–12. See also A. Rinaldi, "Architetture en trompe l'oeil in alcuni giardini toscani di gusto romantico," in *Il neogotico nel XIX e XX secolo*, ed. R. Bossaglia and V. Terraroli (Milan, 1990), 291–99; Zoppi, *La città e i giardini*, 35.

9. *Guiseppe Bezzuoli, "Portrait of Luigi Cambray Digny," 1827 (private collection)*
10. *Emilio Burci,* Vedute del giardino del marchese Stiozzi Ridolfi già Orti Oricellari *(Views of the garden of the Marquis Stiozzi Ridolfi, previously the Oricellari Gardens), Florence 1832, frontispiece*

These devices were in part borrowed from Parc Monceau and Louisenlund, but at the same time they reflected a new use of space that, by eliminating all confines and multiplying the number of recognizable scenes, could be linked to a dimension of sociability that was expressed through yet other elements. Indeed, the itinerary included a hippodrome, a grassy field for *cuccagna,* "the charming game of the balance or *bascule,* brightly decorated with a folding parasol such as the Chinese use, in which as many as six persons could participate at once," the wall "which served as a backboard for the games of ball, *pillotta*, archery, and pistol and rifle shooting" and the "modern gymnasium" constructed on the ruins of a "magnificent amphitheatre" and reserved "for the friends and followers of the Torrigiani family."[30]

The garden therefore became a space dedicated to reflection and diversion, to intimacy and complicity, a space in which the visible elements of its itinerary were tied to the dimension of sociability that constituted one of the fundamental themes of the Masonic movement and its culture. It played an important role in the general transformation of private spaces into public ones, and furthermore contributed a new—and wholly modern—perception of landscape.[31]

It is in this light that various paintings filled with symbolism and containing significant correspondences with the gardens under discussion here must be read, such as the already cited *Portrait of the Marquis Pietro Torrigiani*, in which the garden with Baccani's tower forms the metaphor for a more complex and absorbing cultural and emotional Anschauung, or the *Portrait of Luigi Cambray Digny* painted in 1827 by Giuseppe Bezzuoli (Fig. 9). Against the setting of "un bosco tra rocce e tronchi e cascatelle: paesaggio romanticamente americano [a forest, amid rocks and tree trunks and cascades: a romantically American

---

[30] *Guida al Giardino Torrigiani*, 21, 26–28.

[31] See M. Conan, "The Coming of Age of the Bourgeois Garden," in *Tradition and Innovation in French Garden Art: Chapters of a New History*, ed. J. Dixon Hunt and M. Conan, (Philadelphia: University of Pennsylvania Press, 2002), 182. On Freemasonry as a form of sociability, see Ciuffoletti, *Per la storia della massoneria in Toscana*, 10; Margaret C. Jacob, *Living the Enlightenment: Freemasonry and Politics in Eighteenth-Century Europe* (Oxford, 1991); M. C. Jacob, "Il pubblico diventa il privato: La rivoluzione inglese e le origini della massoneria in Europa," *Il Vieusseux* (1991), 11, 25–70; Cazzaniga, *La religione dei moderni*.

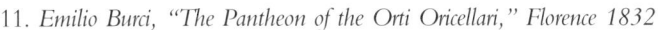

11. *Emilio Burci, "The Pantheon of the Orti Oricellari," Florence 1832*
12. *The Pantheon, Orti Oricellari*

landscape]," Luigi is depicted with his son Guglielmo, pointing to the bust of an uncle who had fought alongside Lafayette and designed the fortifications for Charlestown, a map of which appears in the foreground.[32]

We find the same atmosphere in the series of engravings *Vedute del giardino del marchese Stiozzi Ridolfi già Orti Oricellari* [Views of the garden of the Marquis Stiozzi Ridolfi, previously the Oricellari Gardens] published in Florence by Emilio Burci in 1832 (Fig. 10), which illustrate another important project realized by Cambray Digny. In 1813, the architect was called on to redesign the famous Orti Oricellari for Giuseppe Stiozzi Ridolfi (Figs. 11 and 12), a nobleman with influential political connections (he had served as prefect of the District of the Arno) and supposed but not documented links to the Freemasons.[33] Cambray Digny designed a garden filled with symbolic references that included, in its first section, the "Abbey of Saint Anne" (a Gothic structure embellished with sculpted and polychrome decoration), a lake with an island and a "ruined temple" (Fig. 13), the "remains of a Roman circus," a "small temple dedicated to Venus," and finally a "garden of flowers" in the Italian style that was visually separated by ingeniously conceived landscaped zones. The second part of the garden boasted a baroque statue and a grotto of Polyphemus by Antonio Novelli and a pantheon celebrating the members of the Accademia Platonica, as well as a ruined staircase, a donjon, and a small circular tower built in 1825 (Fig. 14).

Other gardens commissioned in the same period by figures with ties to Florentine Masonic circles appear instead to be somewhat more nuanced, presenting elements that, although they are difficult to interpret as explicit allusions to ritual practice,

[32] U. Ojetti, "Giuseppe Bezzuoli ritrattista," *Dedalo* 1 (1920): 275–76. See also M. Praz, "Gli Orti Oricellari" (1940), now in *Fiori freschi* (Milan, 1982), 305–8; G. L. Mellini, "Bezzuoli pittore emblematico," *Labyrinthos* 3/4 (1983): 63; on the *Ritratto del marchese Pietro Torrigiani*, see also Tosi, *Romantici in giardino*.

[33] L. M. Bartoli and G. Contorni, *Gli Orti Oricellari a Firenze: Un giardino, una città* (Florence, 1991), 57–73. See also E. Burci and T. Salucci, *Vedute del giardino del marchese Stiozzi Ridolfi già Orti Oricellari* (Florence, 1832); L. Passerini, *Degli Orti Oricellarii: Memorie storiche* (Florence, 1875), 44–51; L. Scott, *The Orti Oricellari* (Florence, 1893); Dezzi Bardeschi, *Il linguaggio segreto*; Tosi, "Fruit and Flower Gardens," 216; *Giardini parchi paesaggi*, 99, 198; Cinti, *Giardini & Giardini*, 281–88.

13. *Emilio Burci, "The Lake of the Orti Oricellari," Florence 1832*

do seem to reflect a carefully meditated perception of landscape. Such is the case of the garden of the Count Guido Alberto Della Gherardesca, which was relandscaped in 1811 in the English style by the architect Giuseppe Cacialli, who built for him an "Ionic temple" (whose vault was decorated with allegorical figures painted by Antonio Marini), a Kaffeehaus, and a "Doric temple";[34] and the garden of the Villa di Belmonte near Florence commissioned by the senator Ippolito Venturi, an illustrious agronomist who was admired for his "philanthropic virtues."[35] In other cases, the garden might be chosen as the site for architectonic inventions, as with the architect and poet Bartolomeo Sestini, one of the founders of the Carbonari sect in Tuscany, who in 1812 designed an aviary "in the Chinese style" made of bricks and wrought iron for the garden of the Villa di Celle near Pistoia owned by Carlo Agostino Fabroni.[36]

Furthermore, it must be observed that beginning in the 1820s the popularity of this symbolic repertoire with its more or less overt esoteric allusions began to spread to the rest of Tuscany.

Although none of the projects in this period possess the same conceptual awareness and authority as Giuseppe Jappelli's garden for the Cittadella Vigodarzere, whose Templar chapel and grotto of Baffometto were designed with precise and carefully documented symbolic allusions,[37] the work of Alessandro Gherardesca nevertheless does offer a typical example of this cultural phenomenon. Projects by the architect in the region of Pisa range from his design for the park of the Villa Roncioni in Pugnano to the impressive obelisk of "Parrana travertine" inserted into the itinerary of the garden of the Villa Scotto Corsini at Valdisonzi near Crespina amid a multitude of tablets, niches, memorial stones, statues, artificial ruins, and painted decorations.[38] In the volume *Album dell'architetto e dell'ingegnere, del paesista e del pittore, del giardiniere e dell'agricoltore, del meccanico ecc.*, printed in

[34] M. G. Vaccari, "Il giardino della Gherardesca e gli Orti Oricellari a Firenze," *Quaderni di Palazzo Tè* 5 (1986): 67–74; M. Pozzana, *Firenze: Giardini di città* (Florence, 1994), 42; Cinti, *Giardini & Giardini*, 129–34. On Gherardesca see also Bertini, *La massoneria in Toscana dall'età dei lumi alla Restaurazione*, 148.

[35] Cresti, *Architetti e ingegneri massoni*, 138; Maresca, *Architetti e committenti massoni*, 172–73. See also G. Gazzeri, *Omaggio alle virtù filantropiche del senatore conte cavaliere Ippolito Venturi* (Florence, 1817).

[36] Documents show that from 1814 in the city of Pistoia a cell of the Carbonari secret society existed, one of whose founders was Bartolomeo Sestini, an architect and poet (he wrote the elegy *Pia de' Tolomei*): see C. Francovich, "Le società segrete in Toscana dalla Massoneria alla Giovane Italia," in *Rassegna Storica Toscana* 2 (1963): 122. In 1812 Sestini designed an aviary "in the Chinese style" made of bricks and wrought iron for the garden of the Villa di Celle near Pistoia owned by Carlo Agostino Fabroni. The aviary bore a tablet with the following inscription: "Quest'uccelliera la disegnava verso il MDCCCXII Bartolomeo Sestini che lasciando il compasso e la squadra per l'eloica lira emulò Francesco Gianni nell'estemporaneo canto e si preparò fama più duratura narrando il lungo spasimo della Pia [This aviary was designed around the year 1812 by Bartolomeo Sestini who, when he abandoned his compass and T-square for the eloquence of the lyre, emulated Francesco Gianni in extemporaneous song and paved the way for a more enduring fame by narrating the infinite sufferings of Pia]": see M. Cei, *Il parco di Celle a Pistoia: Araba fenice del giardino* (Florence, 1994), 20, 34; L. Dominici, "Il giardino Puccini di Scornio a Pistoia: Genesi, evoluzione e significati di un'idea romantica," *Ricerche storiche* 3 (1994): 650. On the ties between Freemasonry and the Carbonari cf. G. M. Cazzaniga, "Les origines maçonniques des grades charbonniers," in *Symboles, signes, langages sacrés*, 93–111.

[37] Azzi Visentini, *Il giardino Cittadella Vigodarzere a Saonara*; Mazza Boccazzi, "Simbologia massonica nel giardino veneto tra Settecento e Ottocento," 248.

[38] See A. Rinaldi, *Architetture en trompe l'oeil in alcuni giardini toscani di gusto romantico*; M. A. Giusti, "Natura e cultura nei giardini di Alessandro Gherardesca," in *Il giardino italiano dell'Ottocento nelle immagini, nella letteratura, nelle memorie*, ed. A. Tagliolini (Milan, 1990), 225–39; *Le ville del Valdarno*, ed. M. A. Giusti (Florence, 1996), 51–52; G. L. Bianchini, *Le ville e i giardini*, in *Alessandro Gherardesca: Architetto toscano del Romanticismo (Pisa, 1777–1852)*, ed. G. Morolli (Pisa, 2002), 70–71.

Pisa in 1837, Gherardesca included a lithograph depicting a "Sepulchral cell in the Egyptian style" designed by Pelagio Palagi, a Bolognese painter who amassed a fascinating iconographic repertoire overtly linked to the Freemasons.[39] Other examples of the same tendency may be found, such as the pyramid-sepulcher designed by Agostino Fantastici in 1835—when the popularity of Manetti's pyramid was at its height, and just one year after Bezzuoli completed his *Portrait of the Family of Vincenzo Antinori*—for the garden of the Villino del Pavone, a pleasure house constructed by Mario Bianchi outside the Roman Gate of Siena;[40] or the "Monumental Egyptian Sepulcher" created around 1850 by the architect and painter Giovanni Gambini for the park of the Villa di Celle.[41]

14. *Emilio Burci, "The Fortezza and the Belvedere of the Orti Oricellari," Florence 1832*

Therefore, it is not only the period's singular construal of the universe of symbols—whose influence was destined to spread into the realm of taste, particularly after the expedition to Egypt by Champollion and Rosellini in 1828–29, which made the theme of ancient Egypt more popular than ever—that has opened up intriguing new themes for historiographic research.

Also to be taken into consideration is the fact that after the fall of Napoleon the transformation of the political situation had direct consequences for the role and aims of the secret societies. Beginning in 1814 the moderate tradition of the Order of the Freemasons, with its ties to the Enlightenment and its profound philosophical and literary interests, gave way to new societies such as that of the Carbonari, which retained affinities to Freemasonry in terms of ritual but had more overt political connotations. This process led to a modification of the dimension of sociablity that had characterized Freemasonry during the course of the eighteenth and the beginning of the nineteenth centuries, and therefore requires a more attentive reading of its spaces.

Perfomances in the Garden

The "Temple dedicated to Minerva Medica" was built in 1823 at Montefoscoli (near Pisa) by the surgeon Andrea Vaccà Berlinghieri in honor of his father Francesco, a well-known physician who probably had ties to the Freemasons

[39] The lithograph by Brazzini of a "Cella sepolcrale di stile egizio," "bel pensiero del celebre Architetto e Pittore Sig. Palagio Palagi di Bologna," may be found in *Album dell'architetto e dell'ingegnere, del paesista e del pittore, del giardiniere e dell'agricoltore, del meccanico ecc.* (Pisa, 1837), 8, plate 19. On Palagi and Freemasonry see A. M. Matteucci, "Committenza e massoneria a Bologna in età neoclassica," in *Massoneria e architettura*: 143–53.

[40] Maresca, *Boschi sacri e giardini incantati*, 64. Gherardesca also worked for Giulio Bianchi in Siena; the "Prospetto di cancellata con sedili e fontane per l'Ingresso di Villa o Giardino [View of the gate with seats and a fountain for the entrance to the Villa or Garden]" was prepared by him "per la deliziosa Villa Bianchi nel Senese luogo detto Pagliaia [for the delightful Villa Bianchi in a locality called Pagliaia near Siena]" (*La Casa di delizie, il giardino e la fattoria* [Pisa, 1826], 15, plate 16; see also Bianchini, *Le ville e i giardini*, 78).

[41] Cei, *Il parco di Celle a Pistoia*, 22.

15. *Ridolfo Castinelli, Temple to Minerva Medica, 1823, Montefoscoli (Pisa)*

(Fig. 15).[42] Designed by the "celebrated Pisan architect" Ridolfo Castinelli, the temple was erected "in the midst of a grove of acacias." An emblem of immortality, the acacia tree was invested with a precise symbolic meaning within the Masonic ritual, like the laurel and the olive that also were used as decorative motifs in the temple. The building itself was constructed of terracotta bricks, so that "seen from a distance as the sun was setting, it seemed to be all aflame," and decorated with Ionic columns (Fig. 16). Trees were planted that "surround the temple with a grateful shade and protect the long and winding path by which it could be reached." Within, the building was divided into three stories and contained decoration with symbolic and ritual allusions (vaults frescoed with the starry heavens, butterflies, etc.).

The temple was conceived as a private and secret monument: Giuseppe Montani, man of letters and a close friend of the physician, confessed that he shed a "secret tear" when he visited it together with Pietro Giordani and Giovan Pietro Vieusseux. At the same time, it was an eminently public monument, constructed by the inhabitants of the village: "[s]ince only persons native to the village of Montefoscoli were employed, all of whom needed to learn and perfect their craft,"[43] its construction was an act of commemoration in which the entire community participated, scrupulously seeking to preserve intact the building and its meanings. It is difficult, however, to demonstrate specific and convincing ties to Freemasonry of an architectural project that seems to have been conceived to express sentiments—the love of science, of philanthropy, of friendship—that were broadly shared by the entire culture of the period.

Even more significant are the events surrounding the creation of the Puccini garden at the Villa of Scornio on the outskirts of Pistoia near Florence (Fig. 17). Some quite illustrious figures were involved, including Giuseppe Manetti (who drew up the design, together with the architect Cosimo Rossi Melocchi, for "the renovation of the great Villa of Scornio in the Doric-Egyptian style" around the year 1806),[44] Cambray Digny and his protegé Giuseppe Martelli, the architect-designer Luigi Facchinelli, and the artist Ferdinando Marini. The history of the garden centers around Niccolò Puccini, an intellectual who did not hide his ideological sympathies with the Freemasons and the secret society of the Carbonari and who maintained

[42] L. Vaccà Giusti, *Andrea Vaccà e la sua famiglia: Biografie e memorie* (Pisa, 1878), 111. The temple is also mentioned by Giovanni Rosini, *Tributo di dolore e di lode alla memoria del professore Andrea Vaccà Berlinghieri* (Pisa, 1826), 51, 72. See in addition Cristelli, "Massoneria e società segrete in Toscana nell'età napoleonica," 326; R. Panattoni, *Ridolfo Castinelli (1791–1859) architetto e ingegnere negli anni del Risorgimento: Progetti e realizzazioni per committenti privati* (Pisa, 2004), 69–95.

[43] "Pei dischi di terra cotta dei quali sono formate le colonne del tempio; pei mattoncelli e gl'intagli, pure di terra cotta, furono fatte le apposite forme ed eseguito l'intiero lavoro da quei paesani. Così pure le maniglie degli usci, le quali sono finamente lavorate in ottone, e rappresentano delle farfalle; gli arpioni dello stesso metallo, che figurano dei ramoscelli d'ulivo, furono lavoro e guadagno degli operai di Montefoscoli [For the discs of terra-cotta from which the columns of the temple were formed . . . [and] for the bricks and the carvings, also of fired clay, special molds were made and all of the work was carried out by those villagers. Thus even the handles of the doors, which are finely worked in brass, and represent butterflies; their hinges of the same metal, which are in the form of little olive branches, were the handiwork and gain of the workers of Montefoscoli]" (Vaccà Giusti, *Andrea Vaccà e la sua famiglia*, 115–16).

[44] Dominici, "Il giardino Puccini di Scornio a Pistoia," 650–51.

16. *"Tempio di Minerva" (Temple to Minerva Medica), 1878*

17. Monumenti del giardino Puccini, *1845, frontispiece*

close ties with the members of the "Antologia" of Giovan Pietro Vieusseux.[45] In 1820, at the age of just twenty, Puccini commissioned the painter Ferdinando Marini to decorate his reading room at the villa with a series of portraits of famous writers including Dante, Petrarch, Boccaccio, and Macchiavelli; significantly, he reserved the lunettes for the figures of Benjamin Franklin, the Marquis de Lafayette, George Washington, and America portrayed as Minerva.[46]

For the next twenty years, Niccolò Puccini devoted himself to the construction of a magnificent garden characterized by a symbolic itinerary whose references have justifiably also been interpreted in terms of their links to the ideals of Freemasonry and the Carbonari. These allusions include the Pantheon "dedicated to illustrious men" commissioned from Alessandro Gherardesca around the year 1825;[47] the Tower of Catilina designed by Facchinelli, who used as his model Baccani's

---

[45] Puccini's sympathies with the Carbonari and the Freemasons are clearly expressed in a letter which he wrote to his mother criticising Leo XII's papal bull of 1826, which condemned the members of these two secret societies: see Dominici, "Il giardino Puccini di Scornio a Pistoia," 654. See also A. Linaker, *Niccolò Puccini: La sua villa di Scornio, i suoi amici (con documenti inediti)* (Pistoia, 1899); *Giardini parchi paesaggi*, 100. Edgardo Donati considers it is "very likely" that Puccini himself was a member of the Freemasons: see E. Donati, "Niccolò Puccini, proprietario e patriota nel Risorgimento nazionale," in *Niccolò Puccini: Un intellettuale pistoiese nell'Europa del primo Ottocento* (Florence, 2001), 25.

[46] M. C. Mazza, "Eroi classici, fabbriche romantiche e feste popolari nel Giardino Puccini a Pistoia," *Ricerche di storia dell'arte* 15 (1981): 46: "with a Phrygian beret on her head instead of a helmet, a baton in one hand and an open volume in the other, and sceptors and broken crowns lying at her feet."

[47] Completed in 1829, these wall paintings portrayed Dante, Petrarch, Christopher Columbus, Ariosto, Ludovico Muratori, Raphael, Leonardo da Vinci, Alfieri, Galileo, Alessandro Volta, and Napoleon. An earlier design for the room in the neo-Gothic style was published in *La casa di delizia, il giardino e la fattoria, progetto seguito da diverse esercitazioni del medesimo genere* (Pisa, 1826), plate 38. In the end a classical theme was chosen, perhaps at the suggestion of Puccini himself: see G. Bonacchi Gazzarrini, *Il Pantheon nel giardino romantico di Scornio: Storia e restauro* (Florence, 1999); Bianchini, *Le ville e i giardini*, 75. A plate with 26 "visuali" showing "the principle vistas, and objects that embellish the paintings of that agreeable sitting room, and which one can discover from the Terraces crowning the Building" may be found in Gherardesca (*La casa di delizia*, 18–19, plate 35); the "visuali" include views of Pistoia, Florence, and Prato, as well as the Port, with a cabin housing boats for excursions on the lake; the villa and garden of flowers; the statues of Gaetano Filangeri and Dante; the monuments to Machiavelli and Columbus; the Guelfa Tower, which also houses the Baths, near the playing field of the Giuoco del Pallone; the island in the lake with the remains of the Temple of Pythagoras; the Gothic abbey; the antique castle; café; and restaurant called *At the Sign of the Phoenix*; the Swiss lodge; the remains of an antique Greek temple; the small temple dedicated to Tasso; and the Tower of Catilina.

VEDUTA DEL LAGO ED ISOLA COL TEMPIO DI PITAGORA

18. *"Veduta della Torre Catilina" (View of the Tower of Catilina), in* Monumenti del giardino Puccini, *1845*
19. *"Veduta del Lago e Isola col Tempio di Pitagora" (View of the Lake and the Island with the Temple of Pythagoras), in* Monumenti del giardino Puccini, *1845*

"Torrino" in the Torrigiani Garden (Fig. 18); the Hermitage ("Romitorio") built between 1832 and 1841, which was a small neo-Gothic church decorated with paintings by Bartolomeo Valiani that was intended to serve as the family sepulcher; the Monument to Friendship; Napoleon's Bridge, inaugurated in 1838 and fraught with political allusions;[48] and—as its culminating and most spectacular structure, a conceit that recapitulated the meaning of the whole—an island in the middle of a lake with a Temple and Grotto of Pythagoras (Figs. 19 and 20).[49] This reference to Pythagoras and Pythagorism, which was shared and whose significance was recognized by many Tuscan intellectuals close to Puccini, represented a key theme in the culture and literature of the Freemasons.

"Niccolò Puccini's garden was strewn with monuments, images, and memories, whose scope was not one of vain ornamentation or the creation of scenes of idle delight, but rather the transmission of ideals of the highest nature that would also be intelligible to the humblest visitor," wrote Pietro Contrucci in his "Introduzione" to *Monumenti del giardino Puccini*, a work published in 1845 that introduced the reader—through prose, poetry, epigraphs, and engravings—to Puccini's splendid "garden of images and of memories."[50] Indeed, there were many other elements to be found in this conceptual program, which united a wide range of suggestive elements into a single and complex whole. Thus, columns and busts assumed an emblematic dimension with complex nuances; there were monuments to Gutemberg, Linnaeus, Galileo, and his disciples Torricelli and

[48] Cristelli, "Massoneria e società segrete in Toscana nell'età napoleonica," 332. The Ponte Napoleone was designed by the architect Angiolo Gamberai of Pistoia in the classical style; nearby was a renovated three-story farmhouse called the "Palazzina dei Promessi Sposi" in honor of Alessandro Manzoni, "author of the best novel the Italians ever had" (*Monumenti del giardino Puccini* [Pistoia, 1845], 563–70).
[49] See Dezzi Bardeschi, *Il linguaggio segreto*; Maresca, *Architetti e committenti massoni*; D. Negri, "Il giardino Puccini ed il territorio di Scornio nella cartografia storica," in *La villa e il parco Puccini di Scornio* (Pistoia, 1992), 78–79; Dominici, "Il giardino Puccini di Scornio a Pistoia."
[50] *Monumenti del giardino Puccini*, 24 ("Niccolò Puccini sparse il suo giardino di monumenti, di imagini, di memorie, non ad ornamento, o a scena oziosa, ma con alto concetto che si par chiarissimo anco ai volgari").

Viviani, and the "celebrated engraver" Raffaello Morghen.[51] The monument to Linnaeus—to whom Niccolò Puccini dedicated his garden—acquires particular significance in the context of other works tied to the memory of eminent botanists, such as, for example, the "tomb" of Albrecht von Haller erected in the garden of the Comte d'Albon at Franconville-la-Garenne.[52] Furthermore, it may be noted that not only was an elaborate *Hemicycle of Galileo* erected in Puccini's garden around the year 1840, but also, in 1841, the Napoleon Lodge of Florence was renamed after the great Tuscan scientist, the quintessential symbol of intellectual liberty in opposition to ecclesiastic authority. There were even busts erected at the end of the 1820s—in concomitance with the French-Tuscan expedition to Egypt—of Cleopatra, symbol of ancient Egypt, and Giovanni Belzoni, a contemporary explorer of ancient Egypt, who

20. *The Temple and Grotto of Pythagoras, Puccini garden, Scornio (Pistoia)*

also was a well-known member of the Freemasons with ties to Jappelli that are reflected in the decorations of the Caffè Pedrocchi in Padova.[53]

Niccolò Puccini's garden at Scornio is significant because it constituted the translation into visual form of a system of symbols and settings that was secret but at the same time public. The garden functioned therefore as a space for the expression of themes that were broadly shared by the intellectuals and artists of the period, extending from philosophical reflections and symbolic allusions to philanthropic impulses and the nascent movements of patriotism and unification of the nation. This led to a broader interpretation and use of the garden's spaces and routes that could be experienced by visitors from different social classes, and through its different stages of knowledge.

The Marquis Cosimo Ridolfi, who had constructed a garden on his estate at Bibbiani and in 1835 established an institute for the study of the theory and practice of agriculture on his estate at Meleto, wrote after he had visited Puccini's garden in 1842: "I passed through the gates, and the sheer vastness of the garden, the allure of the monuments, the amenity of the green lawns, the cool woods, the shimmering lake, the beauty of the scene held me for some time, alone with my thoughts, transfixed before the spectacle of nature embellished by art, and filled with admiration for the Patrician who had

[51] *Monumenti del giardino Puccini* contains a self-portrait, which Morghen executed in dry point and presented to Tommaso Puccini "dell'arte amatissimo [a great lover of the arts]," adding the motto "Nec sculpi melius, nec potuit melior."

[52] This epigraph was published in *Monumenti del giardino Puccini*: "A Carlo Linneo principe della bottanica che il regno vegetabile della natura in ventiquattro classi ordinò e distinse consacra il giardino di Scornio Niccolò Puccini MDCCCXXXXIV [To Carolus Linnaeus—prince of botany, who divided the plant kingdom into twenty-four clearly defined classes—is the garden of Scornio consecrated by Niccolò Puccini 1844]." Concerning the "tomb" to Haller erected by the Comte d'Albon see Curl, *The Art and Architecture of Freemasonry*, 185.

[53] *Monumenti del giardino Puccini*, 237–47; Dominici, "Il giardino Puccini di Scornio a Pistoia"; L. Dominici, "Niccolò Puccini e il suo giardino di Scornio nei documenti pistoiesi," in *Niccolò Puccini: Un intellettuale pistoiese nell'Europa del primo Ottocento* (Florence, 2001), 39–56. On the relations between Jappelli and Belzoni see Mazza Boccazzi, "Simbologia massonica nel giardino veneto tra Settecento e Ottocento," 246.

placed at the disposition of all that which in other ages would have been kept exclusive."[54] The Marquis Ridolfi was invited to participate in the "Festa delle Spighe" (Festival of the Wheat Sheaves), a remarkably innovative project conceived by Niccolò Puccini that was many years in the planning. Finally inaugurated in 1841 and held every year until 1846, this event took place on the grounds of the Villa of Scornio and was intended for the general public. Puccini threw open the gates of his estate for three days at the beginning of August and the people poured in to enjoy a carefully planned and skillfully choreographed program that represented much more than a harvest festival. The first day was dedicated to religious ceremonies; the second to events celebrating the virtues of *operosità* and *ingegno* (industriousness and invention), including the exhibition of farm animals and various arts and crafts, and the distribution of prizes; and the third day focused on philanthropy and the furtherance of popular education, with a free meal, games, and the display of paintings and other works of art from Puccini's private collection, including the much-admired sculpture group *Orphans on the Cliff* by Lorenzo Pampaloni.[55] By means of this public event, with its ceremonies and educational activities, the garden gave a collective dimension to ritual, a ritual that, although not abandoning its symbolic repertoire, created links with concepts of a much broader and more complex nature, in which profound pedagogic and social experiences close to the culture of Romanticism played a fundamental role—an employment of the spaces of the garden, in short, that revealed the presence of other, and quite different, kinds of rituals.

Acknowledgments
I would like to express my profound thanks to Margherita Azzi Visentini, Gian Mario Cazzaniga, Bernardino Fiorentini, Lucia Tongiorgi Tomasi, and Luigi Zangheri for their invaluable advice and suggestions.

[54] C. Ridolfi, *Festa delle Spighe 1842*, in *Monumenti del giardino Puccini*, 261 ("Entrai nei cancelli, e la vastità del giardino, le allettative dei monumenti, l'amenità dei prati, il fresco dei boschi, il tremulare del lago, il pittoresco del sito mi tennero per qualche tempo solo coi miei pensieri, collo spettacolo della natura abbellita dall'arte, coll'ammirazione del Patrizio che facea di tutti quel che in altri tempi avrebbe tenuto esclusivo").
[55] Cf. C. Rosati, *La festa delle Spighe: Il sogno di Niccolò Puccini nella Toscana del primo '800* (Pistoia, 1987); Mazza, "Eroi classici, fabbriche romantiche e feste popolari nel Giardino Puccini a Pistoia"; G. Bonacchi Gazzarrini, "Puccini e Leopardi," in *Niccolò Puccini: Un intellettuale pistoiese nell'Europa del primo Ottocento* (Florence, 2001), 204. On the importance of philanthropy, fraternity, and social justice in the rituals of the society of the Carbonari, see Cazzaniga, "Les origines maçonniques des grades charbonniers."

Performance and Appropriation: Profane Rituals in Gardens and Landscapes

Performance and Appropriation: Profane Rituals in Gardens and Landscapes

Performance and Appropriation: Profane Rituals in Gardens and Landscapes

Performance and Appropriation: Profane Rituals in Gardens and Landscapes

Meaning and Change in the Walled
Kitchen Gardens of Ninteenth-Century
Britain

Susan Warren Lanman

Ralph Sneyd, the owner of Kneel Hall in North Staffordshire, gave the following instructions to William Hill, his new head gardener, at their first meeting on 17 October 1850: "Hill, I am particularly anxious to have good Grapes, as they are the only fruit I eat." William Hill (Fig. 1) later noted, "In this respect I have every reason to believe he was perfectly satisfied. For many years we were never without Grapes all the year around."[1] The apparently autocratic and daunting challenge directed at the head gardener might, on initial consideration, be read as the imperious demand of a powerful patron to a subservient underling. However, this exchange resulted in Hill deriving status and substantial benefits from meeting his employer's expectations including winning numerous prizes at the most prestigious horticultural shows in London. This exchange offers a brief glimpse of the complex relationships between elite employers and their gardeners, which were constantly negotiated during the nineteenth century.

As the development of markets for profit accumulation ushered in major economic and social change in Victorian Britain, relations between servants and their employers entered a period of renegotiation. The traditional embedded economy presumed a natural hierarchy embodied in the phrase "the master/man relationship." Elites sought to preserve their privileged position, but they also wished to expand their authority and to control the benefits concurrent with the introduction of new technologies. Conversely, those in humbler circumstances sought to manipulate the new technologies to their own advantage while retaining their customary prerogatives. By subtly altering established rituals and developing new ones, elites and those subject to their control slowly reconfigured the "master/man" relationship. Rituals nurturing renegotiation took place in many settings, but those specifically connected to gardens reveal altered understandings of horticultural spaces and the forces that shaped them.

Understanding the Role of Rituals

Academics from numerous disciplines, and especially ritologists, employ rituals to explore changes in culture and society. This essay draws on the functionalist tradition, in which rituals offer a mechanism for experiencing, affirming, and generating collective beliefs while also promoting social cohesion. In this instance, ritual performances clarify obligation and facilitate social appropriation of goods. Rituals of reciprocity enmesh the economy in social relationships and often help decrease social tensions. The more intensive development of markets for profit accumulation in the nineteenth century proved so corrosive because they undermined the principles of reciprocity and mutual obligation. This resulted in revised and new ritual interactions between social classes to filter, accommodate, and reflect social change. If carefully examined, seemingly simple garden rituals reveal a wealth of information about the transition from the embedded to the market society. Because

[1] D., "Keele Hall Gardens," *Gardeners' Chronicle*, 11 November 1871, 1452–53. William Hill, "British Gardeners— XXXV. William Hill," *Gardeners' Chronicle*, 12 February 1876, 213.

ritual performances followed highly prescribed and expected behaviors, they could potentially either affirm or subvert the existing social order. Quite subtle variations in interactions between gardeners and employers, therefore, may reveal important shifts or cleavages and new meanings in the landscape.

Ritual enactment drawing on formative gestures might function to repair potential rents in the social fabric by drawing on the dialectical process. The ambivalence inherent in formative gestures lent plasticity to social interaction and mediated against abrupt and destructive confrontation.[2] A close study of nineteenth-century garden rituals proves particularly rewarding because of the massive changes occurring in Great Britain. Market forces corroded traditional relationships, engendered anxiety for those at the margins, encouraged labor mobility, and fostered changes in property rights. These changes promoted new horizontal solidarities in competition with traditional vertical loyalties and thus impacted relations between gardeners and their employers. Rituals potentially offered a mechanism for preserving traditional advantages for those seeking new opportunities so they carried the burden of dual and conflicting functions. Rituals may contain or diffuse tension between classes, but they do not necessarily resolve social contradictions. If rituals function to both preserve privilege and facilitate adaptation to change, what do they reveal about the negotiation of social relationships and power between landowners and gardeners, as well as others at the social margins? How did the dialectical process facilitate accommodation to change? What do rituals reveal about the definition and perception of gardens?

1. *Portrait of William Hill, head gardener at Keele Hall (printed in article, "British Gardeners—XXXV. William Hill,"* Gardners' Chronicle, *12 February 1876, 213)*

The rituals explored in this essay follow the "strict" definition proposed by Peter McLaren.[3] Briefly described, McLaren defines rituals as exhibiting distinct forms, and composed of clusters of symbols. Inherently dramatic, rituals facilitate psychosocial integration fostering personality development. They often employ codified language that may exert inherent authority and secular rituals, such as those examined in this essay, often rely on formal qualities of repetition, stylization, and evocative resonance frequently suggestive of staged performances. Rituals represent a possibility of choices and their prescribed codes, frequently unarticulated, closely relate to family and social class. Although rituals invariably draw on different modes, issues of decorum occupy a significant place in the garden. In nineteenth-century walled kitchen gardens, the many aspects noted here—especially clusters of symbols, stylized presentation, and class relations—all converge on the garden as it becomes a stage for interactive rituals.

A synergistic relationship exists between landscapes and the rituals enacted in them allowing gardens to become unique and distinctive. Although garden rituals superficially may appear to mirror other rituals, customs, or traditions, they possess a unique ability to redefine the garden while concurrently altering or adjusting social relationships as a result of their performance. Obviously not every garden ritual will directly result in social change or significantly altered conceptions of space, but cumulatively, over time, they inherently possess dynamic, transformative capacities. Garden rituals among different social classes drew on stylization and ritual codes, and they took distinct forms using symbols and often possessed an inherently dramatic quality. The walls and physical partitions of the kitchen garden provided a "theater" for ritual performances, and gardeners served long and arduous transformative apprenticeships to legitimate their presence in the performative space. Because they

[2] Ronald L. Grimes, *Beginnings in Ritual Studies* (Washington, D. C.: University Press of America, 1982), 59–65.
[3] Peter McLaren, *Schooling as a Ritual Performance: Towards a Political Economy of Educational Symbols and Gestures* (London and New York: Routledge, 1993, 2nd ed.), 42–50.

acquired ritual knowledge linked to an exclusionary language and special technical skills, they sometimes used ritual to ameliorate their position in the social order.

The propensity of interactive ritual performances to subtly alter the social and political balance raises questions about the coherence of intention and reception, as well as shared beliefs. In *Ritual, Politics, and Power*, David Kertzer stresses the importance of ritual in all political entities noting that symbolic systems help people negotiate physical reality and their social universe by manipulating symbolic power, which may lead to actual political power. People live within symbolic systems even when they remain unaware of them so symbols provide content for rituals by condensing meaning, offering alternatives, and retaining ambiguity. Once constructed, ritual practices demonstrate resilience, although they remain malleable. Ultimately political rites may sustain those holding power or become a potent weapon for the powerless. Although ritual may build solidarity, it does not require shared beliefs; and if one further accepts that human beings assimilate and process information through preexisting paradigms, then it follows that variances in education, status, and reference groups will lead to differences in absorbing and interpreting information. Thus, elites find themselves constantly challenged when presenting their views of society in the face of contradictory evidence from the lives of those subject to their dominance.[4]

In the case of landscapes, people engaged in the same gardening rituals may not believe the same thing and, most importantly, may not *see* the same thing. This offers a model for aesthetic understanding as a function of both creative intention and perception. Specifically, rituals offer rich opportunities for analyzing multiple and simultaneously held meanings for gardens. Although interactive rituals in gardens do not appear political in the more obvious sense of the term, they serve political ends by disappropriating some property rights and pressing the economic claims of the impoverished. Additionally, careful study of interactive rituals reveals their function as powerful mechanisms for cohering social groups. Gardeners, with strong horizontal loyalties buttressed by ritual, claimed the working areas of the walled kitchen garden as their own. Even those at the margins appropriated the use of certain garden spaces, and in the case of laboring women, convincing ritual performances ensured survival.

Most analysis focuses on elites and their maintenance of hegemony.[5] A careful investigation of rituals, however, reveals that those in subservient positions also used garden spaces to their own advantage. Interactive rituals could reinforce or challenge accepted relations between the powerful and those dependent on them for protection or patronage to the advantage of either party, and reveal physical, sensory, behavioral, and emotional dimensions of gardens that otherwise remain ephemeral or amorphous. Rituals provide the framework for human intervention in shaping the physical properties of gardens as well as dictating their design, arrangement, care, and presentation. Knowledgeable interpretation of ritual meanings shifts estate gardens from static, rigidly defined entities, ostensibly orchestrated by elites for promoting their cultural hegemony to amorphously, creatively construed spaces.

Rituals of Consumption

Rituals of consumption, such as visits to walled kitchen gardens, functioned to establish and maintain the privileged status of elites among their peers and other ranks in society. These ritual visits took distinct forms beginning with entrance into the performative space at the front gate and culminated with an exhibition of the most valuable horticultural possessions at the height of the experience. Participants demonstrated decorum specifically related to class divisions. The "master," family members, and guests entered the often ornate front entrance gates to the high-walled complexes on broad paths flanked with elaborate borders and then proceeded to glasshouses while duly admiring the flowers. Engaging in the ritual promenade actively influenced elite participants' perceptions as they presented a version of the garden to others. Strolling through long borders at a slowly measured pace mentally enlarged the dimensions of gardens to account for the time consumed in walking through them

[4] David Kertzer, *Ritual, Politics, and Power* (New Haven and London: Yale University Press, 1988), 31, 38, 76, 176.
[5] See Ann Bermingham, *Landscape and Ideology: The English Rustic Tradition, 1740–1860* (Berkeley: University of California Press, 1986); Nigel Everett, *The Tory View of Landscape* (New Haven and London: Yale University Press for the Paul Mellon Centre for Studies in British Art, 1994); and Tom Williamson, *Polite Landscapes: Garden and Society in Eighteenth-Century England* (Baltimore, Md.: Johns Hopkins University Press, 1995).

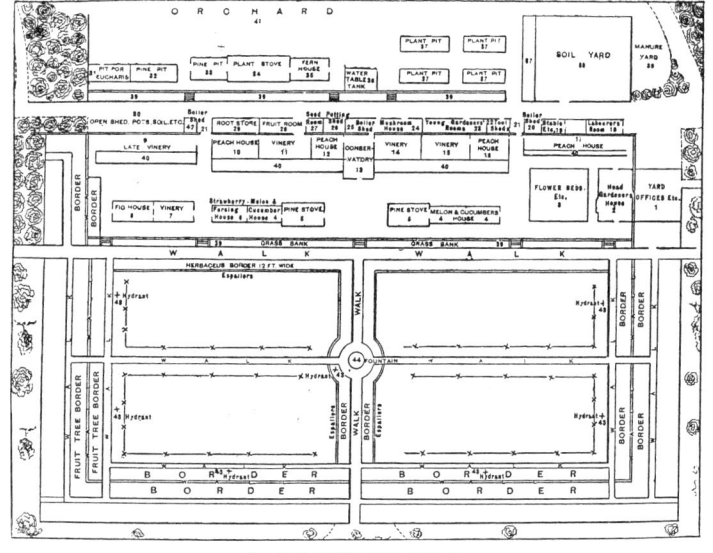

Plan of Fruit and Kitchen Gardens at Thoresby.

2. Plan of the fruit and kitchen garden at Thoresby (plan taken from an article on the gardens at Thoresby, "Kitchen Gardens and Forcing Houses," Garden, *30 October 1880, 428)*

in elaborate, constraining clothing. In some seasons, elite visitors might decide to view the magnificent fruit trees trained flat along the brick or stone garden walls.

The kitchen gardens included propagating houses either within the boundaries or adjacent to the walls, as well as the head gardener's house and office. Because the walled space served as the working domain for the entire estate garden complex, visitors saw a vast range of plants. The displays in the conservatory demanded constant rotation of the plants first brought into bloom in the greenhouses. Flowers for the house as well as arboretums drew on plant material originally propagated in the complexes. The substantial walls and richly manured soil sheltered and nourished fruit trees with heavy crops as well as other fruits and vegetables that the gardeners delivered to the kitchen staff. These men also regularly provided large quantities of flowers and blooming plants grown in the complex when the family occupied the house. The frame yard and glasshouses enabled the staff to produce delicacies out of season, and when the family took up residence in town the gardeners packed and shipped fruits, vegetables, and flowers to them by railway. The head gardener, once alerted to the employer's presence by staff, proffered respectful greetings and offered to accompany the "master" and any guests on their tour. The various glasshouse interiors held plants gathered from around the world. Rare orchids flaunting their exotic and sensual colors with multiple blooms or huge clusters of amethyst-colored grapes luxuriantly dangling under glass provided the culmination of the ritual. The ability to display such rare treasures confirmed the superior status of estate owners.

Spaces and structures omitted from the tour also reveal information about the structuring of ritual garden tours. Utilitarian spaces, often located behind the greenhouses in the walled kitchen garden and accessed by separate back entrances for the gardening staff, contained furnaces, coal shed, and housing for under gardeners as well as tool sheds, potting sheds, storage, fruit houses, and frameyards. Thousands of plants grown in the frameyards furnished the bedding material that changed with the season or more often for special occasions. Mounds of well-rotted compost and manure also stood piled for use lending these back areas an odoriferous presence in warmer weather. Owners, and certainly not visitors, rarely saw these work spaces. Conspicuous consumption, as with the case of many new consumer goods of the nineteenth century, relied on austere production sites and rough labor that remained out of view. The plan of the fruit and kitchen gardens at Thoresby (Fig. 2) clearly depicts the utilitarian sections of the complex in the upper fourth of the image.

Estate owners employing large gardening staffs expected pristine maintenance for the entire complex, and especially the glasshouses. The close proximity of plants required extreme vigilance for any sign of disease or insect infestation, and treatment by hand or chemical occurred immediately to avoid further problems. Staff rapped on endless terracotta pots for the hollow ring indicating the need for more water. Experienced gardeners immediately recognized the sound of dry pots as well as the ineptitude of the ignorant missing it. Each gardening task required expert performance for peer acceptance. Owners expected to see the results of this but rarely observed all this exacting work because class ideologies and decorum discouraged the presence of elites in work areas. Gardeners' rituals occurring in these spaces drew on special conventions, elaborate decorum among ranks, constant negotiation, and specialized language. Elite insistence on their own paradigm of ritual understanding would have shielded gardeners from upper-class comprehension of their robust ritual enactments and vibrant alternative culture.

Only the superb plants, but not the work required to produce them, ever appeared during visits to the glasshouses. Instead, elite visitors focused on their favorite horticultural specimens. One cannot imagine Ralph Sneyd of Kneel Hall, for example, visiting his glasshouses without closely observing the swelling clusters of Black Prince, Sweetwater, and Black Hamburgh grapes destined for both his table and horticultural renown. In the ten years between 1853 and 1863, the magnificent grapes from Kneel Hall took twenty-one first prizes at the Royal Horticultural Society shows in London, twenty-three firsts at the Royal Botanic Gardens Society show in Regent's Park, and fourteen firsts at the Crystal Palace Company exhibitions at Sydenham; and this added up to a tidy sum for William Hill, given that a single dish of Black Prince grapes received as much as £4 in prize money. The head gardener derived at least as much pleasure from his horticultural prowess and prizes as his employer did from eating the grapes.[6] In this instance, the status rituals surrounding privileged consumption provided specific benefits to both parties.

Gardeners' Prerogatives

Many estate owners enjoyed the prestige garnered when plants from their glasshouses captured prizes at prominent competitions. At Glamis Castle, for example, Lord Strathmore proudly displayed the splendid cup won by his head gardener George Johnson on the dinner table in the stately dining room for all his guests to see.[7] Only the most careful pruning, selection, and cosseting produced perfect specimens for the judges' scrutiny, and no one, not even Lord Strathmore, considered plucking a single bunch without the express assent of his head gardener.

Ritual clearly dictated that the gardener should select any fruit to be eaten, cut it, and then send it up to the house for consumption to avoid conflict. However, as the market created new wealth, employers appeared who might not fully understand head gardeners' prerogatives. Indeed, handbooks offering advice and guidance about expected behaviors flourished. One practical guide published in 1894, *The Duties of Servants*, written by "a member of the aristocracy" for ladies hiring household servants and hoping to retain their staff carefully gave the following advice regarding gardeners. "He objects, on principle, to his choicest blossoms being cut by his mistress or her daughters, or the finest bunches of grapes being gathered; when his green-houses and hot-houses are to be rifled, he prefers that it should be done by himself rather than his mistress, and ladies who value their gardeners are inclined to humor this weakness."[8]

Although some employers clearly needed education on gardening protocol, other members of the elite became quite knowledgeable about specific aspects of gardening and the accomplishments of their gardeners. They spent substantial sums subscribing to plant hunting expeditions and enjoyed showing their guests new and unusual specimens. Their glasshouses contained prize plants carefully grown from seed shipped back from other continents. Rare divisions and cuttings grown on and flowered stood like trophies on the glasshouse benches asserting status in much the same way as a fine collection of books in the library or superb paintings hanging in the principal rooms. Ritual visits to the glasshouse complex, particularly if the visitor also collected rare plants, served to affirm the superior status of both parties.

Status Rituals

Other "persons of quality" also might engage in ritual visits to the gardens even in the absence of the owners. Respectable ladies and gentlemen, after being shown around the public rooms of a country house by the housekeeper, then visited the walled garden complex accompanied by a member of the gardening staff. High-ranking visitors expected to be escorted by the head gardener, but those without titles or great positions might find the attention of a foreman or under gardener quite satisfactory because vails (tips) customarily reflected the attention accorded the visitor. Many excursionists found vails particularly unpleasant and complained of the custom in their correspondence and diaries as early as the eighteenth

[6] Hill, "British Gardeners," *Gardeners' Chronicle,* 12 February 1876, 213.

[7] "Mr. George Johnson, Glamis Castle," *Gardeners' Chronicle*, 15 October 1887, 473.

[8] A Member of the Aristocracy, *The Duties of Servants: A Practical Guide to the Routine of Domestic Service* (London: Frederick Warne & Company, 1894), 116.

century. When John Byng visited Chatsworth in 1769, he wrote, "Seeing this little garden, cost us much money."[9] The ritual tip proved difficult to avoid because the gratuity secured the status of those bestowing it. The vail provides a particularly obvious example of an old ritual functioning to reallocate resources. The bestowal of the gratuity generated outward deference and decorum on the part of the gardeners and existed as part of a system of social control. The vail also provides an example of a ritual that at the most obvious level appears practical and might be defined merely as a custom, but given that rituals act to reify the sociocultural world in which they are embedded, the vail turns out to be a ritual when it becomes infused with symbolic meaning for the participants.

As gardeners escorted ladies and gentlemen on visits into the glasshouses and gardens, they pointed out items of special interest and plants in bloom. They also might choose to keep certain items from public scrutiny. Thus, they imposed a specific vision of the garden on those whom they guided around. This is not to suggest that visitors lacked their own perceptions and mental filters but simply to highlight that the interactive ritual of touring the gardens might shape or change their perspective by virtue of the plants brought to their attention.

Outdoor staff followed the example of under servants among the indoor staff and discreetly vanished when the family and their friends made use of the ornamental areas of the gardens. The ritual of invisibility formed a component of psychosocial integration eventually shaping personality development. Garden apprentices quickly learned that they "ceased to exist" at certain social levels. During house parties, perfectly tended hedges, borders, and lawns provided immaculate settings for strolls, teas, and other entertainments. Gravel walks regularly appeared raked, lawns swept, and flowers deadheaded by invisible hands. Gardeners silently merged with the shrubbery at the sound of approaching voices with upper-class accents. The ritual of conjured disappearance cut both ways. Although it offered elite visitors to the gardens a fantasy of magically maintained perfection, it also denied them an understanding of the forces shaping their gardens.

Estate owners, by contrast, expected to see the gardening staff in the kitchen garden, although their servants hastily grabbed coats and doffed caps to greet their "betters." At the same time, the "master" or "mistress" rarely entered gardeners' work areas such as furnace rooms, frame yards, or potting sheds. The combined performances of elites and their gardeners created a kitchen garden compound composed of two distinct zones with closely controlled privileges of entry. In this instance, the construction of garden space depended on social as well as physical divisions.

The knowledge and importance of nineteenth-century gardeners increased as they successfully used innovative technologies to cultivate exotic plant importations, while simultaneously the elite often became less conscious of the technical requirements of gardening. A brief look at a few tasks of head gardeners will make these points clearer. Solving complex engineering problems, manipulating the artificial environments required for continuous production, and discovering the cultivation requirements of a vast range of botanical material all provide examples of how elites could find their comprehension of gardens narrowed by the very rituals of consumption they practiced. Thus, elites often perceived their gardens in ways that did not match the vision of their gardeners.

James Sheppard served for thirty-six years as head gardener to Captain Hugh Berners and subsequently to his son, C. H. Berners, at Woolverston Park, Ipswich, a large and beautiful estate in Suffolk bounded by the River Orwell. Sheppard created a series of dams that carried water for about a mile to supply the local village and the gardens he supervised. He skillfully integrated the project into the surrounding landscape so the artificially luxuriant growth of the gardens appeared "natural" rather than dependent upon his engineering skills. He also developed the heating system for the kitchen garden glasshouses and so successfully grew prize fruit that he later published articles on his techniques, served on the Fruit Committee of the Royal Horticultural Society, and acted as a judge for metropolitan and local shows.[10] The Berners provided the patronage for all the improvements and certainly enjoyed the results, but their aesthetic enjoyment of the landscape did not derive from viewing it as an engineering project. They routinely engaged in garden-related rituals centered on consumption. Afternoon teas admiring flower borders and lavish dinner parties asserted their superior social position, however, their visceral

[9] J. Jean Hecht, *The Domestic Servant Class in Eighteen-Century England* (London: Routledge & Kegan Paul, 1959), 171.
[10] "The Late Mr. James Sheppard of Woolverston," *Gardeners' Chronicle*, 28 January 1893, 107.

enjoyment of the mouth-watering fruit served up for these social occasions required no knowledge about the finer points of growing it.

At Eaton Hall near Chester, fifty-six gardeners reported to Mr. Sellwood, head gardener to the Duke of Westminster. In even more glasshouses than the foremen could count, six miles of hot-water pipes snaked through the estate's substantially built and seemingly endless glass enclosures, which included multiple plant houses and a conservatory 375 feet long that served as the termination point for eight dependent glasshouses projecting from it. Forcing six thousand strawberry plants, cosseting prize melons, and harvesting perfect grapes as well as all other glasshouse work proceeded in tandem with the care bestowed on the terraces, flower gardens, shrubbery, and extensive park bordering the town.[11]

The Duke of Westminster and his family only used Eaton Hall at Christmas time and during hunting season. The duke loved driving through his beautifully tended park, appreciated the flower-filled state rooms and family wing, and took great pride in the ornate iron gates leading to the vast walled garden. He freely shared the estate's park with visitors, who also might be shown in groups around the walled gardens and glasshouses by foremen. As was typical among those with wealth and rank, the duke regularly presented choice flowers and fruit from the greenhouses to friends and relatives. These gifts arriving in estate hampers and boxes exuded far more status than the boxes of the best London florists.

The ritual of touring glasshouses and presenting flowers reached its apogee in cases of royalty. In the early 1830s, the Duchess of Northumberland served as preceptoress to the future Queen Victoria. The duchess brought baskets and bouquets of flowers made up by Mr. Thomson, head gardener at Syon House, to her young pupil at Kensington Palace. The then Princess Victoria and her mother also would visit Syon House frequently and tour the great domed conservatory and hot houses accompanied by the duchess and Mr. Thomson, who quickly made bouquets of flowers attracting royal interest. When the then rare *Vanda teres* orchid first flowered in England at Syon House in 1833, it caught the royal eye. Mr. Thomson, with a silent nod from the duchess, promptly cut the orchid for presentation to the young Princess Victoria. Significantly, when Queen Victoria visited Baron Rothschild at Waddlesdon Manor in 1891, his floral offering to her consisted of a bouquet of *Vanda teres*.[12] These rituals involving rare and valuable plant presentations dated back to at least the Tudor dynasty and affirmed the high status of those offering the gifts. The ritual floral presentations to Queen Victoria functioned as metaphorical political acts.

Only the active cultivation and continued use of the garden allowed the space to fill its intended aesthetic function. Within the logic of Max Weber's model, lavish consumption defined status honor as gentry and an emerging industrial elite copied the behavior of affluent aristocrats.[13] "Effortless" splendor in park and estate gardens, or cap-tugging subservience by the gardening staff as the "master" entered the main gates of the kitchen garden became an intrinsic part of the aesthetic experience of elites. Their perceptions of the garden coincided with their performances projecting power and benevolence.

Rituals Facilitate Evolving "Master/Man" Relationships

Public garden rituals such as glasshouse visits and bouquet presentation affirmed rank and privilege, but private rituals such as review of the garden-account books by owners and estate agents reflected the new dominance of the market. Although the practice of selling excess kitchen garden produce rested on a long tradition going back to at least the 1300s, profit typically remained a secondary consideration.[14] By the 1870s, however, many estate owners saw the abundance of their kitchen gardens as commodities and actively began pressing for increased revenue to the dismay of market gardeners. The latter complained bitterly about the practice since they found themselves disadvantaged by higher tax rates and land-rental costs as they competed in the market.[15] One angry market gardener specifically noted, "Noble lords, baronets, noblemen's factors, and a host of

[11] H. E., "Eaton Hall," *Gardeners' Chronicle*, 13 December 1884, 743–44.

[12] "A Royal Gardener," *Gardeners' Chronicle*, 21 March 1892, 652.

[13] Weber, M, *From Max Weber: Essays in Sociology*, trans. H. H. Gerth and C. W. Mills (New York: Oxford University Press, 1964), 185–94.

[14] John Harvey, *Mediaeval Gardens* (Beaverton, Ore.: Timber Press, 1981), 61.

[15] A. D., "Non-rated Trading," *Gardeners' Chronicle*, 12 December 1885, 758–59.

gardeners" as those involved in the unfair practice.[16] An 1891 legal case affirms that no less a person than the Duke of Marlborough charged his head gardener, Thomas Williams, with responsibility for the sale of garden flowers and the collection of revenues.[17] By the last third of the nineteenth century, estate owners might more fully appreciate the aesthetic satisfaction derived from the fecundity of the kitchen garden with its abundance of vegetables, fruits, and flowers. For some owners concerned with containing expenditures, the visually desirable garden began imperceptibly merging with the dictates of the market. As a result, reviewing gardeners' account books became a nuanced interactive ritual.

In order to understand why reviewing gardeners' account books constituted a ritual, one must remember that in the nineteenth century gardeners received housing, fuel, and food as compensation. Employers monetized only a portion of their earnings. Furthermore, this system made hoarding or saving money difficult often leaving gardeners dependent on employers' benevolence in sickness or old age. Because sociopolitical systems help people negotiate physical reality and find their place in the social universe, money carried both practical and symbolic importance. Monetizing productive tasks and the possibility of savings provided opportunities for social change.

If commissions and profit splitting monetized a significant aspect of the relationship between employers and gardeners, the rituals of negotiation could lead to altered social and political perspectives. As the "master/man" relationship dependent on rituals of class distinction, subservience, and decorum rocked and then slowly gave way in the nineteenth century, new rituals of negotiation tied to the symbolic meaning of money coalesced. Astute employment of ritual modes of decorum attached to monetized value and the increasing pressures of the market enabled some gardeners to slowly transform their position in society. Capitalism facilitated altered rituals drawing on the actual and symbolic power of money to serve as framing devices that shifted perceptions of both gardeners and their employers while it slowly undermined the traditional "master/man" relationship.

Regular meetings to review the accounts meant that gardeners needed to note quantities of various goods sent to the cook, housekeeper, and butler each day, and they demanded initials acknowledging the items on receipt. Whether conducted in the estate office or the head gardener's office in the kitchen garden, the ritual of reviewing expenditures required tact and discretion on both sides. Owners faced with increasingly unprofitable estates needed to curtail expenses without appearing miserly. Head gardeners sought to retain or expand their prerogatives and resources while endeavoring to appear conscientious.

Two practices that dated back to the Middle Ages, "commissions" and profit splitting, could become important considerations during any review of the account books. Briefly described, commissions consisted of a percentage of the money spent by employers being returned to the servants facilitating the purchases. Some viewed this percentage payment, also known as poundage, as blatant extortion; others, including some employers, regarded it as a legitimate augmentation to wages set in expectation of this prerogative. Profit splitting resulted from the sale of estate garden produce and plants to outside buyers and included the subsequent division of the gains between the employer and gardener based on a negotiated percentage.

Both of these practices impacted the review of account books. Mutual acceptance of "commissions" acknowledged the older embedded economy anchored in the "master/man" relationship. The increased prevalence of profit splitting and economic rationalization with rigorous scrutiny of the gardeners' books heralded a shift to the market economy.[18] The ability to skirt the exigencies of the market lent status to employers and their gardeners so their interactive rituals stressed appropriate forms of address, an emphasis on private privilege, and commerce as a secondary consideration. Economic imperatives might force some concessions to the market, but rituals reinforcing status honor cushioned the brutal reality of market imperatives. The importance of these rituals becomes starkly evident when we observe how they failed. Numerous oblique and open

[16] "Unequal Rating of Market Gardeners," *Gardeners' Chronicle*, 25 September 1880, 404.

[17] "Law Notes: A Disputed Account, Duke of Marlborough v. A. E. Mayo," *Gardeners' Chronicle*, 2 May 1891, 568.

[18] "Garden Expenditures," *Garden*, 31 December 1881, 621; "Nisbet's Garden Account Book," *Garden*, 23 June 1877, 522; "Garden Account Book," *Garden*, 23 December 1876, 595; "Mr. Sinclair's Garden Diary," *Gardeners' Chronicle*, 6 January 1877, 18.

references to bitter feelings and lawsuits between employers and gardeners appeared in the horticultural press attesting to failed accord between the parties.[19]

The enumeration of these market developments, however, should not be construed as an argument for a materialist-based understanding of historical development or aesthetic perception. Ritual performances reinforced tradition, status honor, and elite perceptions as they shaped understanding of gardens. Gardeners molded elite perceptions by skillfully manipulating new technologies and plants to make aesthetic appreciation of gardens more dependent on botanical understanding than familiarity with the classics. Examining the rituals of working gardeners illustrates some of the complex motives driving their behaviors and offers new possibilities for aesthetic understanding of nineteenth-century gardens.

Gardeners' Gardens

Long years of apprenticeship and practice made estate gardeners expertly versed in the language, history, and execution of their rituals. They skillfully employed them to sustain their collective identity and reformulate their sense of community, as they concurrently pressed for economic improvement and security in a rapidly changing society. Because the elite owed obligations and responsibilities to those below them in the social hierarchy, gardeners often supported traditional forms of authority and direct questioning of elite power did not necessarily serve their best interests. Alterations would inevitably occur in the nineteenth-century walled garden, but the gardeners perceived themselves as advantaged when negotiating change within the ritual practices they expertly performed and at least partially adjudicated. Gardeners' performances reveal both their conscious and unconscious collective attempts to explore the boundaries of authority, while also elucidating how and why new rituals emerged and their implications for aesthetic perception. Exploring these points requires placing gardeners' rituals within a broad framework of nineteenth-century social and economic change.

Toward the end of Queen Victoria's reign, social norms stressed individual initiative and responsibility in an environment that increasingly monetized more spheres of human activity, but it remains problematic as to whether this shift necessarily constituted an improvement. As E. P. Thompson reminds us in his introduction to *Customs in Common*:

> The conservative culture of the plebs as often as not resists, in the name of custom, those economic rationalizations and innovations (such as enclosure, work-discipline, unregulated "free" markets in grain), which rulers, dealers, or employers seek to impose. Innovation is more evident at the top of society than below, but since this innovation is not some normless and neutral technological/sociological process ("Modernization," "Rationalization") but is the innovation of capitalist process, it is more often experienced by the plebs in the form of exploitation, or the expropriation of customary use-rights, or the violent disruption of valued patterns of work and leisure.[20]

Thompson's perspective on the working class engenders differences of opinion among scholars, but the working lives of gardeners lends much supporting evidence to his interpretation of capitalism. However, gardeners did not constitute a single cohesive group because they drew sharp divisions between themselves and common laborers, and the distance separating apprentices from foremen could become an unbridgeable chasm so cleavage existed within ranks as well as between them. At the same time, gardeners' rituals reinforced horizontal loyalties. Adolescent apprenticeships, use of a specialized vocabulary, segregated housing, and duties of increasing complexity led to slow movement through the ranks creating social cohesion among gardeners. Additionally, many gardeners constituted the

[19] "Gardeners' Discounts," *Gardeners' Chronicle*, 1 April 1871, 418–19; "Gardeners' Discounts," *Gardeners' Chronicle*, 22 April 1871, 516; "Charge of Stealing," *Gardeners' Chronicle*, 16 November 1889, 573; "A Partick Gardener's Action," *Gardeners' Chronicle*, 29 July 1893, 137; Malcolm Dunn, "Gardeners and Their Employers," *Gardeners' Chronicle*, 1 September 1894, 253.
[20] E. P. Thompson, *Customs in Common* (New York: New Press, 1991), 9.

third or fourth generation in their family to follow the occupation so familial tradition reinforced knowledge and shared emotions. Journeymen habitually changed positions on estates in the early years of their careers so shared experiences, living quarters, and extensive social networks further consolidated group identity. As gardeners became increasingly mobile to fit the needs of an expanding market economy, the rituals of bothy life and employment practices reinforced and reinvigorated group- as well as self-identity.

Gardeners also compared employment venues, or alternatively phrased, considered one aesthetic expression in relation to another. They saw and experienced geographically dispersed estates with walled complexes from many periods enabling them to achieve a critical understanding of garden aesthetics. They were the "producing subject"—a fact frequently unacknowledged by their employers and historians because of their social status—but they were also the "consuming subject." Their impeccable grasp of "connoisseurship" and botanical knowledge resulted in aesthetic comprehension possibly broader than that of "their betters." Arnold van Gennep's concept of rites of passage offers help in comprehending the apprenticeship system as practiced on large estate gardens in the nineteenth century. Briefly stated, a tripartite ritual process moved individuals from one social status to another by initially separating them, ensuring a period of transition, and then reincorporating them into their new status group. Victor Turner augmented van Gennep's work with a rich exploration of the intermediate stage, or liminal phase, and presented it as a period when neophytes operate as if in limbo. Once stripped of old roles, they become open to assuming new ones. Garden apprentices in this liminal phase experience vulnerability and uncertainty along with others of the same status creating a kind of "communitas." When living outside fixed norms provided by their former status, they encountered new options, behaviors, and expectations leading to change. This model facilitates a deeper understanding of their rituals.

With improved technologies and transportation options, gardeners began presiding over newly exotic landscapes and glasshouse complexes that gloriously obfuscated climate and geographical plant distribution. Rituals reflected the expansion of apprenticeships to include additional skills and knowledge but also acted to protect the craft from the exigencies of the market. Gardeners carefully used rituals to retain their social and economic distinctiveness from laborers. Employers acknowledging their interactive rituals reinforced vertical loyalties. Dismissive and miserly employers, by contrast, simply strengthened horizontal loyalties as a reaction to the indignities suffered by gardeners. Multiple performances provide vantage points for observing either the consolidation or attenuation of vertical or horizontal loyalties.

Acknowledgement on the part of employers ranged from grand gestures such as building improved gardeners' housing to brief conversations in which employers acquiesced to gardeners' selection of new apprentices. More protracted interactive rituals might focus on discussions of bedding displays required at certain times of the year or for special occasions. The essence of these interactive rituals, from the perspective of gardeners, rested in the visible and verbal tokens of trust given by the estate owner. Simultaneously, the rituals assured the elite that the gardeners remained dependent on their desires and patronage thus ensuring their loyalty. A seemingly simple public compliment on the family crest in a complex bedding scheme for a coming of age celebration served as an acknowledgement of the status and importance of both parties. The estate owner admired the bedding because it proclaimed his family's position, and the gardener saw the favorable attention accorded his masterpiece as a proclamation of his skill and value. This subtle interactive ritual cemented the alliance of both parties, but it rested on divergent suppositions.

Professional gardeners' roles expanded and improved for much of the nineteenth century. With new technologies and transportation systems, they expanded their domain to become masters of a growing variety of plant material in artificially heated glasshouses. New railroad networks increased their labor mobility and made it possible to change employment venues to gain horticultural skills, as well as compete for prizes. As gardeners began growing plants under glass employing greater sophistication and skill, they often became discerning connoisseurs of the exotic. They played with retarding and advancing plants as they manipulated fruits and flowers to reach perfection according to their needs. Top head gardeners skilled at almost any horticultural task earned the complimentary accolade, "all-rounder." These experts made their aesthetic judgments based on tasks of production. Plants requiring the greatest resources to procure and the highest skill to cultivate became, in their eyes, the most desirable. Large spaces containing an array of challenging plants all brought into peak bloom or fruiting for a special purpose excited their particular admiration. They based their approach to aesthetic understanding on "connoisseurship" and carefully sorted out all the elements contributing to the finished effect. Gardeners' gardens became spaces intensively packed with difficult, rare, and challenging plants, all of which bore testimony to their skill and superior status. Their rituals supported the creation of tableaux of exquisite perfection with expertly potted and staked plants silently and motionlessly conveying messages of the gardeners' mastery.

From the perspective of head gardeners, ideal "masters" or patrons would understand enough about horticulture to appreciate their skilled statements of horticultural bravura, but would refrain from intervening or questioning their authority. Gardeners working for titled members of the aristocracy with substantial resources felt fortunate and basked in the reflected glory of their patrons. If elites saw gardens as stages for their performances, the gardeners saw their spaces as the most essential element in the play.

Gardeners felt that a liberal patron steeped in tradition and with substantial resources constituted an ideal employer. Gardens designed and run to show off benevolence and grandeur meant that the gardeners retained a position more removed from the pressures of the market.

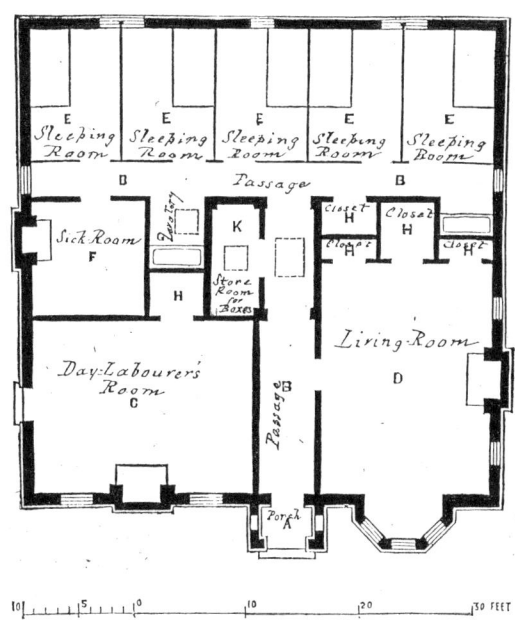

Plan of the Young Gardeners' House at Wimbledon Park.

3. *Plan of bothy at Wimbledon Park (plan taken from article on the gardeners' accommodations at Wimbleton Park, "Under-Gardeners' Lodgings," Garden, 13 January 1872, 175)*

Employers from old families attuned to tradition understood that deference and faithful service required reciprocal acknowledgment in old age and, further, they supported competent sons following their fathers as head gardeners. Both estate owners and gardeners benefited from supporting traditional relationships, but each held differing perceptions and beliefs. Gardeners addressed their "masters" by title and employers used only surnames in answering their head gardeners. Yet, in turn, all members of the gardening staff would affix "Mr." to head gardeners' surnames. This may seem to be a small nicety, but the importance of these interactive rituals may be gauged by gardeners' scrupulous observance of proper forms of address. Ritual language clarified the roles and the hierarchy that participants observed. Some of the best "master/man" relationships existed when both parties used interactive rituals to come to a mutually satisfactory acceptance of their respective prerogatives.

Women's Gardens

If estate owners entered the walled kitchen garden through ornate gates at impressive entrances, the gardening staff controlled the working entrances to the complex as their prerogative. Garden walls symbolically and actually barred laboring men from entering the complex except for the most backbreaking, unskilled labor paid at the lowest daily rates. Hauling manure, double digging, and other types of rough outdoor work fell to these men. A few thoughtful estate owners or head gardeners provided a shed or room with a fire where they might warm their numb hands in the winter; however, as in the case of Wimbledon Park, they often remained segregated from the regular gardening staff. (Fig. 3) These men shared common bonds with the farm laborers and usually led extremely hard lives marked by poverty and a marginal existence. Laboring women also sometimes entered the walled enclaves as domestic servants. In gardens with large staffs, one or more female servants attended to the domestic needs of the gardeners. The household records of the Duke of Westminster, for example, reveal payments for two women, who cooked and cleaned for the men in the bothy.[21]

[21] Gervas Huxley, *Victorian Duke: The Life of Hugh Lupus Grosvenor, First Duke of Westminster* (London: Oxford University Press, 1967), 138.

Laboring women occasionally gained peripheral employment in walled kitchen gardens. "Weeding women" performed mundane tasks, including weeding paths, picking bugs, and hoeing.[22] Some male gardeners adamantly opposed any women within the garden walls even when they worked at such humble jobs.[23] In walled kitchen gardens, neither estate owners nor head gardeners paid particular attention to lowly "weeder women" working on hands and knees.

In spite of their humble position, laboring women understood that the walled kitchen garden existed as a garden within a larger garden that their knowledge and perspective allowed them to identify. While they gained a few badly needed shillings for their weeding, the garden they harvested from lay in the fields and hedgerows full of "wild" food. Because of their experience, traditional knowledge, and unique aesthetic perspective, laboring women conceived of the walled park enclosure and its boundaries as an enormous kitchen garden that frequently only they knew how to nurture and harvest. Most gardeners and estate owners ignored the resources of this space. Ironically, this ancient form of gardening remains largely imperceptible to scholars today because the activities of these women stayed primarily outside the realm of the market.

Gardening requires human manipulation of soil and nutrients to produce plants of some economic or aesthetic value. Land ownership or usufructuary rights are an additional condition often attached to the concept of gardening but are not necessary for horticulture. Understanding the supernumerary nature of property rights allows appreciation of the full range of gardening activities carried out by laboring women without land ownership. Their "ownership" originated in their ability to conceive of meadows and hedgerows as gardens with edible resources. Their ability to mentally construct gardens depended on their lowly status and the rituals of deference.

Laboring women made critical contributions to the family economy by means of plant gathering. Jane Humphries argues that their efforts made a significant difference in the standard of living of laboring families and acted to delay proletarianization.[24] As enclosure and subsequent diminishment of common rights increased in the nineteenth century, access to gathered food became more difficult. The Larceny Act and the Trespass Act, both in 1827, provided summary punishment for the "theft" of plants, shrubs, and trees, including their fruits and nuts.[25] However, in tracing the "custom-to-crime" shift, it appears that women infrequently suffered prosecution for breaches in the new laws.[26] Apparently, in some locations wild food-gathering continued to be a privilege unofficially granted to women and children. On many occasions, those in authority simply made a ritual of ignoring their work.

The economically precarious position of laboring women and children in society provided them with advantages when engaged in gathering wild foods. As long as their shabby, worn, patched, and torn garments matched their rough hands and bony frames, those with property and power usually engaged in the ritual of deliberately seeing through them. At most the poor might receive fleeting acknowledgment for the bobbed curtsey or doffed cap from the landowner if they lived in one of his cottages. Their muddy feet or berry-stained hands aroused no interest and the rough heap of weeds might pass unnoticed. Girls observed the behaviors of their mothers tugging shawls and aprons closer as they modestly and obediently dropped their eyes. Even landowners, who recognized the value of the gathered foods, might engage in rituals of feigned ignorance. After all, if the women and children subsisted off the hedgerows, it kept down the poor rates. A Norfolk woman remembered gathering watercress, wild fruits, and various nuts with her family for extra food. Acquiescing to their seemingly pathetic efforts created an internal sense of benevolence for landowners and fit with older traditions of tolerance for the marginal elements in society.

Ostensibly, collecting wild food did not require gardening skills, but knowledge of growing conditions and informal botanical expertise proved essential to avoid illness or death, as those who have collected wild mushrooms know. A skilled

[22] Jennifer Davies, *The Victorian Kitchen Garden* (London: BBC Books, 1987), 27.

[23] "Obituary, James Maule," *Gardeners' Chronicle*, 17 May 1884, 653.

[24] Jane Humphries, "Enclosures, Common Rights, and Women: The Proletarianization of Families in the Late Eighteenth and Early Nineteenth Centuries," *Journal of Economic History* 50, no.1 (1990): 17–42.

[25] David Philips, "Crime, Law and Punishment in the Industrial Revolution," in *The Industrial Revolution and British Society*, ed. Patrick K. O'Brien and Roland Quinault (Cambridge: Cambridge University Press, 1993), 167.

[26] Hudson, "Women and Industrialization," 36.

wild-food forager recognized a vast range of plants and avoided dangerous ones. She memorized plant locations and carefully gathered her harvest in order to leave sufficient seed or root for reproduction. Many plants such as nettles, sorrel, and dock could only be successfully gathered at certain points in their growth cycle and others, such as cowslip, proved poisonous unless cooked. Identifying the characteristics of growing sites also required skill. Lamb's-quarters, or pigweed, a nitrate lover, needed to be avoided on soils too heavy in natural nitrate fertilizer such as dung. The health of a family partially sustained by gathered foods depended on the botanical knowledge of the homemaker. Young girls served a childhood-long apprenticeship, albeit outside the garden gates, with oral instruction and skills acquired by experience working with their mothers or grandmothers.

The clothing of country women and children, as well as their habits, facilitated their gathering activities. Country women wore print gowns and long aprons with a large kerchief about their shoulders, and girls dressed in frocks with long pinafores. Women carried large printed or checked handkerchiefs along with their market baskets, and children's clothes featured commodious pockets that could be used for collecting food items. Laboring women bought, bartered, and garnered a vast array of difficult-to-trace food items. A "master," "mistress," or local official querying women about the legitimacy of their bulging bundles faced silence and seemingly uncomprehending stares. Any answers came framed in thick country dialect that the "educated" classes might not understand.[27] Convincing interactive rituals involving feigned ignorance or stupidity might protect them and their children from starvation. Kerchiefs came out of pockets to conceal gathered foods that might be hidden under similar handkerchiefs enveloping their shoulders and forearms. In cooler or wet weather, a larger shawl might encase their entire upper body. A stooped position and bowed head with downcast eyes embodied in attenuated form the more formal ritual of rendering obeisance, and it simultaneously functioned to obscure the gathered plants tucked under their shawls. These examples elucidate how rituals exercise a capacity to reify the sociocultural world in which they take place.

Experienced herb hunters gathered such plants as borage, burnet, chervil, chicory, cowslips, field mustard, lamb's lettuce, orach, and wood sorrel.[28] The vast majority of these plants function as antiscorbutics because they contain significant vitamin C. Some, like stinging nettles, also contain nutrients, such as carotene, which the human body manufactures into vitamin A. In addition to pot herbs, women and children gathered a large range of fruit such as bramble, bilberries, elderberries, crabapples, and rosehips that provided excellent sources for vitamin C.[29] From a present-day perspective, it is easy to romanticize or trivialize countryside food foraging, but for a mother with undernourished or sick children the activity could prove crucial for survival.

Because these activities of women so often took place outside the market, even defining them as gardening remains problematic, and yet this form of horticulture proved important for women trying to exist during decades of major economic transition. In a period when working gardeners defined their craft in terms of mastery over nature, ecologically oriented interventions timed with plant growth cycles and pursued in accordance with existing natural environments seemed like the antithesis of gardening. The subtle rituals accompanying their efforts remain frequently ignored because women so often managed to carefully hide their motives.

The marginal economic position and observant mentality of laboring women fostered the broadest comprehension of plant resources distributed according to their preferred ecological niches. If bowed heads reflected their lowly status, the downward gaze also made plant identification and gathering easier. Their foraging gardens existed because laboring women perceived the spaces as resources for sustenance. Whereas children, lowly status, and outward deference often exempted these women from notice as they practiced their skills, the inability of those "above" them to see their "gardens" also protected them from prosecution. Laboring women observed nutritious food where others saw only weeds. Women prized gardens offering

[27] Gertrude Jekyll, *Old West Surrey* (London: Longmans, Green and Company, 1904), 218–28, 248–51, and 265–67.

[28] Ron Freethy, *From Agar to Zenry: A Book of Plant Uses, Names and Folklore* (Dover, N. H.: Tanager Books, 1985), 80, 128, 139; Walter Conrad Muenscher and Myron Arthur Rice, *Garden Spice and Wild Pot-herbs* (Ithaca, N. Y.: Cornell University Press, 1955), 21, 35, 51, 77–78, 137, 167–200; Roger Phillips, *Wild Food* (Boston, Mass.: Little, Brown and Company, 1986), 15, 18, 28, 30, 33, 64.

[29] A. E. Bender, "The Nutritional Importance of Fruit and Vegetables," in *Diet and Health in Modern Britain*, ed. Derek J. Oddy and Derek S. Miller (London: Croom Helm, 1985), 134–47.

nutritional plants distributed according to natural growth patterns suggestive of wild abundance rather than geometrically organized spaces. Furthermore, laboring women employed to perform endless weeding in formal walled kitchen gardens might come to despise the orderly requirements of the impeccability tended "weedless" walled kitchen garden that left their backs aching and their joints swollen.

The interactive rituals of various members of society reveal how production and consumption shaped aesthetic understanding and facilitated alternative approaches to connoisseurship, as well as frequently influenced the appropriation of resources. Most importantly, some performances proclaimed the existing order or reflected and solidified new principles, in this case, those of the market. Only the most careful analysis of the ritual performance might clarify the point. Did the estate owner out for a ride in his park fail to comprehend the activity and intentions of the cottager picking her primroses? Or alternatively, as she looked up and bobbed her curtsy and he acknowledged her gesture of obeisance; did he bask in the thought of his own "gentle benevolence"? Here, intention and reception may become even more entwined. Neither might wish to understand the full meaning of the interactive ritual, but both accepted with complacency the comfort of obfuscation leading to the avoidance of conflict.

Conclusion

Although landscapes may not offer fixed meaning, they do provide multiple perspectives and mirror the fluidity of aesthetic comprehension and its malleability over time. Rituals help individuals comprehend and function in society, and garden rituals literally define space and infuse it with meaning. Rituals among social classes result in very different understandings of the garden. Individuals viewing the same physical space at an estate may see very different gardens.

Several key points emerge from this brief look at interactive rituals in gardens. Members from different social groups benefited from participation in rituals, but they did not necessarily share beliefs or similar aesthetic understandings. Rituals confined to a single group often created mutual social bonds and fostered shared understandings of garden aesthetics. Interactive rituals between social groups eased tensions, and performances steeped in ritual might reshape the perspectives of the performers even as they sought to present their version of the garden to others. Ultimately, rituals functioned to facilitate renegotiation of the "master/man" relationship as market forces corroded the embedded economy. One simply sees an empty stage if viewing nineteenth-century estates without understanding the social and economic forces that shaped them, but thoughtful appreciation of the interactive rituals of elites, gardeners, and laborers infuses the gardens with life and meaning.

Performance and Appropriation: Profane Rituals in Gardens and Landscapes

Performance and Appropriation: Profane Rituals in Gardens and Landscapes

Performance and Appropriation: Profane Rituals in Gardens and Landscapes

Performance and Appropriation: Profane Rituals in Gardens and Landscapes

Sylvie Brosseau

"Le quotidien est parsemé de merveilles, écume aussi éblouissante [Everyday life is spiritualized with treasures, as dazzling as foam]."

Michel de Certeau, *La culture au pluriel*

"We go to see the cherry blossoms, not the willows. We say that we are waiting for the first snow, not the shower or the hailstorm. We miss the cherry blossoms so much that we should give our life for them, but the red leaves, we don't miss them like this."

Kamo no Shōmei (1155?–1216), *Mumyō-shō* (Treatise without title)[1]

Introduction

In Japan, we can easily observe the permanence of the course of nature in urban space and social life. Practices in Tokyo's public parks take place mainly according to a universally known calendar of seasonal events, but we cannot reduce them to mere habits. They refer to values and symbols, they take place in space and time that we may see as "consecrated": the clearly delimited park space with its own aesthetic elaboration, and the time outside daily routine yet rooted in the succession of natural phenomena and social life. These practices also involve the body and the senses through direct contact with some fundamental elements of nature like water, soil and rocks, air and wind, fire, vegetation and animals, and according to specific ways of moving, such as sitting, watching, ways of sharing food and drink, ways of communicating, and so on. Thus, we may see them as significant manifestations of a certain social order. Like ritual practices, they demand a whole combination of formalized acts. They are expressive, symbolic acts, throwing light on a context, and allowing individuals to give meaning to the surrounding world and to transform it by their acts.[2]

Contemplating the Cherry Blossoms

A Sacred Ritual in the Countryside

It is quite striking to observe in Tokyo parks how highly structured and originally sacred rituals have merged into the modernized and westernized society since the Meiji Era (1868–1912). *Hanami*, meaning, "to see flowers" or, rather, "to enjoy

---

[1] Quoted by Michel Vieillard-Baron, *Fujiwara no Teika (1162–1241) et la notion d'excellence en poésie* (Paris: Collège de France, Institut des Hautes Etudes Japonaises, 2001), 297.

[2] To propose a preliminary definition of ritual practices that is not founded on experience would be yielding to (theoretical) prejudice and might lead to an aporia. It might be preferable to start from features observed in Japanese practices and in comprehensive studies of rites and ritual practices by specialists: Gillo Dorfles, *Mythes et rites d'aujourd'hui* (Paris: Klincksieck, 1975); Claude Rivière, *Les rites profanes* (Paris: PUF, 1995); Monique Segré, ed., *Mythes, rites, symboles dans la société contemporaine* (Paris: L'Harmattan, 1997); Martine Segalen, *Rites et rituels contemporains* (Paris: Nathan, 2000).

contemplating the cherry blossoms," provides an example. *Hanami* was originally both a rite of purification, and a rite of welcoming and escorting divinities, which used to take place in the countryside.[3] In the spring, one of the *kami*, the divinities and souls of the ancestors who bestow fertility and dwell in the mountains, comes down to the plain inhabited by the farmers, and becomes a rice-paddy divinity. Villagers used to go on a pilgrimage tour to the nearby mountains when wild cherry trees were in blossom. The blooming of the flowers meant the renewal of the vegetation, the vigor expected of the young plants, and a premise to their fertility. Moreover, that moment of encounter and of conviviality among fellow villagers (sometimes called *hana-mi shogatsu*, "flowers' new year's day")[4] announced the beginning of work in the rice fields, the last occasion of merrymaking (called also *yama asobi*, "to have pleasure in the mountain") before a period of hard work.[5]

Augustin Berque notices the link between the sacred and the feast referring to nature and wilderness.[6] During these ritual excursions, people left the space of daily life (plain and village, fields and work) to reach the mountain (wilderness, sacred space, and feasting), another space and time. It interrupted the ordinary course of life and offered access to a deeper order, arising from nature and able to regenerate society and culture. Today, this still partly applies in the modern practice of hanami, not only in the mountains but in urban parks as well. Yet, during the purifying walk of the pilgrimage, people were not seeking nature as such, but the presence of the *kami*, the divinities, dwelling within it. Bodies and places are intermediate spaces between the material and the immaterial world. The pilgrimage tour is like a course in a territory marked with successive signs that call for interpretation. The mountain, its rocks, springs, waterfalls, and remarkable trees are sacred, replete with stories and presences for everybody able to read and understand them; they are emphasized by statues, sculptures, straw and paper ropes, offerings, and so are appropriated by concrete objects and symbolic meanings. The mountain is neither totally natural, nor really artificial, but it cannot be considered wild.[7] This sacred way of feeling nature, of perceiving the landscape, of appropriating a place, particularly mountains with forests and waters, still applies, and shapes the Japanese perception of space.

Poetry and Formalization at the Imperial Court.

Since the seventh century, Japan has borrowed from China a conception of the world that provided a model for appreciating nature. The Chinese model and aesthetics enriched the Japanese cultural appreciation of nature, as, for example, the praise of *prunus mume* blossoms. *Prunus mume* was introduced to Japan from China in the eighth century, planted in aristocratic gardens, and considered more refined than the indigenous wild cherry. The oldest compilation of poems in Japan, the Man.yō-shū in the first half of the eighth century, contains more than sixteen hundred quotations of plant names. *Mume* is quoted in 118 poems, often related to *sono*, garden; and *sakura*, cherry blossoms, is quoted in forty-two poems, often related to *yama*, mountain.[8] In addition, from the ninth century, the Japanese aristocracy, formed after the Chinese model, became an urban court society installed in the new capital Heian (now Kyoto), which adopted Chinese ways as part of the Japanese identity and saw nature with a new distance. The Heian era (794–1185) also was a period of emancipation for Japanese culture from the Chinese model, when the originality of the national tradition was reclaimed. Poetry gives an example. The *waka*, a traditional Japanese poem, was considered less refined than a Chinese poem, but, in contrast, as spontaneous as frog or bird songs.[9] In the same way, cherry trees, considered simpler, natural, and original—thus, more Japanese—came to be preferred to

[3] Called *mukae*, "welcome," in spring and *okuri*, "see off," in autumn.
[4] Laurence Caillet, *Fêtes et rites des quatre saisons au Japon* (Paris: POF, [1980], 2002), 245–46.
[5] Augustin Berque, *Le sauvage et l'artifice* (Paris: Gallimard, 1986), 70–71.
[6] Berque, *Le sauvage et l'artifice*, 72–73.
[7] Anne Bouchy, *Les oracles de Shirataka* (Arles: Editions Philippe Picquier, 1992), 118–57.
[8] Claude Péronny, *Les plantes du Man.yō-shū* (Paris: Maisonneuve et Larose, 1993), 136–37, 185–89.
[9] Jacqueline Pigeot, *Questions de poétique japonaise* (Paris: PUF, 1997), 12–17.

prunus mume. This new form of appreciation engages an aesthetization of wild cherry trees and an "artialization"[10] of some mountain landscapes, already known and considered important. Aristocrats required to live in Heiankyo enjoyed viewing the cherry blossoms as an occasion to escape from the city and to appreciate the beauty of nature. Thus, cherry blossoms were imbued with new aesthetic and symbolic meanings, such as the impermanence of this world, a major feeling in Buddhism and in Japanese aesthetics.[11]

A renewed appreciation and choice of plants took place,[12] leading to the creation of new landscapes like Yoshino,[13] and at the same time an aesthetic language was elaborated. During the heyday of the Heian court, a peculiar sensitivity to the harmony among plants, places, seasons, and human feelings developed, and plants became a cultural touchstone in particular for poetry.[14] The codification of seasonal themes went hand in hand with the inventory, appreciation, and selection of plants (sometimes accompanied by other natural elements), with the development of a sense of nature, and the creation of landscapes. Poetry developed as a primary medium between people and nature, able to reveal the essence of things. It shaped perception, generating classifications, associations (between a moment / a season / a place / a vegetation / an animal or other natural element like water / a feeling) and a hierarchy of all elements. For example, autumn was associated with evening and melancholy, spring with dawn, the cherry blossoms with clouds or snow, a famous river with a precise type of bird and love, and so on.[15] This systemization did not stereotype attitudes toward nature but, on the contrary introduced infinite variations, through decomposition and recomposition of elements. The hierarchy between these elements gave rise to an infinity of themes, metaphors, evocative images, and allusions, expunging the stylistic constraint.[16] A poem may present a microcosm belonging to the tradition, with a new meaning contained in an ancient expression.[17] This applies not only to poetic words but also to items or places perceived in a landscape, or arranged in a garden or in a park.

The poetic tradition of the Heian court produced norms, instituted models of sensitivity or perception of nature and landscapes, and created an aesthetic of allusion and references that would forever steer the Japanese gaze. This poetic process also informs a global knowledge about nature and natural phenomena, cognitive experiences, meanings, and representations. Culture activated the sense of nature, and nature impregnated cultural and social practices.

In the middle of the twelfth century, the court lost its supremacy to some powerful clans of warriors, called *bushi* or samurai.[18] The military system of government set up since 1185 in Kamakura, a city near present-day Tokyo, instituted the first

[10] Artialization is thus defined: "The artistic process which transforms and embellishes nature, whether directly (in situ), or indirectly (in visu) according to specific models." Alain Roger, "Artialisation," in *La Mouvance, cinquante mots pour le paysage* (Paris: Editions de la Villette, 1999), 45–46. In Japan, poetry has always produced enduring models. It has favored the perception and creation of landscapes that became famous places, *meisho*. These places in turn have nurtured the poetic vision, representation, and creation in situ, engaging in an infinite echo between nature and culture. The space of the lifeworld and its different representations in poems, paintings, etc. are mutually enriching.

[11] Like a sublimation of the unstable physical conditions of Japan, subject to typhoons, landslides, earthquakes, tidal waves, volcanic eruptions, etc, noted Berque, *Le sauvage et l'artifice*, 120. Nature engages in a perpetual metamorphosis, yet the immutable order of nature itself ensures that variation is bearable, and the natural cycle renders present the idea of eternity. The social rituals related to nature represent a way to control the course of time. Natural elements may change form, and yet provide a constant reference and value. For example, in Japan every 20 or 30 years, houses and buildings are demolished and rebuilt, and the way in which the ground is used often changes. In every case of demolition or rebuilding, trees and rocks in the garden are not destroyed but salvaged very carefully. In the same way, with respect to cultural heritage, the preservation of existing architecture is not comparable to the high level of care for gardens.

[12] Plants and vegetation play an essential role in Japanese culture: in the diet, in construction and architecture, in all registers of aesthetics, and in many daily life practices.

[13] Yoshino, near the old capital, Nara, is an important mythical site in Japan and its imperial dynasty. The planting of cherry trees, today more than 100,000, on hills and mountains, is said to have been initiated by a legendary Buddhist monk in the late 7th century. Today, Yoshino is a national park, one of the most visited places and one of the landscapes most admired by tourists.

[14] The poetic form is *waka*, meaning "Japanese song," appearing since the late 8th century. Waka is constituted by five verses of 5/7/5/7/7 syllables.

[15] Vieillard-Baron, *Fujiwara no Teika*, 289.

[16] Ibid., 297, 221.

[17] Ibid., 141, 159, 249.

[18] First the Taira clan, and then the Minamoto clan.

1. *"Ueno Kiyomizudō Shinobazunoike"* (View of Ueno with the pond Shonobazunoike and the temple Kiyomizudō), *Utagawa Hiroshige,* Meisho Edo Hyakkei (One hundred famous views of Edo), 1856.

of a long series of *bakufu,* shogunate governments, who in fact ruled the country until 1867. The new rulers did not participate in the refined taste of the aristocrats but still appreciated the cherry blossoms. A warrior ethics formed, called *bushidō*—the way of the *bushi*—based primarily on the faithfulness of the vassal to his lord. A *bushi* had to have superior moral qualities such as courage, abnegation of self, generosity, and unselfishness. It was encapsulated in a proverb: *"Hana ha sakura, hito ha bushi"* (the flower is *sakura,* cherry blossom, the man is bushi, the warrior). This means that if cherry blossoms are the quintessence of flowers, the samurai are the quintessence of humans. The *bushidō* code of honor, written in the seventeenth century, and still influencing the military mentality, implied that the bushi acquired glory by scorning death and dying for his lord, sacrificing himself and splendidly falling, like a cherry blossom.[19]

The Ritual Spreads to the City

The Edo period (1615–1867), dominated by the Tokugawa Shoguns, was a long period of peace and stability in which the leading class of warriors, samurai and *daimyo,* strictly controlled the social order.[20] The growth of the city of Edo, now Tokyo, was exceptional, with an estimated population of one million in the early eighteenth century. The development of a monetary economy stimulated urban consumption and thus the rise of a rich merchant class. These bourgeois played a major role in the blooming of an urban culture in Edo city.

In early Edo, three places to appreciate one or a few trees (*prunus mume* or cherry blossoms) linked with historical events or stories became famous. In 1624, the third Shogun, Tokugawa Iemitsu, on the advice of a monk, decided to build a large Buddhist temple to protect the city in a place called Ueno, featuring a large pond and a hill with a forest. The temple was called Tōeizan Kaneiji, in reference to Mount Hiei, a famous mountain dominating Kyoto and sheltering an important Buddhist temple, Enryaku-ji. Tōeizan means "the eastern Eizan," in relation to Kyoto, and it is also a branch of this famous Enryaku-ji. It implies several references to the historic capital Kyoto through the toponymy, geographic situation, and affiliation of the temple. Starting around 1625, the *bakufu* (the Shogun's government) began a large planting of cherry trees from Yoshino. This rapidly became the most famous place in Edo to admire cherry blossoms, and became an archetype of Edo's *meisho,* that is "a place with a name," a place of interest, and a noted sight (Fig. 1).

The creation of the urban landscape of Ueno clearly displays a historic, symbolic, and practical grafting of tradition that aimed to bring history to a large new town, Edo. Indeed, until the sixteenth century, Edo was only a little fishing port. It was

[19] From the early Shōwa Period (1926) until the Second World War, the way that the cherry blossom quickly and gracefully falls was appropriated for military purposes to beautify the deaths of suicide units. See Sugiura Yoichi and John K. Gillepsie, *A Bilingual Handbook on Japanese Culture* (Tokyo: Natsumesha ed., [1993], 2003), in a chapter on symbols of Japan, about the national flower.

[20] The samurais constitute the class of the warriors, *daimyō* or shogun vassals. *Bushi* is a general term that refers to any professional warrior. In the Edo period, the bushi were classified according a strict hierarchy, dominated by the Shogun. The Tokugawa *bakufu* is the shogunate, military government, led by a Tokugawa Shogun. All samurai whose revenues were above 10,000 *koku* of rice (180 liters) were called daimyō, "a great name." From 1635, the Tokugawa's shogunate instituted the system of *sankin-kōtai,* alternate attendance, in order to control his vassals: the daimyō had to maintain a residence *yashiki* in Edo, to stay there every other year, and to leave their family there. This rule explains the rapid and remarkable development of Edo, accelerating the concentration of people, goods, money, and information.

meant to foster the legitimacy of the Tokugawa Shoguns, creating a symbolic link between such historic places as the ancient capital Heian, Yoshino, and the new center of power, Edo, by transposing a foundation myth.

In the summer, Shinobazunoike, the pond in Ueno, was covered with lotus flowers, and it became customary to describe Ueno like this: "Cherry blossoms in spring, lotus flowers in the early summer, the full moon in autumn, and the snow in winter." This means that people enjoyed going to Ueno all year long, following a calendar tied to the rhythm of nature. Many little shops, selling food and souvenirs, and teahouses were lined up around the pond. This was the beginning of a truly popular engagement in the hanami.[21] Hanami became an urban mass practice, accompanying the development of a new city landscape, made of cherry groves emerging from the dense roofs of commoners' houses.

The formation of the archetypal meisho of Ueno, and that of other meisho afterward, exhibit several similar features that inform and trigger the gaze and agency of visitors: the geographic substratum of the site, presented by two essential elements highlighted and framed: water and a mountain with forest,[22] framing in turn other elements of the environment around the city;[23] the historical stratum, presented by references to historic places, such as Yoshino, Kyoto, and Mount Hiei, which form a symbolic frame; the social stratum, presented by (a) practices following a precise calendar, which forms a sequential frame generated by natural phenomena according to climate and seasons, and (b) popular stories about real or imaginary events and persons.

These features link names, places, history, narratives, and landscapes into a network of local meanings. A concrete and symbolic geography of the city developed through combinations of these meanings. Some genuine spatial entities were created. First, they were officially appropriated by the power, and then by the people.[24] The constitution of a new urban landscape and the spread of popular practices went hand in hand. The spaces, their perceptions and representations evolved, and the practices did also.

In the middle of the Edo Era (about 1716–36), the growth of the city reached its zenith, and construction density increased.[25] At the same time, places to enjoy *prunus mume*, cherry, or peach blossoms in the spring; wisteria, lotus, or insects in the summer; red maple leaves in autumn; and so on, became more and more numerous. A lot of temples, soon called *hanamiji*—temples to view flowers—or *tsukimiji*—temples to view the moon—selected and started to cultivate some seasonal plants or trees, to take an interest in some natural themes like the moon, the snow, the sunset view, as their own specialties to attract visitors rather than for religious reasons. Meeting together, in a landscape in harmony with the season, to enjoy drinking, eating, and singing in a festive atmosphere and in a collective way, was more exciting for people than poetic celebrations[26] or

---

[21] Tanaka Seidai, *Nihon no kōen* (Public parks of Japan) (Tokyo: Kashima shuppankai, [1974], 1993), 11–34.

[22] "Japan is an archipelago of mountains, forests and rains. No other industrialized country receives more than 1600 mm of rain in one year," says Nakamura Yoshio in "Poétique du territoire" (unpublished text, 1999, with many thanks to Nakamura Yoshio for his article). Abundant water is the first richness of Japan, absolutely indispensable and vital for the rice culture. Rains also impregnate forests, completely assimilated with mountains and representing 67% of the Japanese territory. This humidity associated with warmth also favors a rich flora and fauna. For example, we can find in Japan 160 different kinds of trees as opposed to 85 in all of Europe. Philippe Pelletier, *Le Japon* (Paris: Armand Colin, 1997), 20.

[23] The hill in Ueno offered a view on another mountain, Fuji, which became a new referential mountain in Japan after the transfer of the government in Edo, because it was visible from all parts of the city like a boundary marker, a symbolic and aesthetic landmark, always seen within a framework. In Buddhism, mountains occupy a primary place (center and pillar of the world, for example). Particularly in the veneration of Mount Fuji, evoking Indian and Chinese matrix mountains, Buddhist and Shinto meanings about mountains joined, and Edo's culture added its own aesthetic representations.

[24] Paul Waley, *Tokyo, City of Stories* (New York: Weatherhill, 1991); "A la periphérie d'Edo: La Grande Rivière et sa rive orientale," in *La maîtrise de la ville: Urbanité française, urbanité nippone*, ed. Augustin Berque (Paris: Editions de l'EHESS, 1994).

[25] Edo's inhabitants lived in long rows of wooden houses, called *nagaya*, built along narrow streets, and divided into apartments. One family had the use of 6 tatami (9.7 m²). Tanaka, *Nihon no kōen*, 14. This fact could explain why outside spaces used as public spaces were very important to people. The commoners' areas occupied only about 16% of the total surface of Edo, and a peak of 600,000 inhabitants was concentrated there by the early 18th century.

[26] This observation does not mean that written poetry was absent in the Edo era. During this period, the short poetic form *haikai* (called haiku from the Meiji period and constituted by three verses of 5/7/5 syllables) became an independent genre, no longer produced by the aristocratic court like waka, but by the new middle class of Edo. The high level of formalization offers one of the most remarkable characteristics in the representation of nature, *kigo*, meaning words of season, obligatorily used in haikai/haiku, classified and listed in special dictionaries. In fact, each kigo supports a large power of evocations, feelings, and correspondences. It is really a poetry of daily life. Over the presumed delicate variation of the Japanese climate, kigo expresses the fundamental idea of the return of time, of the perpetual transformation of nature, and beyond, of infinity.

historical records. Hanami has become very popular for all sorts of leisure practices (Fig. 2). For example, dance or *shamisen* masters visited some places and put on disguises with their disciples. Women also wore kimonos in harmony with the place and the moment, and rivaled in elegance with their *hanami-kosode*, "hanami-little sleeves kimono."

In the city of Edo, the renown of many meisho spread quickly, especially with the publication of guidebooks. These woodblock print collections contained pictures representing landscapes and the activities of the people, with written commentaries combining useful information, historic explanations, and poetic descriptions, and then offering various ways of reading and appropriating the space. These representations led to greater renown and

2. *"Nippori" (View of Nippori), Utagawa Hiroshige,* Tōto Meisho *(Sights of the eastern capital), 1835*

greater renown led in turn to further representations. A meisho could be visited in person; seen in pictures; evoked by names of places, poems, or other texts; and transposed in another place as a reference like a landscaped allusion (Fig. 3).

During the Edo era, sacred practices of the countryside and aesthetic practices of the aristocracy were merged into a renewed popular practice, the enjoyment of the cherry blossoms, hanami.[28] Walking, eating, drinking, and enjoying in a group related space (here and elsewhere) to time (historic time and seasonal time), and allowed people to share the moment. At the beginning of spring, the beauty of the cherry blossoms and their ephemeral nature had to be celebrated. The playful aspects of the ritual were reinforced as it became urban, the symbolic meanings (welcoming spring, the impermanence of the world) did not disappear, but a hedonist morale was introduced. At the same time, new varieties of cherry trees were introduced: the wild ones (very tall and somewhat thin), were replaced by larger ones, with more and more spectacular and precocious flowering, selected by grafting and pruned to increase their effect.[29]

During Tokugawa Yoshimune's Shogunate in the eighteenth century (1716–45), the creation of new meisho-like recreational places offering a beautiful panorama on the sea, Mount Fuji, or Mount Tsukuba, blossomed, achieving genuine city planning. Yoshimune was fond of hunting with falcons, and he decided at first to transform hunting woods around Edo city into excursion places. He selected cherry trees, pines, and maples for planting,[30] and allowed people to enter. In fact,

[27] The first guidebook of Edo with authentic descriptions was published in 1662, and presented seventy-nine famous places. It is considered very influential for the following *meishoki*, famous-place chronicles, and local geography. Kokuritsu Kōbunshokan, *Hana to kōraku, mokuroku* (Flowers and pleasure trips, catalogue), exhibition catalogue (Tokyo: The National Archives, 2002).

[28] Iinuma Jirō and Shirahata Yōzaburō, *Nihon bunka toshite kōen* (Parks as Japanese Culture) (Tokyo: Yazakashobō, [1993], 1994), 4–11.

[29] The current most common species of cherry tree was obtained in the city of Edo by grafting, and was named *somei yoshino* (*prunus yedoensis*). Somei is the name of an Edo quarter (now in Toshima Ward) where, during the Edo Period, horticulture developed remarkably, and multiplied new hybrids of many flowers and trees. The large gardens of the daimyō's residences stimulated production, creation, and a flourishing market. Yoshino was added to the name for its evocative power. This cherry tree *somei yoshino* spread throughout Japan from the Meiji Era on.

[30] For example, in a place called Asukayama, near the northern limit of Edo, Tokugawa Yoshimune had 1270 cherry trees, 100 maple trees, and 100 pine trees planted in an elm forest, creating a wood, like a melting pot of different trees, a typical element of the urban landscape, *zōkibayashi*. Tanaka, *Nihon no kōen*, 35.

hunters were a nuisance for farmers, but hanami marked the end of the hunting period and the possibility of selling some products to the visitors. Allowing hunting grounds to be used for leisure helped make hunting acceptable to the people.

Then, during this period, the fiscal pressure on the inhabitants of the city increased, and Yoshimune decided to keep the people quiet by creating some other recreational places. For example, he decided to open one of his private properties, Goten-yama, in the south of Edo, planted with cherry trees and maples (Fig. 4). He also decided to plant cherry trees along the Sumida River, and willows along the Kanda River, in the east of Edo, to create walking paths. To the west, he created a garden open to visitors with peach trees (Nakano Momozono). The location of these places, radiating in every direction from the center of the city, the amenities they provided (recreation

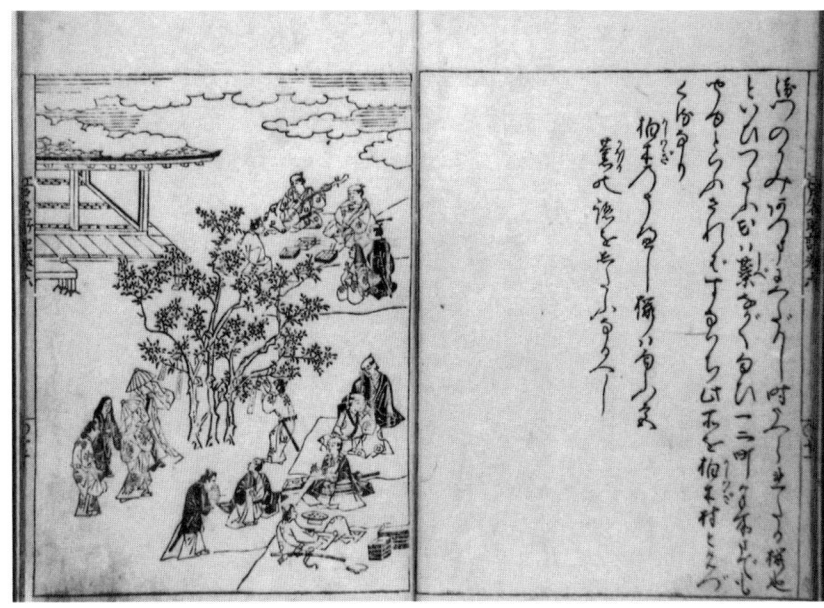

3. Edo Meishoki *(Chronicle of Edo's sights), first guidebook published in Edo in 1662 (photo: courtesy of the National Archives of Japan, from* Hana to Kōraku, Mokuroku *[Flowers and pleasure trips, catalogue] [Tokyo: the National Archives, 2002])*

and security in public places, and also fire protection between dense neighborhoods), and the decision process that was followed, all bear the hallmark of a city-planning endeavor. The Shoguns after Yoshimune followed suit. From the Edo era on, public authorities contributed to the creation of meisho as places of playful recreation, and the encouragement of seasonal open-air practices, because it was a way to exercise control over the spaces and the people's activities.

Finally, in the early nineteenth century, some farmers started to plant *prunus mume* (Japanese apricot) along the lanes, in their gardens, or in orchards, to offset tax increases. Only the fruits were important to the farmers,[31] but around 1820, *umemi*, "to enjoy seeing *prunus* blossoms," grew more popular among the people of Edo, because the *prunus* blossoms come very early and are delicately fragrant, offering a foretaste of the cherry blossoms. Stands selling sweets and tea spread rapidly in *prunus* gardens or orchards, following the already established and ritualized way of the cherry blossoms. Attention to the crops of *ume* invites a look beyond aesthetic and recreational practices, to the economic management of meisho, because a place with local production is easier to manage when the flower season is finished (Fig. 5).

During the same period—the Edo era—many other natural elements became the object of growing public interest, thus establishing places where people love to go; walk; take excursions; see azaleas, wisterias, irises, morning glories, hydrangeas, lotus, chrysanthemums, camellias, and so on; catch fireflies in June; watch dragonflies and listen to crickets in the late summer; contemplate the full moon in September (Fig. 6); admire the snow in winter; and *momijigari*, "to hunt maple trees," has meant to enjoy seeing the red leaves in autumn, marking in a spectacular way the passage into winter, as the cherry blossoms celebrate its end (Fig. 7). The commoner class enriched and spread the urban culture of Edo, and the leading class tried hard to control it. The daily life of Edo's inhabitants was structured according to the rhythm of the seasons, partially reflected by visits to different shrines, temples, and other meisho. The Edo people lived in a world in which some spaces and times fit together.[32]

[31] The fruit, not naturally edible, is conserved in salt and becomes a tasty and much appreciated condiment with rice, called *umeboshi*. In alcohol, it is a fragrant and also medicinal drink.

[32] The sociocultural framework and the religious framework were closely linked. On religious daily practices see Ian Reader and George J. Tanabe, *Practically Religious: Worldly Benefits and the Common Religion of Japan* (Honolulu: University of Hawaii Press, 1998).

4. *"Goten-yama, Hanazakari" (View of the cherry blossoms, Goten-yama), Utagawa Hiroshige,* Edo Meisho *(Sights of Edo), 1834*

5. *"Kameido Ume Yashiki" (Garden of Prunus mume at Kameido), Utagawa Hiroshige,* Meisho Edo Hyakkei *(One hundred famous views of Edo), 1856*

This space–time relation has prescribed the most important part of the social calendar, which dictated ritualized behavior. To this day, the calendar informs, guides, and reflects various seasonal phenomena and practices that organize social time.

Rupture and Institution

The Meiji era (1868–1912) is the period when Japan opened widely to the outside world, and started to modernize itself and to assimilate new techniques and concepts from the West. The rhythm and the scale of the changes exceeded those known in the past, including those resulting from the introduction of the Chinese model. Many foreigners were invited to Japan and delegations were sent abroad to study. But the beginning of the Meiji era was a very unstable period with several political factions struggling to define the way of modernization. This produced great social turmoil and the population of the city of Tokyo quickly dropped to almost half that of Edo.[33]

At the beginning, many of Edo's meisho were destroyed, for at least two reasons. First, the immense enterprise of modernization demanded deep spatial restructuring (enlargement of roads, construction of technical networks, etc.), and the Ministry of Education and the Ministry of Defense requisitioned land to build new and indispensable facilities (military facilities, universities, hospitals, etc.). Second, a certain form of iconoclasm took place and some Buddhist temples were destroyed. Those destructions expressed the rupture with the ancient order, but they obviously served some interests as the surface of temple properties was very important.[34] Afterward, because of the industrialization, some places were destroyed little by little, and disappeared, as, for example, along the Sumida River. The transition did not happen smoothly.

The new urban model was the western city planning. During the second half of the nineteenth century, the urban public park, together with its specific landscape and practices, spread from England throughout Europe and the whole world.

[33] Tokyo had a population of 580,000 in 1872, as opposed to 1,000,000 at the peak of the Edo era.
[34] The case of Ueno is very significant in this period.

As the western city had public parks, the Government of Meiji thought the capital needed such modern facilities for inhabitants and foreigners living in Tokyo. In 1873 (Meiji 6), the government instituted by decree the first modern system of administration of Tokyo's public parks. In fact, five places, very famous and frequented meisho in the preceding era, were designated as parks with a new name: *kōen*.[35] The role of meisho in social life was rapidly reappraised (Fig. 8). The aims of this decree were to constitute a modern city on the western model (precisely London, Paris, Berlin, and Vienna), to provide secure places for recreation, and to preserve some remains of Edo city.

The priority of the Meiji government was industrialization and the constitution of a modern army. The government would have liked to reform city planning and create new parks but could not afford it, so its idealistic projects remained unrealized. It limited itself to reallocating the role of existing places. The new administrative system wanted, however, to keep popular gatherings under control to avoid riots, particularly feared in this period of political and social unrest. Moreover, rapid changes and modernization generated increasing tensions between the government and the city of Tokyo, because Tokyo didn't want to completely lose control of its territory and the management of its heritage. The decree of 1873 achieved a compromise. Thus, some continuity is visible beyond the rupture of the Meiji era:

- continuity in space: new public parks, kōen, were all meisho, famous places, of Edo;
- continuity of practices;
- continuity of control by a central authority: like the bakufu, the modern administration decided the location, name, and later the design of the new parks, to attempt to control the people's activities.

With regard to outdoor public spaces, the early Meiji is more than a rupture with the past, a period of narrowing the range of existing places. This was, however, sufficient to maintain ritualized practices with their capacity for shaping and molding sociocultural consciousness. The accumulative process did not come to an end.

6. *"Dōkan-yama" (View of Dōkan-yama), Utagawa Hiroshige,* Tōto Meisho *(Sights of the eastern capital), 1835. Two women and a child with a cage walk and listen to insects, while three men have a picnic enjoying the September full moon.*

7. *"Kai.anji Momiji no Zu" (The red leaves at Kai.an Temple), Utagawa Hiroshige,* Tōto Meisho *(Sights of the eastern capital), 1835*

[35] *Kōen* literally means "public garden." Three places were Buddhist temples (Asakusa, Shiba, Ueno); another was a Shinto shrine (Fukagawa), and yet another a recreational place founded by the Shogunate (Asukayama).

8. *"Shiba Kōen" (Shiba Park),* Meiji Tōkyō Meisho Zue *(Sights of Tokyo in the Meiji Era), 1897. Shiba Park is one of the first five meisho (famous places) appointed as kōen (park) with a detail of a street performance.*

The first characteristic of the hanami period is its brevity, like a sudden emergence: only a few days, as an expression says: "*Sakura ha wazuka nanoka*" (Cherry blossoms last for seven short days), between the end of March and the beginning of April in Tokyo. It is short but, even today, it is one of the most intense and festive moments in the year. First of all, hanami has an important collective meaning: it marks reentering. Actually, in Japan, the year starts in April for schools, universities, businesses and companies, the Parliament, new TV programs with new hosts and newscasters, the baseball championship, and so on.[36] Thus, the period of hanami indicates an important moment of passage for both individuals and the whole society. This social and cultural passage happens in a specific atmosphere, attuned to the growing rhythm of nature. Thus, it impresses the natural order on society, and anchors the social order in nature. Enjoying cherry blossoms takes different forms; it occurs in the public space of the park, for large or small groups, or individuals. It accompanies the irreversible changes of season and of status, in an intense elation and excitement for the energy of life and nature.

More precisely, new employees, who were recruited in autumn or winter and graduated in March, start work on 1 April, and one of their first tasks may concern hanami: they go to a park, choose a good place under cherry trees, mark it with vinyl sheets and cardboard. Although some of them are buying drinks and foods, others guard the place for a whole day, under very changeable weather, waiting for all the other colleagues to come in the evening to eat and drink for part of the night.

This ritual, which means for everyone the change of season, the beginning of a new academic or professional year, marks the change of status for new employees and evidently has an integrative role. We can see it as a ritual of status elevation, in which the three phases described by Arnold van Gennep and further developed by Victor Turner are clearly visible:

•preliminary phase: separation of the new employees from the group (a company department), as they depart to research a good place under a cherry tree;

•liminary phase: waiting in this separated and outside place, while the others are working normally inside;

•postliminary phase: when all the employees of the department get together, sharing food and drink.

During the first two phases, the group of new employees does the service for their seniors in the company. They are subjected to the weather conditions, sometimes quite bad.[37] Thus, they learn humility and patience. They also show their capacity for finding a good place, and taking the initiative to prepare a happy evening party.[38]

[36] Japan is in the northern hemisphere, and in this part of the world this calendar is an exception. As of a few years ago, the fiscal year begins on January 1st to follow other developed countries.

[37] In this season in Japan, the weather is very changeable (*hana-gumori*, "flower clouds"), sometimes cold (*hana-bie*, "flower coldness"), rainy, and windy. Even if it is raining, hanami is so important that it takes place all the same.

[38] It does not impose any humiliation, unlike, for example, the French *bizutage* (hazing; new arrivals at certain educational institutions or the army are often subjected to an initiation ceremony known as bizutage, which may lead to nasty situations). On the contrary, in Japan, new recruits are sincerely thanked for their help in organizing a great hanami.

As Pierre Bourdieu noted,[39] this ritual institutes an order, that is the established order of the company, assigns a status to the new employee in this order, and encourages the promoted persons to act according to expected principles. We could add that the employees seize territory in the park, like a metaphor of their future role, which is conquering market shares. This practice of hanami is an occasion to ascertain the essential values of the group, that is, the company, and to underline its social features (like the sense of the hierarchy, seniority, respect, and mutual help).[40]

During the last phase, when the entire department gets together, people share food and drink as if sharing in the learning of an ideal manner of being together and communicating, in a confident way. Alcohol more than food plays an important mediating role. In a society as polished and self-restrained as that of the Japanese, people need alcohol to liberate their verbal and corporal expressions. The primordial function of alcohol, admitted by everyone as a general truth in Japan, is to make individuals less tense, to allow them to relax and reach a necessary stage when they can become themselves. In the second stage, Turner noted the relation between frank, even rough, words and purification. Hanami is also one occasion to use direct words thanks to alcohol, which allows employees to unload the resentment accumulated among them inside the company. To speak frankly even against the boss allows the structured group to purify itself and reactivate its community spirit. So cleansed, the community is able to start a new cycle. The hierarchical system is not contested; on the contrary, it is consolidated.

Students practice hanami in a similar way, not within classes but within clubs and circles. This form of community offers many occasions for vertical relations between new and older students[41] in different faculties. These clubs and circles are the basis for an important network of relations and mutual aid during the academic period and continuing for the rest of the students' lives. Hanami also provides a good opportunity to deepen contacts within a constituted group.

The ritualized practices during the hanami period institute a "social drama," in which everyone is both actor and spectator. Spectator of a theatrical landscape with a spectacular decor of cherry blossoms, emphasized by the layout of the park or, at night, by the lights; and spectator of other people; actor in a scenario with a beginning, *kaika*, the opening of the flowers; a middle, *hana-zakari*, *mankai*, full bloom; and an end, *hana-fubuki*, when the petals fall like snow in the wind or *hana-ikada*, when the petals flow downstream. There are many ways to enjoy a hanami sequence: either in an improvised walk, or in an organized way with cooking equipment, music and lamps; with family, among friends for the simple pleasure of being together, or alone to taste the beauty of the moment. The scenario of a hanami sequence goes on for a day or an evening for each group or individual; for the whole country, it goes on for a few days.

All the mass media follow and diffuse information about hanami. For example, the weather forecast gives precise information on the progress of the blossoms. The first official map with forecast dates is published in February, updated every week, and once the first flower opens in the southern part of Japan, every day. Train and subway companies publish brochures describing many places served by their networks, and display posters in every station with lists of places to enjoy the flowers, and news about the state of the blossoms. It becomes truly impossible to ignore this national event.

Institutions such as schools pass on the cultural experience of hanami. Starting in kindergarten, children learn to enjoy and practice hanami sitting together on the ground under a cherry tree and eating their *bento*, box lunch. Thus, the continuity of the generations is ensured, cognitive and didactic values contained in this experience are taught, and relations between culture and nature are transmitted. In a general way, Japanese education takes on and transmits many experiences and knowledge related to nature within a seasonal calendar that distinguishes many flowers, plants, birds, insects, and so on, the better to appreciate them.

[39] Pierre Bourdieu, "Les rites d'institution," in *Actes de la recherche en sciences sociales* 43 (1982): 58–63.
[40] Following Claude Rivière, the rite of passage should have a sense only if the passage is irreversible. Claude Rivière, *Les rites profanes* (Paris: PUF, 1995), 97. In Japan, until recently, the practice of hanami has integrated new employees into a job guaranteed in the same company for life. The rite does not create but underlines and strengthens social continuity. Now, this principle of employment for life is questioned, and perhaps the ritual of hanami practiced by employees will change.
[41] The younger students are called *kōhai*, and the older students, *sempai*.

The ritual of hanami correlates collective time (the changing of seasons concerns all of society) and individual time (concerning access to a new status for employees, students, or new members of specific groups). Every year, hanami synchronizes society and individuality, history and nature in the environment.[42] Society and culture again become impregnated by the order of nature, and social order is instituted as a natural order. The ritual stimulates memory and links the present to a certain past. Social groups are again asserting themselves, reinforcing a strong social continuity as a prelude to renewed activities. The social structure is revitalized by this common experience, and the ritual consolidates integrative links. The ritual of hanami contributes to a better insertion of the individual in his society and his culture, while enchanting his daily life.[43]

A ritual practice, such as hanami, is an aggregate of simultaneous actions, varying according to different groups or individuals. Its polysemy, its plasticity, and its capacity to accompany social changes show that the ancient elements have mingled, after a long historical sedimentation, with more recent ones, and that this transformation is permanent. Some traces of the past linger in the present, such as successive and multiple reemployments. They engender today a vivid tradition, not a folklorization, a tradition that always fosters many practices through metamorphosis of earlier ones. Hanami is a way for the collectivity to constitute and represent itself in a fleeting moment as in an artistic performance. Hanami as a ritual practice shares with an artistic performance its vitality, the force of its presence here and now. Hanami is acted in the present, displaying an ephemeral temporality, and is at the same time evanescent and immemorial. Every year, every time hanami happens, it is the same social ritual, but it is not a mere commemoration; rather, it is a celebration of the present moment. People come to an appointment; they take part in a self-conscious and symbolic drama, and in return, they are molded by the surrounding landscape. Like a performance, hanami concerns multiple sensory levels (visual; tactile, e.g., sitting on the soil; auditory; olfactory; gustatory; emotional, e.g., staying in a crowd under vaults of flowers).[44]

In a symmetrical and complementary way, the glowing red leaves provide the main theme in autumn. This natural phenomenon is particularly visible in Japan in November, because of the contrast of temperatures between a sunny, warm day, and a cold night. On the basis of real observation and experience, Japanese people have developed a cultural appreciation of this autumnal moment. In a way similar to the praise of cherry blossoms, trees with yellow leaves and especially red-leaved trees have been more and more appreciated and favored in plant selection. The most famous are the maple trees, *momiji*, selected, planted, and pruned to let the sun shine more easily through their branches, and thus make them redder. During this period, called *kōyō,* meaning "red leaves," the contemplation of red maple leaves and colored trees accompanies the collective passage toward winter, and perpetuates the memory of the countryside ritual of bringing divinities into the annual cycle from plains to mountains. The seasonal walks concern all society and its culture. Information is as plentiful as that about hanami, but kōyō remains devoid of any meaning concerning social organization (such as the start of a new year in April). Yet this autumn period is very important and appreciated because it means an abundance of colors, of harvests of mushrooms, chestnuts, persimmons, and so on. It is a moment to take in energy and heat from nature and the sun, after an exhausting wet summer and before a cold winter, as the seasons are commonly perceived.

The two important periods in the seasonal calendar (hanami and kōyō) indicate two revolving moments of the annual cycle, marking the growth and the decrease of nature, white and red.[45] Between these two poles, every natural phenomenon in

[42] Berque, *Le sauvage et l'artifice*, 31.

[43] Michel de Certeau, *L'Invention du quotidien* (Paris: Gallimard, [1980], 1990).

[44] Catherine Bell, *Ritual, Perspectives and Dimensions* (Oxford: Oxford University Press, 1997), 159–64.

[45] The association of white and red colors symbolizes happiness in Japan, like white and red links on congratulation cards or on wedding presents. In reference to a famous battle opposing a red and a white army of two clans of samurai, the Minamoto and the Taira in 1185, these two colors mark opposing teams on many occasions. For example, all schoolchildren have a reversible cap with a red side and a white one, to play games and sports competitions; on the evening of 31 December, a very popular TV program called *kōhaku uta gassen* (red and white singing contest) presents for four hours the most famous singers of the year in Japan divided into two teams, red women against white men. Red and white are also the colors of the national flag of Japan, the red sun in the white sky. In poems, the white cherry trees are compared to clouds and the petals are carried away by the wind or a stream; the favorable moment to sing the autumn landscape is the sunset, and the red leaves decompose in the soil or are burnt. Victor Turner noticed the symbolic values of these two colors, associated with fundamental human liquids, particularly blood and sperm. Victor W. Turner, *Le phénomène rituel: Structure et contre-structure*, trans. Gérard Guillet (Paris: PUF, [1969], 1990), 121–22.

relation to vegetation, water, and sometimes animals (such as fireflies, dragonflies, crickets, crayfish, frogs, and various birds) is articulated in appropriate spaces to practices, which cut out, organize, and make social time expressive in present-day Japan.

Throughout the centuries, Japanese culture has built its peculiar relations with nature very close and appreciated, like a meticulous construction starting from concrete experience and real life and ending in conscious codification. People join a very cultured nature in a merging relation. Thus, the most elaborated artistic expressions, such as poetry, gardens, the tea ceremony, have exalted nature to the utmost level. The feeling of nature has always evolved, continues to evolve, and has integrated many contingencies: physical, symbolic, aesthetic, historic, and also economic and political. In this way, practices, even if they seem very traditional and ritualized, are indefinitely changing and they are in part the result of people's creativity. These ritualized practices are forms of representation of society and help to create social links and revitalize the will to be together.

The Modern Public Parks: Renewal and Reuse
  The Creation of an Archetype: Hibiya Kōen
In 1882 (Meiji 15), when the city of Tokyo recovered the population level it had reached before the Meiji Restoration and subsequent period of unrest, the government promulgated an order on the Renovation of Tokyo, which first decided on an administrative reorganization with a new division into districts. As a part of this Renovation order, a decree asserted the creation of forty-nine parks. Their locations and areas were calculated after patterns from London and Paris. In this new list of parks, seventy percent were meisho of Edo, and half of the total were Shinto shrines.[46] Others were originally gardens in residences of ancient feudal lords, daimyō, but in fact were rapidly transformed into housing estates and then disappeared. New creations, strictly speaking, were almost nonexistent. The Renovation order merely achieved the requalifying of some old places, because of economic limits, and because the bucolic characteristics of Tokyo were still evident. Yet one creation was projected: Hibiya Park in the center of the city, next to the Imperial Palace. It was created to aid the modernization of the city's shape, its new monuments and town planning, and to reflect changes, rather than to satisfy the need for outdoor and recreation spaces. Such was the aim of this project for a park in the heart of a city that was rapidly changing at the time.[47] What was really at stake was essential.

However, the municipal commission in charge of the project faced a major problem, since it lacked a precise idea of a modern, Western park. Therefore, development of the plan proved very long and difficult. As a result, the work started only in 1902 (Meiji 35), and the park was inaugurated in 1903 (Meiji 36).[48] Starting in 1900 (Meiji 33), Honda Seiroku, a young agronomist and forestry specialist who studied for two years at Munich University, was in charge of the project. He was neither a garden designer nor an architect, so he tried to avoid criticism and find a consensus by piecing together much advice. He produced a synthesis of different plans drawn up by his many predecessors (architects and Japanese garden designers), some advice from a military doctor about hygiene, from botanists about flower beds, and from many other specialists and engineers

[46] In all, 24 places were Shinto shrines, small in area (from 0.6 to 2 hectares), but very familiar to people because well integrated into the neighborhood and daily life of the local community: places for festivals, playgrounds for children, and all the daily rituals. The Shinto shrines always had exceptional trees (as they still do today), and a beautiful landscape and view. Buddhist temples (4 places), on the contrary, were very large (from 30 to 80 hectares), not used as nearby recreational spaces, but more attuned to individual life, and at the origin of a real development of tourist travels. Tanaka, *Nihon no kōen*, 220–25.

[47] The center of the city was transforming completely with the construction of office buildings, numerous ministries, and a luxurious guesthouse for foreign visitors called Rokumeikan (1883); then the central station (1914); and the Imperial Hotel, open in 1890, rebuilt and designed by Frank Lloyd Wright in 1922. The construction of this new neighborhood in the western style of architecture was not meant only for administrative reasons; the creation of an "honorable urban landscape" also had diplomatic reasons. Bureau of City Planning, *Tōkyō no toshikeikaku no hyakunen* (100 years of city planning in Tokyo) (Tokyo: Tokyo Metropolitan Government, 1996).

[48] From 1893 until 1901 and Honda's intervention, nine projects in Japanese style were refused for this reason, and two projects in western style only (one by a Japanese architect and another by an English architect) were also rejected.

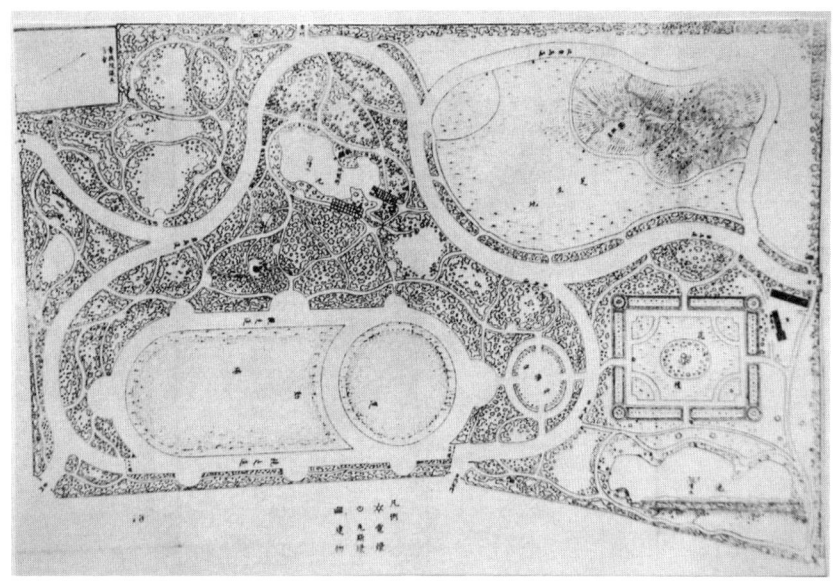

about architecture, construction, urban rules, and so on. German books about Western forests and park design[49]—and, of course, his own direct experience in Germany, particularly in the parks of Munich and in Dresden and Konitz—provided him with another important reference source. Honda himself accounted for all of his references and sources. He didn't want to impose his own personal idea, in order to avoid criticism as he said himself, and perhaps because he lacked a clear one. The introduction of modernity in Japan amounted to patching together diverse elements and sources in this case.

9. *Hibiya Park, original plan in 1900 (photo: courtesy of the Tokyo Parks Association, from Maejima Yasuhiko,* Hibiya Kōen *[Hibiya Park] [Tokyo: Tokyo Parks Association, 1994])*

Honda was the true representative of the authority, ruling on central city projects designed to institute and strengthen the new government structure. This authority also had to transpose and integrate numerous requirements, combining Japanese and Western elements, and different functions. It produced a new space, with Japanese and Western features, but still original in its layout, which resulted from taking apart and reconfiguring landscape elements (Fig. 9). In Europe, nineteenth-century public parks not only provided urban ornaments or facilities for public recreation, but they procured spaces for imposition or at least display of the leading classes' way of life and leisure activities. People could learn polished behaviors and become less ignorant of urban customs in public parks, which were designed to frame the expression of proper behavior. In Germany, building its national unity during this period, parks also offered spaces that enabled people to develop a sense of being a nation. In Japan during the Meiji era, as in Europe at the same time, the sense of national unity was stressed as an important moral theme. The state voluntarily used the landscape and its meanings to re-found the national identity. In the plan of Hibiya Kōen, three essential elements structure the project: a large sport ground, a Japanese garden, and large paths suitable for horse-drawn carriages.

The park's most important space was the grass field in the southwestern part: in the original plan called *undōjo*, sport ground. Honda lifted its form directly from the municipal park of Konitz (today Chojnice in Poland). It shows that sports were spreading in the Meiji era.[50] This field also provided a space for mass meetings on different occasions, not only sports, but also official celebrations. The modern park was clearly meant to contribute to and celebrate a common identity. Rapidly, this ground became used as an urban square for national and official events, and for transgressive uses as well. In 1905 (Meiji 35), at the end of the Russo-Japanese war, a gathering in Hibiya Park against the peace treaty degenerated into a violent riot in which about 300 buildings were destroyed by fire. More recently, during the 1970s, student protest movements and confrontations against the police also took place in this park. More quietly, but reminiscent of an activist past, one ritual May Day gathering

---

[49] Honda's German references were Heinrich Salisch, *Forstästhetik*, 1885; Max Bertram, *Gärtnerisches Planzeichen* (Berlin: Paul Parey, 1891); and G. Meyer's plans.
[50] For the Government during the Meiji era and the Taishō era (1912–1925), sport practices, walking, hiking, and cycling, were encouraged and made easier in the center of Tokyo and in the immediate environs, first to favor the constitution of a healthy and vigorous people, and then, from the Shōwa era on, clearly to make good soldiers. See the catalogue of the exhibition at Parutenon Tama Rekishi Museum: *Kōgaikōrakuchi no tanjō* (Birth of leisure places in the suburbs) (Tokyo: Historic Museum of Parthenon Tama, 2002).

takes place in Hibiya Park, and another in Yoyogi Park. The open grass fields can be used for political and labor union rallies, that originally are an unexpected practice.[51]

Following the Hibiya Kōen model, all Japanese parks have a large central grass field, easy to use in many ways. When Honda conceived and named such a place he meant to introduce a sign of modernity. Yet, even though the form was clearly inspired by a Saxon park (originally derived from a racetrack), he certainly availed himself of its similarity to a figure and a spatiality already known by city dwellers. In the city of Edo, open grass fields, called *harappa*, were not rare; children used to play there, people used to collect herbs and plants, go for a walk, or fly kites there. Moreover, samurai had at their disposal several training grounds, also open to the people, quite large and surrounded by trees (pines and cherry trees), where they could practice horse-riding and archery. On such occasions, these grounds seemed like performance stages, and the rest of the time they were used like playgrounds for children or meeting places, for enjoying cherry blossoms, for example. It was certainly easy for most people in Tokyo to understand and appropriate a kind of place that seemed familiar. Since the creation of Hibiya Kōen, Japanese public parks have had a large and central multiuse grass field, at the same time trace and matrix of new or renewed practices. Imported schemes were selected both to bring a new vocabulary for building the modern Japanese identity, and to continue appreciating what already existed, with a renewed meaning.

The formal flowerbed constitutes another typical Western element of parks. Honda was a forestry specialist, not really attracted to flowers, but the pressure to create this exotic place was so strong that he introduced a flowerbed at the park entrance. His model was the garden of a German hospital published in a book, and the basin in Dresden's park. Two botanists designed the flowerbeds using only Western flowers. At the opening, this part of the park attracted the greatest attention and curiosity of all.

The Japanese garden, entrusted to a specialist, Ozawa, was another important place, planned for since the beginning of discussions about Hibiya Park. It followed the composition of a pleasure garden of the Edo era as found in the feudal lords' (daimyō) residences, called *kaiyū-shiki teien*, "stroll garden" or "transforming garden." All the elements of this pleasure and walking garden are visible: in the center, a pond surrounded by a footpath; all along this path, little streams, stones, lanterns, paving stones, and pruned bushes are arranged. Along the fixed walk around the pond, different atmospheres and landscapes with many references (to the history of Japanese gardens, to famous landscapes, to poems, etc.), follow one another, appearing and disappearing in a succession of fragmented views. The route unfolds sequentially like a narrative, sometimes quite anecdotal, cast into a whole by the landscaping. Just as European public parks presented people with an aristocratic space to rest and to relieve their minds, in which the most elaborated elements were flower beds, Japanese modern public parks also presented everyone with the possibility of enjoying a Japanese garden, previously reserved only for the elite.

In the northeastern corner, called Hibiyamitsuke-ato, some remains of the fortifications and the ditch of Edo's castle were preserved. It wasn't Honda's idea but the botanists', to preserve a trace of an important historical place in the modern city. Therefore, Hibiya Park expresses, like a meisho, some links with history and thus participates in the constitution of the cultural identity, thanks to the Japanese garden, and these archaeological remains. The introduction of modernity in Japan did not proceed from a tabula rasa, but rather from a cumulative process.

The large lanes for carriages and bicycles[52] were meant to allow people to quickly reach the center of the park, giving an image of modernity. At the center, a luxurious restaurant was open to allow the Japanese elite to meet and invite foreign guests in a convenient setting. This restaurant was also an occasion for the Japanese to learn new table manners and corporal customs (to eat sitting on a chair at a table decorated with a floral bouquet, tasting western cooking, and using forks and knives). Today, this restaurant conserves its role of meeting place, and continues to offer formal spaces where French cooking is served. It provides an occasion, rare in Japan, to eat or drink on an outside terrace, as in France. Since the Meiji era, the

[51] At Hibiya Kōen, in fact, the grass field, originally the first modern sports ground in Japan, which permitted so many uncontrollable demonstrations, is surrounded by a low fence, and its access is prohibited with many signs, which is quite unique in Tokyo's modern public parks.

[52] Horse-drawn carriages were very rare in this period (only 270 private vehicles), but the use of bicycles was rapidly spreading.

inhabitants of Tokyo continue to go to Hibiya Kōen "to smell the fragrance of the Western city."[53] These new practices spread rapidly and allowed people to learn ideal models of behavior and appearance: walking in the night under the first electric lamps, drinking coffee at the coffee shop, listening to western music at the music kiosk, enjoying bicycle races, then playing tennis, "like abroad."[54] A public library and a multi-use hall were planned in the original project and were added afterward. As a result, Hibiya Kōen, the first attempt at a public park in Japan, quickly became a new meisho, and an archetype of the modern public park in the Japanese fashion.

With its rich variation of landscapes and its numerous facilities, the public park is an essential space for learning cultural modes of perception (physical realities, representations, behaviors, etc.). Hibiya Kōen is not only a park designed according to functionalist principles, juxtaposing different spaces and functions, but it is also composed like a large kaiyū-shiki teien, a Japanese circular walking garden, integrating different sequences along the main route. The winding movement unfolds a narrative of the constitution of modern Japanese identity in which nature, history, many stories and practices, are linked. The park also brings together as a whole numerous aesthetic values, meanings and feelings of nature, and it has the power to evoke memories and to bring history into the present. And the process is still going on.

The Parks Today

After World War II, the situation of the city was dramatic: almost all the buildings and houses were destroyed and of course, this was also the fate of the parks, transformed into temporary cemeteries or shelter for homeless people, or changed into cultivated fields. The priorities were for a rapid reconstruction and setting up of production facilities, rather than developing the urban environment and public amenities. Since the high growth period of the 1960s, pollution has been intensifying, urbanization spreading, and the rich natural resources of Tokyo disappearing. This phenomenon has particularly tangible effects on the inhabitants: for example, the area in which to see fireflies in June, an indicator of the environmental quality, is always moving farther west. Deterioration and damage were considerable and the rapid downfall directly related to the previous high quality of the natural environment in Edo and Tokyo before the war. Edo's population exceeded one million in the eighteenth century but nature (vegetation, water, and wildlife) was very present. The daimyō's residences with large gardens represented sixty percent of the territory; the temples and shrines fifteen percent, which covered two-thirds of the city's surface; planted riversides and woods were numerous. But now, paradoxically, Japanese cities and Tokyo in particular have the least greenery among cities in industrialized countries.[55]

Under such conditions of degradation, parks have become absolutely necessary facilities for improving the environment, compensating for damages, and proposing an answer to the local citizens' movements that keep gathering momentum. Plans for environmental improvement, protection of nature, and greenspace development have multiplied. In 1981, the Green Space Master Plan indicated for the first time precise and detailed areas to be maintained in the future; it was revised in 1995 and 2000. The goal is to achieve a per-capita park space of seven square meters by 2015. Although the area of Tokyo's green space has tripled over the last twenty-five years, the seven-square-meter goal has not been reached, but as the Bureau of City Planning says, "Charming urban spaces beautified with water and greenery represent a precious social capital that symbolizes the prosperity of a city."[56] The quality of the environment refers to political views about the quality of life.

[53] Suzuki Satoshi and Sawada Seichirō, *Kōen no hanashi* (Narration on parks) (Tokyo: Gihōdō, 1997), 91.

[54] At first, eating or drinking in the garden, sitting on the ground in the traditional way, was allowed only at the designated place, the restaurant. Quickly, popular behaviors regained their rights, and the two ways began to coexist.

[55] The ratio of park space per capita in the main cities gives a seemingly evident classification: Tokyo metropolis: 5.4 m²; Tokyo—only the 23 districts: 4.5 m²; Paris: 11.8 m²; Madrid: 14.0 m²; Seoul: 17.4 m²; Los Angeles: 17.8 m²; Brasilia: 19.4 m²; London: 26.9 m²; Berlin: 27.4 m²; and New York: 29.3 m². Yet these figures have to be considered cautiously. In the case of Paris, cemeteries are included in the total, and conversely in the case of Tokyo, shrines and temples are excluded since the 1947 law separating religions and the state. Figures from *Tokyo no koen-ryokuchi mappu* (Map of Tokyo's parks and greenery) (Tokyo: Tokyo Metropolis ed., 2002).

[56] Bureau of City Planning, *Planning of Tokyo* (Tokyo: Tokyo Metropolis ed., 2002), 37.

At first, starting in the 1970s, the Metropolitan Government of Tokyo worked to develop urban parks on vacant military bases. Today, it is developing parks in the western hill district (conservation of natural areas), and is reconstituting green space such as parks, green areas along rivers, tree-lined streets, and, in the eastern bayside, greenswards along the seaside (restoration of natural areas). The concerns are quantitative but qualitative, too, not only from an aesthetic but also an ecological perspective. It might amount to the same thing, because what is considered beautiful and appreciated by Japanese people is the existence of vivid nature, of wildlife inside the city, and inserted into the daily life and seasonal ritualized practices. The presence of nature is recognized and sought in its particular and concrete expressions.

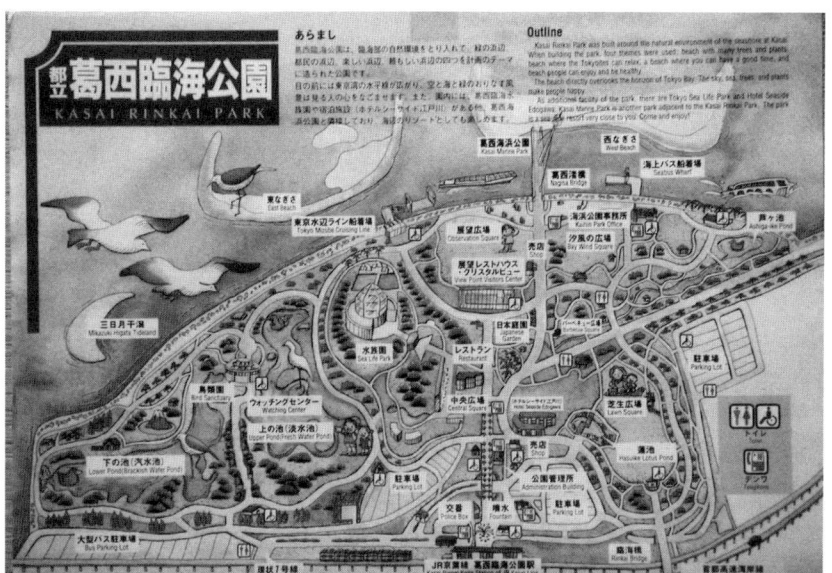

10. *Kasai Rinkai Park, present-day general map*

The very principles set up at Hibiya Kōen still apply in the layout of the new Tokyo parks. They follow a sequence of functional unities: at the entrance, a formal space (tree-lined avenue, fountains, flowerbeds, etc.); a large open grass field in the center convenient for many uses; a Japanese garden around a pond; restaurants with open-air terraces; many specialized facilities for sports, education, and recreation, for all ages. The park is crisscrossed by intertwining routes, with different themes (sport or leisure activities, didactical discovery of nature, historical or cultural walking), offering courses that unfold along many different sequences. The layout neither makes up a visual composition when drawn on a plan, nor offers a global vision, but it frames successive scenes and landscapes. It is a construction of expressive relations that organize space inside closed limits, by means of significant elements seen from some different angles along a course.[57]

For example, Kasairinkai Kōen, developed from 1985 to 1994, is a large park (eighty hectares), located along Tokyo Bay (Fig. 10). It recreates the natural environment of the bay with lagoons, marshes, and sand islands. In these three reconstituted ecosystems, wild birds come back and nest, and frogs, insects, and plants reappear more numerously on completely artificial landfill along the coast. Visitors can observe and study this performing wildlife in a directed nature, and take pictures from overlooks.[58] Bird-watching groups are very numerous and have great success in Japan. It is a new way to enjoy seeing some natural phenomena like birds nesting or migrations.[59]

Bird watching is an activity very much linked to photography. A Japanese person taking a picture may be a cliché, but photography also exercises the traditional way of perceiving landscapes, creating and representing them through cutting and framing. Taking a photograph is a way of catching the instant in a shot, materializing and making visible an ephemeral moment, in its poetic and cultural essence, and making memories similar to a short poem like a *waka* or a *haiku*. In Japanese culture, the way to make a picture has evolved following technical changes. Taking the photo itself lasts a very short instant, a few hundredths of a second, but the shooting session could be very long. It may last a day, or even several days, waiting for the right moment, the perfect light, as a poet looks for the best choice of words and turn of phrase, the best form to find the right unique expression in a short poem and thus catch the essence of a moment. Taking a picture is a quest, a long wait, and a

[57] This definition seems valid for Chinese gardens, such Japanese gardens as kaiyū-shiki teien, and today's modern public parks in Japan.

[58] Observation posts and bird sanctuaries are very frequent facilities in Tokyo's public parks.

[59] In Edo, meisho for listening to or observing birds were numerous. Bush warblers, cuckoos, ducks, and plovers were particularly praised in specific places. Higuchi Tadahiro, *Kōenzukuri wo kangaeru* (Thinking about park planning) (Tokyo: Gijōdō, 1996), 24.

SYLVIE BROSSEAU

111

repetition of the same gestures. It is a way to learn, to feel, to become imbued with the natural or cultural environment, and to capture the essentials of a place and a time.[60]

In Europe, the practices of holiday leisure in the countryside or at a beach set the pattern of practices in public parks.[61] In Japan, these practices, since their appearance in the Meiji era, are signs of both modernity and Westernization: eating Western cooking at a restaurant, drinking coffee on a terrace, playing tennis (since 1920 in Hibiya Kōen), and, recently, playing football. And a park such as Kasairinkai Kōen, along the seaside, allows the discovery of practices stemming from Western beach leisure. For Japanese people who do not have long summer holidays, a park still provides an opening to the world, and favors the assimilation of new practices. In fact, new practices are a way to reactivate some latent dispositions, or to continue expressing deep-rooted attitudes in a different way.

For example, the sea has always been a much-appreciated landscape, and also a very important domain of economic activities such as fishing or collecting shellfish and seaweeds. Yet, because of the industrial development of the Bay of Tokyo, the inhabitants were completely dispossessed of the ocean. It became impossible to access the seaside, and even to see it. A park like Kasairinkai Kōen, however artificial, as the soil was created *ex nihilo*, gives a new existence to the natural coast, some maritime landscapes, contact with the sea and nature, and suits the modern ecological feeling. This park also allows the discovery of new practices such as water sports, resting on a beach, installing such amenities as a beach tent near the water or rediscovering old practices such as shellfish gathering, or enjoying the sight of the bay.

Among all the new leisure practices introduced in the parks, group activities are developing most particularly. For example, a very successful practice today is barbecuing. To have a barbecue at home is impossible, but it is a very significant practice, because it is modern (derived from Western leisure and eating), seems natural (cooking outdoors,[62] using a natural element, fire), familiar, and convivial. Above all, Japanese society very closely associates group activities and nature. To have a barbecue is a new way to enjoy and reactivate a very ancient practice, eating in the open air and roasting food such as sweet potatoes, in a public space. Local propensities select among and selectively adapt new practices from the West. Even groupings are changing form because, on the model of Western holidays, one or several families come together, as for a barbecue. In this example of the barbecue, modernity is expressed in different ways: in the name (*bābēkyū*, from English), in the numerous new accessories (grill, charcoal, etc.), in the food (meat, particularly beef, rather than traditional vegetables or seafood), and in the form of grouping (gatherings of one or several families, friends rather than a local community). Yet the presence of nature is not simply accidental. People also organize many meetings between self-selected groups in indoor sites (restaurants, hotels, banquet halls), but nature recalls to the mind of Japanese people emotions and a long memory of ritual-like practices. The hedonistic drive and the desire of multisensory experiences in contact with nature (a landscaped nature) always are very present in the collective action.

On the contrary, a bodily practice such as sun bathing is not a group but an individual practice, pursued in order to achieve personal distinction rather than integration into society, by falling in line with current practices. The common judgment about physical beauty still values white skin. Recently, as outdoor leisure was booming, sun exposure has been declared bad for the skin and it has been admitted that it would be better to protect oneself. This should stop the spread of sun tanning as a group practice associated with youth, health, liberty, and social distinction, as it was in Europe after World War II. On the contrary, some young people express their individual dissidence against the established order by their appearance, showing off their very dark tans, highlighted for girls by pearly and almost white make up on the mouth and eyes, and with bleached hair, thus proclaiming their individuality and asserting publicly that their body belongs only to them. These girls,

[60] In the parks, almost everybody takes photographs, but video cameras are not as prevalent as in Europe. Japanese people might have a preference for fixed pictures. There are several ways to take a photo: with a very simple or disposable camera to keep a record of the visit, or with very sophisticated equipment, in groups or alone, with a model, etc. Young people enjoy a new way: with portable telephone fitted with a camera, to immediately send pictures to their friends.

[61] Franck Debié, *Jardins de capitales* (Paris: Editions du CNRS, 1992), 226.

[62] The practices accompany social change, and the vocabulary also reflects this change. About some new open-air practices, the Japanese say *autodoa* (from "outdoor"), in place of the local term *yagai*.

called *ganguro*,[63] do not have a good reputation since their fashion deliberately defies common good taste. They value a self-presentation according to an antimodel, turning upside down the dominant model (dark hair/white skin versus bleached hair/dark skin). Sun tanning is an individualizing practice that comes close to a temporary tattoo or a piercing,[64] and it is not done by the natural sun in an open-air place but from exposure to artificial sunlamps in a beauty salon. This example could confirm the fact that Japanese society associates the collective to the natural, and the individual to the artificial.[65]

Conclusion

Let us summarize this presentation of some ritual-like practices taking place in Tokyo's public modern parks, their historical foundations and development, their spatial and temporal configurations.

First, these practices are very numerous, all year long, and first and foremost they bring together groups of people who achieve common feelings through common acts. Society becomes aware of itself and its culture. Thus, the identity and permanence of society and culture are reasserted. Other cities have monuments; a great city like Tokyo instead rehearses its own stories through group practices.[66] These practices, clearly identified, named or related to named places and phenomena (hanami, kōyō, *momiji*, etc.), may be considered ritual practices because they imbue social and collective behaviors with shared meanings and values; they are patterned, repeated and symbolic. They never stop evolving, awakening a sense of memory, and linking the individual and collective present to an eloquent past.

In Japan, society is strongly ritualized,[67] and, for this reason among others, social cohesion, at present, is greater than in Western countries. Ritual practices do not create social cohesion but express it, and in so doing, reinforce it. Japanese society has absorbed many deep and rapid changes throughout its history, particularly since the late nineteenth century. Its high level of ritualization might have favored and allowed much assimilation because rituals, instead of being immobile, are flexible, have diverse meanings, and are integrative: they integrate people into the social framework, and changes into the society. Therefore, rituals could help to control the unsettled and shifting situations, the passages, and the ruptures. In Japan, unlike in Western societies, rituals are always part and parcel of the lifeworld for everybody.

Ritual practices observed in parks bring together individual and collective time. We saw that they integrate individuals into society and they institute the social order as a natural order. They also consolidate the continuity among generations. The parks offer a spatial framework, which favors the unfolding of these practices according to a temporal framework. Even in as big a city as Tokyo, they recreate in the park some local communities. They rehearse ideals of social control and harmony at fixed moments in the cyclical return of time. They reveal some fundamental values and issues of Japanese society, like integration and will of personal commitment to society, the sense and aesthetic perception of nature, the strengthening of the national consciousness.

Some ritual practices have the power to dress diverse elements in traditional garb, and seem to warrant the immutability of society, and yet they result from evolving social forces set in motion at specific times. They accompany social changes. They are more plastic and polysemic than fixed and repetitive. Japanese ritual practices have incorporated different elements borrowed from the West and brought about by a changing social structure, into cultural patterns reminiscent of, but distinct from, the original components. The meanings of the ritual practices are continuously renewed, but hark back to an ancient cultural fund.

These practices fulfill a certain role of exemplarity. They demonstrate some models. They take place in an ideal environment encompassing a fictitious harmony of people and nature, as noted by some critics. According to their judgment, the sense of nature in Japan engages in a fiction, since aesthetics and the lifeworld are completely divorced.[68] Celebrations in

[63] The term *ganguro* is a play on words formed from *gang* in English and *guro* meaning black in Japanese.
[64] See David Le Breton, *Signes d'identité: Tatouages, piercings et autres marques corporelles* (Paris: Métaillé, 2002).
[65] Berque, *Le sauvage et l'artifice*, 203. Another example of individual practice very frequent in public parks in the West is jogging, rare in Japanese parks. Japanese people go jogging on little roads.
[66] Paul Waley, "Power, Memory and Place," *Japanese Capitals in Historical Perspective* (London: Routledge Curzon, 2003), 385.
[67] Japan maintains the oldest imperial dynasty in the world, and this fact is regularly emphasized on diverse occasions.
[68] Berque, *Le sauvage et l'artifice*, 50–52, 205.

praise of nature in haiku poems, in the parks, or in some preserved or restored places in the city can be seen as mere illusions. Yet, people are actors in the construction of this "fictional" sense of nature. They play a role; they are not merely a passive audience. Popular culture does not open itself to outside manipulation but succeeds in inventing itself as a result of popular practices. Social rituals taking place in parks are based on the appropriation of a territory by people who become, in this way, closer to others. The appropriation (or reappropriation) of their environment by local communities or diverse forms of groups takes place through basic sociability: to assemble, to take food and drink in groups outside, enjoying a landscaped nature.[69] Therefore they share emotions, pleasure, satisfaction, spiritedness, and common ideals. They celebrate a common identity in a landscape that stands as a symbol of the group.[70]

Participating in hanami enacts a reading of the world, here and now, making evident its singularity. It is more akin to a dramatic performance than to a ceremony. Every hanami provides a singular interpretation of a spatial and temporal framing, so it achieves the appropriation of this moment and space by its participants. Such framing activities as spreading a vinyl sheet on the soil, disposing some accessories such as sophisticated photography equipment or a beach tent, setting a course for the event and corresponding practices, such as taking pictures, walking, sitting, waiting, eating, engage in the appropriation of a fragment of public space during a delimited time sequence. The appropriated frame creates a sense of condensed totality that explicitly models some values, meanings, and feelings, about aesthetics, nature, social order, pleasure, and links them into a comprehensive ordering of the world.[71]

Through these ritual-like practices, Japanese society and urban spaces maintain an engagement with nature. Japanese culture emphasizes the collective dimension of the perception and enjoyment of nature. As a consequence, people maintain the interest and the means to enjoy nature, even in a vast urbanized region such as Tokyo. City dwellers preserve a strong intimacy with natural phenomena through all sorts of creative expressions. We could say that the quality of the Japanese city (particularly Tokyo because, as a result of historical reasons, its natural resources were very abundant) is essentially located in its nature: a nature diffused in enclaves of agricultural or natural lands among the spread of urbanization, or a nature planned in parks, gardens, courtyards, and tree-lined plantings.[72] These two kinds of natures join, concretely in today's developments (remaining natural or agricultural lands are preserved and used as public parks), and symbolically in the collective perception of nature, its representation in landscape and its aesthetic appreciation. In this landscaped nature, the vivid elements and changing phenomena (plants, animals, meteors, etc.) are rich, numerous, and breathe life into space. That seems paradoxical with respect to the poverty of statistics about greenery but, in fact, it is the result of the conception and schematization of nature by Japanese culture. More explicitly, a Japanese specialist of city history, architecture, and landscape can write: "Nature, the foundation of the Japanese conception of the world, is not as it is, nude. It is a nature cultivated throughout history since the prehistoric times (Jomon and Yayoi periods). This vision of nature shaped all the country as a product of the civilization, and Japanese cities represented its apogee."[73] To say that the Japanese vision of nature reached its apogee in the city (Edo is the reference), also seems paradoxical for a Western mind contrasting city with nature but shows clearly that all the ritual-like practices taking place in today's public parks represent some fundamental ways of organizing the world and social life.

[69] We saw an example of this reappropriation of the environment in Kasairinkai Park, in Tokyo Bay. Every year, six million visitors come to this seaside park, which mixes memory, ecology, and leisure in correspondence with present tastes. Philippe Pons presents a more dramatic example, at Minamata in Wakayama prefecture. There, since the sixties, the sociability and the practices clearly have become acts of resistance against one big industry causing very serious damage; they have become tools of reappropriation of their destroyed environment by the fishermen and their families who have been poisoned by mercury. Philippe Pons, "Japon: Un attachement sélectif à la nature," in *Les sentiments de la nature*, ed. Dominique Bourg (Paris: La Découverte, 1993), 42–45.

[70] Michel Conan, "Conduite d'appropriation," "Rituel social," in *La Mouvance*, 50, 84.

[71] Catherine Bell, *Ritual*, 161.

[72] Christian Rouvière, "La nature dans la ville et la qualité de l'environnement au Japon," in *La qualité de la ville*, ed. Augustin Berque (Tokyo: Maison Franco-Japonaise, 1987), 150–55.

[73] Kawazoe Noboru, *Tōkyō no genfūkei* (Tokyo's original landscape) (Tokyo: Nihon Hōsō Shuppankyōkai, 1983), 10.

Moreover, these ritual practices keep commercial pressure at bay. They introduce a resistance to consumerism, and to the homogenization of time and space in the modern city,[74] opposing a very meticulous calendar, emphasizing sensitivity to variations (of the climate, the light, the season, the feeling, etc.), or offering the possibility of costless indulgence in the pursuit of excess.[75] They allow a degree of liberty because practices are always renewed and extend beyond the functional and limiting order of the park.

Practices such as hanami or those built around other natural facts, are like a feast, a fragment, a sparkle, like a radiance that breaks the monotony of daily life, like the "treasures, as dazzling as foam" mentioned by de Certeau, which keep a popular culture alive. These ritual practices in parks catch the fleeting moments of encounter between nature and society that enchant life again and again.[76]

[74] In Japan, and particularly in Tokyo, many chains of shops, restaurants, condominiums, and other services are spreading their networks and their standardized production, space, and time. The chains of convenience stores open 24 hours a day, very numerous in Tokyo, are a significant example of this homogenization of time and space.

[75] For example, the cherry trees flower profusely, but do not produce a single cherry. And a person waiting day after day to take a picture is also going against the general trend of frantic consumption.

[76] With many thanks to Ignazio Gioè for his precious help and constant support.

Performance and Appropriation: Profane Rituals in Gardens and Landscapes

Performance and Appropriation: Profane Rituals in Gardens and Landscapes

Performance and Appropriation: Profane Rituals in Gardens and Landscapes

Performance and Appropriation: Profane Rituals in Gardens and Landscapes

Silent Performances in Guadeloupean Dooryard Gardens: The Creolization of the Self and the Environment

Catherine Benoît

Introduction

Many institutions were tempted to create "Creole gardens" in the 1990s in the French overseas department of Guadeloupe. "Creole garden" is a recent concept that claims the originality of these gardens in comparison with those in Europe.[1] The specificity of these gardens—the dooryard gardens planted around a house—is supposed to lie in the variety of their plants, grown for food, rather than in their layout, often described as a "hodgepodge." They rightly are perceived as conservatories of biodiversity and horticultural practices expressive of a precise folk-knowledge of nature. Thus, Creole gardens can be viewed as interpretive centers of a regional culture, contributing to the fashion for heritage conservation dear to the French ministry of culture and the European Union (EU). Despite many attempts, no dooryard garden has yet been recreated. I have been asked many times to write about or participate in some of these projects. The story of one such attempted project will serve as an introduction to the difficulties of research on garden rituals, and to the importance of these rituals for an understanding of some vernacular gardens.

I did my Ph.D. fieldwork on Guadeloupean traditional medicines in the mid-1980s as an intern at the National Center of Agricultural Research, INRA (Institut National de Recherche Agronomique—Centre de recherches Antilles/Guyane). The former president of the institute, himself trained in anthropology at the very beginning of his career in the fifties, was the head of a research project on dooryard gardens and provision grounds in the French Caribbean. The other doctoral students working on this project were either agronomists or botanists; I was the only one trained in the social sciences. The staff and the other researchers, who wondered what an anthropologist could bring to the understanding of plant selection, horticultural technology, improvement of soils, and organization of labor, were skeptical of my participation. Most of my colleagues were angered that I documented in a scientific report people's popular knowledge of plants embedded in the world of healing, religion, and sorcery. I mentioned, at a department meeting, people who took into account the phases of the moon for the sowing and harvesting of the plants. The agronomists grew upset at some of the technicians who confirmed my description and mentioned other folk customs. At the same time, these technicians pretended to persuade me that I was describing old ways of life and superstitious beliefs to which nobody paid attention anymore. This meeting had enabled some of the least recognized people of the institute's hierarchy to have their voices heard. When they realized that I was mainly interested in the uses of medicinal plants, one of them, whom I shall call Rose to respect her anonymity, offered to show me her dooryard garden. I visited Rose. Her two-level house was surrounded by a wonderful garden full of ornamental and medicinal plants and some vegetables. I spent hours mapping this garden, learning the creole names and the uses of the plants. Rose, to whom I became

---

[1] L. Degras, "Etude de la polyculture vivrière 'jardins créoles' des Antilles et de la Guyane (1981–1984)." Paper presented at the Systèmes de production agricole caribéens et alternatives de développement, Martinique, Université des Antilles-Guyane, 1985.

close, was undergoing an initiation to become a healer. She had a room to practice in her basement and was eager to introduce me to such traditional healers as midwives, physical therapists who heal with heavy massages (*frotteurs*), and *gadédzafè*, healers who use spirit possession in their art of healing. I eventually brought a botanist there to help me to identify the binomial of the plants. This same botanist asked me to work on an exhibit on dooryard gardens six years later in 1994. He had created a very successful and powerful association dedicated to the preservation and development of the Guadeloupean environment. One of its main projects was a "Parc paysager," or landscaped garden, with a pond, an exhaustive collection of Caribbean cherry trees, a collection of medicinal plants, and a "typical" creole hut within a presumably no less "typical" dooryard garden. This garden, which had been laid out just two years earlier, could in no way be mistaken for a dooryard garden. I learned from this botanist that he had expected Rose to create the dooryard garden and was perplexed when she declined. When I asked her the reason for her refusal, Rose pretended that her partner did not want her to build the garden, because he thought the botanist was her lover. It was only while working on this essay that I began to understand the real motives for Rose's refusal. Why is there such a failure to create any public dooryard gardens? Why is it inappropriate to ask lay people to make a creole garden for public purposes? What does this failure say about the definition of gardens? What is at stake in the creation and experience of gardens? And how can the Caribbean experience of vernacular gardens enrich a theoretical debate on the relations among space, the domestication of nature, and the construction of the self and society?

This long narrative introduces the main themes of this essay. The dooryard garden is a meaningful cultural space, made up of daily practices that are invisible to people who do not have the code to decipher it. The garden is a place for promenades and silent rhetorics that shape people's being-in-the-world. It is a space engendered and created out of practices that also engender people's identities as Guadeloupean. Finally, through the enactment of ritualized actions, gardens are places that participate in the development of a creole culture.

Defining Dooryard Gardens

Dictionaries and most studies define the garden as an enclosed space of ground devoted to the cultivation of flowers, fruit, or vegetables. A garden is called a flower garden, a vegetable garden, or a fruit garden depending on the types of plants that grow in it. It can be a kitchen garden, a market garden, or a botanical garden, depending on its function. No usual definition considers the garden as a place of practices. The garden is understood first and foremost as a space where vegetal species are grown. It is a portion of space perceived through the gaze rather than through the senses of smell, hearing, and touch. In the *Dictionnaire historique de l'art des jardins* we are reminded that the arrangement, the cultivation, and the maintenance of the plants follow general rules of refinement in terms of horticultural technique, function, and types of plants.[2] The choice and the arrangement of the vegetal species follow cultural rules to a point that an academic or cultivated gaze distinguishes different gardens' art forms such as, among others, the medieval garden, Renaissance garden, picturesque garden, Italian garden, or Japanese garden. Nonetheless, when the design of such a cultivated plot is too alien to a Western understanding of gardens, a European gaze cannot distinguish anything. Caribbean dooryard gardens were for a long time considered "mish-mash" or *salmigondis* places surrounding the houses of people of African descent. From a Western perspective not all planted grounds deserve to be termed gardens. An anthropological perspective on gardens does not limit itself to looking at the organization of space, the number of species cultivated in the garden, the type of plants that grow in it, and the functions of the garden; it strives to understand people's experience of the garden. This analysis of the Guadeloupean dooryard garden will illustrate a phenomenological understanding of space by examining the practices of the living space, not merely its design practices.

The dooryard garden that surrounds the house cannot be conceived of apart from the house (Fig. 1). Dividing the dwelling space into garden and house, for analytical purposes, imposes Western categories of space, and disregards the

[2] Michel Conan, *Dictionnaire historique de l'art des jardins* (Paris: Hazan, 1997).

Guadeloupean experience of gardens. It introduces a distinction between house and garden space, between building space and nature, rather than the continuity of their living experience. Thus, the study of Guadeloupean gardens cannot view gardens as spaces only worth a stylistic or species analysis, as Guadeloupean people do not conceive of a garden without people and without a house.

1. *A Guadeloupean dooryard garden: house and yard define the dwelling (Saint-Claude, 2000)*

The Caribbean dooryard garden is a heterogeneous place—a concept developed by Michel Foucault in his phenomenological approach to space—laden with social and cultural tensions, and not a homogeneous and empty place.[3] Each garden is specific, with its own amenities that shape the social interactions, behaviors, and attitudes of its dwellers or visitors, who can include neighbors, strangers, spirits of the dead (who visit the garden at night), and ancestors (who appear on All Saints' Day—1 November). By placing a protective plant at the entrance of the garden, one protects the dwelling against the malevolent intentions of the visitors; one also indicates a definite knowledge of proper behavior, and invites visitors to behave accordingly. Not only people but also spirits of the dead who know the code are able to read the gardens and behave according to their understanding of the place.

The choice and location of plants mediate the inhabitants' relationships with their neighbors, visitors, and the spirits of the dead who can intervene in their life to bring luck or to hurt them. The garden is made of symbolic shells or layers that protect the inhabitants from malevolent forces. Following Gaston Bachelard's *Poetics of Space*[4] and Abraham A. Moles and Élisabeth Rohmer's *Psychologie de l'espace*,[5] the symbolic shells can be defined as the numerous protections that are laid on the body linking it to the environment and protecting it from the outside elements.

The gardens are the architectonic of the world as defined by Bakthin.[6] The architectonic of the world is the world experienced by an acting self who invests space and time with his "flesh and blood,"[7] and not the ideal, abstract world made of mathematical space and time. Acts that define the garden as this architectonic are small acts usually considered superstitious and magical practices, nonrational behaviors that have no bearing on the real world. Misinterpreting daily practices is characteristic of the study of neocolonial societies: the French Overseas Departments (Les départments d'outre-mer—DOM) were until recently considered to be totally assimilated to the culture of the continental center. Yet, seriously studying these practices in the context of creole worldviews reveals their fundamental role in the construction of the creole self, and the definition of cultural and collective identities.

[3] Michel Foucault, "Different Spaces," in *Essential Works of Foucault 1954–1984*, vol. 2, *Aesthetics, Method, and Epistemology*, ed. J. D. Faubion, trans. R. Hurley et al. (New York: The New Press), 175–85. Text of a lecture presented to the Architectural Studies Circle, 14 March 1967. First published in *Architecture, Mouvement, Continuité*, 5 October 1984.

[4] Gaston Bachelard, *The Poetics of Space*, trans. Maria Jolas (New York: Orion Press, 1964).

[5] Abraham A. Moles and Élisabeth Rohmer, *Psychologie de l'espace* (Tournai, Belgium: Casterman, 1972).

[6] M. M. Bakhtin, *Toward a Philosophy of the Act* (Austin, Texas: University of Texas Press, 1993).

[7] Ibid., 59.

The Rhetorics of Walking and of Silence in Constructing an Embodied Place

Boundary-making through Silence

Creole gardens have recently attained the status of an object worthy of scientific study and of being exhibited.[8] They are featured in popular literary works as well,[9] but beyond this public display gardens are cast in silent gestures—gestures that are dangerous to discuss. This silence has direct methodological implications. The difficulty in collecting data and conducting interviews about the practice and meaning of Caribbean gardens reveals what is at stake in laying out a garden, maintaining it, and living in it.

I began to study gardens when I was working on Guadeloupean traditional medicines. I interviewed healers and their patients in the healers' houses and I spent a lot of time in their yards learning the names of the medicinal plants and waiting for the patients. Frustrated by these long hours of waiting, and disappointed by the healers' reluctance to reveal the protective uses of plants, I decided to draw the gardens plant by plant, in the hope that an analysis of the resulting maps would reveal something about the gardens' organization. My training in archaeology had given me a sense of the importance of the analysis of space in the study of social relationships and I was adept at drawing maps. I drew many gardens and analyzed eight of them, whose owners were healers or laypeople whose lives I knew well and who had provided me with the creole names and uses of each plant.

The methodologies of ethnobotany, cartography, and experimental graphics have been crucial in understanding how the inhabitants of these gardens experience them. By cross checking different sources of information, some proceeding directly from the inhabitants, and others from the knowledge that I had acquired elsewhere, I was able to discern an unexpected organization. For example, knowing that silence is meaningful and that people are not supposed to divulge all their knowledge about the uses of plants (because to do so would put into action the world of spirits and unveil the protective strategies of the house), I drew two maps contrasting people's discourse and my own knowledge (Fig. 2). The first presents the inhabitants' discourse about the uses of the garden's plants. The second is the analysis I was able to make of the garden's functions. When I first compared the maps, I thought the inhabitants had told me everything about the uses of the garden. But then the cartographer with whom I worked suggested that I superimpose the two maps, whereupon I discovered that the inhabitants did not mention the uses of the "protective" plants placed at the entrance of the garden. This discrepancy held true for all eight gardens I analyzed. It meant that the inhabitants could not reveal to an anthropologist the kinds of protections they establish against malevolent visitors.

To speak about plants in a Guadeloupean dooryard garden is to participate in a situation of "performative utterances" as Austin describes them: "to say is to make."[10]   In other words, speaking about the plants that provide protection from the spirits of the dead would activate the world of the dead and spirits, thus putting the self at risk. Silence defines a garden in the sense that those who do not know the code cannot imagine that a garden is more than a space for the production of flowers and vegetables. The necessity to "hang around" with the people with whom we work and the "obsessive patience and passionate tact" needed to interact with them characterize the way anthropologists work in order to understand how people

[8] In 1998, to celebrate the 250th anniversary of the abolition of slavery, the French government organized a series of celebrations in the metropolis and in the DOM. The *Musée des Arts et Traditions Populaires* in Paris was asked to develop an exhibition on cultural traditions in the DOM. The exhibition was to include a recreation of a dooryard garden with imported tropical plants. A model of one of the gardens that I studied was designed by a group of architects, although without my input and introduction to the social content of its creation. For a presentation of decontextualized cultural facts in this exhibition see the introduction to the exhibiton catalogue: *Tropiques métis—Mémoires et cultures de la Guadeloupe, de la Guyane, de la Martinique et de la Réunion* (Paris: Éditions de la Réunion des Musées nationaux, 1998).

[9] In 1992, the Goncourt prize, the most prestigious French literary prize, was awarded to Patrick Chamoiseau for *Texaco*. The novel deals with the migration of gardeners' families to the Martiniquan main city, Fort-de-France. P. Chamoiseau, *Texaco* (Paris: Gallimard, 1992).

[10] J. L Austin, *How To Do Things Without Words* (Cambridge, Mass.: Harvard University Press, 1976).

experience the places in which they live.[11] The constraint of silence led to the drawing of the maps; their interpretation relied on the memory of people's practices in the yards that I came to know.

Boundary-making through Spaces Devoted to Walking and Exclusion

My approach to garden practices parallels Michel de Certeau's study of "the practices of everyday life," in an urban space. He was concerned with practices that are foreign to the "geometrical" or "geographical space":[12] "specific ways of operating," "another spatiality," or "an anthropological, poetic and mythic experience of space."[13] Following de Certeau's analysis of the city as a place of "walking rhetorics" that engender the self,[14] modes of walking in Guadeloupean gardens define these gardens as embodied places.

The dooryard garden is made up of symbolic shells that are not merely physical limits. Objects and plants signal them, but above all they result from practices. They ensue from behaviors and attitudes that define forbidden or authorized spaces and corresponding limits (Fig. 3). The first shell consists of the outer limits of the garden with its protective plants. These plants are located at the entrance to the garden, along the boundary with the neighbors, and at the corner of the master bedroom. It has been noted that in the Caribbean there is no clear delimitation between one property and another; fences are not common.[15] A tree can indicate delimitations between two gardens, but the boundaries are actually defined by practices and walking habits based on social interactions among inhabitants, neighbors, visitors, and the dead. People who walk past dooryard gardens without visiting them will not look at the people in the dwelling. Before entering, visitors must signify their presence by calling out to the inhabitants. Visitors who are not related to the family stay in the front part of the yard and do not access the backyard where people actually live during the day. The second shell is the protective cordon around the house. Much has

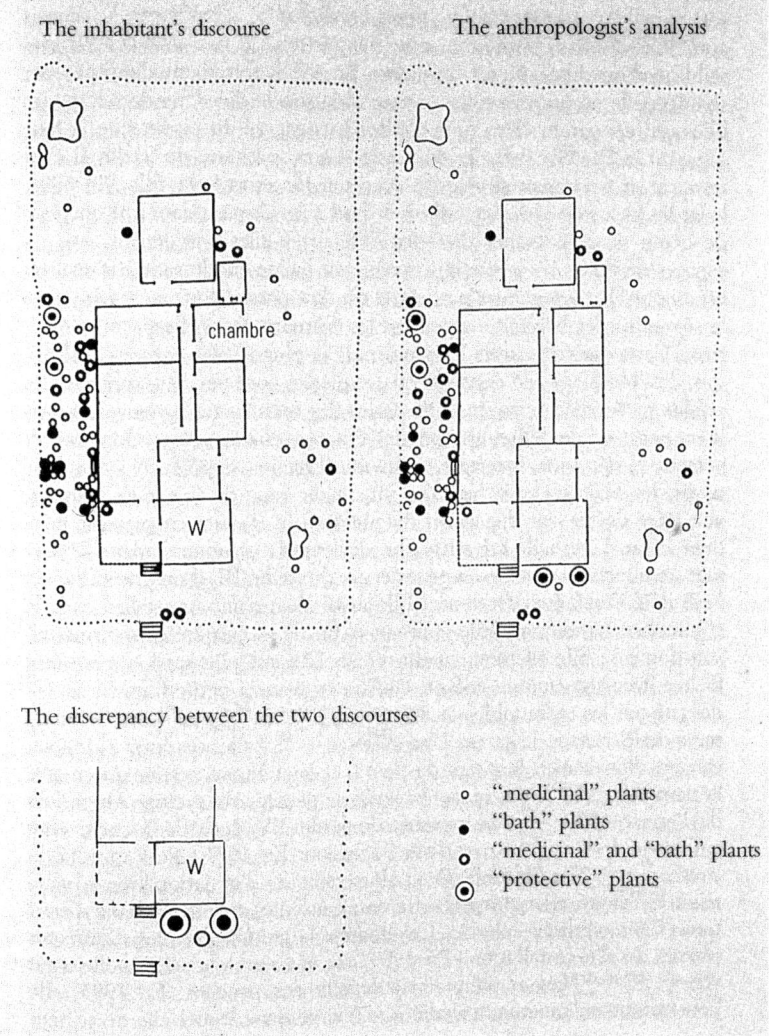

2. *Contrasting the inhabitant's discourse (1) with the anthropologist's knowledge (2) of the uses of therapeutic plants.*

[11] Clifford Geertz, "Afterword," in *Senses of Place*, ed. S. Feld and K. H. Basso (Santa Fe, N.M.: School of American Research Press, 1996), 260–61.

[12] Michel de Certeau, *The Practice of Everyday Life* (Berkeley, Calif.: University of California Press, 1984), 93.

[13] Ibid., 93.

[14] Ibid., 100.

[15] S. Mintz, "Living fences in the Fond-Des-Nègres Région, Haïti," *Economic Botany* XVI, no. 2 (1962): 101–5; A. Peeters, "Le petit paysannat martiniquais et son environnement végétal. Recherches en cours." *JATBA* XXIII, nos. 1, 2, 3 (1976): 47–56; idem, *Le lakou dans la région de Salagnac*. DGRST, GNRP/P, 1979b.

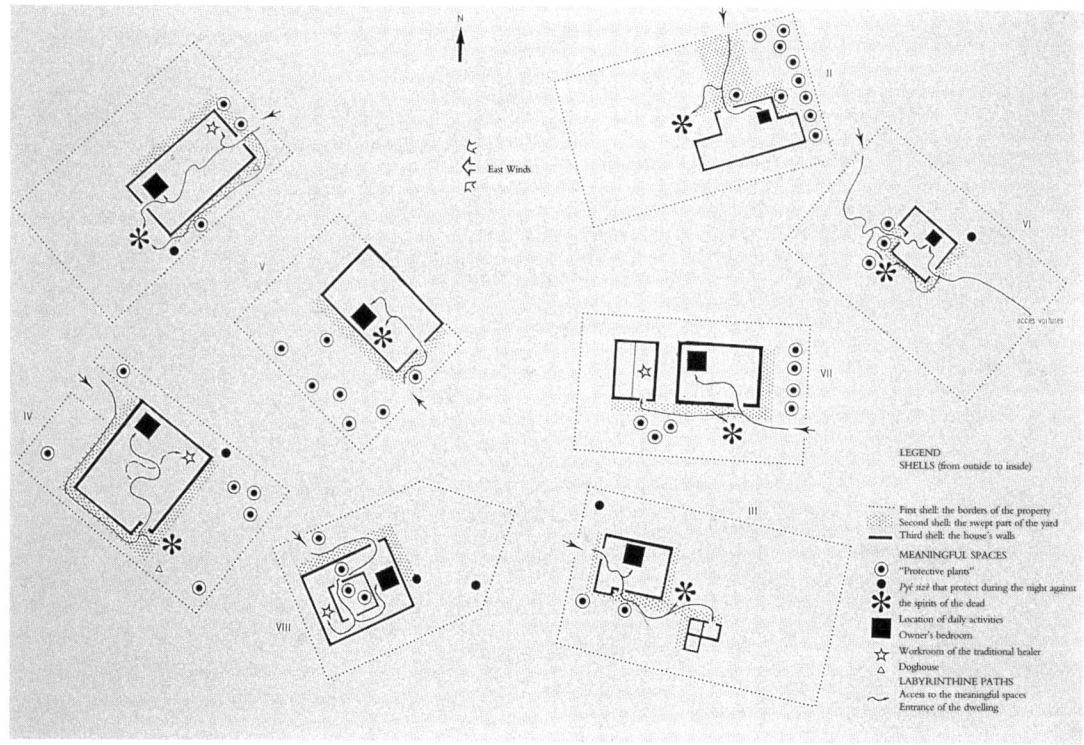

3. The shells of the dwellings

been written about the swept yards of the Caribbean. It is usually proposed that people need a clean area where they can sit outside because their houses are small.[16] This interpretation of the Guadeloupean dooryard suffers from a major difficulty: the swept part of the yard is not big enough for people to occupy. It is a small strip of space surrounding the house. The rear portion is swept every morning in case by any misfortune an evil spirit had visited during the night, or someone had placed malevolent objects there. Visitors do not come too close to the swept part of the yard surrounding the house because of the fear that they could place malevolent objects there. The third shell is made up of the walls of the house: the inside walls are hung with different objects and inscribed figures to protect the house. Visitors who enter the house access the meaningful places such as the bedroom, the room where the healer works, or the backyard where people live via quite labyrinthine paths. There is no direct access: people have to pass by protective plants and follow corridors from one room to another. These paths and positions define excluded spaces.[17] Spatial prohibitions allow for boundary-making that engenders shells to protect the house.

These different shells refer to the humoral conception of the body.[18] Well-being is based on maintaining an equilibrium in the constant exchanges of bodily fluids and the environment but also between the body, the different souls of the self, and other people. In this context, the body is permanently threatened both by external invasive forces and the escape of fluids and the soul from bodily openings. During the weeks that follow birth, the fontanel is massaged to close an opening

[16] C. Kimber, "Spatial Patterning in the Dooryard Gardens of Puerto Rico," *The Geographical Review* 6 (1973): 6–26.

[17] For a discussion of "excluded spaces" as constitutive of the living experience of a place see N. D. Munn, "Excluded Spaces: The Figure in the Australian Aboriginal Landscape," in *The Anthropology of Space and Place: Locating Culture*, ed. S. M. Low and D. Lawrence-Zuniga (Malden, Mass.: Blackwell Publishing, 2003), 92–109.

[18] C. Benoît, *Corps, jardins, mémoires—Anthropologie du corps et de l'espace à la Guadeloupe* (Paris: Éditions de la Maison des sciences de l'homme/Éditions du CNRS, 2000).

that could let spirits enter the body. The skin does not by itself define the body, for the bodily discharges and waste material that contain the vital aspects of the person can be manipulated by sorcery. The body is perceived as being made of many protective shells. Some of these shells are inside the body, such as that created by the drink given to babies after birth or to someone who needs protection against spirits. Others, such as amulets, are worn on the surface of the body. The protective sealing of the body is enhanced by specific massages and by different types of baths given over the course of a lifetime. Because the creation and maintenance of protective shells are grounded in the humoral conception of well-being, they link space and body in another intimate way.

The Construction of the Self through Ritualized Practices

In her works on rituals Catherine Bell stresses the difficulty of defining rituals as either a distinct and autonomous set of activities or as an aspect of all activities. How can we draw a limit between what would seem to be a ritual (speaking to the plants at night to apologize for waking them up when in need of leaves for making tea) and a common interaction with plants (speaking to the plants as a sign of affection during the day and respect at night)? Bell suggests that instead of delimiting what can be considered a ritual, one could construct a model of ritualization of practices, recognizing a range of possibilities between ordinary and ritual practices. Bell highlights four features of ritualized practices: (1) they are situational—meaning that they engage within a specific material and social environment—and strategic—meaning that they impose making choices; (2) they "misrecognize" what they are doing; (3) they refer to the will to act; and (4) they are motivated by the benefits they provide to the actors.[19] The specificity of rituals compared to nonritual practices is generated by ritualization. Ritualization produces a contrast between ritualized activities and other forms of social behavior (i.e., the difference between a Christian Eucharistic meal and an ordinary meal). The main quality of the ritualized actions is "the primacy of the body moving about within a specially constructed space, simultaneously defining (imposing) and experiencing (receiving) the values ordering the environment."[20] According to Bell, a place—ontologically different from Cartesian space—is defined by the body movements of agents who are well apprised of the ritual and who consider themselves to be responding to the environment. Ritualization links in an inextricable way body and space. Thus, the study of Guadeloupean dooryard gardens calls for a phenomenological approach to space. The transformation of the tropical environment into a Guadeloupean dooryard garden is made through the actions of the body. The perception and practices of the place are thus constitutive of the body. The ritualized practices of space and nature and their reenactment transform individuals into agents and initiate men and women into the worldviews of their society. These rituals are performative: beyond their immediate function as perceived by the actors, they participate in the development of people's personal and collective identities that, by the same token, shape space and nature, transforming them into a place.[21] Ritualization creates gardens as places that are not merely Cartesian spaces. Gardens also structure some aspects of the inhabitant's life. Thus, we can see these gardens as embodied spaces, as places with personalities that are structured by the actions of its inhabitants, and that in turn act on their lives.

In Guadeloupe, an individual becomes a person through rituals performed at birth, both on the newborn body and in the garden, binding body to place. The umbilical cord of the newborn is placed at the foot of a breadfruit or more often a fruit tree. People then treat this tree with particular consideration. A first link is thus established between the individual, his birthplace, and his parents, if not his ancestors.[22] In Haiti, the link is closed at death when people are buried in the yard (Fig. 4). This link is maintained through life by taking specific baths in the garden and planting trees for specific purposes.

[19] C. Bell, *Ritual Theory, Ritual Practice* (New York–Oxford: Oxford University Press, 1992), 80–88.
[20] C. Bell, *Ritual: Perspectives and Dimensions* (New York–Oxford: Oxford University Press, 1997), 82.
[21] For a discussion of space/place see Feld and Basso, *Senses of Place*.
[22] When women delivered at home, the placenta was buried or burnt within two to three weeks after birth so it could not be used for sorcery.

4. *Tomb in a Haitian dooryard garden: the living and the dead are definitively linked (Haiti, 1998)*

Baths play a major role in well-being and in communication with the Guadeloupean world of the Catholic saints and the spirits. There are baths taken in the river to tone up the body or to enhance an individual's relationships with the protecting saints. There are baths taken in the sea to relax, ward off fate, or bring luck when taken on New Year's Eve. Finally, there are baths taken in the garden the first Friday of every month to protect oneself against evil and misfortune as well as to ensure good luck and happiness. To take this kind of bath, people sit in a bowl placed in the backyard and pour over themselves water that has been liberally infused with floral plants. Then they scrub the body with these plants before cleaning the house with the bath water. That these baths have to be taken in the yard shows that their effect goes far beyond the body envelope and that the living space has to be taken into account to maintain people in good health in relation to the environment.

There are trees or plants growing at the entrance of the dwelling that are called *plant monté* in Creole, meaning that the owner bound his or her life to the growth of the tree or plant. At the base of these trees or plants, some specific preparations are poured or prayers said to bring luck to the owner, protect him against malevolent forces, or send malevolent forces to others. Through the *plant monté* the future of the owner is sealed to the dwelling and encapsulated in a tree. Members of the landowner's family occasionally suspect the function of some trees and cut them down at his death to free the space from the malevolent intentions of the dead. Other significant garden plants include the "gift plant" (*plant don*), which guarantees a healer's powers. Each healer strongly identifies with a secret *plant don* that he or she uses in all medicinal preparations. Without this plant, the preparations would be ineffective. This plant is removed when the healer dies. Finally, there are the trees that the owners, and, more specifically, females, particularly love and strongly identify with. These trees can be those that bring messages in dreams, or the ones whose appearances are majestic. By embracing and caressing trees such as a coconut, a palm, or a mahogany (*Swietenia mahogani* [L.] Jacq.), females acquire some of the trees' strength.

All the care given to these trees and plants constitutes ritualized practices because these very acts transform the nature both of the plants and trees and of the garden and its caretaker. The lives of the plants, trees, and individuals are inextricably interdependent to the point that when the owner dies, some trees and plants have to be removed from the yard. Their presence and the care given to them mark the garden as a place where the vegetation mediates the inhabitants' social relationships. For example, before a baptism, wedding, or wake, the alleys in the gardens and the front door are sprinkled with sugar and the house is washed with "Bird pepper" (*Solanum americanum* Mill.) to prevent any discord. The garden is an extension of the body: it participates in the definition of the body, it reacts to the movements of the body, and also induces practices on the body.

Gardens as Interworlds, or becoming a Guadeloupean

From a phenomenological perspective, Guadeloupean gardens are interworlds (*intermondes*[23]). They engage their inhabitants in specific experiences of the world. Mastery of these experiences defines belonging to a society and allows for nonambiguous communication between its members. Guadeloupean gardens are cultural objects experienced by people that also shape people's understanding of who they are and how to behave.

The dooryard garden is the place in which some of the fundamentals of culture are acquired during adulthood. In this sense, acquisition of culture is both a "time and space"–based initiation. A family is really founded only when a couple moves into its own house and has to lay out a dooryard garden. Even people with children who live in their parents' house or in an apartment are not considered ready to receive or practice some of the cultural foundations of their society. This cultural foundation is based on the knowledge and the mastery of the relationships among the living, and between the living and the environment, and the living and the dead. When a couple moves into its own house, the mothers transmit this knowledge to them. When a new garden is laid out it is constructed in the following way. The first shell is completed at the time of moving in. Before laying the foundations of the house, the land is prepared by spraying some powder where the foundations are going to be erected. At the entrance and sometimes at the four cardinal points of the property many *pyé sandragon* are planted to protect the dwelling from the spirits of the dead (Fig. 5). A tree is planted with salt at its base in order to secure the inhabitants to the place. For the same reason, salt is spread at the corners of the house. To the contrary, when one is trying to get rid of someone in a house, he will pour salt in the washbowl or the toilets. People will leave the place as the salt melts. When necessary, other plants such as the *pyé sizè* (*Phyllantus niruri* L.) are planted both at the corner of the master bedroom to protect the dwelling against the spirits of the dead (Fig. 6), and closer to the neighbors' side to protect the inhabitants from any malevolent actions on the part of their neighbors. When the wooden roof structure is positioned on the walls, and before it is covered by the sheet metal roof, a bouquet made of red flowers and *cordylline* (*Cordyline fruticosa* [L.] A. Chev.) is hung. The red signifies the victory of having been able to build a house. When the bouquet dries, it is removed and burned. When the owner of the house dies, a black piece of tissue is hung on the roof for at least one or two years. Women are in charge of maintaining the dooryard gardens. Women tend their gardens by selecting the plants, testing them, watering them, and weeding. In André-Georges Haudricourt's terms, a "respectful friendship" links women and plants in a dooryard garden, where every plant is worthy of personalized attention.[24] Plants are living elements that must be addressed with kindness. They must be awakened by nice words when picked at night, to calm the disturbance. Women also contribute every day to the maintenance of the second shell. Every morning they sweep the yard, whereas the men drink what is called in Creole a *dékolaj*—a glass of rum—in order to be in good shape for the day and to cleanse the body of whatever might have gone wrong during the night. If the house has to be swept during the night, the dust is thrown outside while apologizing to the spirits of the dead who are supposed to be present. The third shell made of "pentacles" and religious "pictures" hung on the inside walls of the house protects the dwelling and is created upon moving in or when necessitated during the course of life. Some specific colors such as red, signifying a victory against evil, are used to decorate the house. Ritualization of the dwelling follows the annual calendar. At the end of the year, the furniture is moved around so that the New Year finds everything in a new order. The house is cleansed with leaves of *fruit à pain* (*Artocarpus altilis* [Park.] Fosberg) in order to bring luck and abundance. The garden is cleared of all the bad herbs and useless objects. People also take a bath in the sea on New Year's Eve. The annual progress of the cosmic order is reflected in the microcosm formed by the dwelling and the individual.

Guadeloupean dooryard gardens do not belong to the world of children and are not the places where children and teenagers discover nature and develop their sense of observation, unlike modern bourgeois European gardens.[25] Dooryard

[23] The concept of interworld is introduced by Maurice Merleau-Ponty in his discussion of intersubjectivity and solipsism. Maurice Merleau Ponty, *Phénoménologie de la perception* (Paris: Gallimard, 1997; 1st ed. 1945), 409–19.

[24] A.-G. Haudricourt, "Domestication des animaux, culture des plantes, traitement d'autrui," *L'homme* 2, no. 1 (1962): 40–50.

[25] M. Conan, "'Puer aeternus' in the Garden," *Studies in the History of Gardens and Designed Landscape* 1 (1999): 86–101.

5. Pyé sandragon *are planted to protect the dwelling from the spirits of the dead (Vieux-Habitants, 1987)*

gardens are not places for experimentation and learning activities for children. Boys play and socialize outside the yards, whereas girls stay at home. Children learn about the vegetal world by helping their fathers in provision grounds that are not dangerous places. There, when eight or nine years old, they help by weeding and transporting vegetables and roots. In their teens, they begin to grow food. Children are not introduced to the world of the dooryard garden because they are considered too clumsy. "Plants are delicate," I was told many times. But, actually, this is a half-truth. Children are not allowed in the garden because the garden is a place that mediates the inhabitant's relationships with neighbors, visitors, deceased, and ancestors. This is too dangerous a place to allow children to participate in its maintenance.

Space and the Definition of Creole Culture

Through the ritualization of gardens and through rituals that an individual performs in the gardens, s/he becomes both a person and a full member of Guadeloupean society. The garden is part of the "notion of person," which, in Guadeloupe, is made of the body, the breath, the soul, the guardian angel, and the hidden first name.[26] For healers, the protective saint who granted the gift of healing is another component. The notion of person is usually inscribed in a specific time frame: the origin of spiritual principles is linked to genealogy and ancestry. This notion is never understood in reference to space. The garden introduces this spatial dimension in the definition of person and in the construction of the self. Space is a fundamental element in the construction of Guadeloupean subjectivity. The analysis I propose here is not exclusively about gardens as places where worldviews can be read but as places that create people. Through gardening rituals, constant interactions between people and gardens become essential for the construction of the self and society. Rituals introduce both the experience of space in the development of the person and the experience of time in the living experience of space. By articulating space and time in the gardens, the analysis of rituals leads to a definition of places not only as cultural embodied spaces but also as cultural embodied spaces framed in specific times.

The notion of person is articulated as a worldview according to which relationships between the living and the dead are constant. However, the practice of these rituals does not always signify the adherence to this worldview. When people in their thirties pretend not to believe in this worldview but still perform some of the rituals of foundation for their dwelling, they certainly do so under pressure from their parents. But by doing so, they mark their belonging to that portion of the Guadeloupean community that believes in the interaction of the living and the dead. The rituals are less about performance—in this case, the protection of the dwelling—than about the reception of knowledge and integration into an "imagined" community.[27] When an individual abandons this worldview, the frequency and the intensity of the rituals decline in such a

[26] The hidden name is the name used for the registry office but never in private or public life for fear that it could be used for sorcery. People are called by a name that does not appear on any official papers.

[27] B. Anderson, *Imagined Communities: Reflections on the Origin and Spread of Nationalism* (London: Verso, 1983).

manner that a typology of gardens can be proposed. First, there are gardens that anyone can make. The presence of some protective plants and the practice of rituals show how the inhabitants participate in this worldview and that they know how to protect and to defend themselves. Second, there are hyperritualized gardens indicative of an intense religious life, such as the gardens of healers or people who are victims of sorcery. By contrast, there are gardens that have been destroyed. These are particularly interesting. They are the gardens of people who abandon this worldview, or the gardens of healers transmitting their gift of healing to someone else. Two of the gardens that I drew do not look the same anymore. In one case, the woman who was becoming a healer at the time of the mapping finally gave up healing. There were no longer so many plants in her garden and she pretended not to have had a garden before. The owner of another garden is now getting very old and has transmitted her gift of healing to her daughter. Her garden is reduced to a lawn. She pretends that a *fourmi manioc,* a sort of ant, ate everything in one night. A person's identity is linked to his garden so that when a person changes his worldview the garden will reflect these changes.

6. The pyé sizè *protects the dwelling from the spirits of the dead (Gourbeyre, 2000)*

The very existence of a typology of gardens related to specific worldviews sheds some light on the processes of creolization in a multiethnic society. Guadeloupean society is stratified according to class and ethnicity. The main ethnic groups are composed of the white *béké* of colonial descent, the vast majority of people of mixed African and European descent, the Indians, and the continental French, who most of the time come as temporary public

7. *The creole garden of the Parc paysager with a coconut alley reminiscent of the great houses' alleys (Petit-Canal, December 2002)*

servants. What can the study of a few Guadeloupean dooryard gardens teach us about the definition of Guadeloupean personhood and culture? This is a creole culture—not a unified cultural system, but rather, as noted by Lee Drummond, an intersystem—characterized by internal variation and change. Internal variation points to the multiple meaning of many cultural facts. For example, a plant such as the "paper flower" (*Bougainvillea spectabilis* Willd.) is an ornamental flower in the béké

8. *A creole garden created by Archipel des Sciences (Basse-Terre, Festival "Enfance du monde," March 2002)*

9. *A creole garden designed for public tours (Ste Rose, December 2002)*

gardens, and an ornamental and magical plant used for sorcery by some healers. The notion of change in Drummond's definition stresses that a cultural fact produced by a specific ethnic group can be incorporated into another ethnic group's undersystem (for example, the béké who are not supposed to practice sorcery can under certain conditions have plants used for sorcery in their gardens). Guadeloupeans are aware of the undersytem even if they only identify with a specific part of it. Each group claims a different identity in terms of ethnicity and garden design. Many of the plants found in the Guadeloupean gardens of people of African descent, such as the *Qui vivra véra—Codiaeum variegatum* (hort.)—that brings luck, or the cordylline that protects against the spirits of the dead, are not present in a béké garden. Nonetheless, gardens have a very important significance to the béké population. They also participate, although in a different way, in the definition of the female as a person. Until recently, béké women were not allowed to leave their houses for social encounters. The white endogamous group feared that they might encounter black men and marry outside the group. Therefore, béké women developed two skills to deal with the boredom of their daily life: first, organizing extravagant dinners; second, maintaining a garden. Dinners and gardens are objects for display when receiving guests. The authority of both béké and women of African descent is embodied in their ability to conceive and maintain a garden. The variety of gardens—as cultural productions—thus derives from an intersystem of practices and meanings pervading the entire society. A study of the interactions between béké women and gardeners of African or Indian descent would be a promising avenue for the exploration of creolization as a set of processes in which the different ethnic groups are engaged.[28]

Conclusion

At a time when anthropology studies transnational movements and the effects of globalization, the mobility of people, culture, society, and place are no longer considered isomorphic. It may seem retrograde to focus solely on how people transform space into a place without being interested in their movement across territories. Even anthropologists conduct multisite fieldwork, following the people with whom they work or tracing the networks of which they are a part.

[28] For a discussion of creolization as made up of synthetic and segmentarized processes see O. Patterson, "Context and Choice in Ethnic Allegiance: A Theoretical Framework and Caribbean Case Study," in *Ethnicity: Theory and Experience*, ed. N. Glazer and D. P. Moynihan (Cambridge, Mass.–London: Harvard University Press, 1975), 205–49.

Contemporary anthropological questions on the study of space concern the creation of a "sense of place" by displaced, immigrant, and refugee populations. Actually, Caribbean people belong to the African diaspora, which was dramatically constituted through the enslavement and displacement of African people to the Americas. They were the first people to experience, on such a global scale, definitive displacement without any hope of return to their birthplace, even if they survived the Middle Passage. Since the advent of slavery, Caribbean gardens have played an immense role in the appropriation of a new, imposed environment even under the coercive system of the plantation.[29] Using the produce of their gardens, in addition to work performed in the fields, enslaved Africans could purchase their freedom and, after abolition, could buy land and thus strive for some control over their world. Let me propose that gardens nowadays, as well as during the period when slavery still existed, also expand the frame of consciousness of gardeners, thus contributing to processes of self-definition. The study of experience and practice of space invites a hermeneutic approach to gardens. In addition, gardens are places for social interaction rather than solitary use by only one individual. Therefore, they cast self-definition within a frame of cultural interactions and thus contribute to the production of what Arjun Appadurai calls a "neighborhood" and a "locality." Neighborhoods are "situated communities characterized by their actuality, whether spatial or virtual, and their potential for social reproduction."[30] In this case, the neighborhoods are made up of people linked by the worldview I have described. Locality is realized in the neighborhood as a "phenomenological property of social life, a structure of feeling that is produced by particular forms of intentional activity and that yields particular sorts of material effects."[31]

A few creole gardens have finally been recreated in Guadeloupe. The only dooryard garden is to be found in the "parc paysager" that I mentioned earlier. Yet its layout with neatly ordered beds and rows of palm trees, reminiscent of the alley leading to a plantation's great house, has nothing to do with any real creole dooryard garden. Four gardens altogether have been opened to the public as creole gardens. The first two have already disappeared. In 1989 and 1990, the former president of the INRA was able to create two creole gardens, which were later abandoned when he retired. Today, only the footprint of these gardens remains. They occupied two small strips containing a few square meters of land. Two creole gardens remain that can be visited today. The first is a pedagogical garden that was also conceived by the former president of the INRA. After his retirement, he became very involved in the Archipel des Sciences (Archipelago of the Sciences), which is part of a network of associations linked to the Musée scientifique et technique de la Villette (Science Museum at La Villette). Archipel des Sciences promotes public interest in the sciences. Gardens are considered emblems of local naturalist lore and places where scientific agricultural experiments can take place to increase or improve economic production. Through exhibitions, conferences, and contests of gardens laid out by children and their schools, the association promotes the knowledge of gardens. The absence of a house and the presence of pathways, necessary for walking in the gardens, make this garden space quite different from a dooryard garden. It presents to the public the diversity of plants with different economic functions, characteristic of the horticultural technique used in Guadeloupean gardens. This layout was adopted to replace a former attempt at creating a creole garden made up of beds, as in the case of the Parc paysager, which illustrated the difficulty in a neocolonial situation of thinking of creole gardens as different from French continental gardens. The second garden opened to the public as a creole garden was created between 1989 and 1990 by a Guadeloupean who had returned there from France. He presents the garden as a "page of culture." Walking in this garden, one discovers Guadeloupean vegetation as well as exhibits on the preparation of cassava bread, the butchering of a pig, and the preparation of herbal teas. This garden with its pathways and its displays gives

---

[29] For a discussion of the economic importance of gardens under slavery both in the Caribbean and the U.S. see I. Berlin and P. D. Morgan, *The Slaves' Economy: Independent Production by Slaves in the Americas* (London: Frank Cass, 1991); idem, *Cultivation and Culture: Labor and the Shaping of Slave Life in the Americas* (Charlottesville, Va.: University Press of Virginia, 1993); L. Degras, "Du fouet, des lianes, des liens," *Dérades* 7 (2001): 41–48; S. W. Mintz and D. Hall, "The Origins of the Jamaican Internal Marketing System," in *Papers in Caribbean Anthropology*, comp. S. W. Mintz. Yale University Publications in Anthropology 57 (New Haven, Conn.: Yale University, Dept. of Anthropology, 1960), 3–26.

[30] A. Appadurai, *Modernity at Large* (London–Minneapolis: Minnesota University Press, 1996) 179.

[31] Ibid., 182.

visitors a sense of an older way of life. Yet, it is an interpretive center, not a living garden. The conception of gardens as conservatories of traditional knowledge, or as places that display local techniques and scientific knowledge used for the exploitation of the environment, actually misses the nature of the local knowledge that is embedded in dooryard gardens. To refer again to Appadurai: "Local knowledge is substantially about producing reliably local neighborhoods within which such subjects can be recognized and organized."[32] Because the garden is a place of personal embodiment and social interaction, no institutional garden can be created that will refer to a creole worldview. Nobody would consider building a place that echoes his personal and family identity within an institutional setting. The garden is so much a place, not a mere space, that it cannot be conceived of without reference to a house, to the people who live in it, to their ancestors, and to the spirits of their dead.

[32] Ibid., 181.

Performance and Appropriation: Profane Rituals in Gardens and Landscapes

Performance and Appropriation: Profane Rituals in Gardens and Landscapes

Performance and Appropriation: Profane Rituals in Gardens and Landscapes

Performance and Appropriation: Profane Rituals in Gardens and Landscapes

Performing Hybridity: Wedding Rituals at Japanese-Style Gardens in Southern California

Kendall H. Brown

In 2002, roughly 220 couples said their vows in six public Japanese-style gardens in Southern California. When adding three restaurants and hotels that host weddings in their Japanese-style gardens, the number nearly doubled to about four hundred.[1] Although a small percentage of the total weddings held annually in the region, this figure represents an exponential increase in weddings in Japanese-style gardens relative to a decade earlier. For example, at the Earl Burns Miller Japanese Garden on the campus of California State University, Long Beach, weddings were so rare as to be uncounted in the early 1980s, by 1992 they had risen to 60, and in 2000 they reached 130 (Fig. 1).

The florescence of weddings at Japanese-style gardens has multiple roots. For garden administrators, it signals the importance of raising revenue as well as a shift in attitudes about gardens as social spaces. For brides and grooms, it is part of a trend for weddings outside of churches in general and outdoors, in particular.[2] One popular wedding location guide, itself a reflection of and a spur to this change, lists 78 garden venues among its 210 Southern California wedding sites.[3] In the age of Martha Stewart, people of all socioeconomic groups easily visualize social functions in gardens and elegant outdoor weddings are no longer reserved for the social élite. Statistics from the Condé Nast Bridal Group indicate that people marry later, plan their weddings more carefully, and spend

1. *Promotional photo used by the Earl Burns Miller Japanese Garden to advertise weddings (courtesy of California State University, Long Beach)*

---

[1] Many gardens do not keep annual records of weddings. Thus, some of these figures are approximations based on estimates by event coordinators. The term "Japanese-style garden" designates gardens outside Japan meant to replicate or approximate pre-modern gardens in Japan. For an extended discussion, see Kendall H. Brown, *Japanese-Style Gardens of the Pacific West Coast* (New York: Rizzoli International, 1999).

[2] The trend toward garden weddings is seen in the recent decision of the Huntington Gardens in San Marino, California, to allow wedding photographs. The Huntington is currently debating the suitability of weddings, a germane issue given their construction of a lavish "classical Chinese garden" designed in part to host social events. The other Chinese-style garden in Southern California is the courtyard garden at the Pacific Asia Museum in Pasadena that hosted sixteen weddings in 2002. Weddings comprise 44 percent of the museum's rental events but 60 percent of total event revenue. At the Miller Garden, in 2003, site fees were $1,100 for two hours (wedding only), $1,700 for three hours (reception only), and $2,100 for four hours (wedding and reception). The bargain-priced Tillman garden charged $500 for three hours (weddings only) and $750 for six hours (wedding and reception).

[3] Lynn Broadwell, *Here Comes the Guide* (Berkeley: Hopscotch Press, 2002; 7th edition); also available at <http://www.herecomestheguide.com> (accessed 13 January 2006).

more on them.[4] Increasingly, location is critical as couples stage weddings as their first and greatest opportunity to demonstrate their own style, heritage, values, and experience. Although "destination weddings" to exotic locales rose with the economy in the 1990s then dropped precipitously, ceremonies at unusual sites have continued to increase as couples seek to "personalize" their wedding.[5] The rise of Japanese garden weddings belongs to this larger tendency but is also explained by specific features of the gardens themselves.

Practice, Authenticity, and Japanese Gardens

The exploration of weddings in Japanese-style gardens demonstrates how gardens impact social practice by detailing ways in which they inspire human action. Conversely, it illustrates some means by which garden users, the wedding clients, produce new meanings in these gardens through responses not entirely dependent on the gardens themselves. More dramatically, because most weddings discount the Japanese character of these gardens or leaven them with other cultural attributes, and because premodern gardens in Japan were not used for nuptials, these ritual practices indicate—and themselves are key actors in—an ontological shift whereby these places change from being "Japanese gardens" outside Japan to being American gardens in Japanese styles. The practices enacted in these gardens make them imperfect as Japanese gardens but help redefine them as a type of American garden marked by intense cultural hybridity.

This functional breach between premodern gardens in Japan and modern Japanese-style gardens has been noted with horror by "purists," who hold that gardens in Japan and America should share identical aesthetic values and spiritual content. The conventional sentiment, "A Japanese garden is an aesthetic place, a place to re-attune oneself with the natural world, a place to reinvigorate one's spirit," seeks to deny all social function in Japanese-style gardens in order to restore them to the pure state imputed to premodern gardens in Japan.[6] Widely held by the public and generations of garden historians, this idea erases the history of use. As demonstrated in recent scholarship, however, many gardens in Japan were deployed for a range of social activities.[7] Ironically, social rituals in contemporary Japanese-style gardens link them to premodern Japanese gardens. Despite this connection, the contradiction remains that most persons who marry in Japanese-style gardens do so under the impression that they are "authentic" Japanese gardens—places of abiding tranquillity and spiritual rejuvenation. Paradoxically, the perception of Japanese gardens as spaces of serenity, beauty, and order encourages people to seek them out for ceremonies that both build upon those ideas and ultimately subvert them. Japanese-style gardens engender multiple levels of experience and "forms of engagement," some enhancing the dominant perceptions and rhetoric of the gardens, others contradicting them.

That wedding rituals controvert the orthodox claims made about Japanese-style gardens parallels a larger set of contradictions and tensions in contemporary nuptials. Weddings are about personal feelings and private love but they are also public performances in which guests serve as an audience. In Jaclyn Geller's analysis,

[4] "Brides Pay Princely Sum to Be Cinderellas," *Los Angeles Times*, 2 October 2002, A: 1.
[5] Interview with Gerard J. Monaghan, President of the Association of Bridal Consultants, in Jaclyn Geller, *Here Comes the Bride: Women, Weddings and the Marriage Mystique* (New York–London: Four Walls Eight Windows, 2001), 259.
[6] John Hall in "Viewpoints: Commercialism in Japanese Gardens" in *Journal of Japanese Gardening* 30 (November/December 2002), 6. The persistent idea that Japanese-style gardens are virtually identical to Japanese gardens is witnessed in such articles as Brenda Rees, "Where Peace Meets Quiet" *Los Angeles Times*, 29 June 2000, Calendar: 6.
[7] See Wybe Kuitert, *Themes in the History of Japanese Garden Art* (Honolulu: University of Hawai'i Press, 2002) and the papers "Mythic and Sacred Gardens in Medieval Japan: Mediating the Past in the Saihōji and Rokuonji Gardens" by Richard Stanley-Baker and "Religious and Lay Rituals in Japanese Gardens during the Heian Period (784–1185)" by Michel Vieillard-Baron, delivered at Dumbarton Oaks's Garden and Landscape Studies Symposium, 2002. For published versions of these papers, see *Sacred Gardens and Landscapes: Ritual and Agency*, ed. Michel Conan. Dumbarton Oaks Colloquium on the History of Landscape Architecture XXVI (Washington, D.C.: Spacemaker Press, 2006).

> . . . the contemporary wedding ceremony, with its departures from traditions,
> its ad hoc additions and subtractions, its quirky combinations of incompatible
> relations and materials, and its by now de riguer personal flourishes, embodies
> the values of our age. Its affirms the conjugal couple as the ordering principal of
> society and extols romantic love above all other forms of attachment while
> advertising its principals' uniqueness as individuals. It also champions such
> psychological ideals as self-awareness, mutual support, commitment,
> communication, and respect for each other's space.[8]

For Geller, the "vaguely humanistic" and putatively individualistic qualities implied by the "ethnic flourishes and personal statements" in contemporary weddings should not be read as fundamental innovations or genuine heterodoxy. Rather, many couples employ the wedding as a means of claiming emotional sensitivity and spirituality, of mythologizing their love, and of concealing economic and social motivations for their union by highlighting the ostensible spontaneity of their love through recourse to natural symbols.[9]

Whereas Geller's critique applies to varying degrees, interviews with couples who married in Japanese-style gardens reveal levels of sincerity and sophistication sharply at odds with standard academic assumptions.[10] Thus, this discussion of why couples choose to marry in Japanese-style gardens and how gardens function in those ceremonies does not share Geller's analysis of weddings as manifestations of sexism, capitalism, and other familiar targets. Instead, this study explores how weddings help contour Japanese-style gardens as dynamic social spaces. It exemplifies Henri Lefebvre's idea that "Space is permeated with social relations; it is not only supported by social relations but is also producing and produced by social relations."[11]

One goal of recent urban landscape studies has been to "reclaim" mundane places—ethnic neighborhoods, relocation camps, workers' gardens—as part of the history of those social groups neglected in orthodox accounts of grand structures built by and for élite males. Studies of "counterspaces"—environments built or used in opposition to dominant sociopolitical structures, or to provide relief from urban placelessness—have dramatically expanded the study of urban landscape as public history.[12] Although many scholars have examined the social reproduction of ethnicity and gender through the rehearsal of collective pasts, this essay aims to complicate ideas of "place-bound identities" and univocally ethnic public spaces. It seeks to discover how weddings transform Japanese-style gardens into multi- or transethnic spaces in which both females and males participate.[13] Because roughly half of the couples who marry in Japanese-style gardens are of different ethnicities or religions,

[8] Geller, *Here Comes the Bride*, 256.

[9] Ibid., 269–74.

[10] Interviews were held with fourteen couples who married in Japanese-style gardens in Southern California between 1998 and 2002. Eleven of the couples wed at the Earl Burns Miller Japanese Garden. The couples ranged in age from their mid-twenties to their mid-forties, and in education from those with some college work to several Ph.D.s. About half had at least one member with a graduate degree. A few couples, brides in particular, clearly romanticized their wedding experience and spoke of its symbolic meanings only after some prompting. Others, notably the academics, were analytical and very much aware of the implications of their wedding locale. One theoretically oriented historian of modern art, married to a professor of philosophy, discussed her wedding in terms of "appropriation" and "performance." Another bride and groom, both of whom teach Japanese art history at top Ivy League universities, admitted the pleasure of their garden wedding but declined to have their names used. The author's own marriage took place at the Higashiyama Ward Office in Kyoto.

[11] Henri Lefebvre, *The Production of Space*, trans. Donald Nicholson-Smith (London: Blackwell, 1991), 286.

[12] See, for example, Dolores Hayden, *The Power of Place: Urban Landscape as Public History* (Cambridge, Mass–London: MIT Press, 1995) in which the author analyzes urban spaces associated with African Americans, Japanese Americans, Latinas, and workers. For relocation camp garden studies, see Kenneth Helphand, "Defiant Gardens," *Journal of Garden History* 17, no. 2 (April–June, 1997), 101–21.

[13] Although most respondents stated that bride and groom were equally responsible for choosing the wedding locale, all nine event coordinators interviewed held that the decision on where to marry, and how to arrange the ceremony, resides primarily with the bride. Because all of the event coordinators are female, it can be argued that weddings are feminine social events. Because Japanese and Japanese-style gardens have long been gendered as feminine, the contemporary wedding can be seen as a further manifestation of this gendered history. See Kendall H. Brown, "The Japanese-style Garden at Hillwood and Its Context" in *Antiques* CLXIII, no. 3 (March 2003), 140–45.

this study transcends the focus on group cultural identity by examining how people of different ethnicities, religions, and cultural traditions deploy the same spaces. Instead of rehearsing collective ethnic pasts, most weddings in Japanese-style gardens are performances of the particular identity of the bride and groom as individuals and as a couple, often as based on nuanced ideas of cultural hybridity (Fig. 2).

Objects and Methods of Study

The focus here is on Japanese-style gardens in Southern California, the region arguably at the forefront of contemporary nuptials. Combined with weather that smiles on outdoor events, an ethnically diverse

2. *A mariachi band poses with a wedding couple in the Miller Garden (photo: courtesy of the Earl Burns Miller Japanese Garden)*

population, the status of many residents as recent transplants or immigrants, the lack of a deeply rooted indigenous culture and a prevailing sentiment that possibility is more powerful than precedent, all make Southern California a breeding ground for cultural innovation and the epicenter of Japanese garden weddings.[14] Unconventional weddings in the United States date from the 1920s, but the first permanent fantasy matrimonial locale was likely Forest Lawn Memorial Park in Glendale, California, where in the early 1920s mortuary industry visionary Hubert Eaton built the Wee Kirk O the Heather for funerals and weddings.[15] Disneyland, which, on its opening in 1954, supplanted Forest Lawn as the area's premier tourist attraction and cultural simulacrum par excellence, joined the growing list of wedding locales in May 2001 by offering "fairytale weddings" near Sleeping Beauty's Castle in Fantasyland.

Among Japanese-style gardens in Southern California that host weddings,[16] the Earl Burns Miller Japanese Garden is the most popular and, arguably, the most compelling in the quality of those events.[17] Completed in 1981, it was a gift to the

[14] Weddings are held at Japanese-style gardens in cities across North America—San Antonio, Nashville, Brooklyn, Montreal, Edmonton—and internationally from New Zealand to Germany. Although increasing in popularity globally, the Japanese-style garden wedding is most common in California.

[15] These first heterodox weddings, where couples married on water skis, in cemeteries, or nude at the Garden of Eden at Chicago's Century of Progress Exposition in 1933, are recounted in Marcia Seligson, *The Eternal Bliss Machine: America's Way of Wedding* (New York: William Morrow, 1973), 205–10. The function of Wee Kirk O the Heather for weddings and betrothals is described in Evelyn Waugh, *The Loved One* (New York: Little, Brown and Co., 1948), 123–25.

[16] The five other civic Japanese-style gardens that host weddings are the Japanese Garden at the Donald Tillman Water Reclamation Plant in Van Nuys, the James Irvine Garden at the Japanese American Community and Cultural Center in downtown Los Angeles, Descanso Gardens in La Cañada-Flintridge, the Japanese Garden at the Torrance Cultural Arts Center, and the Japanese Friendship Garden at Balboa Park in San Diego. The three Japanese-style gardens at commercial venues are Yamashiro Restaurant in Hollywood, the New Otani Hotel in Los Angeles's Little Tokyo district, and the Karl Strauss Restaurant at the San Diego Tech Center near La Jolla. The Tillman garden opened in 1984 at a large municipal sewage treatment facility and, after holding its first wedding in 1984 for the daughter of a local official, now hosts as many as forty nuptials per year. The Japanese Garden at Descanso was added to the botanical garden in 1967, but because of its small size hosts only a few intimate weddings each year. The James Irvine Garden was constructed in 1979 and, after a change of management in 2001, now allows small weddings. The garden in Torrance dates from 1991 and saw a significant rise in weddings to about twenty a year beginning in 1997. The Friendship Garden in San Diego was originally built in 1990, enlarged in 1999, and although it only started to host weddings in 2001, it had nearly thirty in 2002. The Hanna Carter Garden at UCLA was open for events of forty persons and fewer until the summer of 2002, but problems with parking and space in the garden have made weddings there rare. Among commercial venues, Yamashiro was built in 1914 as a residence, antique shop, and garden, and has hosted events soon after becoming a restaurant in the 1970s, and now receives about sixty weddings annually in its courtyard garden. The half-acre rooftop garden at the New Otani Hotel was built in 1977 and weddings there have gradually increased in number each year since, with about seventy held in 2002. The garden at the San Diego Tech Center business park dates from 1982, but weddings started in earnest only after the Karl Strauss Brewery began operating the restaurant in 1998. These gardens, except for Descanso, Torrance, and the New Otani, are discussed in Brown, *Japanese-Style Gardens of the Pacific West Coast*.

[17] The Miller Garden is unique because it can host both the ceremony and reception in the garden. It should be noted that the author's status as a faculty member at the university facilitated access to garden personnel and documents.

university from Lorraine Miller Collins in memory of her late husband. Collins selected university landscape architect Edward R. Lovell to design the garden despite his lack of experience with Japanese gardens (Fig. 3). Problems with Lovell's original plan along with the administration's failure to involve the campus's Asian and Asian-American communities led to protests. To resolve the political tempest and improve the garden aesthetically, the local Japanese garden specialist Koichi Kawana was hired to change some stones and relocate garden ornaments.[18] Although far from the most authenticate or most beautiful Japanese-style garden in the region, the Miller Garden has evolved into a successful social space for university luncheons,

3. *Official postcard for California State University, Long Beach, showing the Miller Garden (courtesy of Rockwell Designs)*

educational programs, and dozens of fund-raising cultural and horticultural events in addition to the ubiquitous weddings.

Because our goal is the elucidation of how wedding rituals shape Japanese-style gardens and are shaped by them, this study adapts the anthropological analysis of weddings as a ceremony marking a social transition. As first elucidated by Arnold van Gennep, the wedding, like other "rites of passage," is marked by the symbolic phases of separation, margin or threshold, and reaggregation.[19] Particularly resonant are the elaborations on these stages by Victor Turner and his followers that show how the physical forms of rituals, especially in the middle stage of margin or liminality, symbolize movement through social structure. However, in contrast to Turner's writings, which often present rituals in terms of preexisting forms and meanings, this analysis dilates on the agents that produce these rituals: the gardens (in their physical features and in their rhetoric as presented by garden staff and texts) and the ritual actors (including the wedding couples and the garden's event coordinators). In the words of one coordinator, "The wedding is the play, the bride and groom are the stars, and the coordinator is the director."[20]

At the Miller Garden, the dramatic rise in weddings and sophisticated performative use of the space stem from the vision of Jeanette Schelin. Presently Director of the Miller Garden, Schelin developed it as a wedding venue when she was the event coordinator from 1993 to 1999. An architecture student then traffic planner and interior designer, Schelin claims a "deep connection" with the Miller Garden as an outlet for her creative, entrepreneurial, and spiritual interests. For weddings, Schelin brought to bear her work experience, elements of her Bahai faith, and a fascination with the spatial applications of social psychology. Most relevant was the idea that thoughtful movement through space can lead us to "live wholly in the moment."[21] In designing garden weddings, Schelin applied the ideas of "flow" and "quality experience" formulated by the psychologist Mihaly Csikszentmihalyi.

Csikszentmihalyi defines "flow" as occurring where action and awareness merge in a physical and mental state brought on by the focus of attention within a limited field of sensory stimuli in a circumscribed space, where the performer is in control

[18] The controversy is recounted in Brown, *Japanese-Style Gardens of the Pacific West Coast*, 131–33.

[19] Arnold van Gennep, *Rites of Passage*, trans. Monika Vizedom and Gabrielle Caffee (Chicago: University of Chicago Press, 1960), 116–30.

[20] Interview with Lynette Gahafer, event coordinator at the Earl Burns Miller Japanese Garden, 11 December 2002.

[21] Interview with Jeanette Schelin, 31 January 2003. Schelin also was impressed by Abraham Maslow's ideas of self-actualization through types of mindful physical action, seeing the Miller Garden as a place that people seek out in order to fulfill the desires to "belong" and "share," important categories in Maslow's "hierarchy of needs."

of action and environment, and when the clearly understood demands for action are circumscribed by formal rules. Flow also usually depends on challenges, and the investment of psychic energy. The result of flow is a deep sense of enjoyment or "optimal experience" that creates a landmark memory on which later actions and understandings are structured. The opposite of the "anomie and alienation" that result in "psychic entropy," every flow activity engenders a "sense of discovery" that transports people into a new reality. Because flow is based both on the individual's sense of differentiation from, and integration into, his environment, it adds complexity to his life and stimulates personal growth. More than just a type of hermetic individual experience, flow activities are freely chosen in regard to what is most meaningful, and are a means by which a society can define or shape itself.[22]

Turner found productive links between "flow" and his own notion of communitas as an aspect of liminality, calling communitas "a sort of shared flow." Turner disputed the necessity of formal rules and "circumscription in space and time as preconditions," arguing that flow and the communitas found in liminality may exist in unstructured conditions, but noted that such "framing of sociological processes" may amplify or highlight flow and that "group experience may lead to the selection of certain symbols as the best flow-elicitors." He hypothesized that these would likely be "liminal or liminoid symbols or symbolic actions" associated with those ritual processes that indicate shared human experiences or open up those human relationships, which themselves are beginnings, transitions, and rites of passage.[23] Csikszentmihalyi, too, acknowledged this connection, paralleling his notion of flow in groups engaged in one activity to Turner's liminality.[24]

For Csikszentmihalyi, the necessity of formal structures is essentially moot as his goal is not establishing the parameters of flow but, rather, identifying processes by which it may be achieved. Given Schelin's belief that Csikszentmihalyi's ideas are critical to social evolution as people search for meaning in their lives, she sought to merge his ideas of the "body in flow" with the spatial and spiritual dimensions of the Miller Garden in her wedding choreography there. By underscoring meaningful physical movements as well as visual and aural stimulation, her stated aim was to make the nuptial experience itself a critical factor in the lives of the matrimonial couple and their guests, even as she simultaneously raised funds and exposed the Miller Garden to a large number of potential supporters. In that Csikszentmihalyi holds that the greatest creativity occurs in places where a variety of traditions and perspectives overlap, then a Japanese-style garden in an ethnically diverse area provides an ideal setting for adapting the orthodox wedding ritual.

Diversity: Who Marries in Japanese-style Gardens

Weddings at Japanese-style gardens are transformed by proactive coordinators like Schelin but are created by the brides and grooms who choose to marry there, then arrange their ceremony in accordance with the spatial and formal requirements of each garden. Based on the recollections of the coordinators who oversaw the roughly one thousand weddings at the Miller Garden from 1992 to 2001, and data garnered from a questionnaire sent to couples who married there in 2002, the great majority of wedding clients are college-educated professionals between twenty-five and thirty-five, middle- or upper-middle class, marrying for the first time, and living within twenty miles of the garden. About one quarter had been students at the university or were employed there. Roughly half were Protestant, one quarter Catholic, and the remaining one quarter Jewish, Buddhist, or having no religion. More important, twenty-seven percent of the couples came from different religions, and over

[22] For definitions, applications, and implications of flow, see Mihaly Csikszentmihalyi, *Beyond Boredom and Anxiety: The Experience of Play in Work and Games* (San Francisco: Jossey-Bass, 1975); idem, "The Flow Experience and its Significance for Human Psychology," in Mihaly Csikszentmihalyi and Isabella Csikszentmihalyi, eds., *Optimal Experience: Psychological Studies of Flow in Consciousness* (New York: Cambridge University Press 1988); Mihaly Csikszentmihalyi, *Flow: The Psychology of Optimal Experience* (New York: Harper and Row, 1990); and idem, *Creativity: Flow and the Psychology of Discovery and Invention* (New York: Harper Collins, 1996).

[23] Victor Turner, "Variations on a Theme of Liminality" in *Secular Ritual*, ed. Sally F. Moore and Barbara G. Myerhoff (Amsterdam: Van Gorcum, 1977), 51–52.

[24] He also compares it to Emil Durkheim's idea of "collective effervescence." Csikszentmihalyi, *Flow,* 110 and 262, n. 110.

half described themselves as only loosely affiliated with a church yet also self-identified as moderately or very spiritual. The hybrid religious values of many young couples and their affinity for locales like Japanese-style gardens is demonstrated by how many clients incorporated aspects of their own spiritual beliefs into their weddings at the Miller Garden. For example, a Mexican-American couple, who merged their Catholicism with their indigenous heritage, began their ceremony by having a dancer—channeling the Aztec god Quetzalcoatl—bless the site by circumambulating the garden, reaching into the pond, then facing the sun (Fig. 4).

4. *Dancer channeling the spirit of Aztec god Quetzalcoatl blesses the Miller Garden before a wedding (photo: courtesy of the Earl Burns Miller Japanese Garden)*

Bridal couples come from every major ethnic group in Southern California: Anglo, Japanese, Chinese, Korean, Thai, Cambodian, Vietnamese, Indian, Hawaiian, Filipino, Mexican, Central and South American, Armenian, Russian, Native American, and African American. Despite the garden's name and popular status as "Japanese," Japanese and Japanese-Americans marry there only slightly more often than do other Asians. Of these couples, only a few selected the garden specifically for its Japanese identity.[25] Roughly one third of the couples were Asian or had one Asian partner, forty-three percent were of different ethnicities (Fig. 5), and fourteen percent were of the same ethnicity but different religions. These statistics parallel coordinators' reports that about half the couples who marry in Japanese-style gardens are "transcultural."[26] Given most couples' cultural diversity, it follows that they seek a wedding locale perceived as culturally neutral yet resonant, a space in which they can separate themselves from the values implied by a dominant culture or the conflict imposed by different heritages in order to connect with greater, "universal" values.

[25] There are, of course, exceptions. For one Caucasian bride, who had met her Japanese fiancé in Tokyo, the Miller Garden was a way to make the groom and his family comfortable and to display to them the cultural sophistication of America and her alma mater. The garden also was a positive context in which to introduce her husband to her family and a means of connecting symbolically to her own experience in Japan. A striking example of self-identity and fantasy fulfillment is found in the case of a half-Japanese woman in rural Redding, California, who shared her wedding with guests as well as visitors to her Web site: <http://scarlettrose.com/wedding.html> (accessed 26 January 2006). To create a Japanese-theme wedding in a town without a Japanese-style garden, she had a *torii* gate constructed in the local park where the ceremony was held, dressed the entire bridal party in Japanese clothing, had the reception site (the senior citizen's hall) decorated with bonsai, and commissioned a two-layer, V-shaped cake in the form of a "Japanese tea garden," complete with raked sand, rocks, curved bridge (surmounted by dolls representing the bride and groom), wisteria-covered pavilion, lantern, and cranes.

[26] Of the one hundred questionnaires distributed, fifty-six were returned. Among the 120 couples who married at the garden in 2002 (where records list only the bride's name), nine brides had Japanese surnames, whereas nineteen had other Asian surnames. Fourteen percent of the questionnaire respondents were from couples with an Asian groom or Caucasian or Latina bride. The demographics of the Miller Garden match event coordinators' estimates for the San Diego Friendship Garden and Yamashiro, but there is some regional variation at other gardens. At the Tillman Garden, in a working-class section of the San Fernando Valley, it is estimated that about one-third of the couples come from different religious or ethnic backgrounds. These figures parallel government statistics that reveal a marked rise in interracial marriages. The 2002 Current Population Survey by the U.S. Census Bureau shows that 2.9 percent of the nation's U.S.-born married couples are interracial, compared to 1.8 percent in 1990 and 1.3 percent in 1980. According to the 2000 U.S. Census, in Los Angeles the percentage was nearly triple the national average. Although there are no statistics for interracial marriages where one or both partners were born outside the U.S., certainly when these couples are figured in the percentage of interracial couples is much higher in urban areas. The trend will surely continue as the polling by the Pew Research Center in Washington indicates that 91 percent of so-called Generation Y respondents approved of interracial relationships compared to 77 percent of baby boomers and 49 percent of the World War II generation. Susan Carpenter, "A Cultural Exchange of Vows," *Los Angeles Times*, Calendar Weekend, 23 June 2005, 31–33.

5. *One of the many interracial couples who marry at the Miller Garden (photo: courtesy of the Earl Burns Miller Japanese Garden)*

Separation: The Choice to Marry in a Japanese-style Garden

In van Gennep's formulation, the initial step in the ritual process is separation—real and symbolic behavior that detaches the participants from their previous social status. For the greatest impact, rituals should occur apart from normal places of social interaction. For couples breaking with tradition by marrying outside a church, the appeal of any garden stems from their physical and cultural separation from a normative indoor ceremony and associated ideas of conformity.[27] For Japanese-style gardens, this notion is intensified by the exoticism of their national origin and design—an ostensible singularity emphasized in garden rhetoric. The Miller Garden's wedding information sheet proclaims, "Splashing waterfalls, graceful bridges and a secluded tea house set the stage for a truly unique and memorable event."[28] According to staff at various Japanese-style gardens, most clients "self-select" these gardens because they parallel their own values or desired self-image. Most of the couples interviewed chose the Miller Garden because it was "unique," then splintered the notion of uniqueness into four factors, which demonstrate the precise ways in which the garden serves as a point of disconnection from normative social experience.

Almost all couples interviewed selected the Miller Garden largely because it was a "neutral" ground. For couples from different religions or where at least one person is estranged from their religion, church weddings are inherently problematic. The Miller Garden's Japanese identity usually removes it from the specific culture of either partner. Moreover, in that a wedding is generally conceived as a semi-sacred rite where couples are brought together "before God," or is considered at least vaguely spiritual, Japanese gardens are ideally suited because they are viewed as spiritual places but without specific religious affiliation. In the words of a Jewish bride with a Protestant spouse, both of whom are "spiritual but without the trappings of conventional religion," the Miller Garden "is a spiritual, sacred, holy place; it is an Eden spiritually but is not connected to any particular religion. It is inviting, not excluding."[29] In this way the specific Japanese identity of the garden is negatively valent: appealing for what it is not.[30]

[27] Of couples surveyed and interviewed, only a few considered churches, and most dismissed restaurants and hotels as prosaic. Most, however, strongly considered other gardens or "cultural places," including museums, libraries, and historic buildings.

[28] Similar phrases are found in the wedding literature of other Japanese-style gardens. A brochure for Yamashiro entitled "The Perfect Wedding" begins, "We want to help make your wedding day special in every way—uniquely yours." The San Diego Friendship Garden events Web page calls the garden "a uniquely beautiful setting." By contrast, of the nine (non-Japanese) garden locations advertised in *WedMagazine* (Late Fall 2002), only one uses the word unique, whereas seven deploy "elegant," and six "beautiful."

[29] Interviews with Rebecca Behar Johnson, 17 January 2003 and 21 January 2003. The Johnsons had originally wanted to marry in a natural setting but were "persuaded" by her parents to hold the ceremony in a banquet hall. Thus, when they celebrated their tenth anniversary with a renewal of vows, they chose the Miller Garden, where both had served as volunteers and had been Board members. Through her docent training, Behar Johnson was aware of the specific Shinto and Buddhist associations of some of the garden's design features and statuary yet still felt the Miller Garden was a spiritually neutral locale. This sentiment was directly expressed in their ceremony where the Reverend Janet Hanstead Meadors began the "Welcome" by stating, "This is a special place to Michael and Rebecca, a sacred place, a place of beauty and contemplation. For the two of them, being outside, somewhere open and garden, is one of the most natural doorways to experiencing spirituality."

[30] Of the six reasons listed on the questionnaire for marrying in the Miller Garden, "culturally appropriate" received the lowest score, averaging a response of "slightly important" and, for fully half the couples, it was rated as having "no importance."

Stated positively, Japanese-style gardens are resonant and welcoming to people of every culture, examples of Lefebvre's "counterspaces" or Turner's sites of "ritual antistructure." For many Americans, gardens in Japanese styles are not merely spiritual, they are considered the most aesthetically advanced form of garden art. As such, they are environments antithetical to mundane urban reality. In contrast to the chaos, ugliness, or mere banality of our cities, Japanese gardens have implicit aesthetic perfection and deep symbolism that suggest that being in them is a transcendent experience. The Miller Garden's pamphlet, for example, concludes, "We hope that the beauty and serenity of this oasis continue with you throughout your day."

Premodern Japanese gardens and modern Japanese-style ones are associated with the timelessness construed as a basic component of "Oriental" culture. The most frequent epithet for Japanese gardens is "traditional," whereas Chinese gardens are "classical." Because Japanese gardens are linked to the past, even the young Miller Garden is seen as a portal to another place and time. However, because of the recent fascination for Asian traditions like *feng shui*, Japanese-style gardens are seen as vital, relevant, and accessible. These qualities help account for the unique yet universal appeal of Japanese-style gardens as wedding locales. For Asians, and couples with one Asian partner, these attributes link them personally to Japanese-style gardens even as they welcome non-Asian guests.[31]

If the implicit cultural appeal of Japanese-style gardens depends on their resonant neutrality or openness, their explicit material appeal derives from their physical closure. Most Miller Garden clients are sold the moment they see it—what Schelin calls the "wow factor." The Miller Garden's visceral appeal begins with its disconnection from its environs. Set at the edge of a large campus surrounded by middle-class neighborhoods, the garden is near a two-story dormitory complex and parking lots but separated from them by a drainage canal and access road. Walled and surrounded by mature trees, it is entered by passing through the metal "main gate," turning left into a formal entry area, then turning right through the "Japanese gate" (Fig. 6). In the garden proper, an earthen berm, thick foliage, and absence of adjacent tall buildings serve to shut out the external world.

Because of the Miller Garden's intimate size, 1.3 acres, and arrangement around a central pond, nearly the entire space can be seen from most points in it (Fig. 7). The Moon Bridge, Zigzag Bridge, and Viewing Platform pull the eye around through space. Yet there are a few discrete areas, the teahouse on a hillock at the north end and the "dry garden" screened off by a living fence of podocarpus, that are seen only when entered. The Miller Garden's mix of modest complexity with intimacy in an isolated setting produces rapture in many clients. In one bride's words, the garden evokes "a strong emotion . . . when you are there, the outside world doesn't matter. You're surrounded by beauty, you feel protected. In the garden you are engulfed." Another bride declared that the garden "perfectly served the purpose" of creating a special ambiance because the

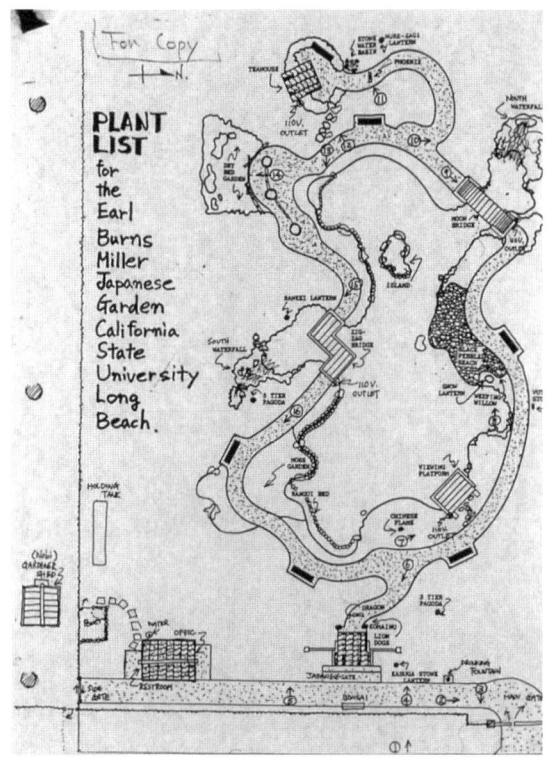

6. *Map of the Miller Garden used for docent training, showing the main entrance (lower right), entry courtyard (bottom), office (lower left), pond with Viewing Platform, Moon Bridge, and Zig-Zag Bridge (center), and teahouse (top center) (courtesy of the Earl Burns Miller Japanese Garden)*

---

[31] For a Protestant Korean-American bride from Southern California marrying a Catholic Polish-American from Chicago, the Miller Garden served as a "middle ground," expressing her long-suppressed "Asian-ness" and sharing something positive with her in-laws who, as "outdoors people," were presumed to like Japanese gardens.

7. *The Moon Bridge seen from the Zig-Zag Bridge (photo by Melba Levick, courtesy of Rizzoli International Publications, Inc.)*

physical disconnection allowed participants and guests to "tune out their mundane thoughts."[32]

Appropriating Liminality: The Garden as a Place Apart

Secluded Japanese-style gardens create a special environment different from that of similarly separated and enclosed gardens without a cultural dimension. An advertisement for the restaurant Yamashiro, which hosts weddings in its courtyard garden, encapsulates this critical physical and cultural dislocation in its tag line, "minutes away, yet worlds apart."[33] These gardens offer not just an isolated setting but also a rich milieu for weddings. Common perceptions of the physical structure of the garden may be divided into two categories: the role played by the general ambiance in setting the mood for the wedding; and the specific symbolic function of garden elements in the wedding ritual. Because of the metaphoric role of gardens as a productive ambiance for weddings, it is worth reviewing some specific ways in which secular rituals work.

Sally Moore and Barbara Myerhoff discuss the creativity of secular ceremonies by underscoring their explicit and implicit purposes and symbols. They begin with Susanne Langer's idea that mental transformation occurs when symbol and object are experienced as an undifferentiated whole, and the important though unpredictable function of ritual in connecting, then transcending, the physical and the psychological in ways that texts typically cannot.[34] At times this transformative power of symbols allows the sense, however fleeting, of a deep understanding of the essential pattern of life. Moore and Myerhoff then underscore ritual's role in creating presence out of void, order out of chaos. They hypothesize that the greatest fear in approaching ritual performance is that its processes, its symbols and subterfuges, become apparent. Rituals thus seek to discourage inquiry by stating their meanings authoritatively as postulates yet cloaking them through symbolic appeal to the senses rather than discursive petition to the intellect. Fearing indeterminacy as well as transparency, rituals act as if their created forms are natural, organically woven from human experience and the physical world.[35] These qualities are central to the liminal aspect of ritual in which the ritual "passengers," the bride and groom in weddings, pass through an ambiguous realm that, for Turner, has few or none of the attributes of their former or future states. Although different in practice from most of the Ndembu rituals studied by Turner, Japanese-style garden nuptials share the qualities of giving mythic and symbolic attributes to

[32] This opinion was voiced by a well-educated and well-traveled woman who had studied Japanese gardens informally. In similar fashion, two M.F.A. students at the university who married in the Miller Garden chose it in part because it functioned physically as an "oasis" ("when you are there, you're only there and nowhere else") and metaphorically as a fantasy space suited to the performative nature of a wedding. As with the art historian bride and philosopher groom, their familiarity with postmodern discourse and even this author's seminar on Japanese-style gardens did not deny the garden's appeal as a "place apart."

[33] Yamashiro undescores the theme in its promotional pamphlet by rhapsodizing about the authenticity of this "magical Mountain Palace handcrafted almost a century ago as . . . an exact replica of a Japanese Palace from the hills near Kyoto," then highlighting the words "timeless," "beauty," "intimate," "rare," "experience," "delicacies," "elegant," and "mystical" to describe the experiences to be had there.

[34] Susanne K. Langer, *Philosophy in a New Key: A Study in the Symbolism of Reason, Rite, and Art* (Cambridge, Mass.: Harvard University Press, 1942), especially Chapter 2, "Symbolic Transformation."

[35] Sally Moore and Barbara Myerhoff, "Introduction: Secular Ritual: Forms and Meanings," in *Secular Ritual*, 13–18.

the ritual participants by blending structure and freedom, differentiation and equality, and temporal specificity with timelessness.

The dominant impression of otherness in the Miller Garden is also the product of its constructed feeling of naturalness—again a difference of degree relative to culturally nonspecific gardens. As is much remarked, most Japanese garden styles use great artifice to suggest nature in its most ideal or symbolic aspects.[36] For persons accustomed to the regimentation of urban and suburban landscapes, even a mediocre Japanese-style garden can seem like nature perfected. More critically, nature is linked to artlessness (naturalness). All couples interviewed expressed a desire to avoid the architectural environments, in which physical structure was associated with the hierarchy of churches or the commerciality of restaurants and hotels. Perhaps because love and matrimony are constructed and tenuous states, there is a desire to cast them as spontaneous and abiding by linking them to nature. Setting a wedding in a garden suggests that the union is neither a result of chance nor susceptible to rupture but grew organically and will endure. Nature is also a trope for humility and informality. Many interviewees stated that they chose the Miller Garden because its simplicity rejected the ostentation of most weddings. As an expression of nature, a Japanese garden is beautiful "just as it is." The ostensible informality of the garden can also be seen as an expression of the wedding couples' personalities. For grooms in particular, "natural" spaces are further associated with the

8. *Bride posing at the Miller Garden in a photo shown to prospective wedding clients (photo: courtesy of Sanderson Studios)*

lack of stress and thus are conducive to spontaneity, or its appearance. In contrast to the formality of European gardens or the generic naturalness of a park, the Miller Garden's asymmetry, waterfalls, and large pond, and variety of carefully pruned trees invest the space with hypernaturalness that heightens its symbolic content.

The naturalness attributed to the Miller Garden is similarly linked to serenity, where its organic orderliness is a break from suburban regimentation and confusion. In the section "How to Enjoy the Garden," the Miller Garden's pamphlet proclaims, "By design, a Japanese garden is a sanctuary for quiet reflection and contemplation. From the first impression to the last, the prevailing sense is one of peace and tranquillity." One bride found the garden's "harmony" an "antidote to the negative energy of the normal world" and a stimulus to the union represented by the wedding. For a hospice worker who renewed vows in the Miller Garden, its tranquility—where "speech is metaphoric, not literal"—paralleled the calm of her marriage. That serenity, combined with the garden's spiritual implications, formed a psychic space where the deeper reverberations of the ceremony were not only more evident at the time but in fact lingered even several years later.

A close relation to serenity is the sense of purity that similarly flows from the definition of Japanese-style gardens as nature perfected, and enhances the Miller Garden's ambiance as a deeply evocative wedding locale. One of the central tensions in the modern white wedding is that between the bride's ostensible chastity and her overt sensuality (Fig. 8). Even before the post–World War II fashion for décolleté bridal gowns and garter tosses, marriage ceremonies represented the joining together of man and woman in a socially sanctioned sexual unit with the goal of procreation. Yet every expression of sexuality in weddings is matched by its opposite. Purity, usually represented in weddings by flowers in addition to the white wedding dress, is

[36] See Kuitert, *Themes in the History of Japanese Landscape Art*; Lorraine Kuck, *The World of the Japanese Garden* (New York: Weatherhill, 1968); and the chapter on Japan in Elizabeth Barlow Rogers, *Landscape Design: A Cultural and Architectural History* (New York: Harry Abrams, 2001).

multiplied at the Miller Garden by the abundant plants, two waterfalls, and flowing water of the clear pond. According to one bride, the garden "radiated harmony and purity—it felt so clean . . . so organic." This purity may be linked to a kind of spiritual and social rebirth. In the renewal of vows ceremony cited above, the minister's "Welcome" associated the married couple and the Miller Garden with Adam and Eve in the garden of Eden. In the short speech, she twice used the words "renewal," "fresh," and "refresh." The imagery is appropriate because the event, she states, is about "rebirth," "reflection and transformation." All gardens engender these tropes, but because Japanese gardens are associated through design and discourse with spiritual purity,[37] the metaphor is more immediate and more potent in places like the Miller Garden.

Several brides spoke of the Miller Garden's beauty in terms of energy. In an age where *feng shui* has become a familiar concept, it is not unusual that some persons feel a similar geomantic power in Japanese-style gardens. A few couples mentioned that garden weddings in general created a charge by the contrast between the casualness of the space and the formality of the clothing. The design of Miller Garden generates its own kinds of energy. One bride found the garden "transcendent, full of flowing energy" manifest most evidently in the waterfall and koi fish. A Brazilian raised near the ocean and with both Catholic and African rituals, she felt that the Miller Garden's "mellow energy" connected to her own life experience and provided her guests with a place where they could breath in "spiritual energy." When the issue was raised in interviews, most couples concurred with Schelin's idea, derived from Csikszentmihalyi, that, more than ambiance this fluid energy was a dynamic force impelling the transformation that is a wedding's essence. The likelihood that respondents were led to these ideas is mitigated by the fact that when similarly asked about the role of the Miller's Garden's "Japanese" identity, most flatly rejected or minimized its relevance.

Performing Liminality: Wedding Ceremonies in the Miller Garden

Although most Japanese-style gardens share some of these attributes, the Miller Garden is unique in the degree to which Schelin designed weddings to fit the garden and manifest "flow." Whereas most garden staffs adapt wedding activities to their site by suggesting open areas for large parties and intimate areas for small ones, Schelin was atypical in staging the ceremony throughout the entire Miller Garden. Although consciously following Csikszentmihalyi, Schelin unwittingly practiced Moore and Myerhoff's paradox that even as rituals seek to "close possibilities," they are open to formal developments. Secular rituals in particular tend to alternate the familiar with the fresh, to juxtapose the general with the particular so that each aspect communicates meaning separately and in tandem. At the Miller Garden, the dialectic involves the clients and the coordinators as well as Schelin's original wedding plan and the variations created by subsequent coordinators.

Schelin presented her processual formula to clients as a way of creating calm and clarity amid the chaos of the wedding day so they could more deeply experience the meaning of the marriage ceremony. Because a wedding involves a substantial "risk element" for brides, who typically dream of the event from childhood yet are challenged by myriad organizational tasks and performance pressures, Schelin believed the properly experienced wedding could constitute a "peak experience." One key was rehearsal of the ceremony's movements, so that the participants would feel completely comfortable in their physical roles and concentrate on the event's meaning. Thus, Schelin mandated a full rehearsal by the entire wedding "cast" the day before the wedding, with each person walking through his part to fully understand it. The formula described here was developed over several years, with the garden slightly altered—paths widened, shrubs removed, branches trimmed—to facilitate new functions. More generally, Schelin sought to maximize the garden's character as a "stroll-type" pond garden *(kaiyushiki teien)*. In so doing, Schelin interpreted the garden as a performance space, which serendipitously presented "elegant solutions" to many of the complex requirements of contemporary weddings.

The Miller Garden's functions as a performance space and a spiritual place are based on its separate entry area, oval design around a waterfall-fed pond, and rear teahouse (Fig. 9). In Schelin's plan, these areas' functions suggest an entry hall or waiting area between the Main Gate and the Japanese Gate, a backstage area for the groom in and around the teahouse on the

---

[37] See, for instance, Maggie Oster, *Reflections of the Spirit: Japanese Gardens in North America* (New York: Dutton Studio Books, 1993).

garden's western perimeter and another for the bride in the office and "friends' garden" in the southeast corner, a viewing area for the guests on the south side of the pond, a processional path along the north side of the pond, and a "stage" in the garden's northwest corner where the "moon bridge" is highlighted by the north waterfall. Because this formula highlights transitions through space, the garden and ceremony work "naturally" to separate then reconnect viewers and participants, and, of course, the bride and groom. The "actors" and "audience" occupy distinct zones, but the garden's "organic" oval design provides an underlying sense of connection and intimacy. Unlike a church's aisle that segregates the bride's side from the groom's, here guests mingle and mix.

In the model ceremony, guests gather in a formal entry courtyard that serves as a transitional space between the mundane world and the ritual space of the garden. The doors of the gate are opened (Fig. 10), and guests file into the south side of the garden reserved for them. The groom and groomsmen, who have arrived earlier, wait near the teahouse, hidden by trees and shrubs. Similarly, the bride and her entourage are sequestered in the Friends' Garden and Office in the front corner of the garden. The ceremony begins with the entry of the parents and other special guests through the Japanese Gate, along the processional path, and over the Moon Bridge to their seats of honor between the bridge and teahouse. The officiant enters along the path, stopping atop the Moon Bridge. The groom and groomsmen then appear from the opposite direction of the teahouse, coming into view as they surmount the bridge. Next the bridal party enters along the processional path to stand along the other side of the bridge (Fig. 11). This preamble, a minute or less in most weddings, can take five minutes or longer, intensifying the guests' anticipation.

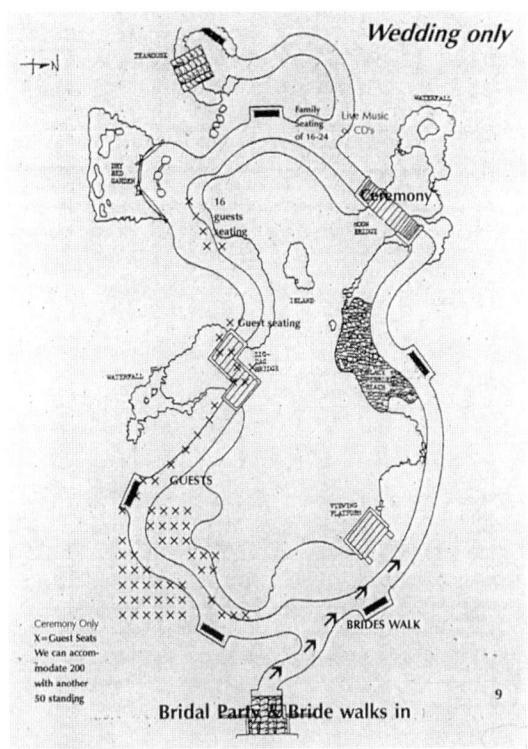

9. *Map showing the Miller Garden's use for weddings, with guest seating south of the pond and the "bride's walk" along the north shore (courtesy of the Earl Burns Miller Japanese Garden)*

After a brief interval, the bride passes through the gate, appearing fleetingly at first then emerging into full view as she rounds the pond (Fig. 12). Like a model on a runway, she is exposed for maximum visibility and to appropriate music.[38] Walking at a measured pace, the procession from gate to bridge takes fully ninety seconds. Given that the bride's appearance is the visual highlight of the ceremony—and a moment for personal reflection—this extended entry prolongs and heightens the experience. The path is defined along the shoreline by several dramatic trees, the Viewing Platform, a lantern, and the stone beach, and flanked on the back by large trees and dramatically pruned pines. Photos and video shown to prospective clients emphasize the bride's journey as both performance and time for contemplation. Several brides noted that the procession allowed them to gaze at family and friends, to speak with their father, to think about their life to this point, and to look forward, literally, to their husband-to-be waiting on the bridge.

With the preamble completed and the wedding party assembled on the bridge (Fig. 13), the nuptial rites begin. As the garden's main focal point, the elevated bridge allows clear sight lines for guests arrayed around the pond. It serves as altar and

[38] Although some brides choose Mendelsohn's "Wedding March," and others opt for "ethnic" music that reflects their heritage, increasingly women select a favorite song. Schelin recommended Debussy's "Claire de Lune" for the entry of parents and officiant, and Pachelbel's "Canon in D Major" for the processional, feeling that both conveyed dignity, joy, and a hint of the "enormous sorrow" that accompanies weddings as one phase of life is entered and another left behind. Recognizing the importance of music to cue actions and emotions, Schelin also hired a technician to make sure that the taped music functioned smoothly.

10. *Guests wearing formal Vietnamese clothing pass from the entry courtyard into the main garden through the Japanese Gate (photo: courtesy of the Earl Burns Miller Japanese Garden)*

11. *The bridal party and officiant wait atop the Moon Bridge, anticipating the bride's entry (photo: courtesy of the Earl Burns Miller Japanese Garden)*

stage, a space set off from but highly visible to the audience in front of whom the ritual actors perform. Some couples decorate the bridge with tulle or floral bouquets to emphasize its importance. It also accommodates the Jewish *chuppa*, the small pavilion used in Hindu weddings, and other ritual structures. The bridge's symbolism is threefold. First, it is connected with the fluid movement associated with water and is free from a fixed or absolute status. Conforming to Turner's core definition of liminality, it is "betwixt and between," touching both shores yet belonging to neither. One bride stated that standing on the bridge, with water flowing beneath her, she felt as if she was being reborn. More obviously, the bridge is a place, and a trope, for connection—an interpretation literally spelled out in one couple's wedding invitation (Fig. 14). The idea of unity is much emphasized in contemporary weddings in which connection rituals such as lighting "unity candles" and drinking from one glass augment the ring exchange. Schelin's choreography, with groom entering from "stage right" and bride from "stage left," underscores this notion of shared experience by literally having them come together to meet each other halfway. Most obviously, the bridge signals the wedding as a rite of passage by underscoring the couple's transition to a new personal and social status. In Schelin's plan, the bridge is traversed by the couple at the end of the ceremony as a physical act and as an emblem of crossing over. So resonant is the bridge's symbolism that it is used by local Girl Scouts for their flying-up ceremonies in which girls "cross over" from one level to the next—and is pictured in the *Junior Girl Scout Handbook* to illustrate the chapter "Ceremonies in Girl Scouting" (Fig. 15).[39]

After the declaration of marriage closes the ceremony, the couple crosses the bridge to greet family (Fig. 16). They continue in counterclockwise circumambulation of the garden—receiving the guests' congratulations in an inverted receiving

[39] *Junior Girl Scout Handbook* (New York: Girl Scouts of the USA, 2001), 12. The bridge at the Tillman garden also hosts Girl Scout flying-up ceremonies.

12. *A bride and her father follow the processional path to the Moon Bridge (photo: courtesy of Tamara Santana)*

13. *A typical wedding ceremony atop the Moon Bridge (photo: courtesy of the Earl Burns Miller Japanese Garden)*

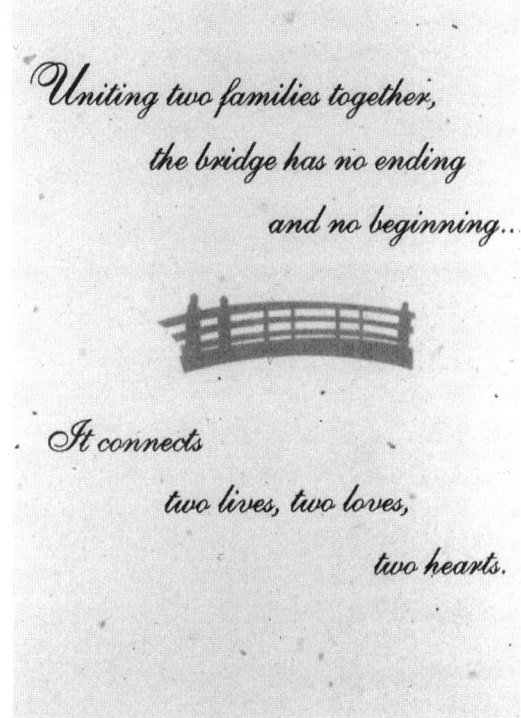

Uniting two families together,

the bridge has no ending

and no beginning...

It connects

two lives, two loves,

two hearts.

14. *A wedding invitation utilizing the Moon Bridge as a symbol of union, and liminality (courtesy of the Earl Burns Miller Japanese Garden)*

Girl Scout Calendar 2002

15. *Photo of Girl Scout "Bridging Ceremony" held atop the Moon Bridge, used on the cover of the 2002 Girl Scout Calendar (photo: Lori Adamski-Peck, courtesy of Girl Scouts of the USA)*

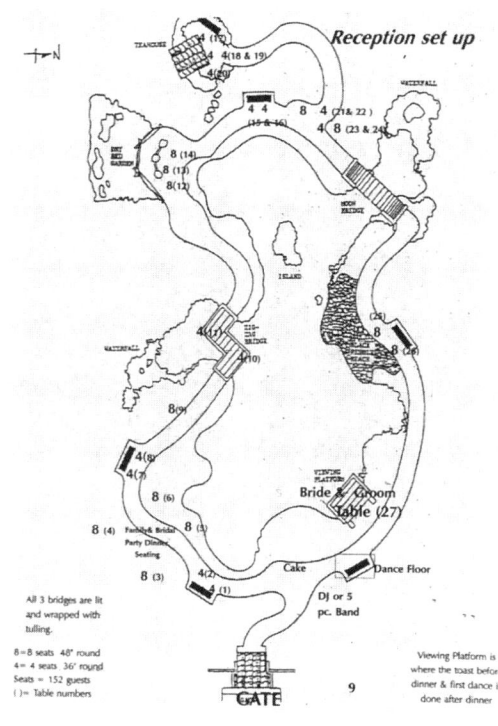

16. *A newly married couple crosses over the Moon Bridge to begin the recessional (photo: courtesy of the Earl Burns Miller Japanese Garden)*

17. *The wedding couple and pairs of ushers and bridesmaids cross the Zig-Zag Bridge during the recessional (photo: courtesy of the Earl Burns Miller Japanese Garden)*

18. *Map showing the reception plan for the Miller Garden (courtesy of the Earl Burns Miller Japanese Garden)*

19. *Bride and groom pose on the Viewing Platform after the wedding ceremony (photo: courtesy of the Earl Burns Miller Japanese Garden)*

line (Fig. 17)—to end up at the viewing platform where photography commences. The bride's round of the pond completes the ritual movement through the garden and symbolizes the "flow" critical to transformative experience.[40] The Brazilian bride who found great energy in the Miller Garden and who made the full circle, described the wedding as a "seamless experience." In van Gennep's formulation, this adaptation of the usual greeting line from the recession would begin the postliminal stage in which the ritual participants reaggregate with society.

Schelin's holistic plan fuses the wedding and reception, the first event flowing into the second (Fig. 18).[41] By bringing consumption of a ritual meal into the space used for the ceremony, the wedding as a rite of separation is joined with the reception as a rite of incorporation, even as their symbolic differences are largely masked by the shared setting. In the usual plan, guests return to the entry court for appetizers while the staff sets up tables in the garden, then reenter the garden now transformed into the scene of a fete, with a dance floor, food, and wedding cake displayed, and decorated tables along the paths. The wedding couple sits on the aptly titled Viewing Platform or utilizes it for the first kiss, first dance (Fig. 19), or other reception events, where they are set apart both physically and in status. As the couple make their rounds of the tables thanking guests, they literally make another round of the garden. With this last performance, their reintegration is complete.

Hybridity: Practicing Imperfection

The Miller Garden serves three roles relative to matrimonial rites: a preliminary place apart that signals the specialness of the event; liminally, as a physical context for and a dynamic actor in the wedding ceremony; and, postliminally, as a site conducive to reconnection. Accordingly, perceptions of the garden shift from eternal tranquillity, to evocative symbolism, then elegant beauty. Just as the garden offers multiple levels of experience and use, wedding couples discover and exhibit multiple aspects of themselves: spiritually centered beings, culturally aware individuals, emotionally sensitive persons, and elegantly beautiful man and woman. These identities for the garden and its clients are negotiated through their interaction and are provisional. For the garden, each wedding reinscribes these values, albeit with slight alterations, and for the married couple these values may return with each viewing of their wedding photos or memory of the experience.

In their role as wedding venues, the Miller Garden and other Japanese-style gardens celebrate not the cultural authenticity and Japanese historicity that dominate their rhetoric but rather appropriation and hybridity. These practices define and in a sense perfect these Japanese-style gardens as a type of modern American landscape. One of the most dramatic aspects of weddings at Japanese-style gardens in Southern California is their radically composite nature in which couples from nearly every ethnic and religious background deploy them in eloquent statements about the fluidity of culture. These vocalizations of hybridity can be relatively simple, as with the ethnically and religiously homogeneous couple who found the Miller Garden conducive to a Hawaiian-theme wedding (Fig. 20). Or they can be complex, as with the Protestant-Jewish couple who used the garden for their vow renewal by adapting elements of the Japanese Tanabata festival and Jewish wedding ritual within a Hawaiian theme. Often these cultural ruptures and aggregations are not clear to the wedding couple; at times, however, every nuance and ramification is calculated. What is perhaps most revealing is not how infrequently Japanese-style gardens actually play the role of Japan, but instead how the Japanese environment of the Miller Garden allows and invites multiple cultural appropriations. In a society in which personal and even group identity is fluid, it follows that people should transform and multiply the valance of cultural spaces.

The refusal of people to see and use Japanese-style gardens in simple, culturally pure ways, does not minimize or invalidate the gardens. Similarly it does not make the feelings or events experienced there less significant or ersatz. To the

[40] Schelin's emphasis on flow and thus the importance of completing the circle was not adapted by Lynette Gahafer, her successor as event coordinator, who advises couples to exit more simply by going back over the bridge and along the processional path.

[41] Because of time constraints, receptions are only held after the last wedding, which begins in the late afternoon, and, thus, they take place during twilight and night. Lights were added to the Miller Garden in 1999 to allow for nocturnal receptions.

20. *A Hawaiian-themed ceremony atop the Moon Bridge underscores the hybrid nature of many nuptials in the Miller Garden (photo: courtesy of the Earl Burns Miller Japanese Garden)*

contrary, it broadens and deepens these sites as our diverse and increasingly "impure" culture finds and creates spaces appropriate to its needs and desires. Far from being anomalies, these gardens are characteristic of Southern California—a region variously described and derided as the land of simulacra, center for "adventures in hyperreality," the capital of the "reel as real," and so on—where the transgression of ostensible cultural boundaries is so commonplace as to be unremarkable for most residents. It is tempting, and easy, to dismiss its values as vagaries and marginalize its meaningful places as parodies. Evidence, however, suggests that not only has the practice of weddings in Japanese-style gardens spread among historically marginal sites like the Miller Garden, it is now so common at Japanese-style gardens across America, Australia, and Europe that it has led to a contentious discussion in the conservative *Journal of Japanese Gardening*.[42] Even in Japan, self-consciously "Japanese" gardens are being constructed as commercial wedding venues to create a romantic ambiance and to serve as a backdrop for photos.[43]

The increase in the number of Japanese-style gardens hosting weddings is no doubt due to their profitability. Although these weddings contribute financially to the institutions that host them, and further create good public relations in the case of a museum or university, do they contribute more broadly to society? Although some gardens employ a transparent rhetoric of tranquil and spiritual nuptials to sell their venues, in the case of Schelin's carefully devised program at the Miller Garden, is there any evidence to suggest that these weddings have any greater effect on the couples who marry there? Even if couples claim some special insight or lasting impact, how do we know that these avowals are not merely designed to boost their image or status? Does a ceremony with "flow" enhance a wedding as a rite of passage, or is it simply a way in which coordinators can justify fund-raising in venues intended as a places of contemplation or education?

If we can accept that social relations are not a zero-sum equation in which economic gain or institutional advantage automatically deny any real value or redemptive potential, then we can productively address these challenges. There is, of course, no concrete way of assessing the sincerity of someone's feelings and of quantifying their psychological growth or spiritual understanding. Even if the future divorce rates of those who married in the Miller Garden using Schelin's formula could be measured against the statistics for society at large, myriad variables would contaminate the results. Anecdotal evidence does suggest that a majority of the couples who marry in the Miller Garden remain attached to it, attending annual events or

[42] See note 6 for the debate over social events in Japanese gardens.

[43] Marriages traditionally took place at Shinto shrines, but beginning in the middle of the twentieth century hotels, restaurants, and wedding halls competed for the lucrative wedding business. In the 1980s, nuptials in Western-style chapels or wedding halls became common, with the surrounding English-style gardens sometimes used for commemorative photos. A study by students of Suzuki Makoto at Tokyo Agricultural University reveals that of the roughly one hundred Tokyo-area wedding venues, twenty-six have gardens or landscapes, most in Western styles. Recently, however, several wedding-hall chains, notably Heiankaku and Nihonkaku, have constructed "Japanese" gardens on their grounds. Although thus far used for photos rather than weddings, the American model and flexibility of Japanese culture suggest that these gardens may well become ceremonial sites.

simply coming with their children to feed the fish.[44] One couple—she formerly a student at the university and he a maintenance supervisor there—met, had their first date, became engaged, and married at the Miller Garden. They have continued this intimate relationship to the site, belonging to the Friends of the Garden, attending most of the garden's events, and bringing their children as well as their friends. Similarly, for the couple who renewed their vows at the Miller Garden, the location was chosen because it resonated with their values and, they claim, the impact of the ceremony reverberates every time they come back. Naturally, couples with a high degree of "spiritual awareness," or desire to connect with such ideas, are more apt to select venues such as the Miller Garden, to be affected by them, and to articulate those feelings. It is far more difficult to ascertain the impact of a wedding at the Miller Garden on the great majority of couples who had relatively little interest in its symbolic potential but, instead, were attracted largely by its ambiance. For these couples, many of whom come from different ethnic or religious backgrounds, the fact of the wedding likely started serious conversation about the difficulties of connecting different traditions. And it may well follow that the practical solutions offered by Schelin and subsequent event coordinators at the Miller Garden for the wedding began to suggest larger strategies for negotiating difference, or at least a constructive forum in which these issues could be discussed. Moreover, for those family members and friends suspicious of unions outside the faith or race, witnessing a fluid, harmonious wedding ceremony in a beautiful setting may well begin to assuage their doubts. In these subtle, immeasurable ways, a wedding venue and a ceremony that smoothly mix disparate realities—Japan and America, past and present, beauty and utility—offer a potentially powerful model of integration for a society increasingly defined by ethnic and cultural hybridity. No hard evidence certifies that the weddings at the Miller Garden successfully reaggregate mixed couples into society, yet there is ample reason to believe that they are dynamic rites of passage as meaningful as the various customs studied by van Gennep.

Just as weddings appeal to garden administrators because of the revenue they can generate, wedding couples are drawn to gardens because of the positive experiences they may produce. Weddings at gardens in general, and Japanese-style gardens in particular, have grown dramatically in the past decade because they give brides and grooms what they want. And although they want many things, some base and others exalted, one fundamental desire is to marry in a place that speaks to their identity, both who they have been as individuals and who they want to be as a couple. In this way, these weddings are not so much about reinscribing extant status but are about suggesting new identities still incipient in a society in the midst of transformation. It is altogether fitting, then, to hold such a rite in an American Japanese-style garden, itself a fantastic cultural hybrid.

[44] This continuing relationship is stimulated in part by the fact that the fee for a wedding at the Miller Garden includes a one-year membership to it.

Performance and Appropriation: Profane Rituals in Gardens and Landscapes

Performance and Appropriation: Profane Rituals in Gardens and Landscapes

Performance and Appropriation: Profane Rituals in Gardens and Landscapes

Performance and Appropriation: Profane Rituals in Gardens and Landscapes

Academy Landscapes and the Ritualization of Cultural Memory in China Under the Mongols

Linda Walton

The Italian Jesuit missionary Matteo Ricci used the term accademia to refer to White Deer Grotto 白鹿洞 when he visited this shuyuan 書院 (literally, "book hall") located on the slopes of southern China's Mount Lu 廬 in 1595.[1] Ricci's familiarity with the centers of learning known as "academies" in sixteenth-century Italian cities likely inspired him to use this name for the institution he saw at White Deer Grotto.[2] Unlike Italian Renaissance academies that flourished in urban settings such as Florence, however, White Deer Grotto Academy was nestled in the lush landscape of Mount Lu, removed from the bustling cities of sixteenth-century China. A mountain range with more than ninety peaks, Mount Lu's mist-enshrouded heights and cascading waterfalls had attracted poets and painters, as well as Daoists and Buddhists, for well over a thousand years before the time of Ricci's visit. By the late fourth century, when the Buddhist monk Huiyuan 慧遠 (334–417) retreated to Mount Lu and founded the famous center of southern Buddhism, Donglin 東林 Monastery, the mountain had already been home to legendary deities and Daoist adepts for many centuries.[3] The landscape that drew religious figures such as Huiyuan to Mount Lu also lured poets and painters, whose aesthetics were inspired by Buddhism and Daoism and whose nature poetry and landscape painting took the mountains and waters of Mount Lu as their subject.[4]

Seeing the natural landscape as the embodiment of spiritual ideals was not limited to Buddhism and Daoism. Beginning at least in the tenth century, Confucians also found inspiration in Mount Lu's landscape. The site of White Deer Grotto Academy had a venerable history that stretched back at least to the late eighth century, when two brothers lived as recluses there.[5] The foundations of the academy dated to the late tenth century and the resurgence of Confucianism that marked the early Northern Song (960–1126). White Deer Grotto's later renown—which led Ricci to visit the site—was largely due to its revival by the famed philosopher, Zhu Xi 朱喜, in the late twelfth century, as part of a widespread academy movement in Southern Song (1127–1279) China.[6] Like White Deer Grotto, many academies throughout the Song were originally founded

[1] John Meskill, *Academies in Ming China* (Tucson: University of Arizona Press, 1982), x–xi.

[2] For recent views on these, see, for example, *Italian Academies of the Sixteenth Century*, ed. D. S. Chambers and F. Quiviger (London: The Warburg Institute, University of London, 1995).

[3] See, e.g., Erik Zürcher, *The Buddhist Conquest of China* (Leiden: E. J. Brill, 1972 [2nd ed.]), 208.

[4] Both Zong Bing (374–443), the author of a famous essay on landscape painting, and Xie Lingyun (385–443), one of China's best-known nature poets (see later in connection with Stone Gate Grotto Academy), were disciples of Huiyuan, and joined his association of lay Buddhists on Mount Lu. See, inter alia, Susan Bush, "Tsung Bing's Essay on Painting Landscape and the Landscape Buddhism of Mount Lu," in *Theories of the Arts in China*, ed. Susan Bush and Christian Murck (Princeton, N.J.: Princeton University Press, 1983), 132–64; J. D. Frodsham, "The Origins of Chinese Nature Poetry," *Asia Major* 8.1 (1960), 68–104; Richard Mather, "The Landscape Buddhism of the Fifth-Century Poet, Hsieh Lingyun," *Journal of Asian Studies* 18.1 (1958), 67–79.

[5] For this and later history, see John W. Chaffee, "Chu Hsi and the Revival of the White Deer Grotto Academy, 1179–1181 A.D.," *T'oung Pao* LXXI (1985), 40–62.

[6] For background on this, see Linda Walton, *Academies and Society in Southern Sung China* (Honolulu: University of Hawai'i Press, 1999).

as private studies or retreats and often located in mountain settings chosen for their scenic landscapes. Because nature embodied philosophical principles, Song Confucian scholars—not unlike their Buddhist and Daoist counterparts—studied and appreciated the landscape as a means of grasping the infinite. Song Confucians also built on their Buddhist and Daoist predecessors in more concrete ways, sometime appropriating sites that had been Buddhist temples or Daoist shrines to create their own sacred space: a shrine or academy dedicated to a Confucian "worthy," scholars honored for their learning and the model lives they led.[7] Even after the Mongol conquest of the Southern Song in the late thirteenth century, many Song academies were restored and new ones were established under the rule of Khubilai Khan and his successors.

Despite its relatively brief reign, the Mongol Yuan (1279–1368) dynasty left an enduring imprint on many aspects of Chinese society and culture. The product of a prolonged military invasion that claimed victims throughout the population, the conquest of Southern Song China by the Mongols in the late thirteenth century had a profound psychological impact on surviving members of the Chinese elite. Their position as leaders of Chinese society was threatened by the new regime, and their traditional role as arbiters of culture was likewise challenged by the Mongol conquest. Faced with a choice between accommodation or resistance, Chinese could either serve as officials in the Yuan government or withdraw to private scholarly life. Such a statement greatly oversimplifies circumstances that varied with individual, family, and region, but it nevertheless suggests in broad outline the dilemmas surrounding cultural accommodation and resistance. Whichever path Chinese scholars followed—withdrawal from public life or seeking office—academies were important sites of social and intellectual engagement, either as private retreats or as one of the few options for official appointment open to them.

Inscriptions commemorating the founding or restoration of Yuan academies regularly drew attention to landscape as a repository of Chinese cultural memory. Composed by Chinese scholars, these texts can help to elucidate their dual strategies of accommodation and resistance in response to Mongol rule. Although writing about landscape in academy inscriptions was not without precedent,[8] it acquired new meaning in the circumstances of Mongol rule. Timothy Brook has explored the impact of the Mongol occupation on the development of a particular genre of public text, the local gazetteers, which contain many examples of academy inscriptions.[9] He asserts that the very conditions of rule by an alien people, in fact, inspired the revival of this native form of local historical recordkeeping.[10] The preservation of local history in the context of alien rule became a subtle and safe means of asserting Chinese cultural identity, as Chinese scholars and local officials compiled records at the behest of the Mongol government, whose administrative needs were served by these local chronicles.[11] Here I will be arguing along much the same lines with regard to one particular kind of record found in local gazetteers or in the collected works of local authors—academy inscriptions—to show how emphasis on the physical landscape in these texts was a narrative strategy that ritualized Chinese cultural memory.

Rites, Ritual, and Ritualization

The veneration of the sage Confucius at White Deer Grotto may have reminded Matteo Ricci of the Accademia Platonica in Florence, where a candle was kept burning day and night before a bust of Plato.[12] During his visit, perhaps Ricci had an opportunity to observe Confucian rites, precisely orchestrated rituals performed at shrines to Confucius, his disciples, and

[7] For a study of shrines honoring Confucian worthies in the Song, see Ellen Neskar, "The Cult of Worthies: A Study of Shrines Honoring Local Confucian Worthies in the Sung Dynasty (960–1279)." Ph.D. dissertation, Columbia University, 1993. For academies and sacred space, see Linda Walton, "Southern Sung Academies and the Construction of Sacred Space," in *Landscape, Culture, and Power in Chinese Society*, ed. Yeh Wen-hsin, China Research Monograph 49 (Berkeley, Calif.: Institute of East Asian Studies and Center for Chinese Studies, 1998), 22–49.

[8] See Walton, "Southern Sung Academies and the Construction of Sacred Space."

[9] See Timothy Brook, "Native Identity under Alien Rule: Local Gazetteers of the Yuan Dynasty," in *Pragmatic Literacy, East and West 1200–1330*, ed. Richard Britnell (Woodbridge, Suffolk: The Boydell Press, 1997), 235–45. See also Peter K. Bol, "The Rise of Local History: History, Geography, and Culture in Song and Yuan Wuzhou," *Harvard Journal of Asiatic Studies* 61.1 (June 2001), 37–76.

[10] Brook, 236.

[11] See Brook's concluding comments, 244–45.

[12] Meskill, xi.

later "worthies." These rites were prescribed in detail in ritual texts dating from nearly a millennium earlier: offerings of silk, food, and wine were presented to images of Confucius and his disciples, accompanied by prayers and hymns. Rituals in the state Confucian Temple and in local Confucian temples or schools—including academies—throughout China were central to the practice of Confucianism. Confucian rites were the performative representation of a key principle in Confucian social and political thought: that social order was maintained by ritual, the external expression of internal humane values. The concept of "ritualization," however, is used here in a sense quite distinct from both the meaning and the practice of Confucian rites. Rather than symbolic representation of transmitted values through the performance of certain acts (sacrificial offerings to venerable persons, etc.), here "ritualization" refers to a dynamic process that both produced and negotiated power relationships. The performance of rites at academy shrines dedicated to Confucian worthies was a vital part of the process described here. Equally important, however, was the act of writing texts that commemorated cultural heroes identified with academy sites. The commemoration of academies—and the cultural memory they represented—in inscriptions written according to a rhetorical formula was as much a ritual performance as presenting offerings to Confucius. Commemorative inscriptions written for academies by Chinese scholars were an important vehicle for the ritualization of cultural memory in China under the Mongols.

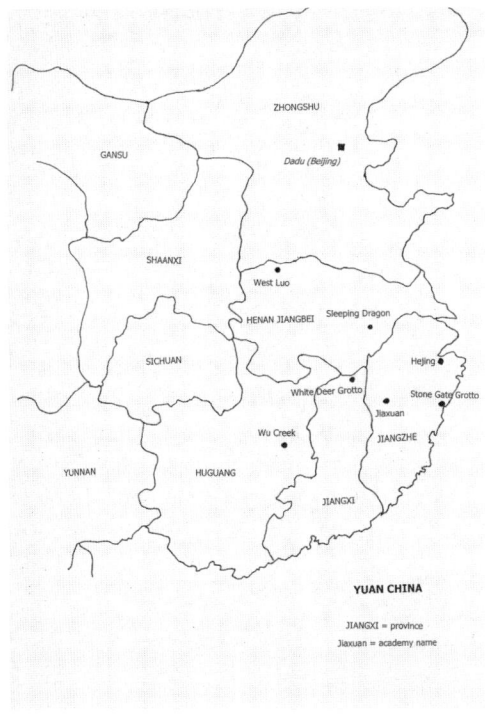

The concept of ritualization as articulated by Catherine Bell provides a useful analytical perspective for interpreting the layers of meaning embedded in our textual sources.[13] Bell suggests that we see ritualization as a "strategic mode of practice" that "produces nuanced relations of power characterized by acceptance, resistance, negotiated appropriation, and redemptive reinterpretation of the hegemonic order."[14] Adapting Bell's concept here, I will argue that the narratives of academy origins and renewal found in Yuan commemorative inscriptions can be understood as a process of ritualization according to the model she describes. First, academy life was characterized by what Bell calls "the differentiation and privileging of particular activities," notably those of lecturing and study, reading certain texts, wearing identifiable apparel, using specialized codes of communication, and performing prescribed rites at academy shrines.[15] Classical texts provided a common educational foundation for scholars, who wore distinctive robes and hats, communicated through an elaborate language of philosophical, historical, and literary allusion, and participated in rituals affirming scholarly traditions associated with Confucius and his disciples. Second, Chinese inscription authors publicized the support of academies by the Mongol regime's representative officials, whose authority sanctioned the recognition of Chinese worthies at academy shrines. Chinese scholars thus engaged these officials in a dynamic process of what Bell refers to as "negotiated appropriation," through which non-Chinese rulers appropriated Chinese historical figures. Finally, Chinese cultural memory was inscribed—both literally and metaphorically—on the landscape, which was read and reinscribed through written commemoration of the building or restoration of academies. The writing of commemorative inscriptions, though not new, in the context of Mongol-ruled China became an act of ritual performance that accomplished the "redemptive reinterpretation of the hegemonic order": the conquerors' position was inverted—becoming culturally subordinate—and thus subverted. In a society in which writing originated as part of sacred ritual

[13] Catherine Bell, *Ritual Theory, Ritual Practice* (New York: Oxford University Press, 1992), 196 ff.
[14] Bell, 196.
[15] Bell, 204.

and was endowed with both meaning and power, writing a commemorative inscription was itself a ritual performance.

The argument here, then, is primarily a textual one, using as the main source commemorative inscriptions written for six academies scattered throughout various regions of Yuan China (see map). Two—Hejing 和靖 and Jiaxuan 稼軒—were dedicated to loyalist scholars of the fallen Song dynasty who, although they belonged to two different generations, engaged the political issues of their day in similar ways; inscriptions for both of these academies were written by the same southern Chinese scholar. Stone Gate Grotto 石門洞 was located at a site associated with the early-fifth-century landscape poet, Xie Lingyun 謝靈運. Wu Creek 浯溪 Academy was a place marked by the poetry and calligraphy of two famous eighth-century statesmen. Sleeping Dragon 龍眠 Academy was named for the mountain villa of the renowned eleventh-century painter, Li Gonglin 李公麟. Finally, West Luo 洛 Academy was located at one of the most sacred sites in northern China, a place associated with the mythical emperor Yu 禹, and also built at the site of the former private garden of the eleventh-century historian and official, Sima Guang 司馬光.

Dai Biaoyuan on Hejing and Jiaxuan Academies

The relations of power produced and negotiated by the ritualization of cultural memory were highly nuanced, as Chinese officials invoked heroes from their own past—even loyalist scholars and statesmen—in the service of the Mongol state's academic agenda. An illustrative example is the establishment of Hejing Academy in 1296 at the grave of Yin Chun 尹淳 (1071–1142), a northerner who fled south after the fall of the Northern Song to the Jurchen Jin state (1115–1234) and was known for his moralistic conservatism and hawkish stance against the Jurchen.[16] In his commemorative inscription, the southern Chinese scholar Dai Biaoyuan 戴表元 (1244–1310) explained that, although Yin Chun was born in the old northern capital of Luoyang, he fled to the south (after the Jurchen invasions) and finally settled in the southeastern region of Yue.[17] When he died, he was interred there, and local people were said to have built a shrine at his grave because they admired him.[18] Dai quotes the Jurchen governor, Wanyan Zhen 完顏真, ordering the school officials to establish an academy at the site of Yin's grave and shrine because of the association of shrines with schools in antiquity.[19] The figure of Yin Chun thus took on a new meaning in the context of Mongol rule of southern China. Because in his own time Yin Chun opposed the Jurchen conquerors of the north, he could be viewed by Chinese scholars living under Mongol rule as a potent symbol of loyalism. At the same time, China's Mongol rulers, whose conquest of the Jurchen-ruled north opened the way for their domination of the whole of China, could honor Yin Chun as a Chinese loyalist who opposed the Jurchen. Even the fact that the governor who supported the academy was himself Jurchen evidently did not undermine the enterprise. This case exemplifies the "negotiated appropriation" described by Bell in her model of ritualization, as the Chinese loyalist Yin Chun was commemorated by a Chinese scholar at the behest of an ethnic Jurchen official of the Yuan government.

In an effort to sanction the academy further, Dai linked the central intellectual figure of Southern Song Neo-Confucianism, Zhu Xi (1130–1200), with radically different cultural heroes of a far earlier time: "Master Zhu held office in Yan; [but] Eremite Dai [Kui] and Right Army General Wang [Xizhi] lived in retirement. Each had his own teaching standards. They were like Yin Chun, who lived and died in Yue and then was buried here."[20] Zhu Xi, who was known for rejecting office many times, held a supervisory post that included the region of Yue at a time when severe famine plagued its people. He

[16] See James T. C. Liu, *China Turning Inward: Intellectual-Political Changes in the Early Twelfth Century* (Cambridge, Mass.: Harvard University Press, 1988), 71–72. For biographical references to Yin Chun, see Chang Bide et al., eds., *Songjen zhuanji ziliao suoyin* (Taipei: Dingwen, 1974–76), I.94–97 [hereafter cited as SRZZ].

[17] Dai Biaoyuan, *Shanyuan Dai xiansheng wenji* (Sibu congkan ed.), 10.3a. For Dai, see Wang Deyi et al., eds., *Yuanren zhuanji ziliao suoyin* (Beijing: Zhonghua, 1987), IV.2063–65 [hereafter cited as YRZZ].

[18] Dai, 10.3a.

[19] Dai, 10.3a. For Wanyan Zhen, see YRZZ I.446.

[20] Dai, 10.3b.

addressed these dire circumstances in part by the establishment of community granaries.[21] Dai Kui 戴逵 (d. 396), who lived most of his life in the Kuaiji (Yue) area, was a landscape painter known also for his musical abilities and for having refused to serve in office.[22] Wang Xizhi 王羲之 (303–361), one of China's greatest calligraphers, for a time held office as governor of Kuaiji, where he hosted a famous poetry gathering at Orchid Pavilion. He ultimately resigned in disgust over the appointment to office of someone he despised, and he retired to pursue his interests in Buddhism, Daoism, and the arts.[23]

One thing that unites all three—Dai, Wang, and Zhu—is their refusal to hold office. The possible exception is Zhu Xi, whose connection to the area was through an official appointment. Even in his case, however, the premier philosophical figure of the Southern Song held regular office as an administrator for only a relatively short period of time, preferring for various reasons to accept sinecures or to withdraw entirely to the company of his disciples and perform his role as a teacher. Like Yin Chun, who rejected holding office out of moral principle, these three figures cited by Dai Biaoyuan similarly withdrew to retirement on different occasions for reasons of moral principle. The linking of these historical figures—all of whom were connected to this place—with Yin Chun is part of a narrative strategy employed by Dai that privileges Chinese cultural associations with the locale. Yue, or Kuaiji as it was also known, was a region famous for its landscape and its literati culture already in the fourth and fifth centuries,[24] and Dai is surely drawing on these associations when he refers to the three historical figures in connection with Yin Chun. The motive behind Dai's strategy is not entirely clear. Was he relying on the Jurchen governor's ignorance of these figures, since they all rejected service to the state in some way? Or was this irrelevant? Was this message perhaps intended primarily for his Chinese scholarly audience, who would have been intimately familiar with the backgrounds of these figures? Whatever the motive, what is striking to the modern reader of this text is the allusion to a range of Chinese cultural heroes—who lived nearly one thousand years apart—in support of this academy.

The privileging of Chinese cultural associations with the local topography is evident even in the rejection of a site for Hejing Academy because of the site's strong Daoist associations, and it is unmistakably present in Dai's description of the power of the physical landscape with its geomantic and historical resonances:

> At first, they deliberated using land beside Dragon Omen Palace for the foundation, but since it was a place where Daoist masters practiced, it was not [considered] appropriate. Wanyan Zhen and Commandery Magistrate Quger 忽哥兒[25] agreed to go and view [possible locations], and so divined the present site. To the north the mountains are cold, and to the south, the sun is hot. To the east is Burning Wind Path, and to the west is Stone Sail [a large rock shaped like a sail]. In the shade of Stone Sail is the grave of Yin Chun. The gullies and creeks wind about and surround it, and the clustered graveyards are continuous and dense. Yue's famous sites include the Qin emperor's "wine jar" [a stone formed like a wine jar], jade quiver, and Yangming 陽明 Grotto Heaven.[26]

A local gazetteer for Kuaiji compiled at the beginning of the thirteenth century provides details on elements of the landscape described here. Dragon Omen Palace was named for the sighting of a dragon there during the eighth century and it was

[21] For background on this, see sources cited in SRZZ I.587–97. See also Zhu's biography by Wing-tsit Chan in Herbert Franke, ed., *Sung Biographies* (Wiesbaden: Franz Steiner, 1976), 285; and Wang Maohong (1668–1741), ed., *Zhuzi nianpu* (Taipei: Shijie, 1984), 297–98.

[22] See Richard Mather, trans., *A New Account of Tales of the World* (Minneapolis: University of Minnesota Press, 1976), 574. Dai Biaoyuan claimed to be related to the famous Dai family of the Han and Jin eras, descended from the branch that moved south to Kuaiji, so he would have been especially eager to mention Dai Kui among these figures. See Jennifer W. Jay, "Negotiating Poverty and Integrity Among the Hangzhou and Mingzhou Literati in Early Yuan," 4–5. Paper presented at the Association for Asian Studies Annual Meeting, 6 April 2002.

[23] For a quick reference to this famous figure, see Mather, 586.

[24] See J. D. Frodsham, "The Origins of Chinese Nature Poetry," 86–88.

[25] For Quger, see YRZZ V.2566. "Commandery Magistrate" was a Yuan title of nobility; according to the biographical sources, Quger held office as Jiangzhe Branch Secretariat Assistant Grand Councilor, so it was undoubtedly in that capacity that he came here.

[26] Dai, 10.3b. For Quger, see YRZZ V.2566.

located at Yangming Grotto Heaven on a branch peak of Kuaiji Mountain.[27] Dai mentions Yangming Grotto Heaven as one of the famous sites of the area, along with two other geological formations linked to the first emperor, Qin Shihuangdi 秦始皇帝 (r. 221–210 b.c.e.). Grotto heavens were Daoist sites that were believed to be part of a subterranean network that provided a gateway to the Daoist heavenly underworld.[28] Yangming Grotto Heaven was number eleven among the thirty-six "official" grotto heavens that were systematized in the Daoist tradition during the eighth century.[29] Despite its strong Daoist connection, however, Yangming Grotto Heaven was also a site associated with the mythical emperor Yu, and said to be his burial place by none other than the famous historian Sima Qian 司馬遷 (ca. 145–ca. 86 B.C.E.).[30] Dai's juxtaposition of these references, including the Daoist ones, reinforce a plethora of Chinese cultural associations with this particular landscape, as he describes it in detail. These associations are rooted in the earliest historical allusions to the mythical emperor Yu, the flood tamer, as well as in Daoist traditions, and Dai adds the dimension of physical topography to earlier mention of Eremite Dai, the calligrapher Wang Xizhi, and the philosopher Zhu Xi. Dai Biaoyuan's references to these figures neatly fit Bell's notion of "negotiated appropriation": iconic personages from the Chinese past recalled by Dai as he promotes the interests of the Yuan government in a process of cultural accommodation.

In the same year that Dai Biaoyuan composed the commemorative inscription for Hejing Academy, he also wrote one for the rebuilding of Jiaxuan Academy, dedicated to the Southern Song patriot poet, Xin Qiji 辛棄疾 (1140–1207).[31] Known as the foremost lyrical poet of his time, Xin was also a determined irredentist, who tried without success to convince the Southern Song court to support efforts to repel the Jurchen in his home region of Shandong. After his move to the south, he held a number of government posts before his political career essentially came to an end in 1182. He retired to Xinzhou's Shangrao county, where he built a villa and named one of the buildings "Farming Pavilion [Jiaxuan]." This became his sobriquet and was later used to name Jiaxuan Academy. When the villa was destroyed by fire, Xin moved to a nearby site and built another dwelling, also called "Farming Pavilion," at a place called Gourd Spring. A generous host to a circle of friends that included the most prominent thinkers and poets of the time—Zhu Xi, the philosopher Lu Jiuyuan 陸九淵, the statesman and thinker Chen Liang 陳亮 the poets Fan Chengda 范成大 and Lu You 陸游—Xin Qiji enjoyed his retirement from official life. Much of the poetry he wrote during this period reflects the powerful influence of the landscape of mountains and streams that surrounded his dwelling at Gourd Spring.

Dai's inscription for Jiaxuan Academy initially focuses on the region as a central place that drew large numbers of sojourning scholars who were forced to move south with the fall of the Northern Song.[32] He refers to the famous debate between Zhu Xi and Lu Jiuyuan at Goose Lake in Xinzhou as an example of the concentration of scholarly culture here during Xin Qiji's lifetime. After his death, however, the Xin family was unable to maintain the property of Farming Pavilion. It became overgrown and abandoned until a local official turned it into government land and built a retreat on the property to house students.[33] A Confucian shrine was added to the retreat, along with a shrine to Song Confucian scholars. Completed in the spring of 1274, it was called Guangxin 廣信 Academy, named for the region. In 1298, the name was officially changed to Jiaxuan, to honor Xin Qiji, and five years later the restoration of Jiaxuan Academy was undertaken by the headmaster, Zhao Ranming 趙然明.[34] Dai's description of the renovated academy emphasizes both the landscape and the productive qualities of the transformed estate:

[27] Shi Su (1150?–1213) et al., comps., *Jiatai Kuaiji zhi* (Song Yuan difangzhi congshu ed.), 7.5b; 11.8a.
[26] See, for example, Susan Naquin and Yü Chün-fang, eds., *Pilgrims and Sacred Sites in China* (Berkeley and Los Angeles: University of California Press, 1992), 17, 154. See also, e.g., Judith M. Boltz, *A Survey of Taoist Literature, Tenth to Seventeenth Centuries*, China Research Monograph 32 (University of California, Berkeley, Institute of East Asian Studies and Center for Chinese Studies, 1987), 117–18.
[29] Shi Su, *Kuaiji zhi*, 11.8a. See also Naquin and Yü, 17.
[30] Shi Su, *Kuaiji zhi*, 11.8b.
[31] For biographical background on Xin Qiji, see Irving Yucheng Lo, *Hsin Ch'i-chi* (New York: Twayne, 1971.
[32] Dai, 10.6a.
[33] Dai, 10.6a.
[34] Dai, 10.6a; for Zhao, see YRZZ III.1753.

In my leisure time, I used to go together with Master Zhao, roving among the hills and peaks. The elms and willows grew thickly together, and the long lake made a sash across the front of it. Numerous passes ornamented and flanked its backside, and [its beauty] made a deep impression. I asked about the pond and [Zhao] responded: "In it [Xin Qiji] farmed multitudes of fish. Today it's used to store excess water." I asked about the Pine Estrade, and [Zhao] responded: "It is the remaining traces of 'Farming Pavilion.' Formerly 1000 cypress trees were planted there, and now we've added to it to make a grove." I asked about the mulberry garden and the official reservoir, and [Zhao] responded: "It is the place where Xin Qiji farmed and fished, and now we have made it 'public'." I asked about the gate on the lake and [Zhao] responded: "The old path went from the west, following the lake to the southeast, and now we have begun to restore it." I asked about the new well and [Zhao] responded: "This is the old excavation [site]. Now we have removed all the residue and the water has refilled it. It is not a new well."[35]

This dialogue illustrates Xin Qiji's engagement with the rural life of the farmer, absorbed in the productive activities of tilling the soil, harvesting fruits and vegetables, and fishing. When he withdrew from official life and took up the rustic occupation of a gentleman farmer suggested here, he was following a well-established tradition that included forebears such as Zhuge Liang 諸葛亮 (181–234), whose reputation endowed retreat with a powerful moral dimension. Zhuge Liang lived for twenty years in a thatched hut, tilling the soil, until he was persuaded to come out of reclusion and join forces with one of the generals struggling for power after the fall of the Han (207 B.C.E.–220 C.E.).[36] The poet Tao Qian 陶潛 (365–427), whom Xin greatly admired, also was known for his steadfast devotion to the simplicity of rural farming life, even at the expense of his own and his family's welfare.[37] Dai Biaoyuan wrote a poem about Tao Qian's life as a hermit poet, and the description of Tao Qian's family circumstances could well have described Dai's own life:

> While books of poems and letters filled his house
> His wife and children never got much food.
> He would gaze up where breezes swayed the branches
> And look below at valleys filled with clouds.
> Who could bear, just for the sake of foodstuffs,
> To suffer being fettered and tied down?[38]

Dai, who received his *jinshi* degree in 1271 under the Southern Song, held office as prefectural professor in Xinzhou, the site of Jiaxuan Academy, at the time he composed the inscription. His post, though modest, provided the means to escape poverty for Dai and his family, who had lost most of their property with the Mongol conquest of southern China.[39] Dai's dilemma—shared with many former Southern Song literati—was one of material deprivation coupled with intense cultural nostalgia. As Jennifer Jay has pointed out, Dai adopted the revitalization of the literati (*shi* 士) as his personal mission: *zhenqi siwen weiji ren* 振起斯文為己任.[40] In his inscriptions for these two academies dedicated to Southern Song loyalist figures, we can glimpse Dai's efforts to find his way through the cultural and political shoals navigated by former Southern Song literati under Mongol rule. In the case of Jiaxuan Academy, in particular, Dai's homage to the poet Xin Qiji reflected his own commitment to poetry

[35] Dai, 10.6b.
[36] See, for example, Alan J. Berkowitz, "The Moral Hero: A Pattern of Reclusion in Traditional China," *Monumenta Serica* 40 (1992), 19, 31.
[37] Lo, *Hsin Ch'i-chi*, 8. For background on Tao Qian, see, e.g., James Robert Hightower, *The Poetry of T'ao Ch'ien* (Oxford: Oxford University Press, 1970).
[38] *The Columbia Book of Later Chinese Poetry: Yuan, Ming, and Ch'ing Dynasties (1279–1911)*, trans. and ed. Jonathan Chaves (New York, N.Y.: Columbia University Press, 1986), 17.
[39] See Jay, "Negotiating Poverty and Integrity among the Hangzhou and Jiang-Zhe Literati in Early Yuan."
[40] Jay, 4.

as the purest form of cultural endeavor, even though Dai himself wrote only traditional style *jueju* 絕句 and *lüshi* 律詩 poetry rather than the typical Southern Song *ci* 詞 lyric, the style mastered by Xin.[41] By commemorating Song loyalist poets (both Yin Chun and Xin Qiji) under the approving eye of Yuan officials, Dai was able to contribute to the symbolic revitalization of the literati at the same time that he participated in the "negotiated appropriation" of these poets' legacies by the Mongol rulers of southern China. In both cases, Dai's inscriptions on academies dedicated to these two poets emphasize the landscape as it resonates with multiple cultural and historical associations.

Stone Gate Grotto Academy

Founded around the same time (1294) as Hejing and Jiaxuan Academies, Stone Gate Grotto Academy was located at a site associated with the medieval landscape poet Xie Lingyun (385–433).[42] Liu Guan's 柳貫(1270–1342) inscription describes the place and links it to Xie:

> The region is remote, but the land is scenic. The records of former men and the maps and records of the states [show] its crooked division into counties aligned with the [contours of the] landscape. So, observing [Xie] Lingyun, investigating [his poem] "[On Climbing] the Highest Peak [of Stone Gate Mountain], and his newly built dwelling— all these works were no more than "waxing clogs."[43] He loved to wander and explore in the mountains and open trails through them. In each thing it was like this. [He] looked up and embraced the clouds and sleet, bent down to bathe in the cascades. In this way [he] comprehended the principles of humanity and knowledge, movement and stillness, and obtained the technique of inner and outer exchange and nourishing. Such was the deep and secret investigation of learning that he achieved on his own. How did Lingyun acquire the capability to comprehend these things? [It was when] he went south to Yongjia during the [Liu] Song Jingping era [423–4], 933 years before 1294.[44]

Not long after the death of his patron in 422, Xie Lingyun was exiled from the capital of Jiankang (modern Nanjing) to remote Yongjia along the southeast coast. Liu implies in this passage that Xie's ability to understand the principles of nature and humanity manifested in the peaks and waterfalls of mountain landscapes was related to his sojourn in the south.[45] On his journey to Yongjia to take up office, he passed through Qingtian, the site of Stone Gate Grotto. Centuries later, in 1294, an official visited Stone Gate Grotto and determined to build an academy there.[46] The academy was to be modeled on Zhu Xi's famous White Deer Grotto Academy on Mount Lu and, like its predecessor, was to be dedicated to teaching and study in order to "uphold the state, nurture classicism, and nourish talents."[47] Subsequently, in 1336, Assistant Surveillance Commissioner Lu Zhidao 魯至道 (1321 *jinshi*) came to visit the shrine at the site of Stone Gate Grotto Academy and discovered it in disrepair.[48] He allotted funds and engaged local elders and officials to help rebuild it; Route Commander Lu Jing盧景 (1283–1343) oversaw the completion of the academy's renewal.[49] When it was finished, the students were assembled

[41] Jay, 14.

[42] Liu Guan, *Zhongke Liu taizhi wenji* (1883 moveable type ed.), 15.28b–31b.

[43] This phrase is an allusion to Ruan Fu (278/9–326/7), whose obsession was waxing clogs, so the meaning here is to belittle these activities in contrast to what comes after. See Liu Yiqing, *Shishuo xinyu* (Taibei: Hualian, 1973), 67. See also translation of this passage and biographical notes on Ruan Fu in Mather, trans., 185, 538.

[44] Liu Guan, 15.28b–29a.

[45] See J. D. Frodsham, *The Murmuring Stream: The Life and Works of the Chinese Nature Poet Hsieh Ling-yun (385–433), Duke of K'ang-lo* (Kuala Lumpur: University of Malaysia Press, 1967), 34.

[46] For this official, named Wang Wu, see YRZZ I.92.

[47] Liu Guan, 15.29a.

[48] For Lu Zhidao, see YRZZ III.1950; see also YRZZ IV.2282 for the Dashman [Muslim] Beg Duludin, who is the same person (see later).

[49] For Lu Jing, see YRZZ III.1959.

for a formal announcement by Lu in which he reflected on the importance to learning of both the landscape and the academic community embodied in the school:

> The academy depends on the flourishing of lofty forests and snowy cascades, and so we have renewed its beauty. You roam and chant here. With the convergence of propriety and principle, [but] without the appearance of luxuriance, [you] embrace [your] endeavors and raise [yourselves] up, fulfilling propriety and thus obtaining [it]. Obtaining [it] lies within the self; seeking it lies with others. This is simply the humanity fulfilled by sages and teachers, and it is also the purpose of the rulers' and ministers' encouragement of schools.[50]

At this point, the headmaster made a formal request of Liu Guan to write an inscription commemorating the rebuilding of Stone Gate Grotto Academy. Liu then takes over the narrative, interjecting his own commentary on the role of scholars, education, and academies and linking them to both landscape and history:

> By comparing things, scholars know the categories. In seeking humanity and virtue, [they] must always have [the opportunity for] lecturing and practice, and what more do they need than the special perspective provided by the mountains and waters? Education in local schools was revived in the Tang and flourished in the Song, thereby connecting, joining together, and fully completing [the scholarly tradition]. But the creation of the four academies even more has an ancestral lineage of its origins, like Li Bo 李勃 at [White] Deer Grotto and Zhu Dong 朱洞 at Marchmount Hill.[51] [These men] frequently selected scenic forest shade and lodged at [the sites of] springs and rocks, cherishing the unrolling scrolls of the clouds and observing the coming and going of the clearing sky and the sun obscured by clouds. That whereby the high was made deep and the flowing stored up is one and the same with the principle of the falling and rising, waxing and waning, of *yin* and *yang*. For those who desire to investigate together with others the "limitless" learning, how can there be techniques apart from examining these [phenomena seen in nature]?
>
> Stone Gate's layered peaks stand erect; the *qi* 氣 that drains clear and cold from the cascading waterfalls freezes men's flesh and bones. Daoist writings call this the "Dark Egret Grotto Heaven." In the Song Shaosheng era (1095–98), Liu Jing 劉涇 (1075 *jinshi*) commanded the district and had [the description of] its landscape recorded in stone, but Mi Fu 米芾 truly wrote it. [Liu] sent Magistrate Zhu 朱 to make a pavilion. The time when Wang Anshi 王安石 led [our] culture astray was not yet distant when Liu Jing's works were already lost, so how can one depend on works of earth and wood [to preserve records]?[52]

After surveying the historical lineage of academies as scholarly institutions and the importance of the natural landscape to their founders, Liu Guan names a Song local official, Liu Jing, who was known for his works in wood, stone, and bamboo as well as his writings.[53] He also attributes the stone inscription depicting local scenery that was commissioned by Liu Jing to the famous Northern Song calligrapher, Mi Fu. Liu Guan concludes his narrative by paying homage to Lu Zhidao, also known as Beg Duludin, a Muslim "tribal person of the western regions," thus connecting Northern Song figures with a contemporary non-Chinese official and suggesting once again the process of "negotiated appropriation" as a mode of cultural accommodation.[54]

[50] Liu Guan, 15.29b–30a.
[51] These were the two most famous of the four academies of the Song.
[52] Liu Guan, 15.30a–30b.
[53] For Liu Jing, see SRZZ V.3862.
[54] Liu Guan, 15.31a.

In addition to Liu Guan's naming of founders of famous Northern Song academies, a local Northern Song official, and the most famous calligrapher of the Northern Song, there are many strands of cultural history interwoven here with the specific landscape surrounding Stone Gate Grotto Academy. There were several sites in southeastern China that were known by the name Stone Gate. The poem cited by Liu Guan at the beginning of his inscription was written by Xie Lingyun about Stone Gate near his family estate in Kuaiji; he also wrote a poem about Stone Gate Mountain in Yongjia, and probably visited Stone Gate Grotto, the site of this academy, when he was journeying to exile in Yongjia and stopped at Qingtian. In addition to multiple sites known as Stone Gate, as Xie's biographer, J. D. Frodsham points out, there also were numerous places associated with Xie scattered throughout southeastern China.[55] The flowering of Xie's poetic talents began with his exile in Yongjia and his appreciation of the power of landscape both to inspire the poet and to reveal philosophical truths. As Liu Guan suggests at the beginning of his inscription, Xie's activities before his exile to Yongjia were no more than frivolous obsessions. His poetry was deepened and enriched by his experience of the landscape in Yongjia, and after his return north to the Xie family estate, he continued to mature as a poet and a philosopher. Xie was heavily invested in the evolving Buddhism of his time,[56] but he also was drawn to Daoism, having been temporarily adopted by the family of a Daoist master in his youth.[57] Stone Gate Grotto is a site that resonates with powerful Daoist imagery. One Southern Song geographical work describes a pavilion filled with Daoist books at the site of Dark Egret Grotto Heaven here.[58] For the Confucian scholar Liu Guan, however, the beautiful landscape was a means to understand the principles of the Confucian sages, which were reflected in the natural transformations of *yin* and *yang* and in the movements of the waterfalls cascading down the stone precipices. The inscription narrative argues for the importance of an institutional environment—the academy—to appreciate fully the power of the landscape to aid students in understanding the concepts of *yin* and *yang*, propriety and principle. It also exemplifies the ritualization of Chinese cultural memory through the negotiated appropriation of this famous poet's legacy.

Wu Creek Academy

Around the same time (1331) as the renewal of Stone Gate Grotto Academy described by Liu Guan, Wu Creek Academy was built and commemorated in an inscription by Su Tianjue 蘇天爵 (1294–1352).[59] One of the outstanding scholars of his day, Su, a northerner, garnered first place in the 1316 provincial examinations and rose to the highest academic circles of the Yuan court. Wu Creek Academy was located far to the southwest of Stone Gate Grotto, along a small tributary of the Xiang River in Qiyang county. Su's narrative of the building of this academy follows a pattern we have seen elsewhere: an official visits a place and finds inspiration in some aspect of the landscape either to establish or to restore an academy:

In 1337 Surveillance Commissioner Yao Fu 姚紱 came to the borders of Qiyang. He crossed Wu Creek by boat and observed the ruins of former worthies. He sighed and said: "Formerly in the latter days of the Tianbao era [742–756], loyal and upright scholars struggled with the hardships of the times [An Lushan Rebellion], and accordingly rebuilt the two capitals [Chang'an and Luoyang] and called it a 'restoration.' Yuan Jie 元結 [719–772] wrote an elegant ode [on this], which was widely praised. Fuzhou prefect Yan Zhenqing 顏真卿 [709–784] wrote some phrases [of the poem] in his calligraphy and these were inscribed on the cliff wall [above Wu Creek]. Although 400 years have passed, those who pass by and observe the brave phrases and strong strokes are still fully inspired [by them]. The moral rectitude and

---

[55] Frodsham, *The Murmuring Stream*, 10.

[56] Frodsham, *The Murmuring Stream*, *20,* 34–35, 45–47 ff.

[57] Frodsham, *The Murmuring Stream*, 5 ff.

[58] Zhu Mu, *Fangyu shenglan* (1984 reprint of the Shanghai Library woodblock print edition of 1265–74; edited with Beijing Library photolithographic edition), 9.10a.

[59] For Su, see YRZZ IV.2114–17. For the inscription, see Su Tianjue, *Ziqi wengao* (1997 Zhonghua ed.), 2.19–22.

the cultural talents of the two gentlemen have never been equaled in their impact on people." The Lingling county sheriff Zeng Gui 曾圭 came fo rward and said: " My family is from Hengshan, where for generations we have followed the Confucian profession. Whenever we read the records and see the excellence of the words and conduct of the ancients, our hearts admire and love them. How much more [do we admire] the influence of the two gentlemen [Yuan and Yan]! In this mountain fastness, it is appropriate that we build a shrine to make offerings to them. Moreover, we should build a school and invite scholars, and everyone in distant places will hear of it and come."[60]

With Yao's approval, Zeng and his family thereupon personally contributed materials and labor to build the school, and after it was completed, Zeng Gui donated land to support students. In addition to a lecture hall, flanking the central hall where sacrifices to Confucius were held, two separate shrines were dedicated to Yuan Jie and Yan Zhenqing. Su continues:

> When I was young I read the Restoration Ode, which says: "When the emperor made his southern inspection tour, the court officials skulked away and offered themselves to the brigands as ministers." It also says: "Honorable rank was given the meritorious, the names of the loyalist martyrs were immortalized, and the imperial favor flowed over their sons and grandsons."[61] [The poem] is so great that people cannot help but know the importance of moral rectitude [from reading it]. Now, to collect a salary and yet neglect one's lord—is this not just like dogs and swine? During the most flourishing time of the Tianbao era, there were said to be multitudes of officials and clerks. [But] when a crisis came, those who died on the altars of the state were only a few more than ten, and there were only two who did not receive 'false' appointments [i.e., by the rebels]. How can this be the loyal ministers' and upright scholars' [way of] meeting hard times?[62]

1. Characters zhong xing (restoration) from ink rubbing of Yan Zhenqing's "Paean to the Restoration of the Great Tang Dynasty," detail, 771, Qiyang, Hunan. From Shodō zenshū, 3rd ed. (Tokyo: Heibonsha, 1966–1969), vol. 10, pl. 45. Reprinted in Amy McNair, The Upright Brush: Yan Zhenqing's Calligraphy and Song Literati Politics (Honolulu: University of Hawai'i Press, 1998), p. 55.

Having made his point about loyal service to the state, Su recounts Yuan Jie's administration of nearby Daozhou, where he rebuffed incursions from non-Han peoples to the south.[63] Su then links the upright conduct of men in the Tang—personified

[60] Su, 2.20. For Yao, see YRZZ II. 730; for Zeng, YRZZ III.1389.
[61] Translation of these passages is by Amy McNair, The Upright Brush: Yan Zhenqing's Calligraphy and Song Literati Politics (Honolulu: University of Hawai'i Press, 1998), 51. Original source: Quan Tang Wen, ed. Dong Gao (Tainan: Jingwei reprint, 1965), 380.7a–7b.
[62] Su, 2.20.
[63] For a brief description of this, see Indiana Companion to Traditional Chinese Literature, ed. and comp. William H. Nienhauser, Jr. (Bloomington: Indiana University Press, 1986), 952.

by Yuan Jie and Yan Zhenqing—both with a general commentary about loyalty and moral responsibility and with particular local issues:

> Alas! The talents that Heaven produces are sufficient for the needs of an entire generation; in uneventful times, human talents perhaps cannot be manifested, but when it comes to decisive events of great importance, then the loyal, upright, talented, and able scholars begin to show themselves. . . . This being so, then, can those who hold the empire not consider the virtuous and talented for service? Now, schools are the means by which human talents are nurtured, and those in charge of administration are responsible for encouraging those who teach. In past years, in the south of Hu-Xiang, the Yao people have many times taken up banditry—they have even attacked walled cities and towns, and killed clerks and people! The court has repeatedly attempted to mollify them, but in the end the effort was unsuccessful. Now there are those like the two gentlemen who have come to administer, and who will follow orders and request to punish them without cease. Furthermore, whoever dares to be seditious will suffer the consequences! Even more, [as with] this land's mountain peaks rising up and clear water flowing [being a product of nature], in the birth of men, who is not loyal and upright by his nature? At present, the state has been at peace for a long time, virtue and favor inundate and spread [over the land], and even though distant commanderies and districts all have schools, still those in charge, when they come to their posts, also seek out the remains of former worthies in the scenic landscapes of mountain fastnesses in order to expand places for study.[64]

Finally, then, Su links the places that are associated with moral heroes of the past with the need to build schools in order to nurture ideals of loyalty in the present generation. The appreciation of the landscape is not just for its beauty but also because it carries the imprint of these past heroes. Even administrators with heavy official responsibilities seek out sites like Wu Creek because of their association with such figures as Yuan and Yan. They choose these places because they evoke for the people who come to the academy the models of Yuan and Yan. These men are almost physically present, particularly so here because of the actual inscribing of Yuan Jie's famous poem in Yan Zhenqing's calligraphy on the cliffs above Wu Creek (see Fig. 1). Both men were paragons of Confucian loyalism and, in Yan's case, martyrdom,[65] and their literary and artistic compositions lived in the landscape of Wu Creek for Su Tianjue to capture in the context of his own times. As Su came from a family whose lineage can be traced back at least five generations in the northern cultural center of Zhending, it is unlikely that Su intended any subtle criticism of scholars in his day serving the Yuan; rather, I think we must read Su's evocation of these late Tang men as an effort to draw the thread of Chinese cultural continuity from the Tang to the Mongols. By evoking these heroes of the past in his narrative of the academy landscape, Su participated in the ritualization of cultural memory by repeating and thereby transmitting the themes of Confucian loyalty and moral conduct attributed to the ideal scholar in retreat and official in service, themes personified by Yuan Jie and Yan Zhenqing in the Tang. He effectively negotiated the appropriation of these figures by the Yuan regime, as Chinese icons of loyalty now venerated by Mongol rulers.

Sleeping Dragon Academy

Places associated with famous painters, as well as poets and calligraphers, also could be invested with meaning as sites for the ritualization of cultural memory embedded in a particular landscape. The site of the former villa of the Northern Song painter Li Gonglin (ca. 1041–1106) in the Longmian (Sleeping Dragon) Mountains of modern Anhui province provided the

[64] Su, 2.21.
[65] For this, see McNair, 140–42. The Northern Song scholar Ouyang Xiu (1007–72), a connoisseur of calligraphy, actually saw Yan Zhenqing's strength of character represented in his powerful calligraphic style. See Ronald C. Egan, "Ou-yang Hsiu and Su Shih on Calligraphy," *Harvard Journal of Asiatic Studies* 49.2 (December 1989), 371–72.

2. Opening scene of riders entering the Longmian Mountains, section of Mountain Villa, *copy after Li Gonglin (Villa I Tatti, Settignano). Reprinted in* Robert E. Harrist, Painting and Private Life in Eleventh-Century China *(Princeton, N.J.: Princeton University Press, 1998) (illustrations).*

foundation for Sleeping Dragon Academy.[66] The building of this academy in 1330 was commemorated in an inscription by Jie Xisi 揭傒斯 (1274–1344), who had just been appointed along with Su Tianjue and other distinguished scholars—both Chinese and non-Chinese—to service at the Yuan court as a member of the Academy of the Pavilion of the Star of Literature.[67] This scholarly agency was designed as a kind of think tank of Confucian scholarship for the purpose of transmitting Chinese culture—Confucian classics, history, and literature—to the reigning *khaghan*, Tugh Temür, and to the Mongol elite.[68] Jie's inscription reflects this mission by describing the Mongol administrator who established Sleeping Dragon Academy as an exemplary Confucian official who shouldered the responsibility for the education of the people under his jurisdiction:

> The way of governing the people is simply to enable them to know the rites and propriety. To enable people to know the rites and propriety, first show them what to look up to; when people know what to look up to, then they will know what to strive toward. The head of Shucheng in Luling is Seli Buqa 爕理普化. Using the Huguang quota, he took a *jinshi* degree in 1327, whereupon he came to govern this district. He used his learning to teach and lead the people, and so people began to know whom among men to regard as noble and whom among Confucians to regard as important, and thereby restored knowledge of how to nourish life and send off the dead. After residing there for two years, he said: "The people can certainly be taught!" Thereupon he arranged to acquire the old foundation of Li Gonglin's mountain villa in the eastern part of the district.[69]

According to Jie, Seli Buqa, scion of a distinguished Mongol lineage, donated his salary to build the academy. Jie further relates that the villa foundation lay between a Chan Buddhist temple and a shrine to a local deity, and that the villa itself had earlier been destroyed by monks from the temple. Included among the academy's buildings was a shrine to Li Gonglin, who painted a

[66] See Liu Zuoyuan, comp., *Longshan shuyuan zhi* (first preface, 1774), vol. 8 of Zhao Suosheng, Xue Zhengxing et al., comps., *Zhongguo lidai shuyuan zhi* (Nanjing: Jiangsu jiaoyu chubanshe, 1995). This Qing era compilation contains material on the Yuan.
[67] For Jie Xisi, see YRZZ III.1385–87. For the inscription, see Jie Xisi, *Jie wen'an gong quanji* (Sibu congkan ed.), 10.4b–6a.
[68] For this, see *The Cambridge History of China*, vol. 6, *Alien Regimes and Border States, 907–1368*, ed. Herbert Franke and Denis Twitchett (Cambridge: Cambridge University Press, 1994), 554.
[69] Jie, 10.4b–5a. For Seli Buqa, see YRZZ IV.2604–5.

long handscroll entitled "Mountain Villa," with separate frames depicting in sequence the landscape of his garden residence in the Longmian Mountains (see Fig. 2).[70] Because the Northern Song poets Su Shi 蘇軾 and Huang Tingjian 黄庭堅 spent time with Li at his mountain retreat, they were also enshrined together with him.[71]

The site of Li's mountain villa and of Sleeping Dragon Academy was a place that "depended on the confluence of the mountains and rivers where worthies in ancient times wandered" and "looked out on Longmian Mountain's foothills and peaks, which put forth clouds and rain to inundate the subcelestial realm."[72] The name of the mountain range was drawn from the appearance of the landscape: the shape of the mountains resembled a slumbering dragon.[73] These qualities—strong mountain peaks and myriad waters—are evident in Li's painting and in the poetry of his companions, Su Shi and Huang Tingjian. But the landscape also resonates with powerful historical images tied to place:

> Shu was [a place name] in the Spring and Autumn period, and this is the reason why there is a mountain named Spring and Autumn and there is the Shu River. At first it was part of [the state of] Sui and later it was together with [the state of] Chu. Its people are brave and love propriety. It is not only Shu that is like this. All of the places of Chu are like this. Therefore, Chu was always a strong state. Finally, when the Song court moved south, its people hid themselves in Jiang-Huai for nearly 200 years. In such circumstances, even though people desired to learn, how could they?[74]

Jie thus links this place with the history of the Spring and Autumn and Warring States era, up through the fall of the Song; in doing so, he juxtaposes the reclusive posture of Li Gonglin and his comrades with the heroic military and political forces that shaped the territories of states over the course of nearly fifteen hundred years. Conjuring a relationship with the past through the physical landscape draws on both the geographical boundaries that circumscribed historical states and on the topographical features that were celebrated in the premier cultural forms of poetry and painting.

West Luo Academy

Far to the northwest of Sleeping Dragon Academy, West Luo Academy was founded in 1314 at one of the most sacred sites in north China: a place along the Luo River where the mystical symbols known as the Luo Writings 洛書, inscribed on the back of a tortoise, were said to have been revealed to the mythical emperor Yu.[75] The location of West Luo Academy was close to the ancient capital of Luoyang, where the Yi 伊 and Luo Rivers converged, and also home to the Song Confucian patriarchs, the Cheng brothers, Cheng Yi 程頤 (1033–1107) and Cheng Hao 程顥 (1032–85). West Luo Academy was actually built on the foundations of a "charitable school" (*yixue, yishu* 義學, 義塾) established by the local man Xue Youliang 薛友諒 (fl. ca.1314–20) to fulfill the intention of his deceased father, Xuan 玄 (d. 1271).[76]

Cheng Jufu's 程鉅夫 (1249–1318) commemorative inscription for the academy celebrates the tradition of Confucian scholarship associated with this area, naming the famous Jin poet, Yuan Haowen 元好问 (1190–1274) and the Confucian

[70] For an excellent introduction to this painting, its artist, and its art historical context, see Robert E. Harrist, Jr., *Painting and Private Life in Eleventh-Century China: Mountain Villa by Li Gonglin* (Princeton, N.J.: Princeton University Press, 1998).

[71] Jie, 10.6b. For one perspective on the relationship between these two poets and the painter, Li Gonglin, see Stuart H. Sargent, "Colophons in Countermotion: Poems by Su Shih and Huang T'ing-chien on Paintings," *Harvard Journal of Asiatic Studies* 52.1 (June 1992): 263–302; see also Ronald C. Egan, "Poems on Paintings: Su Shih and Huang T'ing-chien," *Harvard Journal of Asiatic Studies* 43 (1983): 413–51.

[72] Jie, 10.5a.

[73] Harrist, 61. See also Zhu, *Fangyu shenglan*, 48.3a; Wang Xiangzi, *Yudi jisheng* (Zhongguo gudai dilizhi congkan ed.), 45.10a.

[74] Jie, 10.5b–6a.

[75] See inscriptions on this academy by Yuan Jue, *Qingrong jushi ji* (Sibu beiyao ed.), 18.3a–3b and Cheng Jufu, *Chuguo wenxiangong xuelou Cheng xiansheng wenji* (Siku quanshu ed.), 22.1a–2b.

[76] For Xue Youliang, see YRZZ IV.2016; for his father, Xuan, see YRZZ IV.2012.

adviser to Khubilai Khan, Yao Shu 姚樞 (1201–78), among others, as predecessors who lectured here.[77] According to Cheng, after the death of his father, Xue Youliang allocated income to support the establishment of a charitable school that "imitated the structure of an academy."[78] Xue appointed someone to supervise teaching and students gathered at the school. He later expanded it by purchasing the former site of the Sima family's Solitary Pleasure Garden 獨樂園, where he built a Five Worthies Hall in order to sacrifice to the "Yi-Luo Famous Classicists."[79] The incorporation of Sima Guang's (1019–86) Solitary Pleasure Garden site into the school was more than a physical expansion of property: the place brought with it an important historical and cultural legacy.[80] The great Northern Song historian and statesman, Sima Guang, bought the property and built a garden there in Luoyang after he left the Northern Song capital, Kaifeng, in disgrace following his failed political struggle against the New Policies of Wang Anshi (1021–86). Sima Guang built and named structures in his garden to commemorate figures from the past with whom he identified and whom he desired to emulate. Fishing, gardening, and other activities pursued in the garden were commemorated by specific sites associated with men from the past who had withdrawn to a bucolic life to avoid political strife. When this school was declared an academy in 1314, the Five Worthies Hall, built on the site of Solitary Pleasure Garden, was renamed the Yi-Luo Retreat. The new name commemorated still the Confucian patriarchs of the Song venerated in the Five Worthies Hall but also called attention to the sacred geography associated with the Yi and Luo Rivers. A headmaster was appointed and Hanlin Academician Liu Geng 劉賡 (1248–1328) wrote the name plaque in his own calligraphy. Auspicious signs accompanied the transformation of the charitable school into West Luo Academy.[81]

A second inscription, by Yuan Jue 袁桷 (1266–1327), while also attributing the origins of West Luo Academy to the Xue family and its emphasis on education, makes other associations with Northern Song predecessors and more directly identifies physical aspects of the landscape in relation to the traditions represented by West Luo Academy:

> Henan Xue [Youliang] honored [the intention of] his deceased father and established a charitable school at Yongning. There is a trace [of this school] left at Dragon Head Mountain, where the green cliffs are precipitous. During the Song Yuanyou era (1086–94) Luo Shi 羅適 from Tiantai inscribed on them the words: "Place where Yu received the Luo Writings." Luo Shi was a disciple of Hu Yuan 胡瑗 (993–1059), and he was skilled at water conservancy. According to the gazetteers, Yongning adjoins Changshui county, and the eastern border of Changshui is near the Luo River. The records say that this is where the Luo Writings were produced, and now there is a newly established shrine to Yu at Dragon Head Mountain. Since Xue looks up to it, he has come forward to request that the court make an academy [there] and accordingly name it West Luo Academy so that posterity will know the sincerity of Yu and the Luo Writings.[82]

Several of the traditions surrounding the sage-king Yu, who was said to have founded the first dynasty, the Xia, in the third millennium B.C.E., are relevant here. According to the *Hong fan* 洪範 (Great Plan) section of the *Book of History*, one of the five canonical Confucian texts, Yu succeeded in taming the flood waters, regulating rivers and bringing order to the land. Having proven himself, Heaven bestowed on him the Luo Writings, which provided guiding principles for governing. Luo Shi

---

[77] Cheng Jufu, 22.1a. Among sources for Yuan Haowen, see Stephen H. West, "Chilly Seas and East-Flowing Rivers: Yuan Hao-wen's Poems of Death and Disorder, 1233–1235," in *China under Jurchen Rule: Essays on Chin Intellectual and Cultural History*, ed. Hoyt Cleveland Tillman and Stephen H. West (Albany: State University of New York Press, 1995), 281–304. For Yao Shu, see Chan Hok-lam, "Yao Shu (1201–1278)," *Papers on Far Eastern History* 22 (1980): 17–50.

[78] Cheng Jufu, 22.1a.

[79] Cheng Jufu, 22.1a.

[80] See the description of the garden and its meaning in Harrist, 50–54.

[81] Cheng Jufu, 22.1a.

[82] Yuan Jue, 18.3a. Recall the references to the mythical emperor Yu in the landscape at Jiaxuan Academy.

(1029–1101; *jinshi* 1065), a native of the southeast, served as prefect of Kaifeng, the Northern Song capital, and gained a reputation for his efforts at water control.[83] After he completed his service and left the area, local people erected a shrine to honor him; he was also enshrined after his death in his southeastern birthplace.[84] His contribution to the site of West Luo Academy was his inscription on the cliffs of Dragon Head Mountain identifying it as the place where Yu received the Luo Writings. Luo's own career also links him, on the one hand, to Yu's controlling the waters and, on the other hand, to the numeric cosmology of the Luo Writings, as Luo Shi also wrote on the *Book of Changes*. Cheng Jufu not only does not mention Luo Shi, but also barely mentions Yu, whereas Yuan Jue places the veracity of the tradition of Yu receiving the Luo Writings at the center of his inscription. Cheng centers his on the various northern classicists who transmitted the doctrines of neo-Confucianism and on the Xue family's place in this tradition. Both Cheng and Yuan allude to the transmission of the lost Way by the neo-Confucian patriarchs of the Song, and Cheng also mentions the shrine to Yu built by Xue Youliang, which must be the same shrine referred to by Yuan. Threads of cultural continuity embedded in this place, then, stretch from remote antiquity up through the most recent times.

Conclusion

Spanning the middle decades of the Yuan dynasty, records of several academies scattered across Mongol-ruled China reveal a remarkably consistent rhetorical pattern that relates the origins of these academies directly to Chinese cultural memory embedded in the landscape. The narratives these texts offer were performances that contributed to the ritualization of Chinese cultural memory. The theoretical premise of this argument derives from Catherine Bell's precise definition of ritualization as a "strategic mode of practice" that "produces nuanced relations of power characterized by acceptance, resistance, negotiated appropriation, and the redemptive reinterpretation of the hegemonic order." Moving well beyond the classic Durkheimian sense of ritual as a means of social control, Bell argues that ritual does not control but, rather, constitutes a particular dynamic of social empowerment.[85] Her concept of ritualization rejects the notion of ritual activity as merely an instrument for more basic purposes—power or social control—and views ritual practices themselves as a means to produce and negotiate power relations. Bell's perspective provides an analytic framework that illuminates the complex interaction between Mongol rulers and their Chinese subjects.

Asserting that the argument here is essentially a textual one, I refer to Michel de Certeau's notion of narrative transforming space into place or place into space.[86] Narratives of academy origins and renewal transformed landscapes rich with historical and cultural meanings into spaces where both nature and the Confucian canon were texts to be read and studied. In Liu Guan's inscription on Stone Gate Grotto, for example, he referred to founders of the great academies of the Song who selected scenic places to explore the phenomena of nature. Several of the inscriptions make explicit reference to roaming within the landscape surrounding the academy, further reinforcing the idea of transforming the place into space. For example, Dai Biaoyuan relates his "roving among hills and peaks" at Jiaxuan Academy, and Liu Guan recollects Xie Lingyun's love of wandering and exploring in the mountains as a prelude to describing what the students at the academy do: "You roam and chant here." The narrative of a visit by an official to the place or the recalling of earlier visits rendered static places into living spaces. The space of the academy became meaningful through its association with the past, and it was made into the exclusive domain of the scholarly élite.[87]

Beginning with the inscriptions of Dai Biaoyuan on academies dedicated to two Song patriot-poets, we can identify a process of negotiated appropriation of symbols: men who were icons of Song patriotism are appropriated through narratives of

[83] See biographical sources on Luo Shi in SRZZ V.4273. He discussed water management with Su Shi, who served as prefect of Hangzhou.

[84] For the latter, see Ye Shi, *Ye Shi ji* (Taibei: Hetu luoshu, 1974), 11.192–93.

[85] Bell, 171.

[86] Michel de Certeau, *The Practice of Everyday Life* (Berkeley and Los Angeles: University of California Press, 1984), 91-110.

[87] See Thomas Keirstead, "Gardens and Estates: Medievality and Space," *Positions* 1.2: 289–94.

academy landscapes written by Chinese scholars for their new rulers. The voluntary or forced political exile of both poets is commemorated in the places associated with them, and their symbolic legacy is inverted, making them central to the educational enterprise of the Yuan state. The tradition of patriotism and loyalty to the fallen Song is reinvented in the context of Mongol rule. Both accommodation—serving the Yuan state—and resistance—recalling Song patriots—on the part of the Chinese scholarly elite, represented by Dai Biaoyuan, can be read into the narrative of these academy landscapes.

The Northern Song painter, Li Gonglin, and his poet companions, Su Shi and Huang Tingjian, were enshrined at Sleeping Dragon Academy, where they embodied a rich tradition that associated retreat with cultural creativity. Li's painting of his mountain villa was a material artifact that attested to the power of the landscape, as the poetry of Su Shi and Huang Tingjian equally conveyed the visual and physical experience of the place. This cultural memory was transmitted both through Li's painting and through texts of poems, and was appropriated by one of the foremost Chinese intellectuals of his day. Jie Xisi's inscription on Sleeping Dragon Academy transforms these Song cultural icons into symbols of high Yuan culture through a narrative of the landscape that transmits a Chinese cultural legacy as it reinvents it.

The narratives of the landscape at West Luo Academy range over a lengthy span of time, from earliest semimythical antiquity to the Song, and invite the reader to engage with an broad group of figures, including the sage-king Yu, the Northern Song statesman and historian, Sima Guang, and a local scholarly family. The physical incorporation of Sima Guang's Solitary Pleasure Garden into the academy landscape makes concrete the notion of appropriation of cultural symbols and their transformation into edifices that bolster the claims to cultural legitimacy of the Yuan government.

Reaching further back, the association of Xie Lingyun with Stone Gate Grotto Academy draws attention both to Xie's poetic legacy and to the importance of the southern landscape as a source of philosophical enlightenment. Despite his compromised political career, Xie's reputation as the first landscape poet heightens his value as a cultural symbol. Both poetry and the allied art of calligraphy come together in the landscape at Wu Creek Academy, where the legacy of loyalty in service to the state is highlighted through the model careers of Yuan Jie and Yan Zhenqing in the Tang. Here, as elsewhere, Chinese cultural icons are invoked in the service of the Yuan by Chinese writers who by this means simultaneously resist and accommodate themselves to the Mongol regime. They display their own cultural legacy, capture and remake it in a strategy of negotiated appropriation made visible in the narratives of academy landscapes. In this way, Chinese inscription authors ritualized Chinese cultural memory and accomplished the "redemptive reinterpretation of the hegemonic order" that was China under Mongol rule.

Performance and Appropriation: Profane Rituals in Gardens and Landscapes

Performance and Appropriation: Profane Rituals in Gardens and Landscapes

Performance and Appropriation: Profane Rituals in Gardens and Landscapes

Performance and Appropriation: Profane Rituals in Gardens and Landscapes

British Naumachias: The Performance of Triumph and Memorial

Patrick Eyres

Introduction

Since the mid-eighteenth century, the lakes of particular English landscapes have been appropriated to accommodate the pleasurable and patriotic naumachia—a performative mock naval combat, "fought" in celebration of naval supremacy and empire. "Appropriation" proves to be a useful keyword for discussion of the naumachia. Landscapes were seldom designed for their performance and, in addition to the appropriation of space within gardens and parks, this genre of garden theater has undergone a succession of appropriations by, for example, English aristocrats from the courts of Italy and bourgeois entrepreneurs from the elite Georgian landscape garden to the populist Victorian public park. "Performance" is another usefully discursive keyword. Performance of the naumachia not only emphasizes that designed landscapes serve a theatrical function but also acknowledges the willing participation of the initiators, performers, and audience in a ritualized spectacle that revalidates societal norms. To consider the naumachia as a secular ritual similarly acknowledges that garden spaces can become, or be redesigned as, sites of large-scale social interactions leading to consensual and collective cultural identities. Within the broad context of the appropriateness of gardens and parks as naumachia sites, the two keywords—"appropriation" and "performance"—will provide a focus for discussion. This will engage with origins and definitions, with theoretical interrelationships between theater and ritual, and with analysis both of the Georgian fashion and the contemporary naumachia known as *Naval Warfare*.

- I -

The term, naumachia, acknowledges not only the precedent of antiquity but also the issues of appropriation and performance. Naumachia is the Romanized version of the Greek word for a naval battle. Roman appropriation of the term constructed specific meanings. One signified the reenactment of sea fights as grandiose public entertainments. Another described the architectural basins and lakes designed for naumachias.[1] Roman naumachias were staged as populist celebrations of imperial supremacy and the cult of the emperor, and were performed as epic spectacles of waterborne gladiatorial combat, to the death, between fleets manned by convicts or prisoners of war. However, the term naumachia also described a mock battle between

---

[1] The antiquarian and architect Pirro Ligorio confirmed the naumachia as architectural basin and aquatic performance in his reconstruction of ancient Rome, *Anteiquae Urbis Imago* (1561). For reproductions, see Robert W. Gaston, ed., *Pirro Ligorio: Artist and Antiquarian* (Florence: Silvana Editoriale, 1988), 65, pl. 4, the naumachia basin by the Porta Portuensis; 81, pl. 69, detail of the Porta Portuensis naumachia basin; 81, pl. 67, a naumachia performance underway within the architectural basin on the Via Flaminia. Other plates reproduce Ligorio's sketches of classical coinage showing naumachia performances within architectural basins: 81, pl. 68, a Greek coin of Domitian, and 81, pl. 70, a Greek coin of Tiberias.

1. *The Amphitheater, Boboli Gardens. The Pitti Palace is on the left with the courtyard in shadow*

miniature and manned, replica warships. As such, the naumachia became an aquatic drama performed for the elite within imperial villa gardens.[2] It was the latter that was revived in Italy during the mid-sixteenth century, and that flourished into the early eighteenth century as an integral component of the baroque repertoire of courtly theater.[3]

It was the cultural authority that the Italian Renaissance invested in the forms and practices of classical antiquity that legitimized appropriation of the Roman naumachia. However, these courtly events appear to have been performed within preexisting sites temporarily adapted for the purpose. For example, on occasions during the seventeenth century, the Teatro Farnese in Parma was flooded for these performances.[4] The Medici naumachia appears to characterize the Italian baroque phenomenon. It was performed in Florence during May 1589 as one of the many lavish entertainments devised to celebrate the wedding of Grand Duke Ferdinando I de' Medici of Tuscany to Christine de Lorraine, niece of Henry III of France and granddaughter of the king's mother, Catherine de' Medici.[5]

Significantly, the Boboli gardens of the Pitti Palace exemplify the baroque acknowledgment of the garden as a site of courtly theater. Indeed, the rear of the palace overlooks the amphitheater designed for the performance of spectacles such as those that commemorated this marriage (Fig. 1). However, it was the palace courtyard that was temporarily appropriated for the naumachia because it could be flooded to accommodate the eighteen "warships."[6] The Florentine performance epitomized the modernity of the Italian naumachia as a celebration of contemporary naval prowess. It promoted the potent role of the Medici in the naval alliance forged between the Mediterranean Christian powers to combat the encroachments of the Islamic

[2] See Patrick Eyres and Michael Cousins, "Naumachia: The Parkland Phenomenon of Mock Naval Battle," *New Arcadian Journal* no. 39/40 (1995): 13–29 (13–14).

[3] J. D. Loach, "Pageant and Festival Arts: General Characteristics and Constraints," L. Macy, ed., *The Grove Dictionary of Art Online* (accessed 19 January 2006), <http//www.groveart.com>.

[4] Roland Wolff, "Theatre, III, 3(i): Baroque Italy, b) Stage design and costume," L. Macy, ed., *The Grove Dictionary*. Pirro Ligorio participated in designing the theatrical apparatus for staging a naumachia, *L'isola beata*, in Ferrara in 1569—see David R. Coffin, "Ligorio, Pirro, 3. Tivoli and Ferrara," L. Macy, ed., *The Grove Dictionary*. Ligorio also was known to employ the plan and form of the Roman naumachia basin in his architectural designs, as may be seen in his Casino di Pio IV, of 1558–60, in the Vatican gardens. See David R. Coffin, "Ligorio, Pirro, 2. Papal Service," L. Macy, ed., *The Grove Dictionary*. For reproductions of Ligorio's Casino di Pio IV, see Caterina Volpi, *Pirro Ligorio e I giardini a Roma nella seconda metà del cinquecento* (Rome: Lithos Editrice, 1996), figs. 1, 2, 12, and Isa Belli Barsali, *Ville di Roma: Lazio I* (Milan: Edizioni Sisar, 1970), 211–15.

[5] Another well-documented naumachia was staged in Parma in May 1690 by Ranuccio II Farnese, sixth Duke of Parma and Piacenza, to celebrate the wedding of his son, Odoardo II Farnese to Dorothea Sophia, Princess of Neuburg-Pfalz. See Clare Robertson, "Ranuccio II Farnese, 6th Duke of Parma and Piacenza," L. Macy, ed., *The Grove Dictionary*.

[6] The water came from the Boboli Gardens through the pipes that fed the fountain in the sculpture grotto on the garden side of the courtyard. For details of the Medici naumachia, see James M. Saslow, *The Medici Wedding of 1589: Florentine Festival as Theatrum Mundi* (New Haven, Conn., and London: Yale University Press, 1996), 1, 19, 35–36, 96–97, 127, 168–169, and 257, pl. 87 by Orazio Scarabelli.

Turkish empire. The naval victory at Lepanto in 1571 had become an iconic moment for the Christian alliance, which was to be consistently referenced by the Italian courtly naumachia. The relationship between Ferdinando and the alliance was signified by the dress code of the "Christian" combatants. Some wore costumes bearing the colorway of Ferdinando's livery, whereas the design of others identified the geographical extent of the alliance: a contingent from the Medici villa at Poggio a Caiano, another from the Tuscan port of Pisa, and others from Corfu, Crete, Cyprus, Marseilles, Genoa, and Naples. Characteristically, the "enemy" were armed and costumed *à la turque* and "fought" beneath the Ottoman flag.

The formulaic construction of this Medici naumachia would have been equally familiar to Seicento Italians and English Georgians,[7] and strikes a chord with aficionados of *Naval Warfare* in Scarborough's Peasholm Park. Animated by fireworks and explosions, the naumachia unfolds with a prolonged naval battle in several acts, in which "our side" (the Christian fleet) defeats the "enemy" (the Turks). It continues with a naval bombardment of "the enemy" base (the Turkish castle), whose robust defense is finally overwhelmed by the assault of troops landed from the fleet. Having stormed the fortification, "our side" tear down the "enemy" flag and run up "ours" to signify victory. It was this model of courtly spectacle that was subsequently appropriated by elites in France and later in Britain. By the 1750s, the British naumachia had become a pleasurable fashion enacted on the lakes of aristocratic and gentry landscape gardens in patriotic celebration of the Royal Navy as the agent of Britain's imperial expansion.

The Georgian heyday appears to have been framed by the royal celebrations at Cliveden in 1739, and in London's Hyde Park in 1814. The garden naumachia appears to have been symptomatic of the ways in which patriotism was commodified in the interests of the state and the landowner. Subsequently, the entrepreneurial agendas of Victorian country landowners and bourgeois civic institutions enlarged the repertoire to include static firework naumachias mounted as profitable popular entertainments in the landscape garden, in municipal urban public parks and in the parks and gardens of seaside resorts. Clearly, the seaside firework naumachia stemmed from the decisions in the 1760s by aristocrats and landowners to put their estates on show for a price.[8] During the twentieth century, the Yorkshire seaside resort of Scarborough uniquely developed the garden naumachia. Twice a week during each summer season since 1929, mock naval combat has been staged on the lake of Peasholm Park for the delight of holidaymakers, day-trippers, and residents. Choreographed to a dramatic narrative and patriotic anthems, a diminutive fleet of manned, scale model ships performs the aquatic spectacle and firework display entitled *Naval Warfare*.

However, whether in Georgian landscape gardens or Scarborough's Peasholm Park, it is unlikely that the initiators, performers, and audiences regarded themselves as participants in ritual, doubtless because the term is usually associated with occasions that are more solemn than a jolly-up. Although the Scarborough naumachia has been regularly performed since 1929, its present incarnation as *Naval Warfare* has been underway for the past forty years, and documented through advertisements, newspaper, and television coverage and by the souvenir booklet. As we shall see, this publication details the history, practices, function, and content of *Naval Warfare*. As such, it codifies the prescribed order and narrative as performed since the 1960s. By comparison, the Georgian experience is problematic. Evidence from diaries and publications is largely anecdotal and points to a diverse range of practices. Many examples are of one-off performances, and the longevity of those performed regularly is unclear. Sources tantalize with remarks such as "during" and "throughout" a particular decade. Nevertheless, the British naumachia functions within the broad contexts of consumerism and leisure. For Georgians, it was an elite cultural practice performed in the landscape garden, whereas *Naval Warfare*, performed in the populist Edwardian Japanese–style Peasholm Park, is firmly in the domain of popular culture.

[7] For a comparison between contemporary naval commemoration in the Boboli Gardens, Florence, and Castle Howard, North Yorkshire, see Patrick Eyres, "Castle Howard: Landscape as Political Manifesto," *New Arcadian Journal* no. 29/30 (1990): 32–65 (48–49).

[8] Fred Inglis, *The Delicious History of the Holiday* (London and New York: Routledge, 2000), 44–45. Inglis cites as examples, Prince Leopold of Anhalt-Dessau at Wörlitz, Sir Francis Dashwood at West Wycombe, and the partnership between "Governor" Joseph Pocklington and "Admiral" Peter Crossthwaite at Derwentwater.

Clearly, gardens and parks have been perceived as appropriate spaces for the affirmation of collective identities that bond participants through a physical social communion. As the British naumachia has been staged exclusively within gardens and parks, or in direct relation to them, the performance confirms these sites as theatrical spaces. *Naval Warfare*, in particular, has been discussed as an aquatic drama by Christine Richardson in *Theatre Quarterly*,[9] and by myself as a pantomime in the *New Arcadian Journal*: "the patriotic panto of Peasholm Park."[10] However, even though a landscape may not have been designed for theatrical rituals, it can become appropriated for these purposes. In this way, garden design not only provides the environment for these practices but also occurs as a consequence of them. Although none of the gardens and parks discussed here was purpose-designed as a performative site, architectural and landscape features were developed at each one to enhance the staging and experience of naumachias. Forts, batteries, islands, docks, and viewing stations were added, lakes were enlarged and new ones floated. In addition, at Peasholm Park, an entire hillside was redesigned to provide seating for the audiences of the aquatic music hall theater that included the naumachia.

Stowe provides a useful distinction between these naumachias and the leisured, gardenist pastime of messing about in boats.[11] One of Jacques Rigaud's images of 1734 shows an orientalist romp underway with turbaned party-folk in a boat of sort-of Levantine rig,[12] and, by 1759, it was reported that Stowe's lake sported a "Model Man of War with all her Rigging," dedicated to the contemplations of fishing.[13] The boathouses for these activities were distinct from the garden features designed to accommodate naumachias. At Peasholm Park the naval docks that house the miniature fleet exemplify this distinction, and the naumachia itself has evolved from another form of messing about with boats—the public displays of model boats on the lake in the late 1920s.[14]

Although the British naumachia clearly articulates an integral relationship between garden and performance, the interrelation between theater and ritual has been usefully discussed by Victor Turner and Catherine Bell. Turner considered that ritual created a willing transition from the familiar daily environment, a release into the here and now, into a space out of time and out of the social structure. Within this space, participants experience a spontaneous, immediate togetherness, a bonding that he terms "communitas," which, no matter how momentary, enables them to return revitalized to the everyday world.[15] The garden naumachia may be located within Turner's "genealogy of genres," which he discusses in familiar terms: "Once a genre has become prominent, however, it is likely to survive or be revived at some level of the socio-cultural system, perhaps moving from the elite to the popular culture or vice-versa, gaining and losing audiences and support in the process."[16]

[9] Christine Richardson, "'Naval Warfare' at Scarborough: An Aquatic Drama for the Eighties," *Theatre Quarterly* IX, no. 36 (1980): 82–88.

[10] Patrick Eyres, "The Patriotic Panto of Peasholm Park," *New Arcadian Journal* no. 39/40 (1995): 73–99.

[11] In addition, there was the occasional waterborne pageant, such as the one performed with fireworks and music on the River Thames in London to commemorate the peace of 1749. See *A View of the Fire-Workes and Illuminations, at his Grace the Duke of Richmond's at White-Hall and on the River Thames, on Monday 15 May 1749* (London: Victoria & Albert Museum).

[12] See Jacques Rigaud, "View from the Head of the Lake," 1733–34, pl. 134 in Peter Willis, *Charles Bridgeman and the English Landscape Garden* (Newcastle: Elysium Press, 2002).

[13] Benton Seeley, *Stow* [*sic*], *A Description* (Buckingham, 1759), 13–14. See also Eyres and Cousins, "Naumachia": 20–21. Perhaps fishing was the function of the replica warship in Thomas Badeslade's *A Prospect of Stainborough, and Wentworth Castle in the County of Yorkshire* of 1739 (London: British Library), in which the vessel is stored in the fruit garden. Wentworth Castle was the estate of Thomas Wentworth first Earl of Strafford (second creation), who had been first Lord of the Admiralty—see Michael Charlesworth, "Elevation and Succession: The Representation of Jacobite and Hanoverian Politics in the Landscape Gardens of Wentworth Castle and Wentworth Woodhouse," *New Arcadian Journal* no. 31/32 (1991): 7–65, and "Thomas Wentworth's Monument: The Achievement of Peace," *New Arcadian Journal* no. 57/58 (2004–5): 31–63.

[14] Patrick Eyres, "'Naval Warfare': The Battle of Peasholm Park," *New Arcadian Journal* no. 39/40: 33–69 (48–50).

[15] Victor Turner, *The Ritual Process: Structure and Anti-Structure* (Harmondsworth: Pelican Books, [1969] 1974), 113–16, 155–56. Turner identifies two models for "human interrelatedness, juxtaposed and alternating," which he describes as social structure and "communitas" (82). Of the three types of "communitas"—existential or spontaneous, normative and ideological (120)—it is the former that is operative in the context of this discussion: "Spontaneous communitas is richly charged with affects, mainly pleasurable ones. Life in 'structure' is filled with objective difficulties. . . . Spontaneous communitas has something 'magical' about it" (127).

[16] Victor Turner, *From Ritual to Theatre: The Human Seriousness of Play* (New York, N.Y.: Performing Arts Journal Publications, 1982), 78–79.

Whether the audience is elite or populist, the genre of the naumachia remains constant, as does the repertoire of garden features that have already been discussed. The significance lies in the composition and content of the performance. Here, Turner's definition of ritual is useful—as "prescribed formal behavior for occasions . . . having reference to beliefs in invisible beings or powers regarded as the first or final causes of all effects."[17] By identifying the articulation of beliefs as the purpose of the activity, Turner is able "to think of ritual essentially as performance, enactment, not primarily as rules or rubrics. The rules 'frame' the ritual process, but the ritual process transcends its frame."[18]

By applying Turner's model, we can appreciate that the naumachia generates a transcendent "communitas" that embraces belief in the sacrality of the British Empire and of the role of the Royal Navy as the agent of the grandeur of Imperial Britain. Thus, the naumachia's "communitas" acts as a social intensification that bonds participants through reinforcement of a national identity forged through naval warfare with European rivals. This indicates that the naumachia is no idle whimsy of an elite social function, or of a populist seaside entertainment. Rather, it is a serious ideological engagement. Certainly, it is this ideological bonding that locates these naumachias as paradigms of Britain's imperial identity through their combination of participatory entertainment with endorsement of the dominant national myth. It is interesting to note that, during the 1930s, there was a correlation between the naval events performed during the warship visits to Scarborough each summer and the development of the Peasholm Park naumachia.[19] Equally significant is Turner's acknowledgment that the relationship between "communitas" and this sort of ideological bonding indicated that "Cultural performances may be viewed as 'dialectical dancing partners' . . . of the perennial social drama, to which they give meaning appropriate to the specificities of time, place and culture."[20] This remark implies that agendas and meanings can change, and that "communitas" can be experienced as a diversity of transcendences—as well we shall see.

The collective transcendence of "communitas" is facilitated by the estrangement from daily life experienced through the exotically "other" environment of the garden. For example, the Georgian neoclassical pastoral was designed as a cultural appropriation of a "natural" setting to create a paradoxical, fantasy environment within which imaginative possibilities became so enhanced that estrangement would cultivate the liminality through which actors and audience willingly participated in the illusion of the naumachia's mythic drama, and in which the modernity of naval warfare became fictionalized. At Peasholm Park, the audience's estrangement within a place constructed as a Japanese fairyland orientalizes fictional experience to such an extent that a physical sign of Englishness has been introduced through the theatrical form of a painted representation of the White Cliffs of Dover.

Catherine Bell complements Turner by observing that "In recent years, much attention has focused on what ritual has in common with theatrical performances, dramatic spectacles and public events. Most of these comparisons rest on a recognition that the performative dimensions *per se*—that is the deliberate, self-conscious 'doing' of highly symbolic actions in public—is the key to what makes ritual, theater and spectacle what they are."[21] Bell identifies particular characteristics of ritual-like activities, namely: formalism, traditionalism, invariance, rule-governance, sacral symbolism, and performance. All these characteristics are evident in *Naval Warfare* and in certain Georgian naumachias as well as, variously, in others.

By applying Bell's model, we can see that the naumachia's process of ritualization operates in a way that recollects Turner. The rules that frame the ritual process encompass a restricted code of speech and movement, rigidly structured by rubrics and taboos, which encapsulate a disciplined sequence of actions marked by precise choreography, physical repetition, and the self-control of performers. The way that the ritual process transcends its frame is through its purpose, which is to summarize complex ideological messages that engage consensus between the raptly attentive audience and a legitimized

[17] Turner, *From Ritual to Theatre*, 79.
[18] Ibid.
[19] Eyres, "Naval Warfare," 55.
[20] Turner, *From Ritual to Theatre*, 78.
[21] Catherine Bell, *Ritual: Perspectives and Dimensions* (Oxford: Oxford University Press, 1997), 159.

2. *Stebbing Shaw, "South West View of Batchacre Park," engraving, 1802 (courtesy of the Trustees of the William Salt Library, Stafford)*

tradition invented to endow the present with the authoritative appeal of the past; a transcendence facilitated by deployment of sacral symbols, such as the national flag, naval ensigns, and iconic warships, that encompass histories, loyalty, and a collective identity. The ritual-like action creates an explicit, partisan differentiation between the sacred, or national, "us," and "them," the profane. However, sacrality is not only attributed to objects but also to places, so that the garden or park where the flag is raised and where the navy goes into battle becomes the symbolic site of the living nation.[22] Through the naumachia's performance within the sacral landscape of garden and park, we can appreciate that Bell, like Turner, offers a conjunction between garden, theater, and ritual.

We shall see that this ritual-like, performative transcendence was revalidated by the consistent modernity visualized by replicas of contemporary warships that reenacted recent events. We also shall see that commodification of these sacral landscapes confirms the historical and cultural specificity of distinct audiences. For example, the late Georgian print by Stebbing Shaw promotes Bathacre Park within the elite market for country house and garden tourism, and clarifies that the naumachia is one among a variety of gardenist pleasures (Fig. 2). The mass-produced postcard is among the merchandizing retailed as souvenirs of *Naval Warfare* in Peasholm Park (Fig. 17). The Scarborough naumachia performed a populist celebration of empire as symbolized by a powerful navy that had been victorious in two world wars. Although the British naumachia served an imperial function for two and a half centuries, its present manifestation as *Naval Warfare* is in a state of metamorphosis and, because of Britain's postimperial membership in the European Union, the symbolic coherence of mythic representation has become fractured and the invented tradition may appear to have become emptied of meaning. Before focusing on *Naval Warfare*, it is useful to exemplify the problematic variety of practices encompassed by the Georgian naumachia.

- II -

Elite identity was enhanced by the development of the landscape garden as a site of high culture. The costly production of the naumachia's ships, weaponry, theatrical explosions, and architectural props complemented the role of garden design as a display of conspicuous consumption, wealth, status, and leisure. Stebbing Shaw's print of Batchacre Park (Fig. 2) exemplifies the evidence of garden design as a consequence of a site's appropriation for the performance of naumachias. Miniature and manned, replica warships (a sloop in sail, a barge, and, right, a frigate) adorn a lake populated with islands (center), a fort (center right), dock, earthworks, and batteries (to right of frigate). Reception accounts would generally applaud the "beautiful appearance" of a "little Fleet"[23] as "richly ornamental" and creating "a pretty effect."[24] Stimulated by imperial

[22] Bell, *Ritual*, 138–69.

[23] Thomas Phillibrown, Diary, 1754, cited in Sir Francis Dashwood, *The Dashwoods of West Wycombe* (London: Aurum Press, [1987] 1990), 226–27.

[24] Thoroton, *History of Nottinghamshire* (1795), cited in Nigel Aston, "The Navy Lark," *Country Life* (1 August 1991).

victories during the warfare that preoccupied forty-six of the years between 1739 and 1815,[25] the naumachia reinforced perception of the landscape garden as a representation of patriotic virtue. It also promoted the interrelationship of landed dynasties with the expansion of commercial empire. Many naumachias were performed in landscapes embellished with wealth acquired either from the booty of naval victory or from the returns on investment in mercantile and colonial trade. The uniformed figures manning Bathacre Park's rooftop observatory indicate that this site exemplifies the naumachia as a celebration of naval affiliations and the achievements of family members as career officers in the Royal Navy. Although Georgian naumachias shared the patriotic function of pleasurable social intensification,

3. *William Hannan, "A View of the Landscape at West Wycombe, Buckinghamshire," oil painting, ca. 1751 (courtesy of Sir Edward Dashwood; photo courtesy of the National Trust Photo Library)*

which rallied particular groupings to the imperial project, there is seldom sufficient documentation to fully explore the correlation between liminality and "communitas." Consequently, I shall note a few examples in order to emphasise the variety of agendas that encapsulated interests as diverse as expediency, entrepreneurialism, denial, and transition.

The royal naumachias overtly marked the nation's transition from peace to war (1739) and from war to peace (1814). In September 1739, Frederick Louis Prince of Wales ordained the Cliveden naumachia as an entertainment for Princess Augusta's birthday, and in anticipation of victory in the imminent war with Spain. The prince constructed the relationship between garden-as-belvedere and naumachia-as-eyecatcher so that, from the heights of Cliveden, the appreciative court could applaud the drama performed on the Thames River below by a "fleet" of hired commercial sailing barges. This concluded by reenacting the capture of Gibraltar during the previous war (1704).[26] The prince's agenda appears to have been in the interests of Whig Party politics, as a means of claiming the cachet of patriotism in order to reinforce the promotion of naval warfare as an instrument for the enlargement of commercial empire.[27] However, the Whig-oriented Prince of Wales was simultaneously lionized by influential Tory politicians as the "patriot" king-in-waiting. Consequently, this event not only seems to have stimulated the fashion for naumachias but also appears to have legitimized the practice for Tory landowners.

[25] The War of Austrian Succession (1739–48), the Seven Years' War (1756–63), the War of American Independence (1775–83), and the Great War against Revolutionary and Napoleonic France (1793–1815). I am grateful to Keith Goodway for drawing my attention to the views of Batchacre Park. Careful scrutiny of Georgian parkland maps and views illuminates the fashionable naumachia. For example, see these illustrations in Judith Roberts, "'Well Temper'd Clay': Constructing Water Features in the Landscape Park," *Garden History* 29: 1 (2001): fig. 11 (Anon., "View across the Great Water to Grimsthorpe Castle," n.d.), plate III (Francis Vivares, "The Upper Cascade at Exton Park, Rutland, ca. 1739), and plate IV (John Gundy, "A Plan of the Great Waters and Park of Grimsthorpe Park, 1767).

[26] William Kent, letter to Selina, Countess of Huntingdon, 25 September 1739 (HA 8045), in Peter Willis, "William Kent's Letters in the Huntington Library, California," *Architectural History* 29 (1986): 158–67 (164). War was declared in October 1739. Possession of Gibraltar was an issue between Britain and Spain. Kent records that the bargemen were paid half a guinea each to perform the naumachia. See Willis, *Charles Bridgeman*, for two engravings from Heckell and Mason's (1749) views on the Thames that record barges by Marble Hill house, wafted by breeze and current (pl. 71), and by Pope's villa, quanted in the still air (pl. 76).

[27] For the first performance of the masque, *Alfred*, in the garden at Cliveden on 1 August 1740, see Paul Whiteley, "Images of Empire: James Thomson's Rule Britannia," *New Arcadian Journal* no. 35/36 (1993): 46–59.

4. *William Hannan, "The North Front of the House from across the Lake at West Wycombe, Buckinghamshire," oil painting, ca. 1751 (courtesy of Sir Edward Dashwood; photo courtesy of the National Trust Photo Library)*

5. *West Wycombe, one of the guns from the naumachia frigate, with the nymphs framing the cascade in the distance*

Whereas this royal naumachia exemplified ritualization of national transition, naumachias as ritualized expediency may be regarded as opulent whimsies motivated by a dynastic need to cash in on the cachet of patriotism. Those at West Wycombe and Newstead Abbey exemplified the naumachia as an exclusively elite peer-group bonding. The repertory of aristocratic bonding at West Wycombe encompassed naumachias, bacchanalian revels in antique fancy dress, and the rakish goings-on of the exclusively male Hell Fire Club.[28] Although characteristic of the leisured dilettante lifestyle affordable to a dynasty whose inherited fortune derived from seaborne trade with Turkey and India, Sir Francis Dashwood nonetheless adroitly promoted his garden within the elite tourist market by commissioning conventionally patriotic representations of West Wycombe. While the set of four paintings by William Hannan (ca. 1751) were displayed in the house, the garden was commodified by the reproduction of each one as a print by William Woollett (ca. 1752). One view by Hannan (Fig. 3) encapsulates the house, garden, and lake with the agricultural estate beyond and, to the right, the town and hilltop church. Gardeners toil in the foreground and visitors promenade around the lake, which is adorned with warships of the four-strong "little Fleet": the sloop and the sixty-ton frigate whose flag-emblazoned stern can be seen on the right. The fort that will be assaulted by Dashwood's "fleet" is just visible above the cascade, to the left. One particular "engagement" demonstrated the advantages of mock battle over the real thing. When a ship's captain "received damage" from the wadding of a blank cartridge, "which occasion'd him to spit

---

[28] For these rakish goings-on, see Wendy Frith, "Sexuality and Politics in the Gardens at West Wycombe and Medmenham Abbey," in Michel Conan, ed., *Bourgeois and Aristocratic Cultural Encounters in Garden Art, 1550–1850.* Dumbarton Oaks Colloquium on the History of Landscape Architecture XXIII (Washington, D.C.: Dumbarton Oaks, 2002), 285–309.

blood," Dashwood was able to "put an end to the battle,"[29] thus sparing the wounded and enabling the combatants to reengage another day. Another painting (Fig. 4) reveals the frigate in full view. Its brass carriage guns came from a captured French privateer and three have recently been positioned around the lake (Fig. 5). The grottoesque cascade was later replaced by Nicholas Revett with the pair of reclining neoclassical nymphs.

At Newstead Abbey, the fifth Lord Byron expediently claimed the patriotism of his family's naval service for the naumachias staged between the 1750s and the 1780s (Fig. 6). In the context of anxiety about dwindling timber stocks for warship construction, Lord Byron's attempt to camouflage his "unpatriotic" felling of old oak trees to pay well over £5,000 worth of gambling debts, became the subject of Horace Walpole's swingeing censure in 1760: "In recompense he has cut two baby forts (Fig. 7), to pay the country in castles, for the damage done to the navy."[30] Although the naumachia generally celebrated change, symbolized by naval victory as signifier of imperial enlargement, the Gibraltar genre ritualized resistance to change. Newstead Abbey, along with Larchill and Dangan,[31] seems to have exemplified this ritualization of denial that occurred during the 1780s, when patriotic triumphalism camouflaged an imperial trauma that had become a taboo. Gibraltar had been besieged from 1779 to 1782, during the War of American Independence, and these naumachias commemorated relief of the garrison by the Royal Navy and defeat of the French and

6. *Newstead Abbey and lake*

7. *Canon Fort, circa 1750, and The Fort, circa 1770, Newstead Abbey (drawing: Mark Stewart, courtesy of the New Arcadian Press)*

[29] Phillibrown, Diary, 1754, cited in Dashwood, *The Dashwoods*, 227—see Eyres and Cousins, "Naumachia": 20. In recent years, the West Wycombe naumachia has been revived as an annual summer event. In June 2005, the naumachia was fought to commemorate the bicentenary of Admiral Lord Nelson's decisive victory over the Franco-Spanish fleet at the Battle of Trafalgar.

[30] Horace Walpole, 1760, cited in Barbara Jones, *Follies and Grottoes* (London: Constable, [1953] 1989), 374–75. The forts remain extant. The fifth and "Wicked" Lord Byron had been a teenage naval officer and was the great uncle of the poetic sixth Lord—see Eyres and Cousins, "Naumachia": 18–20.

[31] The fifth Lord Byron intended Lake Sherwood, south of Newstead Abbey, to become a second naumachia site, which would contain a rocky isle doubtless to symbolize Gibraltar—see Eyres and Cousins, "Naumachia": 20. The *ferme ornée* at Larchill, County Kildare, is undergoing restoration. One of the lake's two island forts was named Gibraltar. Larchill was modeled on neighboring Dangan, in County Meath, where the lake was equipped with a detailed miniature fort and a fleet of several vessels including a "complete man-of-war"—see Olda FitzGerald, *Irish Gardens* (London: Conran Octopus, 1999), 16–17.

Spanish forces. However, they resist straightforward triumphalist interpretation. Instead, they exemplify the selectivity of invented tradition and may be read as denying the humiliating loss of the North American colonies.[32] Although loss of the first British empire was denied by promotion of a single European victory, Gibraltar naumachias also reformulated the flawed authority of the ruling oligarchy through representations of a victorious warrior elite.

Alongside denial and reformulation, expediency and transition, entrepreneurial ritualization was exemplified by those naumachias staged as spectacles for paying visitors, as at Thoresby during the 1760s.[33] Motivated by commercial investment in consumer culture, these capitalized on the

8. *John "Warwick" Smith, "Pocklington's Island, Keswick Lake," engraving from* Views of the Lakes in Cumberland, *1971–95 (12. Tab. 36, by permission of the British Library)*

profitability of patriotism through an inclusiveness that embraced the social groups of the middle classes. To create such a naumachia as the climax of the Keswick Regatta throughout the 1780s, the northern expanse of Derwentwater in the English Lake District underwent a series of appropriations. To facilitate the increasingly popular fashion of Lakeland tourism, Derwentwater had already been "gardenized." In the manner of a landscape garden, stations had been created at visually strategic points so that tourists could revel in the lake's mountainous sublimity by enjoying a prescribed sequence of views. As the epicenter of the naumachia, Pocklington's Island became not only a feature for the viewfinders' gaze but also one of the "gardens" to be visited. Formerly known as Vicar's Island, it had recently been renamed after purchase by Joseph Pocklington with proceeds from his family's banking interests (Fig. 8). The view by John "Warwick" Smith shows the new house that presided over the "gardenized" island, replete with boathouse, fort, and "Druidic" stone henge. For the purposes of the Keswick Regatta, Derwentwater was invoked as the lake of a monumental landscape garden whose naumachia was enjoyed from the designed landscapes of the shoreline. These included the viewing stations of Crow Park, Cock Shot, Pocklington's Fawe Park, and the Duke of Portland's boathouse—all of which focused the audience on Pocklington's island garden, and had been identified on *An Accurate Map of the Matchless Lake of Derwent*, published in 1784 by Peter Crossthwaite, Pocklington's business associate and a retired naval officer. Every regatta day, "Governor" Pocklington performed a resolute defence of his island against the determined assault by "Admiral" Crossthwaite's fleet. Certain accounts valued this epic naumachia for stimulating a sublime sensibility in the hundreds of spectators lining the shore. The cannonading of broadsides echoed off the surrounding mountains and miniature men-of-war sank in flames, before the bombardment of Pocklington Island and the storming of its purpose-built fort.[34] However, taste and patriotism were contested by the resident and touring aesthetes of polite society who frowned on this parvenu and vulgar spectacle, and demeaned it as a sordid intrusion of commerce.

[32] For a similar privileging of Gibraltar and denial of the loss of the North American colonies, see Patrick Eyres, "Kew and Stowe: The Late Georgian Redesignation of the Temples' Iconographies," *New Arcadian Journal* no. 51/52 (2001): 96–100.

[33] For Thoresby, see Eyres and Cousins, "Naumachia": 22–24. For other Georgian naumachias, see 14–16 (Virginia Water), 16–18 (Clumber Park), and 20 (Exton Park). For Victorian examples, see 22 (Leigh Park and Stapleford Park), 26 (Surrey Zoological Gardens), and 24–27 (Enville).

[34] One witness considered that Milton had missed a chance for inspiration: "Had the poet who described the battle of the Gods seen a Regatta-day at Keswick, it would have very much enriched his muse for the subject"—see Malcolm Andrews, *The Search for The Picturesque: Landscape Aesthetics and Tourism in Britain, 1760–1800* (Aldershot: Scholar Press, 1990), 182–84 (184), which also cites examples of the reception of Pocklington's Island (now Derwent Island). Crossthwaite's map of Derwentwater is also reproduced in this chapter. See also Eyres and Cousins, "Naumachia," 24.

The Georgian naumachia appears to have been brought to a crescendo in the name of George III during 1814 in London's Hyde Park. Another transition from war to peace was marked by a royal and national celebration to honor the centenary of the Hanoverian monarchy—a tadge prematurely, because Napoleon's escape from Elba deferred peace until his defeat at Waterloo in 1815. Nonetheless, throughout the night of August first, a plethora of spectacular consumerist pleasures were deployed within the three adjacent parks of central London: Hyde Park, Green Park, and St. James's Park. These were designed to tickle the fancy of the elite, the middle classes, and "the crowd," and thus ensure an occasion of apparent social inclusiveness. They were engraved by Clark and

9. *M. Dubourg, after J. H. Clark, "The Fleet on the Serpentine River," engraving in Orme, 1814 (808 M7, by permission of the British Library)*

Dubourg for the publisher, Edward Orme, and included the illuminated Chinese Bridge and the illuminated and revolving Temple of Concord which, through a fantastical *coup de théâtre*, would become transformed from a military tower that symbolized the ravages of war, into a dramatic representation of peace that visualized the victorious union of the army, the navy, and the Hanoverian crown.

However, the event that Orme deemed to be the most spectacular, the most triumphalist and the most popular was the gargantuan naumachia staged on the Serpentine in Hyde Park to valorize the Royal Navy as the agent of imperial ascendancy, and to commemorate the anniversary of Admiral Lord Nelson's victory at the Battle of the Nile on 1 August 1798.[35] Orme's account of the celebrations enables an attempt to perceive the experience of "communitas." The audience, which had gathered over two days from sites out-of-town and within the metropolis, was managed by the organizers' attempt at social segregation. While "the crowd" gathered around the fair in Hyde Park, the various social orders of polite society—the middle classes, gentry, and aristocracy—assembled within the ticket-only enclosure in St. James's Park, which had been designed "for those who dreaded the . . . promiscuous intermixture with . . . an indiscriminate crowd."[36]

Despite the variety of spectacles that competed for attention, the banks of the Serpentine became the space shared by spectators who enjoyed the common experience of anticipation, heightened by the final preparations for the naumachia. The entire length of the Serpentine had been prepared for the epic reenactment of Nelson's annihilation of the French fleet in 1798 (Fig. 9). Two armadas of purpose-built, replica, manned warships had been assembled: "the grand [French] fleet . . . had by noon floated into deep water, and formed the line . . . the Kensington shore was lined with fireworks . . . a balloon was prepared to rise in the rear with the first bulletin of the victory."[37] Preliminary anticipation was further heightened by a tableau

---

[35] To create this metropolitan naumachia, the government chose to mobilize public knowledge and experience of two distinct patriotic genres: the county tradition of the naumachia and London's theater tradition of the aquatic drama, whose familiarity was recorded by George Cruickshank, among others (for example: an overexcited sailor in the audience "participates" in "sinking" the enemy, to the consternation of the proprietor). Both practices had flourished throughout the quarter century of the Great War and had become familiar as representations of naval and imperial commemoration.

[36] Edward Orme, *An Historical Memento representing the Different Scenes of Public rejoicing, which took place the First of August, in St. James's and Hyde Parks, London, in celebration of the Glorious Peace of 1814, and of the Centenary of the Succession of the Illustrious House of Brunswick to the Throne of these Kingdoms* (London: 1814), 60, 45, 46.

[37] Orme, *An Historical Memento*, 54.

that commemorated naval feats of the current war with the United States (1812–14), during which British forces had burned the White House in Washington: "First, we saw a frigate from the English fleet sailing majestically down the Serpentine, with the wind abaft the boom, to attack two ships of similar force, which lay at anchor also, detached from the French fleet, under American colours (*the stripes*)."[38] Thus, on London's Serpentine, these "American" frigates were engaged, boarded, captured, and towed as prizes to the English fleet.

Gradually the preliminal gave way to the liminal:

As evening fell, a new and dreadful note of preparation awoke; sails were bent, flags hoisted, cannoneers embarked, and tow-ropes launched through the hawse-holes. The sun now approached to his setting; and, in the warlike conceptions of the time, the immense multitude that crowded the shore, in rank upon rank, and thousand upon thousand, gleaming in that deep and coloured night, might pass for an army waiting to see the contest of the fleets decided.[39]

It was in this state of liminality that the togetherness and social leveling of "communitas" would forge a collective identity experienced by participation in the performance of the awesome might of imperial Britain: "The headmost ship of the British line got under way, and bore down on the starboard tack; and, in ten minutes, opened her fire, which was immediately returned from the whole French line. The British van followed in succession, each ship opened its fire as it dropped beside its antagonist."[40] After two hours, the spectacularly explosive "combat" was brought to a dramatic climax by the fireship assault on the French fleet:

The awful grandeur, and the still increasing splendour of the scene, drew forth bursts of enthusiastic acclamations from both shores of the Serpentine; and, in a few minutes, the first ship . . . was set on fire, and added to the magnificence of a scene, which, in its real occurance, has been universally allowed to exceed all others in terrific pomp, viz. that of a ship of war on fire at sea. This first frigate was followed by a second; and, by the two, the whole French fleet were set on fire and demolished. The effect produced by their blaze was such as to make the whole water appear on fire.[41]

The consensual state of "communitas" would doubtless enable the audience to perceive the lake as a metonymy of ocean, and warships engulfed in flame as a metaphor of the sublimity of empire. This liminal crescendo passed into postliminality with the visual paradox of fireworks in competition with "the superior splendour of the expiring fleet [which] eclipsed, for a long time, every thing that could be produced by pyrotechnic ingenuity."[42] As the flames of naval warfare ebbed, the spectacular water rockets marked the postliminality of an audience that had become incorporated within an imperial identity emblematized theatrically within the spatial domain of these urban parks. The display of water rockets marked the point when the socially leveled and heightened collectivity of "communitas" began to dissolve once again into the hierarchical patterns of daily life.

- *III* -

It was the entrepreneurialism of these naumachias that created precedents for the commercial practices that spawned the Scarborough performance. This continues to function within the context of the seaside holiday as a site of consumer and

[38] Ibid.
[39] Ibid., 55.
[40] Ibid.
[41] Ibid., 56.
[42] Ibid., 56–57.

popular culture, and flourishes within a public park specifically designed for the consumption of populist leisure.[43] The pleasures of boating and promenading in Peasholm Park were exoticized by evocation of "The Orient," through the design that articulated the modernity of the Japanese craze that had been reinvigorated by the Japan-British exhibition mounted in London during 1910. The repertoire of Japanese features exemplified by the Underground poster (Fig. 10) was, during 1911 and 1912, translated into the amphitheater, boating lake, and island of the park, and into the styling of the floating bandstand, island pavilion, bridge, rowboat kiosk, lakeside lanterns, tearooms, and sculpture. Presiding over this seaside "Orient" were the pagoda and cascade that were constructed as the culminating features in 1929 (Fig. 11).[44] During the 1930s, the ambience of a "Japanese fairyland" was consistently promoted by the resort's guidebooks,[45] and pictured by postcards (Fig. 12).

Although not designed as a music-hall stage set, nor as a naumachia site, Peasholm Park became appropriated in 1922 as a public space for the performance of populist entertainments. In addition to boating and promenading, these included slapstick comedy sketches and clowning, brass band concerts, firework displays, and aquatic and often comic races, such as swimming, rowing, canoeing, boxing, and tub sailing, as well as mop tournaments and walking the greasy pole. It was among these diverse entertainments that the naumachia emerged in 1929.[46] The appropriation of Peasholm Park for performative entertainment has been successfully sustained. Now, lodged within the complex of North Bay Leisure Parks, it offers a putting green, motor launch trips, boating, a 1980s Japanese-style garden on the island's summit, the floating bandstand,

10. *John Henry Lloyd, Underground poster for Japan-British exhibition, 1910 (courtesy of London's Transport Museum)*

the *Naval Warfare* ships, an aviary, a mini-golf course, and a woodland walk. Posters advertise a variety of entertainments, from *The Amazing Water Ski Circus Show* and brass band concerts (Fig. 13), to *Naval Warfare*—"a sea battle in miniature with fireworks."[47]

[43] For confirmation that public parks were part of the commercialized seaside environment, see Inglis, *The Delicious History of the Holiday*, 51. See also Eyres, "Naval Warfare," 33–38. Scarborough is a fishing port on the North Sea coast of England in the county of Yorkshire. The medieval castle indicates that it was once a military site whose strategic importance was first appreciated by the Romans. During the eighteenth century, the town's economic base broadened as it burgeoned as an elite spa and, since the development of the railway network during the nineteenth century, it has sustained a reputation as a rather superior seaside resort. This distinction over its rivals on the east coast was partly reinforced by successive waves of municipal investment in the public parks and gardens that adorn the resort. Around 1900, in order to capitalize on the resort's popularity and to relieve the pressure of the number of holidaymakers on the harbor and spa town in the South Bay, the town and its gardens were extended into the North Bay, beyond the castle's headland. The focal point of the newly designed constellation of sites for overtly populist entertainment was to be Peasholm Park.

[44] In the national context, Peasholm is unique as the solitary example of a public park designed exclusively in the Edwardian Japanese style. See Patrick Eyres, Editorial, *New Arcadian Journal* no. 39/40 (1995): 5–9. Tragically, the pagoda was burned to the ground by vandals in the autumn of 1999. Scarborough Borough Council intends a reconstruction, possibly with financial assistance from the Heritage Lottery Fund. See *New Arcadian Broadsheet* no. 50 (2000): "Pagoda to Rise like a Phoenix." The national significance of Peasholm Park has been recognized by English Heritage through its recent listing on the *Register of Historic Parks and Gardens of Special Historic Interest in England*.

[45] See Eyres, "Naval Warfare," 39–46 and 64–65, n. 25: *The Scarborough Magazine Holiday Annual* (1930), 12, *Scarborough* (1931), 14, and *Scarborough* (1933), 10.

[46] See Eyres, "Naval Warfare," 33–38, for detail of the park's design and development, the variety of interwar entertainments, and the naumachia's evolution.

[47] Scarborough Borough Council, *Naval Warfare* poster, circa 1993.

11. *Peasholm Park, overview (drawing: Chris Broughton, courtesy of the New Arcadian Press)*

12. *Peasholm Park, 1930s postcard (collection: the author)*

Initiated in 1929, the naumachia's audiences have been consistently invited to participate actively in a ritualizing process that has eschewed passive consumption in favor of vocal, ideological engagement through hearty sing-alongs, the cheering-on of "our side," and demonization of "the enemy." Since 1929, the naumachia has undergone three distinct historically specific formulations. The first was known as the *Naval Battle* that, during the 1930s, refought victories of World War I. The second, during the 1950s, refought victories of World War II and was known first as *The Battle of the River Plate* and then as *Naval Warfare*. It is the third and contemporary version that, in the 1960s, reformulated *Naval Warfare* to acknowledge Britain's postimperial status.[48]

The narrative of the originating *Naval Battle* capitalized on Scarborough's wartime experiences to perform a ritualization of retribution, which simultaneously valorized the Royal Navy and reinforced its role as guardian of empire. In December 1914, Scarborough had been among the east coast towns bombarded by the German navy. This assault had been reported with an outrage fuelled by the toll of civilian casualties and physical damage. Judging by local press reports, Peasholm Park's miniature fleet engagement ritualized a particular phase of the Battle of Jutland in 1916 (Fig. 14), when the British battleships *Barham* and *Malaya* had inflicted a near fatal drubbing on the German battlecruisers *Von Der Tann* and *Derflinger*, which had bombarded Scarborough in December 1914. Similarly, through reenactment of battles between Q-Ships and submarines,[49] the municipal ritualists also scripted a symbolic revenge for the harassment of Scarborough's fishing fleet by predatory German U-boats.

The *Naval Battle* was suspended in 1940. After World War II, a new fleet was assembled and the naumachia relaunched to commemorate the Festival of Britain in 1951. Updated as *The Battle of the River Plate*, five ships reenacted the first

[48] See Eyres, "Naval Warfare," 47–69, for detail of the naumachia's different phases.
[49] See Eyres, "Naval Warfare," 51. Q-Ships were merchant vessels equipped with camouflaged weapons that patrolled as bait for submarines. The intention was to lure the submarine into a surface attack, whereupon the ambush of superior firepower would enable the Q-ship to destroy the U-boat.

13. *Peasholm Park, poster display, including* Naval Warfare

14. *Peasholm Park, reconstruction of the 1930s* Naval Battle *(drawing: Howard Eaglestone, courtesy of the New Arcadian Press)*

and legendary naval victory of the war. The postcard exemplifies the commemorations of the action in December 1939 (Fig. 15), through which the cruisers *Exeter*, *Ajax*, and *Achilles* had terminated the surface-raiding mission of the German pocket battleship, *Admiral Graf Spee*. In Peasholm Park, the battleship stalked and sunk a merchant ship in an encounter symbolic of the fate of the *Graf Spee*'s numerous victims. Enter the cruisers that intercept and engage the more powerful warship off the mouth of the River Plate (Fig. 16). The *Graf Spee* is driven into Montevideo harbor. Finally, it steams out to self-destruct as a volcano of fireworks. During the mid-1950s, ever alert to the possibilities of further spectacularizing the naumachia, the municipal ritualists began to introduce further merchant ships, and a submarine, and an aircraft carrier and aircraft. Retitled *Naval Warfare*, it combined reenactment of the Battle of the River Plate with episodes from the Battle of the Atlantic (1940–43).

Both the pre- and postwar versions of the naumachia demonstrate the selectivity of an invented tradition. In elaborating this ritual-like characteristic, Catherine Bell referred to Eric Hobsbawm's comment that tradition can be invented through a "process of formalization and ritualisation, characterised by reference to the past, if only by imposing repetition."[50] The Scarborough naumachia exemplifies this process. The *Naval Battle* of the 1930s had chosen to represent the "retributive" intervention of the *Barham* and *Malaya* during the Battle of Jutland, and to ignore the shocking destruction of three British battlecruisers: *Indefatigable*, *Invincible*, and *Queen Mary*. Similarly, the postwar naumachia has chosen not to represent the sinking of the *Jervis Bay* by the pocket battleship, *Admiral Scheer*, nor the loss of the aircraft carrier, *Ark Royal*, to a U-boat. Even though *Naval Warfare* features HMS *Exeter* and is performed in a Japanese-style park, the fate of the *Exeter* remains unperformed—sunk in the Battle of the Java Sea by the Imperial Japanese Navy.[51]

During the 1960s, Britain's imperial status became reoriented through decolonization toward membership of the European Union in 1975. Nonetheless, when the connotations of wartime triumphalism were contested in the 1960s and again

[50] Eric Hobsbawm, "Introduction: Inventing Traditions," in Eric Hobsbawm and Terence Ranger, eds., *The Invention of Tradition* (Cambridge: Cambridge University Press, 1983), 1–4; cited in Bell, *Rituals*, 48. Bell also draws on the example of the reinvention of the British monarchy in the late nineteenth and early twentieth centuries, as argued by David Cannadine, "The Context, Performance and Meaning of Ritual: The British Monarchy and the 'Invention of Tradition'," in Hobsbawm and Ranger, *The Invention of Tradition*, 108.

[51] For the fate of the *Jervis Bay*, *Ark Royal*, and *Exeter*, although not mentioned during the performance, see "The Ships," in David James, *Naval Warfare: Peasholm Park—Scarborough* (Scarborough: Department of Tourism and Amenities, undated), unpaginated. The other sections of this ten-page illustrated souvenir booklet are: "A History," "How Does It Work," and "The Battle." See also Eyres, "The Patriotic Panto," 85–86, for *Jervis Bay*; 86, for *Ark Royal*; 90–92, for *Exeter*.

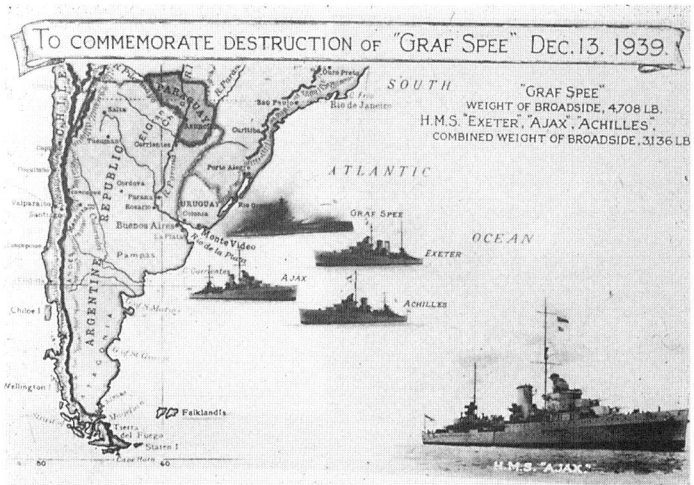

15. *The Battle of the River Plate, 1939 postcard (collection: the author)*
16. *Peasholm Park, reconstruction of the 1950s* Battle of the River Plate *(drawing: Howard Eaglestone, courtesy of the New Arcadian Press)*

in the 1980s, the naumachia's metamorphoses sustained the invented tradition symbolized by *Naval Warfare*. In the 1960s, criticism from alienated German tourists prompted a taboo on the identity of the wartime enemy. Yet, even though the names of the "enemy" warships were neutralized and the spectacle emphasized as innocuous seaside fun, the essential ritualization of partisan Britishness was maintained by retention of "our" iconic warships, which would remain victorious over "Them," the "enemy." During the Falklands War of 1982, the controversial sinking of the Argentine cruiser, *General Belgrano*, prompted calls for *Naval Warfare* to be discontinued, apparently because of the narrative's alleged similarity to the jingoistic triumphalism of the tabloid press. Through another metamorphosis, *Naval Warfare* became repositioned within the nostalgic arena of heritage culture. By the 1990s, the reconstructed semiotics denotationally promoted "family fun for boys and girls, mums and dads," through a rip-roaringly thrilling spectacle of "cowboys and indians in boats" in which "everyone lives to fight another day."[52] Connotationally, the invented tradition had become reencoded as a display of "our naval history,"[53] which revalidated wartime triumphalism as memorialization. Clearly, the conjunction of liminality and "communitas" might appear to be problematic.

However, it is interesting to note that Fred Inglis, writing about the liminal, transitory experience of the seaside holiday,[54] emphasizes the pleasurable, preliminal anticipation of escape from the usual routine and return to a beloved place, by noting that a child's "unbearable excitement of return . . . is ritualised by precious landmarks."[55] In the same spirit, my own experience as a day-tripper is breathtakingly punctuated by the preliminal pilgrimage to the sacral landscape; the liminal "communitas" experienced through participation in the performance of group singing and cheering on the naumachia; and the postliminal fracture of the nostalgic illusion through reassurance that we have participated in a theatrical entertainment.

Anticipating a heady spate of nationalistic rituals during June 2002, I timed my annual pilgrimage to *Naval Warfare* to coincide with the golden jubilee of Queen Elizabeth II and English victories in the World Cup. I was curious to see whether

[52] The MC's commentary, *Naval Warfare*, 15 June 2002.

[53] See "The Battle," in James, *Naval Warfare*.

[54] Inglis, *The Delicious History of the Holiday*, 9, 37.

[55] Inglis, *The Delicious History of the Holiday*, 10. The invented tradition of British naval supremacy was similarly sustained during the bicentenary celebration of the Battle of Trafalgar in the Solent off Portsmouth (2005). These culminated in a *son et lumière* and pyrotechnic mock naval battle between seventeen tall ships. The press commented on the controversial way in which Admiral Lord Nelson's decisive victory was simultaneously reaffirmed yet denied. See, for example, Ben Macintyre, "World Armada Recalls a Day of Victory and Death," *The Times* (29 June 2005): 6–7: "To avoid offending French and Spanish sensibilities, the Navy continued to insist that this was not a re-run of Tafalgar but 'the re-enactment of a sort of naval battle that would have taken place at the time.' The rival fleets were described as red ('enemy') and blue ('friendly')."

these might have any impact on the mythic connotations of *Naval Warfare*, or the experience of "communitas." The outpouring of media-induced royalist enthusiasm that marked the various rites of the queen's jubilee weekend (8–9 June 2002) had been preceded by an orgy of nationalistic fervor: England (7 June 2002) had vanquished Argentina in the victorious 1–0 ritual of retribution that eliminated Argentina from the World Cup competition, redeemed the Argentine defeat of England in 1998, and assuaged Maradonna's ever-hated "Hand of God" goal that had sealed England's fate in the 1986 World Cup. The jubilee was followed by the twentieth anniversary of the Argentine surrender in the Falklands (11 June 2002), which had already prompted jingoistic rites in a number of English pubs after the football victory, as characterized by chants of "Stand up if we trashed the Argies in the Falklands." The morning of my pilgrimage (15 June 2002) produced another World Cup victory as England defeated Denmark. Consequently, the train journey from Leeds was animated by a crocodile of euphoric youths processing up and down the carriages adorned in English flags and chanting "Three Nil to the Ing-ger-lan." Clearly my own ritual had become enmeshed in another. In Scarborough, the streets were awash with crowds adorned with the ritual sign of St. George's red cross in a variety of fetishistic forms: the painted face, the team shirt, the t-shirt, and the flag. The repetitive chant that filled the air was sung, with raucously bucolic but good-natured gusto, to the tune of Sousa's *Stars and Stripes*:

> Ing - ger - lan,   Ing - ger - lan,   Ing - ger - lan,
> Ing - ger - lan,   Ing - ger - lan,   Ing - ger - la - an,
> Ing - ger - lan,   Ing - ger - lan,   Ing - ger - la - an,
> Ing - gerrr - lan.

This generally continues until exhaustion or drunken collapse intervenes, and may be translated as:

> England, England, England,
> England, England, England,
> England, England, England,
> England.

My familiar pilgrimage continued with the descent by funicular to the prom and a stroll past the arcades to the harbor for the customary meal in Winking Willy's fish 'n' chip restaurant: "Willy's Special," comprising haddock and chips, bread and butter, pot of tea. Satisfactorily prepared, I join the throng at the bus stop by the port, where every fishing boat in the Scarborough fleet is adorned with the red and white English flag. Basking in sunshine, I ride on the top deck of the open seaside bus from Arcadia to the Orient.

Ensconced in the floating bandstand, the organ-playing Master of Ceremonies begins the ritual punctually: "Welcome to Scarborough's Peasholm Park for our unique entertainment, *Naval Warfare*. Imagine you were at the England game this morning: stand up, clap your hands and sing along . . . . Cheer like you did this morning." With these words, our preliminal rites are concluded. We are on the threshold of liminality. The MC orchestrates audience participation and, in so doing, cultivates a state of "communitas." First we are warmed up with a sing-along of popular tunes, including, from prewar days:

> If you're happy and you know it, clap your hands
> If you're happy and you know it, clap your hands
> If you're happy and you know it, and you really want to show it
> If you're happy and you know it, clap your hands

and, after Rod Stewart:

> I am sailing, I am sailing, home again, 'cross the sea
> I am sailing, stormy water, to be near you, to be free

and, of course, the essential rehearsal of cheering and booing, as well as the promotion of consumable and fetishistic objects such as souvenir postcards, badges, baseball caps, and the booklet (Fig. 17). Across the lake, a wader-clad Gulliver assembles the Lilliputian fleet. To the right, behind the Peasholm Naval Docks, a painted screen theatrically represents the White Cliffs of Dover (Figs. 18 and 25) and functions as an icon of the Englishness of the performance we are about to experience.

Everything we are told is detailed in the souvenir booklet that codifies the formalism, invariance, rule-governance, traditionalization, and sacral symbolism of this performative ritual-like action. Of the ten ships, seven are operated by a "captain" concealed within the hull and superstructure, and the three to be "sunk" will be remotely controlled from the island pavilion.[56] Once each ship has been introduced with a flourish on the organ and a eulogy from our MC, the fleet performs a naval parade accompanied by the rousing strains of "Heart of Oak."[57] As the performance gets under way, each of the MC's "captains" must be attentive to his commentary because it cues maneuvers and action. Once snug within the superstructure, the visibility of each "captain" is limited to what is immediately in front. Consequently, their scripted choreography is assisted by the MC's narrative over the public-address system. At the flick of a switch on the control panel in each vessel, the gun turrets will "fire," "direct hits" will explode, "fires" will break out on deck, and the underwater charges will be detonated as the "near misses" that throw up plumes of water. Although the warplanes swoop into the attack from high above, and behind the audience (to general surprise, consternation, and delight), they are, in fact, ingeniously suspended on "invisible" wires.[58]

A haze veils the lake as vessels "steam" and stricken ships pour smoke. The prescribed order comprises a sequence of engagements dramatized by our MC's organ music. His narrative engineers the enthusiastic participation of the audience, and reveals the paradoxical slippage between the denotational presentation of warships as aquatic cowboys and Indians, and the naval heritage connotations of wartime triumphalism signified by the names and histories of the iconic British vessels. We are reminded that the cruisers *Exeter*, *Ajax*, and *Achilles* were the heroes of the Battle of the River Plate. We are told that the aircraft carrier, *Ark Royal*, the transatlantic liner, *Asturias*, and the armed merchantman, *Jervis Bay*, had performed heroically during the Battle of the Atlantic.[59] The doomed and fictitious tanker, *British Pride*, is cited as a representative of all the merchant ships torpedoed during the Battle of the Atlantic. The performative content, and narrative, that has been repeated twice a week each summer season for almost forty years, is enshrined in the souvenir booklet, whose centerspread, "The Battle," also anchors this public park as a sacral landscape. On the map, the boating lake has become transformed into the site of the "Battle of Peasholm," and the floating bandstand into the "commentary point." "Dock Island" stands adjacent to Peasholm Island, which now hosts the "Enemy Arsenal" and "Enemy Harbour Installation." The words announcing the presence of "Enemy Submarine Patrols" and the "Route of Convoy" transform the lake into a metonym both of ocean and empire. Similarly, the text that encapsulates the traditionalizing narrative relayed by the MC, begins: "The thirty minute battle stirs memories of brave and heroic deeds which are part of our naval history and our heritage . . . . Suddenly it is a December day out in the battle of the Atlantic. . . ." It concludes with the typographic banner: "Maritime history has been reenacted. Rule Britannia!"[60]

---

[56] See "How Does It Work" (with cutaway illustration), in James, *Naval Warfare*.

[57] The MC's proudest description was reserved for the latest version of the liner, *Asturias*, painstakingly replicated by Scarborough Marine Engineering and fitted out by the *Naval Warfare* team. See also David Garner, "New Ship Troops in Ready for the Battles," *Yorkshire Post*, 27 May 2000, and Andrew Martin, "Patter of Tiny Fleet," *Independent on Sunday*, 20 August 2000.

[58] See "How Does It Work," in James, *Naval Warfare*.

[59] See "The Ships," in James, *Naval Warfare*.

[60] See "The Battle," in James, *Naval Warfare*.

17. Naval Warfare, *merchandizing, circa 1997: badges, baseball cap, postcards, booklet, ticket (collection: the author)*

18. *Peasholm Park*, Naval Warfare *(drawing: Chris Broughton, courtesy of the New Arcadian Press), with (left to right) the second enemy battleship, the* submarine, *the* Exeter, *the* Jervis Bay, *the* White Cliffs, *and the* British Pride

19. Naval Warfare, *the* Exeter, *and the first enemy battleship*

20. Naval Warfare, *the* Jervis Bay, *and the submarine*

21. Naval Warfare, *the* Asturias

22. Naval Warfare, *the* Ark Royal, *the* Ajax, *and the* Achilles

Naval Warfare proceeds apace. Amidst the gunfire, explosions, fireworks, and smoke of the action we boo, cheer, hiss, and hurrah on cue (Fig. 18). The convoy is attacked by an "enemy" battleship: "Booooooo!" The *Exeter*, *Ajax*, and *Achilles* fight off the surface raider: "Hurrah!" (Fig. 19). However, the "enemy" submarine sneaks up on a convoy straggler: "Boo! Watch Out! Hiss!" Struck by torpedoes, the merchantman is set ablaze and explodes: "Booo! Hisss!" Planes from the aircraft carrier, *Ark Royal*, are scrambled and scream into the attack. Supported by the armed merchantman, *Jervis Bay*, they destroy the submarine: "Hurrah!" (Fig. 20). The transatlantic liner, *Asturias*, now a wartime troopship, steams safely onward: "Hurrah! Hurrah!" (Fig. 21). Another enemy battleship threatens the convoy: "Booooooo! Look Out Behind Youuuuuuuuuu!" Suddenly, aircraft swoop out of the sky and, together with the warships, go into the attack. The battleship is overwhelmed by the combined air and fleet assault: "Hurrah!" (Fig. 22). It "explodes" in an eruption of fireworks: "Hurrah! Hurrah!" (Fig. 23). In a tumultuous crescendo of explosions, fireworks, and the swelling strains of "Rule Britannia," an air and sea assault storms the enemy base and the Union Jack is run up: "Huge, Huger, Hugest Hurrahs!"

Throughout the performance, our MC has emphasized that *Naval Warfare* is fun! It is not serious! During the concluding naval parade, before the vessels steam off to port, the togetherness of our reaffirmed collective identity is tickled by the incongruous sight of hands waving through portholes as certain captains bid farewell to their appreciative audience. Another captain removes the concealing superstructure to wave, revealing himself seated in the hull as he motors the model ship across the lake. These sights intentionally fracture the authority of the illusion and reassure us that *Naval Warfare* is "only" a seaside entertainment. In so doing, the performers usher us from liminality into the postliminal stage when, as "communitas" fragments, we wonder what we have become incorporated into. In the days of empire, this would have been a straightforward question. But now, as postimperial consumers, do we wonder whether we have been rallied into a nostalgia for the past, for empire?

Naval Warfare is the flourishing survivor of that long-standing cultural tradition, the British naumachia. It exemplifies not only the successful appropriation of a theatrical garden genre but also of the parkland space for its ritual-like performance. In addition, it exemplifies the role of garden design in sustaining the practice. The continuity and longevity of this success reiterates the appropriations that sustained particular Georgian naumachias, for example, those at West Wycombe, Newstead Abbey, Thoresby, and Derwentwater. However, *Naval Warfare* is rooted in Britain's imperial past and, like its Georgian predecessors, it has served to rally audiences to Britain's imperial mission. Despite the ambiguity of the contemporary postliminal experience, the positioning of *Naval Warfare* within heritage culture doubtless rallies modern consumers to a nostalgia for the imperial past. The fashion for historical reenactments has escalated since the 1980s with the growth of the heritage industry. The *English Heritage Events Diary* exemplifies the ubiquity of reenactments as well as the variety of historical periods, which range from the Roman occupation to World War II.[61] *Naval Warfare* now sits so comfortably within this phenomenon that it is tempting to read the naumachia as a paradigm of that industry's nostalgic relationship with the imperial past—even as a reformulation of history to construct simulacra that can assuage the complications of the present.

Conclusion

The contribution of *Naval Warfare* to the commodification of an invented tradition is self-evident, despite ambiguity in the promotional agenda, and it is this that introduces a reflective conclusion. Although the resort reinvests in the invariance of its principle sacral symbols, the iconic warships, the posters that registered a World War II battle (Fig. 13) have been redesigned to emphasize a neutralized modernity, as signified by naval imagery as "warlike" as the display in a model shop's window (Fig. 24), and a colorway that eschews any resonance of the national flag. It is possibly this ambiguity that enables members of the audience to appropriate *Naval Warfare* for their own subjective purposes and to create their own meanings.

For myself, I was left wondering about my anticipations of a nationalism reinvigorated by the royal Jubilee and World Cup victories. But these had proved to be ill founded. The way that our MC narrates the script of *Naval Warfare* continues to

[61] *English Heritage Events Diary 2003* (London: English Heritage, 2003).

be a model of English restraint! The only concession to these events had been the Union Jack in the floating bandstand and the exhortation to cheer as heartily as if we had been at the morning's football match! Similarly, I have speculated about the European-ness of *Naval Warfare*. In the context of a contested europhile ideology, I have wondered whether the tradition that had "othered" continental Europe had become transformed into a "Little England" ritualization of eurosceptic resistance. However, I have preferred to regard the combination of movie cowboys and Indians who never actually die, with promotion of "naval history" to memorialize wartime heroism, as a fine example of the regional diversity cherished by the European Union.

23. Naval Warfare, *the* Ajax, *and the second enemy battleship*

We have seen that, as a nationalistic phenomenon, the British naumachia has been consistently shaped by contemporary events that, through metamorphosis and appropriation, have produced new meanings. In March 2003, Britain's largest naval task force since the 1982 Falklands War took part in the invasion of Iraq. Although European consensus became fractured, this intervention illuminated the kind of triumphalism that, historically, had stimulated the naumachia's development. It also confirmed my appreciation that individuals within an audience appropriate the naumachia to create personal meanings. Certainly, the synthesis of naval action with the sacrality of an iconic warship has the potential to create a perceptional metamorphosis by subjective appropriation.

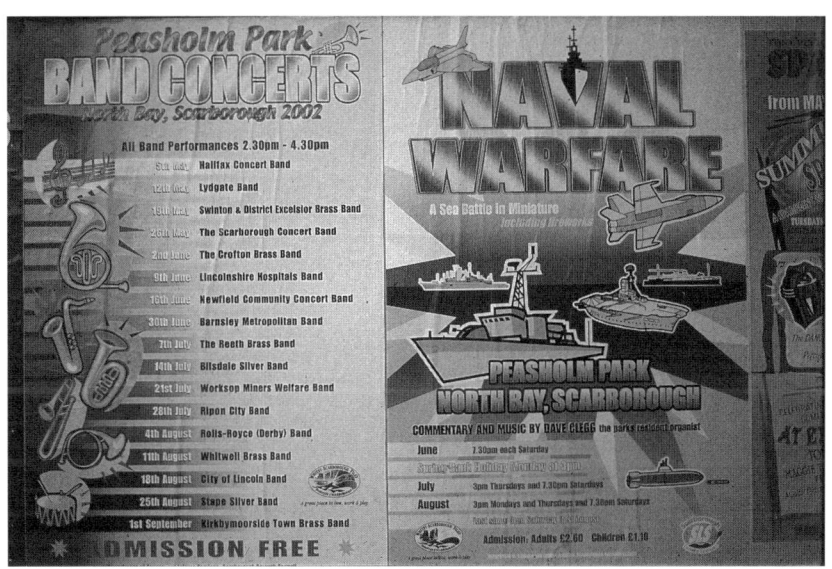

24. *Peasholm Park, poster display, including the redesigned* Naval Warfare

The naming of British warships contributes to the invention of tradition. For almost five hundred years, a capital ship has been named *Ark Royal*. Since the early twentieth century, these have been aircraft carriers, and the present *Ark Royal* also was the flagship of the task force in the Persian Gulf. For British audiences, the first days of April 2003 were characterized by media images of the ceremonial repatriation of the bodies of naval aircrew who had perished in the opening hours of the invasion. Their coffins, draped in Union Jacks, lined the flight deck of *Ark Royal*. The association of the *Ark Royal* with contemporary death in action was emphasized during August by the three-part television documentary *Ark Royal*, which charted the carrier's role in the invasion. This association was reiterated on 12 October 2003 by the national memorial ceremony for the fifty-one British servicemen killed, by that date, in Iraq.

25. Naval Warfare, *the* Ark Royal, *with (left to right) the* Asturias, *the* Ajax, *the White Cliffs, and the* Exeter

The transhistorical resonance of *Ark Royal* (Fig. 25) may enable members of the audience to appropriate *Naval Warfare*'s ritualization of "naval history" for their own purposes. As in 1982, this may encompass the differing perceptions of triumphalism, opposition, and memorialization. These likelihoods have introduced a further possibility for this member of the audience: that *Naval Warfare* could be perceived as a countermemorial that, as outlined by James Young,[62] requires the participatory engagement of an audience with the site that activates memory in a process that bears the hallmarks of Catherine Bell's characteristics of ritual-like activities, combined with Victor Turner's formulation of "communitas."

Acknowledgements

This material has been developed from, and remains complementary to, the subject of *New Arcadian Journal* no. 39/40 (1995): "Naumachia—Naval Warfare in Peasholm Park, Scarborough: Flourishing Survivor of the British Parkland Tradition of Naumachia, or Mock Naval Battle." I am most appreciative of the comments made during the discussions generated by successive versions of this essay: at the Staff Seminar, School of Art and Design, Bradford College (April 2003), at the symposium on landscape and garden architecture, Dumbarton Oaks (May), and in the Faculty of Art and Art History, University of Texas at Austin (November). Conversations with Michel Conan have been particularly helpful in developing this chapter. My thanks are also due to Margherita Azzi Visentini for her generous introduction to the work of Pirro Ligorio and the various uses of the naumachia within Italian baroque culture (Dumbarton Oaks, 30 April 2003).

[62] See James Young in W. J. T. Mitchel, *Art and the Public Sphere* (Chicago: Chicago University press, 1992).

Performance and Appropriation: Profane Rituals in Gardens and Landscapes

Performance and Appropriation: Profane Rituals in Gardens and Landscapes

Performance and Appropriation: Profane Rituals in Gardens and Landscapes

Performance and Appropriation: Profane Rituals in Gardens and Landscapes

Rituals of Transgression in Public Parks in Britian, 1846 to the Present

David Lambert

Introduction

When in 1926 Reg Speller photographed a gang of skinny-dippers being chased away from the Serpentine in Hyde Park by a cane-wielding policewoman, he probably hoped to sell the image as a humorous piece about the naughtiness of children and the varied work of the London bobby (Fig.1). Yet the image also hints at the nature of outlawed pleasures in public parks; in particular, that some rule breaking did not represent merely random acts of transgression but was often part of a ritual-like leisure activity that had its own cultural legitimacy.[1] In the performance—and Speller took a companion photograph of the boys moments before, as they were leaping with abandon into the lake—a kind of appropriation of the place occurs, but it is a performative ritual the grounds of which are temporary, contingent, more or less informally negotiated and frequently broken up by the authorities, in this case with a rattan cane.

1. *Reg Speller, "Skinny-Dippers," 1926 (collection: Fox Photos; copyright: Getty Images)*

The urban parks of the industrial towns of mid-nineteenth-century England and Scotland, Ireland and Wales, were formed as a response to the massive increase in the urban population, the threat to public health, and the threat to the political status quo that this posed. From 1846, when Manchester developed three parks by public subscription, through to the 1890s, parks were seen in many industrial cities, such as Leeds, as a utilitarian necessity: "It is the duty of the Corporation or other public bodies to provide what is in reality a moral, intellectual and physical sanatorium for the ailments that unavoidably attack

---

[1] Catherine Bell examines what she calls "ritual-like" activities and groups them according to certain shared characteristics: leisure activities such as the illicit skinny-dipping can, for example, be seen as formal, traditional, invariant, rule-governed (see Catherine Bell, *Ritual: Perspectives and Dimensions* [Oxford: Oxford University Press, 1997], Chap. 5 passim.)

crowded communities."[2] In 1833, the MP Richard Slaney called for a Select Committee to inquire into the need for open spaces in populous towns, on the grounds that "the want of recreation generated incipient disease, discontent; which in its turn led to attacks upon the Government."[3] They were also the subject of organized pressure from those urban populations. As Martin Hoyles wrote: "The history of public parks . . . has been a history of struggle, both to create and preserve the parks, and also to determine how they should be used."[4]

My starting point in this essay is Catherine Bell's insight into ritual-like activities, in which she observes that "The body acts within an environment that appears to require it to respond in certain ways, but this environment is actually created and organized precisely by means of how people move around it."[5] That is, the space is appropriated by the activities within it. A public park's design and regulation required certain patterns of behavior, but in practice the way in which it was used, in accordance with rules or transgressing them, actually affects and even defies those original intentions.

Space and Carnival

The informal open spaces that predated nineteenth-century urban parks were traditionally places of carnival: places of fairs, horse-trading, assignations, dueling, unlicensed public meetings. As Mikhail Bakhtin said of carnival in writing about Rabelais: "No dogma, no authoritarianism, no narrow-minded seriousness can coexist with Rabelaisian images; these images are opposed to . . . every ready-made solution in the sphere of thought and world outlook."[6] In reading of informal urban open space, one is reminded of this image of carnival: "a world of topsy-turvy, of heteroglot exuberance, of ceaseless over-reaching and excess where all is mixed, hybrid, ritually degraded and defiled."[7]

Battersea Park was created by an Act of 1846 and incorporated Battersea Fields, which for centuries had been a popular venue for informal recreation. In 1870, by which time their Rabelaisian, carnival character had been obliterated by the Park, the Fields are still vividly described by a missionary, Thomas Kirk:

> That which made this part of Battersea Fields so notorious was the gaming, sporting, and pleasure-grounds at the Red House and Balloon public houses, and Sunday fairs, held throughout the summer months. These have been the resort of hundreds and thousands, from royalty and nobility down to the poorest pauper and meanest beggar. And surely if ever there was a place out of hell that surpassed Sodom and Gomorrah in ungodliness and abomination, this was it. . . . I have gone to this sad spot on the afternoon and evening of the Lord's day, when there have been from 60 to 120 horses and donkeys racing, foot-racing, walking matches, flying boats, flying horses, roundabouts, theatres, comic actors, shameless dancers, conjurers, fortune-tellers, gamblers of every description, drinking-booths, stalls, hawkers, and vendors of all kinds of articles. It would take a more graphic pen than mine to describe the mingled shouts and noises and the unmentionable doings of this pandemonium on earth.[8]

Given this genealogy, it is hardly surprising that the new parks found themselves in a tension between order and disorder, pleasure and policing, anarchic pastimes and "rational enjoyment."[9]

[2] Land Use Consultants, "Roundhay Park [Leeds]: Historic Landscape Study and Restoration Management Plan" (1999), 7.
[3] *Hansard*, 14 July 1833, speech by Richard Slaney, MP for Shrewsbury.
[4] Martin Hoyles, *The Story of Gardening* (London: Journeyman Press, 1991), 168.
[5] Bell, *Ritual*, 139.
[6] Mikhail Bakhtin, *Rabelais and His World*, trans. 1968, quoted in Peter Stallybrass and Allon White, *The Politics and Poetics of Transgression* (London: Methuen, 1986), 3.
[7] Stallybrass and White, *Politics and Poetics of Transgression*, 8.
[8] *London City Mission Magazine*, September, 1870, quoted in J. J. Sexby, *The Municipal Parks, Gardens and Open Spaces of London: Their History and Associations* (London: Elliot Stock, 1905), 10–11.
[9] The phrase was used by Joseph Strutt, donor of the land for Derby Arboretum, quoted in Hoyles, *The Story of Gardening*, 149, in contrast to what Strutt called "brutalizing pleasures" such as cockfighting.

A carnivalesque response to the park environment was held in check by bylaws and park policing, generally with a good deal of popular support. Nevertheless, resentment of overt displays of authority was a hallmark of much correspondence about parks, and the park-keeper was a figure of more or less good-natured resistance (Fig. 2).[10] The public park was an arena in which, for physical and cultural reasons, social control was often looser than in other public domains such as public reading rooms, so acceptable behavior was an area of continuous negotiation, as it is to this day.[11] But with new laws, on the one hand, and age-old patterns of behavior, on the other (such as picking flowers), enjoyment of the park could easily veer into what became defined as transgression. Hazel Conway, for example, quotes *Blackwood's Magazine*, which in 1839 reported seeing children crowding round to see the fowl on the lake in St. James's Park, and "the verdant-coated verderers of the Office of Woods and Forests, cutting away with ratans at poor little nursery girls and their helpless charges."[12]

2. *The park keeper at Hampden Park, Eastbourne, 1937 (author's collection)*

Law

The bylaws, railings, and prohibitive signs on which the order of public parks depended were established to exclude the constant threat of behavior deemed unacceptable to the authorities that created the parks. The social program behind their creation in the nineteenth century was based on consciously promulgated ideals of social inclusion but also on the exclusion of improper behavior or individuals.[13] In contrast to the temporary appropriation by transgressive rituals, these places were created or appropriated by the authorities, which then insisted, with the force of law, on a ritualized version of pleasure.

Many parks required formal dress—in Manchester the park-keepers could "exclude any person from the park . . . not dressed in decent clothes"—and were open only at specified times of the week. Drunkenness was generally forbidden, as were many forms of apparently harmless recreation, such as eating, smoking, informal games, lectures, or sitting on the walls.[14] The first bylaws for People's Park in Halifax in 1857 forbade "games . . . of any kind, nor yet dancing" (Fig. 3). Bathing in the lakes

[10] The park-keepers at the Waterworks Park in Belfast had to be given police protection in 1865 as they tried to enforce a prohibition on people taking shortcuts through from Antrim Road to Oldpark (Robert Scott, *A Breath of Fresh Air: The Story of Belfast Parks* [Belfast: Blackstaff Press, 2000], 39).

[11] Scott, *A Breath of Fresh Air*, 53 reports a story of a gang of boys raiding the currant bushes in the Botanic Gardens, caught on the railings by the seat of his pants: the Superintendent, Charles McKimm, "lifted the culprit down, examined the damage, and pronounced judgement. 'The Lord has castigated you on the place provided—but next time He'll probably leave the job to me.' He gave the crying child an apple and sent him on his way."

[12] *Blackwood's Magazine*, vol. 46, August 1839, quoted in Hazel Conway, *People's Parks: The Design and Development of Victorian Parks in Britain* (Cambridge: Cambridge University Press, 1990), 205.

[13] The report of the opening of Baxter Park, Dundee, stressed inclusive ownership to what might be seen as an inflammatory extent: "The people of Dundee entered yesterday into possession of *their* estate. To-day the workman can say to his wife, 'Let us take a walk in *our* Park, and see what the gardener is doing, and how the flowers are thriving.' To-day the mechanic may put on his walking face and his walking coat, and stroll through *his* grounds; and, when he is weary of wandering between banks of flowers, he may rest himself in *his* pavillion, which will be none the less enjoyed for being enjoyed in common by his fellows" (*Dundee Advertiser*, 10 September 1863; original emphases).

[14] All, except eating, forbidden in the 1904 bylaws for Baxter Park, Dundee. The bringing in of "edible provisions" was, however, banned from the Botanic Garden, Belfast (Scott, *A Breath of Fresh Air*, 8).

3. *The genteel landscape of People's Park in Halifax, as depicted in 1857* (Illustrated London News)

was strictly prohibited as was straying from the gravel walks on to the grass, and no dogs were admitted.[15] At Philips Park in Manchester, a year after the park opened without bylaws, the Corporation realized the urgent need for some rules, and in 1847 introduced "a plethora of elegant black notices with gold letters which began outside the park" exhorting [users] to preserve the trees, shrubs, and property from injury, not to walk on the grass, not to touch plants or flowers, segregating the male and female playgrounds, and prohibiting "all gambling, indecent language and disorderly conduct"; subsequent signs also warned against throwing stones at the swans and pulling straw out of the thatched roof of the new summerhouse.[16] At Longton Park near Stoke-on-Trent, the superintendent banned bicycles, tricycles, and dogs in September 1888, and the following year advised against the installation of swings for children and against provision for football and cricket. He also took proceedings against those caught picking flowers, and had notices issued "warning persons against dancing on the grass or otherwise causing damage during band concerts."[17]

Control and Outlawing

The creation of parks was very often a means of controlling an *unruly* space such as Battersea Fields or Kennington Common, which, before its enclosure to form Kennington Park, had been the venue for mass meetings and rallies (Fig. 4). The introduction of bylaws—today seen widely as ineffective and token—was a real means of social control. Social control and the new rituals of correct leisure were also implicit in the park design itself. Natural "desire-line" paths, that is, paths formed by habitual use, replaced by artfully meandering serpentines can be seen as a formal channelling of the potentially threatening dynamics highlighted by Richard Slaney in 1833. When the Commons in Armagh, Northern Ireland, were converted by the Bishop of Armagh into the Mall in 1773, a new symbolic landscape was created. In place of a space in which markets, fairs, and horse-trading could take place informally and unlicensed, the Mall comprised rigid tree-lined walks, and strictly regulated exercise—in this case, a cricket field. At the same time, the Courthouse was built at one end of the oval space and the Gaol at the other and later a Crimean War cannon was erected facing the length of the park (Fig. 5). This was a landscape of occupation, and one in which the forces of law and order ensuring no transgression were palpably demonstrated.

On a different scale, in Prince Consort Gardens, Weston-super-Mare, the construction of formal walks in 1882 was seen as a way of discouraging transgressive behavior: as the landowner's agent remarked, "If a good shelter were supplied for

---

[15] *A Handbook to the People's Park* (Halifax, 1857).

[16] Alan Ruff, *The Biography of Philips Park, Manchester, 1846–1996*, University of Manchester School of Planning and Landscape, Occasional Paper 56 (2000), 57.

[17] Ian Lawley, *Parks for the People*, City of Stoke on Trent Leisure and Recreation Department, nd., no pag. Galen Cranz, *The Politics of Park Design: A History of Urban Parks in America* (Cambridge, Mass.: MIT Press, 1982), 10: "All park departments sponsored music, though not all kinds. Administrators excluded German polkas—'oompah' music—on the grounds that they were undignified, overly stimulating, and associated with dancing. By contrast classical music was edifying. . . ."

4. *The Chartist rally on Kennington Common in 1848* (Illustrated London News)

5. *The Mall, Armagh: common land appropriated for the new ritualized forms of correct leisure*

the Band & the walks were furnished, like the Esplanade, with seats, it would be a very pleasant lounge & an improvement to adjacent property. . . . No nuisance would arise from Excursionists. An open green would always be used for noisy games & the like, but walks are not open to that objection."[18]

The landscaping of Bristol's Brandon Hill in 1840 was similarly tendentious. The 1830s saw the Bristol riots, the burgeoning Chartists' movement, and the campaign for parliamentary reform, in all of which the Hill had played a significant role as a venue for rallies and political meetings (Fig. 6). In 1840, the Corporation began a program of "improvements" to Brandon Hill, comprising new gravel walks and planting, which included the creation of bylaws, and it is clear that improvement, both the physical design and the introduction of regulations, was a strategy against working-class organization, dependent as it was on a large, unregulated, public open space.

Although political and religious meetings were either prohibited or subject strictly to consent from the authorities, parks were often used for military drilling, for example, during the 1860s when there was widespread fear of a French invasion, and parade grounds were incorporated in park designs such as that of R. H. Vertegans in 1879 for West Park in Wolverhampton (Fig. 7).

The use of parks for public meetings, and in particular, political meetings, offers a paradigm of rituals of transgression; they are rituals in the sense Catherine Bell describes when she refers to "the 'social' work of ritual activities: the formation and maintenance of the social bonds [and power relations] that establish human community."[19] The bylaws formulated in urban parks founded in the 1830s–1850s reflected a desire to allay and control social unrest: political agitation was clearly incompatible with this aim and the new bylaws almost universally forbade the use of parks for religious or political gatherings. In 1848, at the peak of Chartist activity, the Duke of Wellington recommended the closure of all London parks. These transgressive rituals were marginalized, failed attempts at appropriating the spaces. But by the 1890s, the growth of the Labor movement, and the

[18] David Lambert, *Historic Public Parks: Bristol* (Bristol: Avon Gardens Trust, 2000), 33.
[19] Bell, *Ritual*, 59.

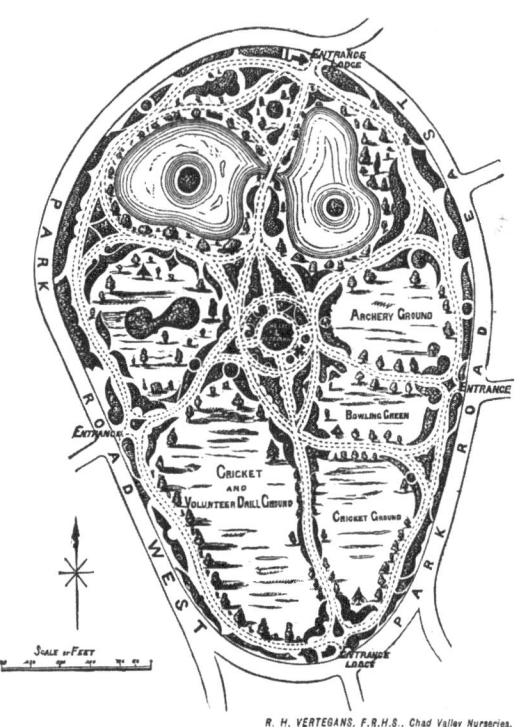

6. *George Rowbotham, "The Grand Reform Dinner on Brandon Hill," (Bristol City Museum and Art Gallery)*
7. *R. H. Vertegans, design for West Park, Wolverhampton, 1879, including a Volunteer Drill Ground in the south-west quarter (Wolverhampton Public Libraries)*

R. H. VERTEGANS, F.R.H.S., Chad Valley Nurseries.

presence of Labor members on Corporation committees, had changed the climate of opinion. What had been seen as transgressive behavior, to be outlawed and resisted, was recognized as a legitimate part of the rituals of working-class cohesion.

In Bristol, where public parks were laid out in a relatively short period in the 1880s and 1890s, public meetings were only to be allowed in two of the parks, and then only by permission. The omission of a general right of assembly in the new parks was highly controversial: on 23 June 1891 the Bristol Labour Emancipation League sent in a resolution to the Corporation, strongly protesting the proposed interference by the Corporation in "the rights of the Citizens of Bristol to hold public meetings in their large parks," while the Bristol Socialist League also protested "emphatically . . . against any restriction of the Citizens' undoubted rights to hold public meetings in our large Parks and Public Spaces."[20]

In Manchester, in the 1890s, the labor movement challenged the prohibition of meetings in public parks. The Manchester and Salford Trades and Labour Council was not satisfied with the offer of specified locations for meetings, the Corporation's first response retorting that the proposals were "incomplete" insofar as they "do not set apart certain public parks of this city in which public meetings can take place." The symbolic importance of meeting in a park was strongly felt, and after further lobbying of the Home Secretary, the Corporation relented and in 1897 earmarked Philips Park, Queens Park, Alexandra Park, Boggart Hole Clough, and five recreation grounds for such purposes.[21] By the beginning of the twentieth century, the park superintendent, William Wallace Pettigrew, was able to see the use of public parks for political meetings as a safety valve "wherein disgruntled folk are enabled to air their grievances."[22] Similarly, consent to hold political meetings in Glasgow Green was described in 1898 as "giving free course and comparatively harmless outlet to sentiment and opinions which otherwise might sometimes attain explosive force. It is a safety valve which should find a place in every great community."[23]

[20] Ibid., 42.
[21] Ruff, *The Biography of Philips Park, Manchester*, 115.
[22] Quoted in Hoyles, *The Story of Gardening*, 164.
[23] R. King, *The People's Palace*, Glasgow, 86, quoted in Conway, *People's Parks*, 189.

In a recent classic example of the politics of parks, the Royal Parks Agency, a quasi-autonomous arm of Government, initially tried to ban the 2003 antiwar rally from being held in Hyde Park, with the Secretary of State herself making the announcement—an attempt withdrawn in the face of public indignation.

The Problem of Inventing Tradition

What park authorities were trying to do was social engineering; encouraging patterns of rational amusement in place of what they deemed irrational or vicious (Fig. 8). In order to achieve this, they invented tradition in the way explored by Hobsbawm and Ranger, and in particular by David Cannadine in his analysis of the contemporary invention of monarchy under Victoria and Albert.[24] Social control was dressed up in ritual-like patterns of prescribed leisure—ritual-like in Bell's sense of formalized, traditionalized, rule-governed, and invariant—the promenade, archery, drilling, Sunday School pageants, civic ceremonies, or music (Fig. 9). These were the activities chosen to feature in the flood of engravings and photographs published to promote the new parks and their amenities.

The authorities went to extraordinary lengths to establish, rapidly, a tradition of correct usage. The opening of Baxter Park in Dundee, on 9 September 1863, was marked by an extravagant neomedieval procession of guilds, societies, militia, bands, and councilors, through verdure-decked and banner-hung

8. *The epitome of rational amusement: an image of West Park, 1910 (author's collection)*

9. *Listening to the band in Princes Gardens, Torquay, 1948 (author's collection)*

[24] Eric Hobsbawm and Terence Ranger, *The Invention of Tradition* (Cambridge: Cambridge University Press, 1992), passim. Catherine Bell cites the same example of late-nineteenth-century monarchism when she wrote of "traditionalization" of activities (Bell, *Ritual*, 145). For Cannadine's analysis of Victoria, see *Rituals of Royalty: Power and Ceremonial in Traditional Societies*, ed. David Cannadine and Simon Price (Cambridge: Cambridge University Press, 1987).

10. *Opening of Baxter Park, 19 September 1863* (Illustrated London News)

streets (Fig. 10).[25] Similarly, the opening of the People's Park in Halifax, on 14 August 1857, was a huge set piece, and included the Sixth West Yorkshire Militia Staff and Band, escorting two Russian Guns taken at the fall of Sebastopol, processions of friendly societies, the mayor and corporation, and workpeople from the factories of the donor, Francis Crossley.[26] Although one-off events, they partook of generalized characteristics repeated on countless occasions—openings, jubilees, and so on—in countless parks throughout the land.

These are classic examples of Bell's "social work of ritual," mentioned earlier.[27] Natural forms of pleasure were corrected, ritualized into performative rituals—the promenade replaced the aimless wander, admiring the floral displays replaced picking the flowers. Public parks rapidly became the locus for commemoration of national or local dignitaries, pageants, jubilees, thanksgivings, parades, even military training.[28]

The new park was a locus for rituals, which can be illuminated by Arnold van Gennep's model of separation, transition, and incorporation. The special quality of the new park environment, heightened by symbolic design elements such as imposing gate piers, elaborate bedding, and statuary, made entry into the park a rite of separation; the experience of the park was a rite of transition, in theory—if not in practice—ending with incorporation of the willing visitor in the dominant ethic of the authorities, transformed and pacified by the rational enjoyments on offer. In practice, carnivalesque inversion often defeated the ritual program intended by benefactors and managers. At Philip's Park in Manchester, the reformers' motto, written on signs in the park, that "This Park was Purchased by the People, was Made for the People, and is Given to the People for their Protection" was frequently quoted derisively at park-keepers by those flaunting the bylaws.[29]

[25] "Opening of the Baxter Park," *Dundee Advertiser,* 9 September 1863. "The streets were bridged with arches, the route from the Seminaries to the Park became one continuous chain of tasteful triumphal erections . . . a great new business in banners, flags, colour poles, transparencies, and evergreens—a business of decorators, colour makers, gasfitters, gardeners, and busy wrights, employed the energies and attention of the people. Great walls of verdure sprang up in the streets. Arches in Gothic, in Norman, and in floral architecture arose within pistol shot of each other, and the great mills came out in an eruption of colour poles, prepared to look as gay 'as an army with banners.' . . . Dundee is all bunting and bravery—the air pulses with the sounds of commingling bands of music—the railway stations are hives of men, and every hive is throwing off its swarms until they blacken the streets; there is mustering and marshalling of men at the shore, mustering of men under glittering new banners, red sashes, green sashes, white sashes, and there is much haste and crowding. . . . The Volunteers in their new blouses are one blaze of brilliant scarlet, . . . The bakers in their picturesque and lively costume are gathering to their place of rendezvous, ... The Freemasons, aproned, sashed, rosetted, and dressed from head to foot in the sleekest of broadcloth, are picking, with hasty steps, their way among the crowd. The trades, in generous rivalry, are, in their sashes and favours, as brilliant as so many tropical birds; and as they move with a forest of silk banners overhead to the starting place, each a link in the great pageant of the day . . . the wonder is . . . how, when once started, it is ever to end. . . ."

[26] *A Jubilee History of the Halifax People's Park* (Halifax, 1907), 11. The official brochure concluded that "this was by far the most splendid procession, and the most costly, ever seen in the town of Halifax."

[27] Bell, *Ritual*, 59.

[28] In the 1890s, the Sanitary Committee granted permission for the use of Greville Smyth Park, Bristol, for drilling by schoolboys from Ashton Gate Board School. In 1860, the Rifle Corps of the Birmingham division of the Warwickshire Regiment was given permission to drill and do field exercises in Calthorpe Park during the summer months.

[29] Ruff, *Philips Park*, 78.

Resistance and Rule Breaking

It is clear that there was never a golden age in which bylaws were unquestioningly obeyed, vandalism was nonexistent and gentility reigned as the park-makers had hoped.[30] On the contrary, early park history is peppered with spicy stories of resistance to bourgeois rituals of correct leisure.

The daybook of the head gardener of Philip's Park Manchester is full of the frustration of trying to impose a notion of "rational exercise and amusement" on users.[31] In December 1865, he made an official complaint to the Manchester Parks and Cemetery Committee: "In fine weather [the park] was frequented by a number of exceedingly ill behaved young men and women whose dress and language was both disgusting and filthy . . . any remonstrations were only received with laughter and sneers, offensive remarks were often addressed to . . . [p]ark servants by these persons and they dare not resent them."[32]

Despite bylaws, what counted as proper behavior was open to negotiation: when a park-keeper reprimanded a man sitting on a bench with his arm around his female companion's waist, he was castigated in the local press for his officiousness and for exceeding his powers.[33] Working-class couples were often seen as using a "wholesome" space in an "unwholesome" way: lighting was often seen as a way to discourage couples without access to indoor privacy, in search of privacy out of doors. One reason given for the decision of the Society of Merchant Venturers to hand over responsibility for Victoria Square in Bristol to the Corporation was that by 1874, the trees were overcrowded and there were no keys to the gates, so that the public used the garden "often, we fear when dark . . . for immoral purposes."[34]

Even the introduction of public conveniences was controversial in terms of notions of correct behavior. When they were first proposed for Philips Park in 1846, one member of the Manchester Parks Committee objected on the grounds that: "It is not desirable at any time to have too much accommodation of this kind, nor are the public parks the proper place for such matters. Besides I do not think encouragement should be given to such occupation and I conceive that there is indelicacy in the very idea."[35]

As in England, in America there was strict exclusion of certain forms of leisure activity. Galen Cranz's study of park development in New York, Chicago, and San Francisco remarks: "Some activities were widely popular but excluded from park life: these exclusions further describe the ideal of enjoyment and reveal its class bias." Cranz refers to the prohibition of "folk entertainment like horseshoe pitching, tomahawk twirling, and bullet throwing [which] were not refined enough for city parks despite their popularity. . . . Workers pouring into the city from rural areas and peasant immigrants from other countries did not share, of course, standards of behaviour in public places, so that rules against spitting, swearing, drinking, raising of the voice, or running underscored the need to create a civic order."[36]

Reading of the contemporary texts has led Sarah Schmidt to show how, in the development of public parks in Montreal between 1855 and 1912, "two particularly disenfranchised groups, the vagabond and the 'improper' courting couple, class-, gender-, and age-specific constructs who embodied economic disorder, social unrest and moral chaos, were ideologically

[30] For example, Scott, *A Breath of Fresh Air*, 56: "From an early stage the public parks were open to abuse. Alexandra Park suffered badly shortly after its opening and in the later years of the nineteenth century the Public Parks Committee received regular reports of trouble and wrecking. In 1897 the flower beds in Dunville Park were badly damaged, and crowds of youths—smoking, spitting and using bad language—were reported to be 'hanging around' the entrance to Botanic Gardens. The shelters in Ormeau and Botanic Gardens were also gathering places and the local constabulary had to be called in on numerous occasions. Complaints were lodged in 1907 about frequent card playing in public and warning notices were displayed after several birds' nests were destroyed."

[31] Words used by Mark Philips at the official opening, quoted in Ruff, 29.

[32] Manchester Parks and Cemetery Committee, vol. 122, December 1865.

[33] Sarah Schmidt, "'Private' Acts in 'Public' Spaces: Parks in Turn-of-the-Century Montreal," in T. Myers, K. Boyer, M. A. Pontanen, and S. Watt, eds., *Power, Place and Identity: Historical Studies of Social and Legal Regulation in Quebec* (Montreal: Montreal History Group, 1998), 142.

[34] Patrick McGrath, *The Merchant Venturers of Bristol*, 341.

[35] Ruff, *Phillips Park*, 53: Manchester Parks Committee Scrap Book MS352–7.

[36] Cranz, *The Politics of Park Design*, 19.

and physically removed from parks."[37] She points out the irony that "the vagabond, the most in need of 'civilizing', was . . . banned from the very space constructed as that which civilized."[38] It is notable how nonlegitimized use, whether by unaccompanied children, vagabonds, or minorities, continued to flourish despite the efforts of those who sought to exclude them.

Provision for children, now seen as integral to good park management, was also controversial. Many parks excluded unaccompanied children: children under the age of eight were not permitted to enter Saltaire Park, near Bradford, without an adult. When Alexandra Parade Gardens were created out of an informal open space of asphalt in the center of Weston-super-Mare in 1909, it was hoped that the laying-out of gardens would reduce the

11. The shelter in Grove Park, Weston-super-Mare, ca. 1910 (author's collection)

noise created by children playing and by musicians in the summer, which had "become a serious public annoyance."[39] Similarly, a correspondent to the *Weston Mercury* in June 1902 complained of the shelter in Grove Park in the same town: "At present the shelter is useless to invalids and visitors by reason of a lot of noisy children being allowed to make it their play place. I have many times seen ladies and gentlemen driven away by the racket" (Fig. 11).[40]

Archery, with its overtones of obeisance to the lord of the manor, or polite country-house amusements, was permitted in Victoria Park in East London, along with cricket, rounders, and boating, but football was not allowed until 1888, forty-three years after the park was opened. Football, although played since the Middle Ages, had no set rules until 1863 and often generated large numbers of players and watchers.[41] It was generally among the last sports to be permitted in public parks.[42]

The games in Philips Park were the source of much controversy. The playgrounds and other facilities were felt to have marred the central valley and they were removed very soon after the park opened; some altogether, some to peripheral areas of the park. An 1849 guide commented: "It was far from agreeable to find this charming section of the park occupied by men shouting under the excitement of the skittle ground, or the unrestrained merriment of the factory girls who used the swings. It is now quiet and tranquil, and will be a favourite spot for the adult population."[43]

The 1852 report of the Committee for Peel Park in Bradford stated: "The first step in raising the working man was to see him thoroughly clean . . . let their motto be 'Touch not, handle not', and if they do that they will enjoy all the pleasure it

[37] Schmidt, 129–49.

[38] Ibid., 138.

[39] David Lambert, *Historic Public Parks: Weston-super-Mare* (Bristol: Avon Gardens Trust, 1998), 10–11.

[40] Ibid., 30.

[41] Steen Eiler Rasmussen, *London: The Unique City*, first published 1934, abridged edition (Harmondsworth: Penguin, 1960), 226.

[42] Football was finally permitted in Victoria Park, Belfast in 1922, by which time "unofficial football games had been taking pace for over twenty-five years" (Scott, *A Breath of Fresh Air*, 50).

[43] *A few pages about Manchester*, circa 1849, quoted Ruff, *Phillips Park*, 57.

is possible to have without doing any harm whatsoever."[44] One is reminded of the insight of Denis Cosgrove in commenting on the mass trespass on Kinder Scout by working-class ramblers in 1935: the intentions of organizers such as Tom Stephenson, he remarks, "were not to *see* landscape so much as to experience it physically—to walk it, climb it or cycle in it."[45] For the working-class users, for whom public parks were ostensibly designed, full experience of the landscape often involved inevitable transgression of the rules.

Transgression as Legitimate Use

So, while clearly in Bell's sense conformity was often ritual-like, to what extent did transgression also take ritual-like form? We can see it historically in the mass games of football that were complained of in superintendent's reports,[46] in the defiant use of parks for political meetings and rallies, and indeed in their place in popular culture during the 1960s; the popular song, "Itchycoo Park" by the Small Faces is typical of the regard in which these informal urban spaces were held by a generation devoted to transgression, spaces in which feeding the ducks and getting high were seen as perfectly complementary.

Going back to Reg Speller, we can see it in the persistent use of lakes for bathing. In 1849 it was estimated that, in three hours on one summer day, three thousand people bathed in the eastern lake of Victoria Park, a use condemned by the park's designer, James Pennethorne, because bathing costumes were not used. Swimming was illegal and people did so "at their own peril, sometimes being taken into custody for it."[47] And yet they persisted in what Bell would call a "traditionalized," ritual-like activity. Steen Eiler Rasmussen has described the love of swimming as a long-standing English trait when commenting on the ponds on Hampstead Heath: "The English love the raw sensation of the elements, to feel the wind and the moisture in their faces. That is why they swim in the lakes, dive down to muddy depths—becoming fish in the coolness of the water."[48] The first park constable in Alexandra Park Hastings had to control among other activities, "skipping, leap-frog (and) kiss-in-the-ring," suggesting in the individual itemization that the prohibited activities were as ritual-like [traditional, invariant, and rule-governed] as those permitted.[49]

When Philips Park, Manchester, opened, the most common transgression of the bylaws was one rich with cultural associations. The day-book of the head gardener, Jeremiah Harrison, records his frustration over the picking of flowers, particularly by young girls and women but also by boys and men: "visitors seem determined not to go out without a posy as they call it."[50] The use of the formal, courtly term "posy" suggests that the transgressors and indeed Harrison were aware of the traditional significance of the flowers, huge in Victorian times as a symbol of love and innocence, even when picking them in the park was illegal.

Card-playing also was prohibited in Philips Park, but the prohibition was resisted. "Tuesday a young man told one of our men that four young men were playing cards in the bandstand, they were caught but were not playing at the time. I sent for a police officer and he advised me to reprimand them and let them go, also a plain clothes police officer caught one on Saturday, three got away, that were playing cards in the bandstand, with only one being caught. For four afternoons last week I got a plain clothes officer from 4 p.m. to 9-15 p.m. but he did not catch anyone they were all very quiet, they turned up again last night."[51] It would be reasonable, given the repeated nature of the offence, to infer that card playing had an important role

[44] Quoted in Stuart Rawnsley, "Saltaire: From Old Paternalism to Romantic Capitalism," in *The New Arcadian Journal* 25 (Winter 1987–88), 25–37.

[45] Denis Cosgrove and Stephen Daniels, eds., *The Iconography of Landscape* (Cambridge: Cambridge University Press, 1984), 268.

[46] Lambert, *Bristol*, 58: in St. George's Park in Bristol, the use of the park for unofficial games of football, even at night, was damaging the turf according to council minutes of February 1897.

[47] Select Committee on Public Walks, Report, p. 355, quoted in Conway, *People's Parks*, 198–99.

[48] Rasmussen, *London*, 239.

[49] Hastings Borough Council, *Alexandra Park*, 1982, quoted in Conway, *People's Parks*, 204. See Bell, *Ritual*, 153 on the "ritual-like" characteristics of many games and forms of play.

[50] Quoted in Ruff, *Phillips Park*, 75.

[51] Manchester Parks and Cemetery Committee, July 1910, quoted in Ruff, *Phillips Park*, 123.

in the social life of the transgressors, and that the park seemed a legitimate location for it, despite the law. The illicit use of the bandstand for this social ritual was a form of appropriation, albeit furtive and unsuccessful.

Correct and Incorrect—Two Sides of the Same Coin

How then did transgressive behavior relate to permitted behavior? I would like to suggest that it was, in some intimate way, complementary, that transgressive behavior was fundamental to public parks. Much of this behavior, when it is not purely antagonistic to the park but in some way a utilization of and engagement with its facilities, should be termed "symbolic inversion." As defined by Barbara Babcock, this covers "any sort of expressive behaviour which inverts, contradicts, abrogates or in some fashion presents an alternative to commonly held cultural codes, values and norms."[52] But, as she continues, "all symbolic inversions define a culture's lineaments at the same times as they question the usefulness and the absoluteness of its ordering."[53] There is a relationship between the intended ritual program and the rituals of transgression: as van Gennep observes, rituals cannot be interpreted outside the whole system of rituals to which they belong.[54]

Moreover, we can see how far the transgressive binds together correct behavior and those who behave correctly. In the Montreal parks in the mid-nineteenth century, debates over single women users illustrates how, in Barbara Babcock's words, "What is socially peripheral is often symbolically central."[55] Fear of prostitution or of fornication was used to define the bounds of correctness. We see today in English and Scottish parks how the disproportionate fear of violence, paedophiles, or of discarded needles rallies a community. (Outside parks, the current hysterical reaction to asylum-seekers again illustrates how what is socially peripheral to the vast majority of the population becomes symbolically central via the mass-circulation tabloid press.) Transgression and conformity are intimately entangled: the margins define the center:

> It has been noted in literary theory how high discourses, with their lofty style, exalted aims and sublime ends, are structured in relation to the debasements and degradations of low discourse . . . how each extremity structures the other, depends upon and invades the other in certain historical moments. . . . A recurrent pattern emerges: the 'top' attempts to reject and eliminate the 'bottom' for reasons of prestige and status, only to discover that it is in some way frequently dependent upon that low-Other (in the classic way that Hegel describes in the master-slave section of the *Phenomenology*).[56]

Right behavior was continually defined in the nineteenth century by its opposite; it existed in its difference from transgressive, was legitimized by it.

Stallybrass and White go further and refer to "hierarchy inversion as a ritual strategy on the part of subordinate groups."[57] The media reporting of vandalism in Philips Park, Manchester, immediately after World War II, intriguingly dramatizes just such ritual strategy. Access and vandalism had been hugely facilitated, of course, by the removal of railings and gates as part of the war effort (a purely symbolic gesture, as most such railings were not melted down for ordnance but were either sold as scrap or simply dumped). The *Manchester Evening Chronicle* reported on 5 November (Guy Fawkes' Night) 1947 that:

---

[52] Barbara A. Babcock, ed., *The Reversible World: Symbolic Inversion in Art and Society* (Ithaca, N.Y.: Cornell University Press, 1978), 14.

[53] Ibid., 29.

[54] I am grateful to Michel Conan for this gloss on van Gennep.

[55] Schmidt, "'Private' Acts in 'Public' Spaces," passim. Babcock is quoted in Stallybrass and White, *The Politics and Poetics of Transgression*, 20.

[56] Ibid., 3–5.

[57] Stallybrass and White, *The Politics and Poetics of Transgression*, 4.

Piled high on bonfires in Clayton and Bradford tonight, will be trees, privets and wooden fences taken from Philips Park. Operation Destruction has been carried out in a thorough manner by two gangs of school children, ages ranging from 10 to 13, who call themselves the Bradford Commandos and the Clayton Commandos. The "commandos" carry out most of their operations on the way home from school and employ ingenious devices to avoid capture. Armed with axes, knives, and even small saws and crowbars hidden under their coats and jerseys, these youngsters have their own calls, whistles and signals when danger—in the shape of policemen, park-keepers and watchmen—looms on the horizon. Fred Shaw, a greensman for over 17 years at Philips Park said they even used trip wires against us. The matter has long ceased to be humourous."[58]

    The description, both alarmed and indulgent, portrays the children's activities as an elaborate miniature version of adult behavior associated with the wartime victory, with its own codes and practices, a form of ritual-like behavior.[59]

    We can see the ritual-like character of transgression again in an undated article from the *Daily Chronicle* that describes how "Feeding the rats in Peckham Park has become as popular as feeding the animals in the zoo." The rats were a health hazard and the authorities had a policy of destroying them, but feeding them became a ritual of leisure for users:

This little park . . . is one of the prettiest in London, and the rats have made it also one of the most popular. You can find peacocks and pigeons in the park. But if you discover a little group of children with paper bags in their hands, you may take it for granted that they are there not to feed the birds, but the rats. One of the park keepers told a "Daily Chronicle" representative yesterday that he has never seen anyone run away from a rat. "The rats are most friendly," he said. "They don't care for crowds, but on a quiet day they like to see the children, and the children love coming here to feed them."[60]

To the despair of park managers, feeding the vermin in public parks, nowadays Canada geese and squirrels, continues unabated, despite continuing to be against the law, a performative transgression ritualized over generations.

Transgression and the Withdrawal of Law

    This ritual-like nature of transgression is also evident in the later history of public parks from places of legislated order to places abandoned by law (Fig. 12).Despite the physical dereliction, public parks have continued to be places in which ritual-like patterns of leisure, such as hanging out away from adults, have developed (Fig. 13). Transgression continues to take ritual form, for example, in the new role of public parks such as Russell Square that had been largely abandoned by the authorities and their representatives, as meeting-places for homosexuals.[61] In Corporation Park, Blackburn, a tree growing near the neighboring school is known by both schoolchildren and park staff as "the cigarette tree," as the habitual gathering place for break-time smokers among the pupils. The tradition has been going on so long that the tree is beginning to suffer from the nicotine absorbed by its roots and it can be seen as a ritual in van Gennep's terms, separating the participants from the everyday world of school, a transitional stage of participation ending in incorporation in the outlaw group.

[58] Ruff, *Phillips Park*, 148.

[59] Catherine Bell notes that "both the scholar and the unschooled observer are apt to appreciate something ritual-like in many games and forms of play" (Bell, *Ritual*, 153).

[60] John D. Beasley, *Peckham Rye Centenary* (London, n.d., [ca. 1995]), 84–85.

[61] The proposal to "restore" the square in 1997 as a Heritage Lottery Fund project, which involved locking its gates at night, was greeted with highly articulate opposition by the local gay community. Similarly, there were objections from the police to nighttime closure of Forbury Gardens, Reading, in the HLF restoration plan, because, with the gates open, "at least they knew where the dealers were" (information supplied by Dr. Stewart Harding, former head of HLF Urban Parks Programme, 2003).

12. *The rose garden in Horton Park, Bradford, in 1999*

13. *Youths enjoying Derby Arboretum, ca. 1996 (from Glenn Kerr Associates, "Derby Arboretum Management Plan," 1996)*

The world of transgressors is inevitably hard to find written up, but this grafitti in Baxter Park in Dundee gives hints of a glorious struggle fitting to a warlike race (Fig. 14).[62] When Central Park in New York was being restored, the number one priority was grafitti removal, because of its role in ritual territorializing of the park by rival gangs, and as early as the 1920s Robert Park of the University of Chicago School of Social Ecology was analyzing "the significance of group bonding in distinctive juvenile gangs."[63] The debate on dog-walking in many public parks has been ferocious in the last twenty years, attacked and defended with equal passion on both sides, with the transgressors claiming to have "a right to take our dogs there."[64]

As described by Eileen O'Keefe, Norbury Park, near Reigate in Surrey, exemplifies the juxtaposition of correct and transgressive rituals of leisure:

> The graffiti in the grim underpass, crossing from Box Hill to the Norbury Park side of the
> A24 would not look out of place in the environs of Kings Cross. Smack on the doorstep
> of the good folk of Mickleham, in a car park on the A24, is the meeting place for the
> motorcycling fraternity who congregate in their hundreds from across the South East to
> celebrate their passion for a visual and sound culture of their own.[65]

Transgression such as this rally may be viewed as purely antisocial; it may, by contrast, represent part of a legitimate negotiation over use. Ken Worpole has demonstrated how in today's post-bylaw public parks "arguments over dog mess, loud

---

[62] See Dick Hebdige, *Hiding in the Light: On Images and Things* (London: Comedia, 1988). Hebdige has concluded that the ritualistic levels of display especially in Punk-era England, were part of a subculture that "translates the fact of being under scrutiny into the pleasures of being watched" (p. 35).

[63] Hebdige refers to Robert Park and the University of Chicago School of Social Ecology, which in the 1920s explored "the significance of group-bonding in distinctive juvenile gangs" (Hebdige, *Hiding in the Light*, 8).

[64] Beasley, *Peckham Rye Centenary*, 61.

[65] Eileen O'Keefe, "Leaving Arcadia: Rites of Passage," in *Arcadia Revisited: The Place of Landscape*, ed. Vicki Beger and Isabel Vasseur (Surrey County Council and Black Dog Press, 1997), 160.

radios, teenage hanging out, scramble bikes, free festivals, all contribute to the problem of a confusion of appropriate activities for appropriate spaces."[66]

Similarly, in America, the revival of parks at the end of the 1960s was seen to lie in encouraging an "anything goes" approach to programming.[67] But the new uses, deeply embedded in social ritual outside the park, were again threatening to the older ideals of rational enjoyment: "The new and vigorous use of the parks, especially during the Vietnam War, was sometimes disruptive, threatening to conventional sensibilities or downright illegal." The café by the Bethesda Fountain in Central Park, New York, was allowed to become a center for marijuana smokers and despite experimental tolerance, "the result was considered unsavoury and the café disbanded."[68]

14. *Grafitti in Baxter Park, Dundee, 2000*

As Galen Cranz has observed, "these rumblings represented a deeper upheaval, indicated by a slogan of the era, Power to the people."[69] From a historical perspective, there is an irony in the echo of the taunts of transgressors in Philips Park a century before, and it epitomizes the conundrum at the heart of the public park.

Resistance to dominant ritual forms and promotion of alternatives has continued to this day. For example, in the 1990s, there was a strain of protest against the new forms of order represented by park restoration. In a critique of the restoration of Victoria Park, in Bow, East London, Iain Sinclair described the heritage vision of the park as "a homage to the dominant ethic": "As transients (non-voters) we are here on sufferance. The park is a manifesto: life could be like this, disciplined leisure, controlled enlightenment. Uniformity, cropped grass and fresh paint on the railings. . . . Zero graffiti. The park repels it. We keep our heads down and our hands in our pockets."[70] The new ritual route, the heritage trail, is vehemently denounced: "Every artefact within the kidney outline of the park must align itself with the gonzo concept of the 'Bow Heritage Trail'. This is not a path that can actually be walked, it's a metaphor, a conceit, meandering aimlessly. . . ."[71] By contrast to the polite and correct promenade along the heritage trail, carnivalesque use of the park, even when licensed, is still presented as a transgression and provokes fury from the establishment's watchdogs: the *East London Advertiser*'s reaction to the Gay and Lesbian Pride Festival held in the park was to rage at the litter of "paper, cans, bottles and used condoms" under a headline denouncing the participants as "Mucky Devils!"[72]

[66] Comedia and Demos, *Park Life: Urban Parks and Social Renewal* (Comedia and Demos: Stroud and London, 1995), 11. The report also quotes Deborah Karasov, *The Once and Future Park* (Princeton, N.J.: Princeton University Press, 1993): "While some park users stroll along the paths and sit quietly among the manicured gardens—the image of bourgeois leisure to which nineteenth-century reformers hoped everyone would aspire—others feel just as comfortable using parks as places to fix their cars, dance to music, or just hang out."
[67] Cranz, *The Politics of Park Design*, 138.
[68] Ibid., 142.
[69] Ibid., 142–43.
[70] Iain Sinclair, *Lights Out for the Territory* (London: Granta, 1997), 38.
[71] Ibid., 213.
[72] Ibid., 212.

In conclusion, "the people's park" was and is a much more complicated cultural structure than is now perceived. The very notion of a people's park is fraught with potential conflict. To whom does it belong, and who decides how it should be used? The way in which it is to be used has been the subject of continuous struggle and negotiation. In the people's park, a lacuna exists between the appropriation of the authorities designed to impose civilizing performative rituals, and the reappropriation implicit in people's actual behavior. But transgression is often far from a random, negative response to the park; on the contrary, it represents older, carnivalesque ways of engaging with place and community; and because it shares the same cultural lineaments, it is very often the corollary and complement to the dominant rituals, expressed in recognizably ritual forms.

Performance and Appropriation: Profane Rituals in Gardens and Landscapes

Performance and Appropriation: Profane Rituals in Gardens and Landscapes

Performance and Appropriation: Profane Rituals in Gardens and Landscapes

Performance and Appropriation: Profane Rituals in Gardens and Landscapes

Contributors

Catherine Benoît is a Professor of Anthropology at Connecticut College. She received her Ph.D. in cultural and social anthropology from the Ecole des Hautes Etudes en Sciences Sociales (EHESS) in Paris. She was first trained in landscape archaeology at the Sorbonne and the EHESS. For fifteen years she has developed research on the construction of the self, space, and collective identities as related to religions and the environment in different islands of the Caribbean. Following the publication of her book *Corps, jardins, mémoires: Anthropologie du corps et de l'espace à la Guadeloupe* (2000), she was a fellow at Dumbarton Oaks in 2000 and in 2003 to work on her next project. She is currently working on a book on the experience of space and nature in the African diaspora in the Americas.

Sylvie Brosseau arrived in Tokyo, Japan in 1988 after obtaining her diploma in architecture and studying city planning in Paris. She was a fellow at the Tokyo Institute of Technology in their architecture department, and she studied the culture of representation at Tokyo University. Her first study in Japan focused on a holiday resort founded by Westerners in the late nineteenth century, at which new practices and a renewed appreciation of landscape were introduced for the first time. She then became interested in public parks, their conditions of creation and their purposes, their different urban and historical contexts, and their specific features. She began to study more precisely the Japanese way of feeling nature, of building particular relations between nature and urban space. At present, she is an Associate Professor at Waseda University, School of Political Sciences and Economics.

Kendall H. Brown is Associate Professor of Asian Art History at California State University, Long Beach. His research on Japanese-style gardens outside Japan includes the book *Japanese-Style Gardens of the Pacific West Coast*, published in 1999, and an article on the contested history of the Japanese Tea Garden in San Francisco's Golden Gate Park for *Studies in the History of Gardens & Designed Landscapes* (18: 2 [1998]). Brown also has published widely on modern Japanese prints and painting, often focusing on the ways in which aspects of Japanese "tradition" were constructed and deployed for both domestic and foreign audiences. He is working on a comprehensive social history of Japanese-style gardens in North America.

Michel Conan is a sociologist. His research has focused on processes of architectural design, evaluation of public programs, and the cultural history of garden design. He was instrumental in stimulating a renewal of garden history in France beginning in the mid-1970s with the publication of several reprints, with a postface, of works by Salomon de Caus, 1620; André Mollet, 1651; Charles Perrault, 1677; William Gilpin, 1799; and René Louis Girardin, 1777; and he has been an active contributor to journals, edited volumes, and symposia. He recently published the *Dictionnaire Historique de L'Art des Jardins* (1997) and *L'Invention des Lieux* (1997); edited numerous Dumbarton Oaks symposia, including *Perspectives on Garden Histories* (1999), *Environmentalism and Landscape Architecture* (2000), and *Bourgeois and Aristocratic Cultural Encounters in Garden Art* (2002); and contributed to the catalogue for the exhibition *The Triumph of the Baroque: Architecture in Europe, 1600–1750*, at the National Gallery of Art in Washington, D.C. (2000). He is presently Director of Garden and Landscape Studies and Curator of the Contemporary Landscape Design Collections at Dumbarton Oaks.

Erik A. de Jong is a former professor of Garden History and Landscape Studies at the Bard Graduate Center in New York. He now holds the position of senior lecturer in the History and Theory of Garden and Landscape Architecture at Wageningen University as well as the Clusius Chair in the History of Garden and Landscape Architecture at the University of Leiden (The Netherlands). He received his M.A. (cum laude) from the University of Utrecht, and his Ph.D. from the State University Groningen, The Netherlands. He was a fellow in Garden and Landscape Studies at Dumbarton Oaks in 1993 and 2001 and a research fellow at the Netherlands Institute for Advanced Studies in 1997. He has been a senior fellow in Garden and Landscape Studies at Dumbarton Oaks since 2002 and is an honorary member of the Swedish Society for Dendrology and Park Culture in Stockholm, Sweden. Professor de Jong has written extensively in the field of garden and landscape studies (sixteenth through twentieth centuries) and architectural history (late eighteenth through twentieth centuries). He has lectured and taught widely in Europe and the U.S. and is an advisor for design, research, preservation, and education on several landscape projects in The Netherlands. He has curated several exhibitions on architectural and garden and landscape history.

Patrick Eyres is Senior Lecturer in Theoretical Studies at the School of Art and Design, Bradford College, where he is responsible for postgraduate studies in visual representation. He also is managing editor of *The New Arcadian Journal* and, in 2002, published the twenty-first anniversary edition on the poetic gardening of William Shenstone at The Leasowes and Ian Hamilton Finlay at Little Sparta. He is a member of the Little Sparta Trust, which seeks to raise funds to sustain Finlay's unique garden. As a member of the Wentworth Castle Trust, he helps to supervise the £15-million restoration (grant-aided by the Heritage Lottery Fund) of the exemplary Georgian house, gardens, and park—which is the subject of the 2004–5 edition of *The New Arcadian Journal*. His collection of essays on sculpture and the garden in Britain, 1700–2000, co-edited for the Henry Moore Foundation, is due to be published in 2006.

David Lambert is co-director of the Parks Agency, a not-for-profit consultancy specializing in urban parks. He has been involved in the campaign to raise the profile of urban parks in the United Kingdom for well over a decade. He is the author of *Public Prospects*, one of the first reports to draw attention to their plight, and advised the House of Commons Select Committee inquiry into public parks in 1999. He was also part of the team that ran the Heritage Lottery Fund's Urban Parks Programme from 1995 onward, and that so far has channeled over £350 million into urban park–regeneration schemes. He has been a research fellow at the University of York's Centre for the Conservation of Historic Parks and Gardens, and at De Montfort University's Centre for Conservation Studies, and is currently the external moderator for the M.A. in Garden History at the University of Bristol. For many years he was Conservation Officer for the Garden History Society, and is now an adviser to both the National Trust and English Heritage. He has lectured and written widely on the politics and practice of heritage conservation.

Susan Warren Lanman is an assistant professor in the Department of History at Metropolitan State College of Denver. She obtained her Ph.D. in Comparative History from the University of Denver, and her publications focus on nineteenth-century British and American society and culture with particular emphasis on the impact of new technologies in the garden. She currently is writing a book on the development of commercial floriculture in America.

Alessandro Tosi is Professor of Art History at the Faculty of Letters of the University of Pisa. His area of research is the history of the visual arts between the sixteenth and twentieth centuries, and the relationship between the arts and sciences. He has focused particularly on naturalistic illustration and garden history. On these subjects he has written more than eighty scholarly works, including books on the painter Giuseppe Zocchi and on the naturalist Ulisse Aldrovandi. He has collaborated on research projects organized by various institutions, including the Istituto e Museo di Storia della Scienza and the Gabinetto Vieusseux of Florence. He has delivered papers at many national and international symposia and conferences and has organized exhibitions at the Gabinetto Disegni e Stampe degli Uffizi, Florence; the Italian Institute of Culture, Washington, D.C.; and the Palazzo Lanfranchi, Pisa.

Linda Walton is Professor of History and International Studies at Portland State University (Oregon). Formerly Director of the Institute for Asian Studies, she is currently chair of the History Department. She received her B.A. from Wellesley College (1969) and her Ph.D. from the University of Pennsylvania (1978). She has lived and studied in Japan, Taiwan, and China. In addition to her book *Academies and Society in Southern Sung China* (Hawaii, 1999), she has published journal articles and book chapters on the social and intellectual history of Song and Yuan China (tenth–fourteenth centuries). Recent research includes a study of academies during the Mongol Yuan dynasty (1279–1368), local history of the Ningbo region in southeastern China, and Sino-Japanese cultural relations during the tenth to fourteenth centuries. She is coauthor of *In the Balance: Themes in Global History* (McGraw-Hill, 1998), and one of two lead scholars for the multimedia web-based world history project, *Bridging World History*, sponsored by Annenberg/CPB and launched in 2005.

Dai Kiu (d. 396) (Eremite), painter and musician, 156, 157, 158

daimyo, 98, 98n, 109, 110

Dangan naumachia, 179, 179n

Daoist sites, 158

Daozhou, 163

Dark Egret Grotto House, 161, 162

Darnton, Robert, 53

Dashwood, Sir Francis, garden of, 178–179

de Certeau, Michel, 115, 121, 168

de Chartres, Duke of, 60

Decker, Coenraad, engraver, 26–27

de Courtin, Antoine (*Nouveau Traite de la Civilite*), 30

de Hooghe, Romeyn, cartographer, 21f

de Jongh, Ludolf, 31f, 32f

de la Court, Pieter (*Consideration on the State*), 38

de Lairesse, Gerard, author, 22

de Leth, Hendrik, artist, 36f

Della Gherardesca, Count Guido Alberto, garden of, 70

della Robbia ceramics, 67

de Monville, François Racine, architect, 60

Denon, Vivant (*Voyage dans la Basse et la Haute Egypte*), 66

de Oude, Gerard ter Borch, artist, 25

Derby Arboretum, 208f

der Laan, A. van, artist, 24f

Derwentwater naumachia, 180, 190

Descanso Gardens, La Cañada-Flintridge, California, 136n

Le Desert de Retz, 60, 61

Desprez, Louis Jean, architect, 60

destination weddings, 134

de Velde II, Jan van, artist, 25f

Dezallier d'Argenville, Antoine-Joseph, author, 45

dialectical process, 80

Discourses of the Tuileries Garden in Paris (Sebastien Mercier), 52–53

Disneyland fairytale wedding, 136

Divers Desseins de Figures (Sebastien Le Clerc), 30

divinities, in Japan, 96, 106

dogs in public parks, 198, 208

domestic servants, 89

Donald Tillman Water Reclamation Plant Japanese garden, Van Nuys, California, 136n, 139n

Donglin Monastery, center of southern Buddhism, 153

dooryard gardens (Caribbean), 118; described, 121–123; public displays of, 117, 118, 127f, 128f, 129; as too dangerous for children, 125–126

Dordrecht Synod, 23, 25

doxa concept, Aristotelian, 49

Dragon Head Mountain, 168

Dragon Omen Palace, 157

Drottningholm garden, Stockholm, 60

Drummond, Lee, 127–128

Dubourg, M., artist, 181

Du Camp, Pierre, sieur d'Orgas, author, 48

Duchess of Northumberland, 85

Duin en Daal landscape park, 20f

Duke de Chartres, 60

Duke of Marlborough, 86

Duke of Wellington, 199

Duke of Westminster, 85, 89

Dunville Park, 203n

Durkheimian view of ritual, 168

Dutch culture, 21; concepts of leisure, 23; country life, 28; French influence, 30; middle class, 23, 26; social groups, 37; urban environment of, 22; weaving, 25

Dutch landscape art, 22, 24–29, 31

Dutch New Church (reformed), 25

Dutch Religious Creed, 25

The Duties of Servants, 83

E

Earl Burns Miller Japanese Garden, Long Beach, California, 133, 135n; described, 141; elements of nature in, 143–144; Girl Scout ceremonies in, 146, 147f; history of, 136–137; map of, 141f, 145f, 148f; as performative space, 144; popularity as wedding site, 136, 138; promotional pamphlet, 143; symbolic aspects of, 143–144; uses of, 137; wedding ceremonies in, 144–149; wedding client characteristics, 138

Eaton, Hubert, 136

Eaton Hall, Chester, 85

Edo (city), 98, 99; fields in, 109; meisho in, 100–103; population size, 110

Edo period (1615–1867), 98–102; culture of, 101; growth of Edo city, 99; importance of nature during, 101

Edwardian era, naumachia in, 173, 183n

Egyptian expedition, 71

Egyptian Revival, 60, 64, 65f, 71, 75

Elisa, Grand Duchess of Tuscany, 62

Elisa Lodge, Florence, 63

elite class in Victorian Britain, 79, 81; knowledge of gardening protocol, 83; prestige from prize plants, 83

embedded economy, 79

embodied places, gardens as, 120–121, 123, 126, 130

embodiment, 57; idea of, 55n; public gardens and, 49; royal gardens and, 52, 57

emic point of view, 57

emplacement, 43, 48, 54–57; defined, 54–55

Emryaku-ji, Buddhist temple, 98

English Heritage Events Diary, 190

Ermini, Pietro, engraver, 62

etic point of view, 57

European Union, 185, 191

excursion rituals. *See* pilgrimages

F

Fabbroni, Giovanni, naturalist, 61

Fabre, François-Xavier, 63, 64f

Fabroni, Carlo Agostino, garden of, 70

Facchinelli, Luigi, architect, 72, 73

Falklands War, 186, 191

Fan Chengda, poet, 158

Fantastici, Agostino, designer, 71

Farming Pavilion (Jiaxuan Academy), 158

Fatherland (Dutch), 35

feng shui, 141, 144

Festa dell Spighe, 76

Festival of Britain, 184

Flanerie, 20

Yuan Jie (719–772), poet, 162, 163, 164, 169
Yuan Jue (1266–1327), scholar, 167, 168
Yue, southeastern region of, 156, 157

Z

Zeeman, Abraham, artist, 34f
Zeng Gui, Lingling county sheriff, 163
Zhao Ranming, headmaster of Jiaxuan Academy, 158
Zhending, 164
Zhu, 157
Zhuge Liang, farmer and general, 159
Zhu Xi (1130–1200), philosopher, 153, 158; neo-Confucianism and, 156
Zong Bing (374–443), author, 153n